Red Thunder, Tropic Lightning

RED THUNDER, TROPIC LIGHTNING

The World of a Combat Division in Vietnam

ERIC M. BERGERUD

Westview Press

Boulder • San Francisco • Oxford

Cover photograph: John Youngblut; objects in the cover photograph courtesy of Dennis Abbey and the author.

Photographs are reprinted with permission of photographers C. W. Bowman, Bradford D. Bromley (courtesy Gary Silva), R. F. Broyles, Dale Canter, Todd Dexter, Thomas A. Giltner, Jerry A. Headley, Jerry A. Liucci, William E. Noyes, Gerry S. Schooler, and Morgan J. Sincock.

Copyright © 1993 by Westview Press, Inc.

Published in 1993 in the United States of America by Westview Press, Inc., 5500 Central Avenue, Boulder, Colorado 80301-2877, and in the United Kingdom by Westview Press, 36 Lonsdale Road, Summertown, Oxford OX2 7EW

Library of Congress Cataloging-in-Publication Data
Bergerud, Eric M.
  Red thunder, tropic lightning : the world of a combat division in
Vietnam / Eric M. Bergerud.
    p. cm.
  ISBN 0-8133-1128-4
  1. Vietnamese Conflict, 1961–1975—United States. 2. United
States. Army Infantry Division, 25th. I. Title.
DS558.B463 1993
959.704'34—dc20   92-30656
                                                                            CIP

Printed and bound in the United States of America

The paper used in this publication meets the requirements
of the American National Standard for Permanence of Paper
for Printed Library Materials Z39.48-1984.

10   9   8   7   6   5   4   3   2   1

To Those Who Served in
the 25th Division
During a Hard War

Contents

Illustrations

Maps

Photographs (Center Section)

Preface

THIS BOOK EXAMINES the world confronted by the men of an American combat division during the Vietnam War. Although the unit in question is the 25th Infantry Division, this is not a unit history or standard military chronology. Instead, I try to view all of the major parts of the soldiers' world—including subjects as diverse as climate, living conditions, deadly combat, and morale. The world inhabited by the soldiers of the 25th Division was not theirs alone; the men and women who served with other frontline units in Vietnam will immediately recognize the major landmarks. Using the 25th Division as a focal point, I hope to help the people of today better understand what the Vietnam War was like in fact, not fiction.

This work is based on a variety of sources. The documentary foundations come from a great number of 25th Division records generated during the war, the most important of which are the large quarterly Division reports. They, in turn, are complemented by the quarterly reports that came from II Field Force, Vietnam, the Army headquarters for the units operating in the provinces near Saigon. The Center of Military History, Department of the Army, provided these documents to me while I was doing research on the village war in a Vietnamese province. I used this research to write *The Dynamics of Defeat: The Vietnam War in Hau Nghia Province* (Westview Press, 1991), which deals with the political and military struggle waged by both sides in an important part of the 25th Division's area of operations.

The most important resource is a collection of tapes and correspondence from veterans of the 25th Division. But tape transcriptions and informal correspondence rarely take a form that readers are used to seeing in print: People do not speak the way they write. In addition, the context for events described was often developed through very lengthy narratives. If some of the quotes appear long, bear in mind that I transcribed several tapes that were over four hours in length. Consequently, I did edit the transcriptions. I also arranged sentences so they followed a clear chronology. I did not indicate where one part of the transcription ended and another commenced; had I done so, the responses would have been covered with ellipses (. . .) and much harder to follow. And though I changed a few terms so the lay reader would understand what was described, I was extremely careful not to alter the meaning of any person's account. Overall, the majority of the accounts are very nearly true transcriptions: I made few, if any, changes in the words used, though I did alter grammatical forms that sound perfectly fine but look like errors on paper. Rather than employing footnotes, I have injected a small number of comments explaining points that might not be clear to the reader (comments are found within brackets followed by my initials [—EMB]). If most accounts appear well put, that reflects the intelligence and sensitivity of the respondents.

Although the matter never came up, I would not have accepted anonymous accounts. Any author who contends that men and women who served in Southeast Asia will not discuss Vietnam publicly is dishonest. I did, however, alter many accounts myself. When men described the deaths or injuries of comrades, I deleted the names of the victims, and I omitted names in any descriptions of embarrassing or tragic episodes. Details like this could only hurt people and would do nothing for the story I present in these pages. In any case, all the tapes and letters that were used in this research are in the public record. For the moment they are in my possession, but I hope they will find a permanent home where they can help other students of the war. Only a small percentage of the accounts I compiled appear in this book, yet they encompass a broad range of issues concerning Vietnam. In a genuine way, I am privileged because I was able to listen to these accounts. I have tried to do them justice, but the intense feeling and sheer power of the voice cannot be duplicated.

I must deal with the accuracy of accounts given twenty years after the fact. No doubt, time has eroded some of the details and thrown a fog around some chronology. Remarkably, however, I do not think this happened very often. In this regard, possessing the 25th Division's documentation was invaluable. When men remembered the exact date of an action, it appeared in the records every time. Furthermore, between the records and a large body of oral evidence, I became fairly well immunized from outright falsehood. I am a trained researcher and skeptic, but only on a handful of occasions did I decide someone was creating fantasy. Perhaps some of the details are wrong. On the other hand, war is extraordinarily intense, and it etches some moments deeply in the mind.

Twenty years is not too long a time to try to put the war into perspective. I have seen hundreds of letters written by young soldiers during the war, but though they are very interesting, they reveal an unavoidable lack of mature judgment. If time is an enemy in the realm of detail, it is a friend in the more important area of context. Twenty years ago, the men and women I interviewed could have perhaps done better at describing what happened; today, however, they have a much better idea of *why* things happened. That is a trade well worth making.

Inevitably, I have made errors somewhere. Nevertheless, I sincerely believe that this volume is based on the most honest historical data I have ever used. The motivation of the respondents is beyond reproach: There is no financial gain involved, none has a public reputation to rescue from critics, and no respondents attempted to glorify themselves. They want to teach, and they want the truth about Vietnam as they saw it to be known. Few researchers are as lucky as I have been.

Although the 25th Division lacks the widespread reputation of some of the elite Army units, no other division can match its literary pedigree. After World War II, 25th veteran James Jones recounted wartime life in his famous trilogy. More recently, some aspects of the 25th's tour in Vietnam have been well portrayed. Al Santoli, author of two splendid oral histories concerning Vietnam—*Everything We Had* and *To Bear Any Burden*—served with the 25th. Two British journalists, Tom Mangold and John Penycate, wrote *The Tunnels of Cu Chi,* an interesting account of the war that developed around the enemy safe zone in the Ho Bo and Boi Loi woods. Director Oliver Stone was with the 25th in Vietnam and relayed his views of the war in the movie *Platoon.* Larry Heinemann was another 25th Division veteran; his powerful novel *Paco's Story* won the National Book Award. Heinemann's earlier work, *Close Quarters,* is a vivid chronicle of field life in the Tropic Lightning Division and, in my opinion, one of the greatest of American war novels.

I would like to thank the people at Westview Press for taking on this project. Senior Editor Peter Kracht gave good advice and encouragement throughout. Project Editor Deborah Lynes did an excellent job of bringing order out of chaos. Copy Editor Joan Sherman has made me appear a better writer than is the case.

I also wish to express my deep gratitude toward the 25th Infantry Division Association. In particular, Morgan Sincock, editor of *Flashes,* the association's wonderful newsletter, helped me far above and beyond the call of duty. Most of the veterans who helped with this research are members of the association, and many helped me contact other veterans who do not belong. Obviously, all who participated shared things that touched their lives deeply. It was not, I know, always easy. I think almost all shared the same motivation: Simply put, they want other Americans to know more about the war as it actually happened. They did a splendid job. Any faults in this presentation are mine alone. Below is a list of people who helped me.

Eric M. Bergerud

Lily Adams
Sgt. Maj. Charles Albridge, U.S. Army (Ret.)
Mickey Andrews
Col. John Bender, U.S. Army (Ret.)
Henry Bergson
Col. Carl Bernard, U.S. Army (Ret.)
Mike Blackwell
Richard Blanks
Phil Boardman
C. W. Bowman
Charles Boyd
Dan Breeding
Col. R. F. Broyles, U.S. Army (Ret.)
Michael Butash
Michael Call
Dale Canter
Dennis Casola
Anthony Cavender
Lt. Col. Frank Chance, U.S. Army (Ret.)
James Cipolla
Robert Conner
Samuel Crouch
Todd Dexter
Gary Ernst
Col. Thomas Ferguson, U.S. Army (Ret.)

Larry Fontana
Herbert Garcia
Dave Garrod
Thomas Giltner
Kenneth Gosline
Dennis Hackin
Dr. Robert Hanson
Ronald Hart
Jerry Headley
Lt. Gen. Harris W. Hollis, U.S. Army (Ret.)
Glenn Jeffers
Robert Julian
Bill Kestell
Robert Knoll
Gerald Kolb
Jay Lazarin
Rick Lewis
Jerry Liucci
Brig. Gen. E. M. Lynch, U.S. Army (Ret.)
Eddie Madaris
William McDill
Roger McGill
Maj. Gen. Thomas Mellen, U.S. Army (Ret.)
Richard Mengelkoch
Mike Miller
Roberto Molinary
James Murphy
Hector Nadal

Alan Neill
Col. Carl Neilson, U.S. Army (Ret.)
Bill Noyes
Lawrence Obrist
Richard O'Hare
Gen. Glenn K. Otis, U.S. Army
    (Ret.)
John Pancrazio
Lt. Col. Donald Pearce, U.S. Army
    (Ret.)
Del Plonka
Gregory Pybon
Lt. Col. Carl Quickmire, U.S. Army
    (Ret.)
Gordon Reynolds
Lee Reynolds
Bill Riggs
John Riggs
Jim Ross
Lt. Col. Andrew Rutherford, U.S.
    Army (Ret.)
Larry Rutt

Gerry Schooler
Justice Selth
Gary Silva
Morgan Sincock
Sidney Stone
Hugh Stovall
Sgt. Maj. Kenneth Stumpf,
    Congressional Medal of Honor
    recipient
Dr. Kenneth Swan
Mario Tarin
Gene Trask
Dan Vandenberg
Col. Jack Weissinger, U.S. Army
    (Ret.)
John Welna
Maj. Gen. Ellis W. Williamson, U.S.
    Army (Ret.)
Michael Willis
Col. Duke Wolf, U.S. Army (Ret.)
Sgt. Maj. Jack Wood, U.S. Army
    (Ret.)

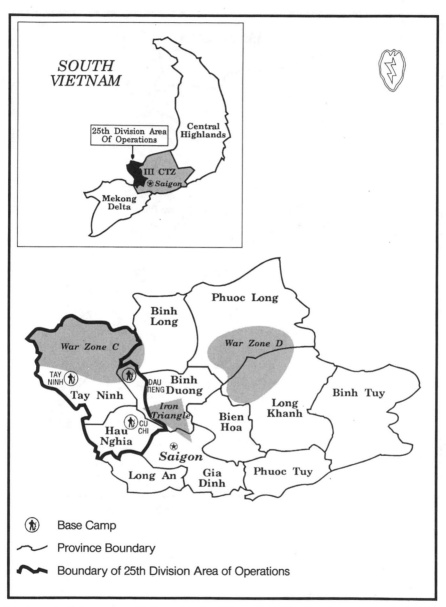

Provinces in Saigon area: III Corps Tactical Zone (III CTZ)

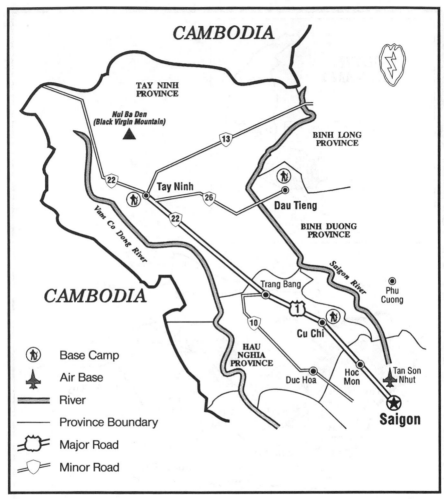

25th Division Area of Operations (AO): Administrative Boundaries and Lines of Communication

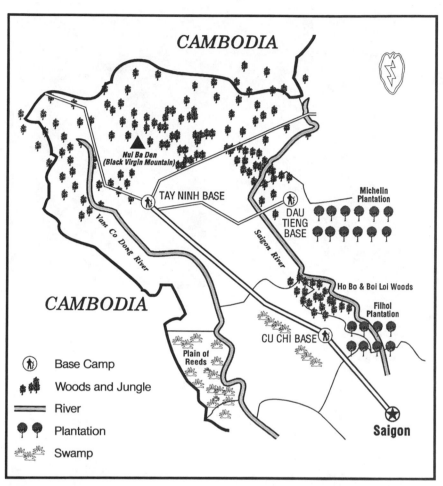

25th Division AO: Terrain

Introduction

W<small>AR MAKES HISTORY</small> move very quickly. In 1965, U.S. armed forces embarked for Vietnam. In 1975, American military helicopters retrieved a final handful of individuals from the roof of the U.S. Embassy in Saigon, signaling the total collapse of a foolish and tragic enterprise. In those ten years, a blink of the eye to a historian, the United States changed greatly. American political institutions were shaken. The government lost will and confidence. American society, already in a state of great flux before the war, was put under greater stress because of it. The economy, once dominant and robust, began to show structural weaknesses so profound that many Americans and foreigners began to predict the eclipse of the United States as a significant economic power. Although not a single battle was fought on American soil, the United States suffered badly because of the Vietnam War. Indeed, the impact of the conflict was so great that it is still impossible to gauge its full magnitude.

Vietnam had such a great impact, I believe, because it simultaneously touched so many national nerve endings. It was like a lightning rod that drew to itself all the negative impulses of a hyperactive time. Because the war's cause was, at best, ambiguous and the conflict was conducted so miserably, millions of Americans questioned the country's world role in the past, present, and future. Moreover, racial change and turmoil in the domestic arena spilled over onto the war. Racked with racial guilt, many Americans accused the government of waging a racial war abroad. And many members of racial minorities argued that their true enemies were white people in the power structure at home, not other people of color far away. The youth culture, the most visible manifestation of the great sea change taking place in some areas of traditional morality, became intertwined with the war. Many in the antiwar movement unmistakably were also waging generational civil war. Although disorganized and often incoherent, the movement's most radical spokespeople seized the spotlight for

1

a very long time. They questioned the value of the American past, and their questions were quickly echoed by many intellectuals and makers of popular culture in the United States.

On the other side were millions of Americans who did not so much support the war as support the men and women fighting it and the proud image of the American past they represented. The generation that fought World War II also created the extraordinary prosperity that followed the conflict. Ironically, this prosperity was a prerequisite for both the military power needed to wage a foreign war and the enormous college system that served as a focus for opposition to that war. Understandably, millions of Americans who had spent their youth in the Depression and war were stunned and embittered at the turn of events. Their sons fought the Vietnam War, and many did not return. But if the people who accepted the idea of wartime service for their sons expected honor or understanding, they were mistaken. The youth of America's privileged and their older counterparts on faculties and in the media routinely vilified both the values held by members of "the silent majority" and the world that they created. The Vietnam War served as a weapon to use on the innocent for reasons that had little to do with the conflict itself. And the weapon was extremely powerful because the war was futile and mismanaged. Inexorably, the bitterness of the war's original supporters turned toward both the government and the war's most vocal critics.

The Vietnam era was a vile period in American history. And the pain was so great that it lingers still. During the nightmare, a flood of books, articles, television shows, and movies dealing with the war began. After the debacle, neatly tied in with Watergate—the greatest domestic political calamity of the recent past—the flood continued. The various works dealing with the war were overwhelmingly critical, many to the point of national self-flagellation. Many critics searched the distant and recent past for the war's antecedents and concluded that it represented a deep malignancy inside the United States itself. What type of country, after all, would wage a criminal war? And the war was portrayed not only as criminal in intent but also as criminal in conduct. The critics' image of Vietnam was dominated by a monstrous war machine spewing death impersonally and indiscriminately. Bravery and tenacity, they suggested, were shown only by U.S. opponents. And the brave and barefoot peasant guerrillas vanquished the technological beast because they had souls that represented the best of the human spirit while the beast was a hollow shell.

As one might expect, the image has changed to some degree over time. Any serious student of the Vietnam War today would dismiss the vast bulk of the books written and the films made during and immediately after the war as hopeless rubbish, despite their huge numbers. Yet, enormous damage has been done. One thing lost in all the sound and fury, unfortunately, was a real desire to understand the war as it actually took place. Anyone searching the past to make a political point risks creating "seek and ye shall find" history. So much takes place in any complicated chain of events that a clever individual can find anecdotes and many bits and pieces of evidence to support almost any contention. And just as someone can maintain any number of unethical arguments with selective quotes from the Scriptures, so can a hack scholar or journalist forge a warped picture of a great tragedy. The truth, naturally, only gets in the way and consequently becomes the first casualty in a war not against the past but against some aspect of the present.

Fortunately, in recent years, some extremely good books have appeared concerning Vietnam. They join a handful of useful accounts written during the war itself and a small number of astoundingly good works of fiction. Some of these books have been compassionate and insightful oral histories. Others, such as the "official" history volumes slowly coming from Washington, are laying the groundwork of objective narrative that is required for any body of historical literature.

Nonetheless, it seems to me that too few people have tried to answer an obvious but important question: How was the war in Vietnam fought by the U.S. Army? Assumptions concerning this subject abound, but many of these assumptions are based on scant evidence. The image of the war that I sketched earlier continues to color the efforts of many honest people.

I know that this is true because I was one of those people. Immediately after the war, I began a Ph.D. dissertation concerning the American pacification campaign in a small Vietnamese province. Ultimately, I had to reverse my original thesis because the evidence pointed unmistakably in a different direction. It was a humbling but useful exercise to realize that many of my assumptions concerning Vietnam—at that time, yesterday's news—did not correspond to reality. Some years later, I picked up the project again, tore it apart, and made a book out of it. As is often the case with dissertations, mine dealt with dramatic events but was abstract, academic, and lifeless. Hoping to remedy some of that, I began to get in touch with a few of the American soldiers who served in the area I was examining. The number soon grew to several dozen. These men did much to make my monograph tolerable. Regrettably, I could not possibly use all the material I had received. And much of that material was pure gold.

Slowly but steadily, I began to collect evidence that created a powerful picture of the war in Vietnam from the perspective of those who fought it. As the picture took shape, I started questioning, one after another, the assumptions that I held about the war. A good number of them I discarded outright, remnants of a lie fashioned intentionally or unintentionally by many before me. I also found that many things I believed were largely true but required deeper thought and frequently reflected impulses that I had not properly identified. Furthermore, it was very clear that I was on the tip of an iceberg, and I knew that if I asked for it, far more material was out there, much of it extremely insightful. With their keen minds, great candor, and deep humanity, the scores of men and women I contacted opened the door to the grim but intense and extraordinary world of the battlefield in Vietnam.

This book is the story of the war in Vietnam as experienced by the men of a combat division—the 25th Infantry. Based in Hawaii, the 25th is also called the Tropic Lightning Division, a nickname alluding to both its home base and its steadfast service during World War II. The Division's insignia, worn as a patch by all its soldiers, is a stylized taro leaf with a lightning bolt streaking down the middle. (The men called it the "electric strawberry," among other things.) Deployed in Vietnam to the area between Saigon and Cambodia, the men of the 25th Division experienced nearly every facet of the war, from tiny skirmishes to the great battles of the Tet Offensive. They confronted a hostile land and climate, fought guerrillas, and traded blood with the fierce North Vietnamese Army (NVA). They operated in rugged enemy-fortified zones and in heavily populated rural areas. They knew the Vietnamese as the enemy, as tenuous allies, and as everything in between. The 25th had a very long tour. The first units began arriving in January 1966, and its last unit left in the spring of 1971. Between those dates, the men of the 25th saw the tempo of battle swing back and forth. Much of the violent reality, however, remained constant from beginning to end. The price paid was heavy: Some 5,000 soldiers were killed, and many times that number were wounded. The 25th's losses were among the highest in the Army.

I chose to concentrate on a single division for several reasons. First, because most American units served either in one area or in a very small number of areas throughout the war, the soldiers developed a very deep sense of place. It is extremely important to somehow duplicate that sense because it provided the framework for the wider experiences the men confronted. The geography, the base camps, and the enemy fortified zones all remained the same. Consequently, although the war lacked fronts and thus had a haphazard nature, looking at one unit in one area provides an element of coherence to the story. Second, because of my earlier research, I possessed huge quantities of documents from the 25th Division, including almost all the quarterly reports. I am probably the only person on earth who has read them all. In any case, the basic narrative this provided was invaluable. It allowed me to detect instances when time played tricks on the memory of some of the respondents. More often, it allowed me to see, in retrospect, some larger patterns that the individuals involved could not have recognized or would not have been told about. The war, after all, lasted five years for the 25th Division, but individual soldiers served one year, or less in the case of wounded. Knowing the basic story from start to finish, I have tried to identify whether aspects of the men's experience illustrated something unique about a particular time or place or whether they illuminated something more general. Last, my previous work gave me some familiarity with the political situation in the area where the 25th Division fought. I am therefore able to show how the enemy troops operated and what their overall intentions were for each phase of the war. I can also show where, in theory, the efforts of the 25th Division fit into the grand scheme of things, such as it was in Vietnam.

This book is not a narrative history of the war. Instead, I have approached the subject topically. I cover several subjects, including the physical surroundings, weaponry, battles big and small, the medical effort, relations with the Vietnamese, and morale. In each chapter, I have relied heavily on the testimony of the men and women who were there. It will quickly be apparent that no completely consistent image of wartime Vietnam emerges in this book: Although the respondents are sensitive, intelligent, and honest, each has an individual perspective. I thought it important, therefore, to give a representative range of views. Indeed, I am as much an editor as an author here.

Although I concentrate on the 25th Division, the experience of the Tropic Lightning's men, though different in some particulars, was essentially the same as that of all American fighting men in Vietnam. Along the way, I have spoken to hundreds of Vietnam veterans from all services. They shared a common background. They shared a common enemy. And they confronted many of the same psychological and physical obstacles. This books deals with matters that any veteran would find very familiar.

Ultimately, this work covers issues that combat veterans of any modern war would quickly recognize. This is a picture of men and women in war. At the center lie death, fear, and pain. Yet, the value of the story comes not from the violence but from observing how decent individuals, most very young, could adjust to a vicious and malevolent environment and remain human beings.

The accounts of the men and women involved are clear and well put and involve human, rather than narrowly military, concerns. I have purposely avoided the use of technical terms. Consequently, the reader need not have any background in military matters to understand this book completely. Nevertheless, military organizations have a language of their own, and some simplified definitions might be helpful. A division, for example, is a military tactical and administrative unit that combines all necessary arms and services required for sustained ground combat. In theory, a division should be able to fight a major engagement with its own assets, and therefore, it is the most important single component of modern land armies. Divisions are also the basic building blocks for larger units, such as the corps and the army. The 25th Division had an authorized strength of 17,000 men during the Vietnam War.

A division in Vietnam had three brigades. When American involvement in Vietnam began in 1965, brigades were a recent development designed to give flexibility to the division. Although each brigade had a commander and staff, there was no set strength: Division commanders shifted combat units from one brigade to another as events demanded. Normally, however, the brigades, named First, Second, and Third, each had approximately one-third of the division's combat strength. The combat strength of the division was based on ten combat battalions. Six of these battalions were standard "leg" infantry; three were mechanized infantry; and one was the division's powerful armored cavalry squadron. (Cavalry is organized somewhat differently than other units, with a great emphasis on speed and firepower. The cavalry's term for a battalion is a squadron; its term for a company is a troop.) The battalions had approximately 950 men. Mechanized infantry battalions also had seventy armored personnel carriers (APCs). The division had forty tanks assigned—some in a separate unit, some in the cavalry—and the 25th also had five artillery battalions. Four of these possessed four batteries of six standard 105mm field pieces; one had twelve heavy howitzers. The Army authorized seventy Huey utility helicopters and nine Cobra gunships to the 25th, and higher command frequently allocated more helicopters to the Division. Air Force and Navy jets were available if ground action required their support.

Unfortunately for the lay reader, battalions had a strange nomenclature. For purposes of historical continuity, battalions retained the numbers of the older regiments that they had served with earlier in American history. Some of the regiments were very old, and many had nicknames. These names were long and consequently put into military shorthand. For instance, the 2/27th refers to the 2d Battalion of the 27th Regiment, nicknamed *The Wolfhounds*.

Six companies constituted a battalion. Four were maneuver companies, named A, B, C, and D (Alpha, Bravo, Charlie, and Delta). In addition, there was a headquarters company and a smaller company E, which had the battalion's mortars. With an authorized strength of approximately 160 men, companies consisted of four platoons of roughly 40 men each. Each platoon was broken down into four 10-man squads. In practice, combat units were invariably understrength.

The 25th Division also had several support units, ranging from cooks to lawyers. Among the most important were the engineers, who frequently were in the midst of combat, and the attached 12th Evacuation Hospital at Cu Chi, which served as the hub of a large medical apparatus. A roster of the 25th Division appears in the Appendix.

I also should note some words that refer to the Vietnamese. I have termed the South Vietnamese regime as "Saigon" or "the government." All Americans called the South Vietnamese army ARVN, an acronym for Army, Republic of Vietnam. Regarding U.S. opponents, I use "the Front" to refer to the National Liberation Front, the revolutionary apparatus based in South Vietnam. I refer to the Communist leaders of the Front as the Party. Although the Party had a southern branch, the politburo in Hanoi controlled everything of importance. The well-armed and well-trained military units fighting under Front command were referred to by Americans as Main Force units, to distinguish them from less well-armed guerrilla units. The North Vietnamese Army was called the NVA by Americans. Naturally, U.S. soldiers often used nicknames and referred to their opponents as "the VC," "the Viet Cong," or "Charlie."

I would like to explain why I frequently refer to the "men" of the 25th Division. It is true that thousands of women served in Southeast Asia during the Vietnam War. As illustrated in this account, women played a critical role in the medical effort on the front lines. Red Cross volunteers likewise rendered deeply appreciated service in a time and place of great danger. Nevertheless, the military of the late 1960s was not the military of today. During the Vietnam War, far fewer women served in sensitive and important positions close to combat units than do now. With very few exceptions, the Vietnam battlefield was a male environment. No doubt, the military's policies on this issue during Vietnam led to a poor utilization of human resources, particularly in a place where intelligence and sensitivity were in such demand. Yet, I am writing about a period, however recent in time, when use of the term "men" was accurate. As recent events in the Persian Gulf illustrate, no potential future conflict featuring U.S. armed forces will be like Vietnam in this regard.

1

A Setting for War: Coping with a Strange and Hostile World

MILITARY PERSONNEL, regardless of rank, study and deal with terrain. Whether in training or in war itself, officers and troops are taught how to use or adapt operations to the layout of the land. It is easy to see why. The nature of combat, whether defensive or offensive, is largely shaped by the topography of the battlefield. But considerations of terrain go much further than this. The physical relationship between the battlefield and the rear, together with the climate involved, will have an extraordinary influence on the complex process of moving forces and supplies. Furthermore, the physical environment shapes the experience of the soldiers involved to an exceptional degree. Although violence and fear are constants in war, soldiers pounding each other on the frozen steppe near Stalingrad experienced something very different than did the men fighting in the foul terrain of Burma or New Guinea. The implications for morale, a crucial component in the grim chemistry of war, are obvious.

All of this also was true in Vietnam. Later, I will examine the impact of terrain, in its military definition, on operations. Here, however, the objective is different. To the extent possible, we must try to see in the mind's eye the physical world surrounding the men of the 25th Division if we are to deeply understand the nature of warfare in Vietnam. Ignoring the physical environment and the ways in which the men coped with it on a daily basis would be akin to writing a biography of Charles Dickens and not discussing London.

Recreating the world surrounding the men at war is particularly important when dealing with Vietnam. In the first place, Vietnam was a very foreign and extraordinarily exotic place to almost all Americans who served there. And war itself turns the individual's world upside down: What is normally considered good becomes bad and vice versa. In Vietnam, even in the absence of war, military life was nearly the exact opposite of civilian life in the United States. The land and climate, vastly different from those found at home, were rarely considered pleasant by the Americans. Moreover, the men had almost no relationships with women in the normal sense. There were prostitutes in huge numbers but few real girlfriends, fiancées, or wives—a major adjustment for young men. Living conditions that soldiers came to consider soft, such as those in the big base camps, would have been considered well below the poverty level in civilian life. Privacy, control over one's actions, jobs (a soldier at war may *do* a job, but he certainly does not *have* one in the civilian meaning of the term), and a familiar social life were all absent. In their place were a strange land, a strange people, and the ever-present possibility of violence and extinction.

Second, unlike most soldiers in other wars, the men of the 25th Division developed an extraordinary sense of place that strikes anyone who has the privilege of talking with them. This situation was a natural consequence of the military realities that developed in Vietnam. The Division was given an area of operations (AO, in military jargon) in an area west and northwest of Saigon, extending to Cambodia. The precise boundaries were often changed, but the location of the battlefield remained essentially the same from beginning to end. The experience was somewhat comparable to that facing the soldiers on the western front during World War I (had their rear been 6,000 miles from home). But during that war, units were often moved from one part of the line to another. By contrast, the 25th Division— except for the 2d Brigade at the very end of U.S. involvement—stayed in place throughout the war. Regardless of the fact that helicopters and armored personnel carriers gave units extraordinary short-term mobility and that men frequently did not have the slightest idea where within their AO they were on a given operation, soldiers returned again and again to the same places, whether friendly or hostile. The camps at Cu Chi, Tay Ninh, or Dau Tieng would become as familiar to these soldiers as Central Park is to someone living in Manhattan. So, too, would areas like the Ho Bo–Boi Loi woods, the Michelin Plantation, or the banks of the Vam Co River. These were the rugged and fearful places the men continually returned to in search of a skilled and brave enemy. Thus, the soldiers of the Tropic Lightning Division not only lived in a country at war, they lived in a very particular part of a country at war—an area that was, in essence, theirs. For a period, regardless of matters of sovereignty, the relatively small part of

Vietnam in which the Division lived and fought for the entire war belonged, in human terms, to the soldiers as much as it did to the native inhabitants. Americans were interlopers in Vietnam, but their stay was a long one. And though the confined world of the 25th was a battlefield, in a strange way it was also home.

Land and Climate

Vietnam is a quintessential tropical country. To most Americans from milder climes, the fertility and fecundity of that land were unknown. So, too, was the heat. Initial confrontations with this climate made deep impressions on many of the soldiers, and they are a major part of their first memories concerning service in Vietnam. Infantryman Gerry Schooler, who reported just before the Tet Offensive of 1968, arrived in Vietnam, like most of his comrades, on board a civilian airliner. His description of the experience illustrates the point:

First thing I remember was flying in an airliner. They tilted a wing and, as they announced it, we flew right over Iwo Jima. Getting ready to go to war gives you a lot to think about, and it was a long flight. It was beautiful and extremely clear that day. You could see Surabachi and everything. But I remember that island being totally covered with this triple canopy vegetation, all kinds and shades of green. It was just beautiful. It really struck me because every scene I had ever seen of Iwo Jima was of destruction, the trees down, not a leaf standing. At least, that's how I thought of it. And now it was totally docile and beautiful. It reminded me that wars do end and things come back.

When we came over Vietnam, it was very clear. We saw lots of water. We didn't know what to expect but thought from that height, we might see firefights, bombs going off, artillery firing, tanks going down the road. But you couldn't see anything, just a lot of green and a lot of brown water. It looked very serene. It didn't look like a war zone from the air. Of course, I found out later that when you are 2,000 feet up, it looks a lot different than from 20,000. [2,000 feet would be a typical altitude for a helicopter on a combat operation.—EMB]

When we landed, we walked off this ramp, and this hot humid air just surrounded us as though we were prisoners. I felt this heavy wet air that just struck my body after coming out of that air-conditioned environment on the plane. It was just amazing. You were sweating right away. At Bien Hoa, where we came in, I smelled something sweet, which I later found out was incense. You would smell it around the villages, especially at night. It was strong at the airport. As I dragged my duffel bags toward the buses that would take us to Long Binh, everyone was soaking wet coming from the air conditioning. It took more effort to carry a duffel bag than I had ever encountered before. That effort was a preview.

James Cipolla was on his way to the same unit as Gerry Schooler—part of the famous *Wolfhounds*—ironically in time for the Tet Offensive of 1969. He had similar impressions:

I arrived in Viet Nam on a TWA 707. Your first impression is, what a beautiful country. There is what looks to be a white coastline, brilliant greens, the rice paddies etched on the land. It's beautiful from the sky. When the plane lands at Bien Hoa, the first thing you see when you taxi over to the hangar there is a group of men and women getting ready to get on your aircraft. And the thing you notice about them is the look in their eyes: like they know something you don't. And you say to yourself, what have I gotten myself into?

Once they finally open the door, you begin debarking. I was in an aircraft with mostly officers and just a few enlisted personnel. It had been my twentieth birthday when I left for Vietnam. And the first thing that hits you is the heat and the incredible, oppressive humidity.

Capt. R. F. Broyles, before serving his tour at Cu Chi during 1968, was also unprepared for the relentless heat:

I remember how interesting and tropical the place looked when we circled and made ready to land. When we landed and the door opened, my first impression was heat: the kind of heat that you didn't think you'd ever really come to grips with. And you don't, at least not for a while. It was nearly six months into my tour when it dawned on me that I was not as uncomfortable as I had been. I stepped out of the air-conditioned airplane into the sauna. And there is the activity. So busy, so deliberate, yet sometimes it seemed— and I felt this right off the plane—somehow futile. I don't know why I thought that at the time, but I did. It was ironic that I felt that during one of the great military victories of the war [the Tet Offensive of 1968—EMB]. It was a nagging undercurrent, never at the forefront of my thoughts but always there. Obviously, I was thinking about what was going to happen to me, how well I would function, and what the next year would hold.

Engineer Michael Butash recalls that accommodation to the extreme temperatures proved difficult or impossible for many:

When we were out with a mech [mechanized—EMB] unit or grunt unit, you dug in every night. You slept in a poncho liner, which was a camouflage-colored, real light, waffled cotton. You wrapped up in it even if you sweated like a dog because the mosquitoes couldn't bite through it. The mosquitoes were awesome. During the monsoon season, you were just all wet all the time. The biggest thing was just a dry pair of socks. The heat was just indescribable. No one wore any underwear, except socks.

As I shall demonstrate in a later chapter, the climate had a major influence on the military environment in Vietnam. Presently, however, I must record something intimately connected with the heat and mentioned by virtually every veteran interviewed for this project: the smell of Vietnam.

Most of the Americans serving in Vietnam came from towns, cities, or suburbs; few had ever been on a working farm. But anyone who has lived in a rural area knows that smells are very prominent due to close proximity of animals, living and dead, and plant life, whether growing or decaying. This was amplified in Vietnam. The heat, the rural makeup of the population, the burning of wood and incense, and the poverty of the country combined to give it a distinct odor.

Bob Conner, one of the first to arrive in the spring of 1966, describes his reaction to a world previously unimaginable to him:

The country was amazing. I looked around, and I said, "My God: I have never in my life seen anything like this." I would never dream in a million years that they still used ox carts: And these things they call water buffalo—big, great-looking animals with rings in their noses, always snorting, with a funny way of looking at you. . . . The air stunk: like a room that's been closed up for a long time and it's been so damp, and when you open the door, the mildew would hit you in the face. Dirty, grayish, stuffy smell. You really want to turn around and get a breath of fresh air. The country was stinking and poor; it was from another era.

James Cipolla was also struck by the smell of Vietnam. As he notes:

The tropics have an aroma all of their own. Even in Thailand, it smells that way out in the jungle. It's the smell of growth; it's the smell of death. Decay, of stuff growing, of stuff dying. The oppressive heat and humidity make that smell stronger. There was very little sanitation the way we know sanitation. Sewers were open in Bien Hoa, so your first impression is of a dirty place. They put you in a chicken-wire bus so grenades can't get into the windows, and you ride to the replacement battalion. You look out the window and see a mama-san squat and go to the can.

Infantryman C. W. Bowman, who had the misfortune of arriving just as the Division began to face its most difficult and violent time in 1967, remembers his trip to Cu Chi, which passed through Saigon:

Landed in Viet Nam in January 1967. I was assigned to the 25th Division at Cu Chi. They put us on a convoy. The convoy came up with 5-ton trucks that had steel plating welded all over them. All the trucks were sandbagged and had a .50-caliber machine gun mounted on the top. As I stood there and looked, I wondered what the hell I was getting myself into. They gave us M14 rifles without any ammunition. They had the ammunition locked up in an ammo box in the back of the truck in case we got hit; if we were hit, then they would pass out the ammo, which I thought would be kind of late in the game. It took us several hours to get up to Cu Chi. New in-country, I was either in a state of shock or naive or I just didn't know what was going on. When we left Tan Son Nhut going to the 90th Replacement Battalion in Long Binh, we had to go through Saigon. There were gigantic piles of garbage in the streets, and you could just smell the decay and maggots growing in the garbage. Some of the canals we crossed smelled like open sewers, and the odor would just about knock you out. You can only wonder how people managed to live in those areas. . . . I was fascinated by the country and the people. Everything stank to me. It either smelled like human waste or garbage or both mixed together, which it probably was. The people were interesting. Little kids were begging along the road and taking care of smaller children. We didn't see any young men: only the old or young, nobody in between.

Gary Ernst, who served with the Division's company of armor until wounded during the Tet Offensive of 1968, gives a vivid description of the combination of odor and poverty noticed by everyone who served outside the air-conditioned luxury billets in the big cities. He adds another element known to all combat soldiers from both sides, the smell of death:

I had trained at Fort Knox, Kentucky, in the summer, so the heat was not unexpected. What struck me was the smell. Everywhere, it was like an overflowing septic tank or something rotting. You'd get used to it, but every now and then, the wind would shift and remind you. We used to ask people what it was, and they just said it was Vietnam: The place stank, it was as simple as that. The poverty that I saw when I just arrived was unexpected. Around Bien Hoa, there were shacks of corrugated iron, mud, what have you. I wrote home that this place made Tijuana look like Palm Springs.

A few months into my tour, I was on a convoy, and we passed through an area that had a firefight right before we got there. There was one dead VC on the side of the road. We were a little surprised because the infantry would usually pick them up for their body count, but we didn't think much of it. The next day, we came by on another convoy, and the body was still there and had started to decompose. For the next week, our convoys passed by it as it got riper and riper. That smell was just terrible: We used to cover our faces when we came near the bend with bandannas. That's when it hit me that the stench and rot of the dead body was the smell of Vietnam. I grew to associate the smell of decay with the country itself. I am sure, looking back on it, that it was rotting vegetation and lack of sanitary facilities. When people had to pee or take a crap, they would do it on the side of the road. But I still thought of death as being the smell of Vietnam.

Although the heat is relentless and present throughout the year, Vietnam has two very distinct seasons. The precise timing varies from year to year and place to place, but the winter and spring are generally bone dry. The summer and fall, however, are the time of the life-giving monsoon rains. Both seasons created unique and unavoidable challenges for the men of the 25th Division.

Most of the Division's AO was flat. Although two major rivers and numerous canals passed through it, it did not have much of the rich, black, and saturated soil typical of the Mekong Delta. Instead, much of the land was of poorer quality, with a reddish hue. Laterite, a red clay, was used to make roads. When the ground dried out, which would happen quickly because of the heat, it would turn hard and grow dusty. In short order, marching men and hundreds of vehicles created a dust bowl loathed by virtually all Americans soldiers. Gary Ernst, a crewman on an APC, describes the situation:

We were stationed in Tay Ninh and often escorted convoys between the base camps at Tay Ninh and Cu Chi or Tay Ninh and Dau Tieng. During the dry season, our tracks would just tear up the clay and create a cloud of red dust. At the end of the day, everything was covered with it: our weapons, our goggles, everything. If you had sunglasses on and took them off, you would look like a raccoon. We had to continually clean our weapons to keep them in order.

C. W. Bowman spent his tour with the infantry and experienced the same phenomenon:

During the dry season, the temperatures frequently reached 110 degrees or more during the day. You can only imagine how the heat intensified the odors of garbage, compost, and manure. The ground would get so dry that the dirt would turn to dust. When the trucks and other vehicles would drive down the roads, there would be great clouds of fine red dust, and you'd just be coated with it. You were already soaking wet from sweating, so the dust would just soak into your clothes and your skin. After a time, it would even get into the pores of your skin, so if you'd take a bath, you'd still be dingy gray or red, depending on the area you were in. It would actually stain your body.

Even in the more comfortable base camp at Cu Chi, the dust was an unwelcome companion, as related by R. F. Broyles, a captain at the time:

When it was dry, I mean, it was dry. When you walked across the compound, it was like walking across a box of talcum powder. There was a layer of fine dust: Your feet sank into 3 inches of fine powder, and it was everywhere. When you perspired, it stuck to you. At night, when Charlie shelled us, you'd roll out of your bed, put on your flak jacket and steel pot, and dive into the bunker. You were just filthy all of the time. The grunts out in the jungle thought we were always spiffy and clean, but they were sadly mistaken.

Naturally, most men did what they could to keep clean. It was a futile battle for many and frequently impossible in the field. Yet, the large streams fed by the rivers did not dry up, and there was a transitional period between the seasons when rain was sporadic. Troops tried to take advantage of the situation, as C. W. Bowman remembers:

Out in the field, we were constantly sweeping the jungle during the day. At night, we would go on ambush patrol or sit in a foxhole or listening post. You wore the same boots, the same fatigues. The only time you took a bath was when you crossed a stream or if you set up near a creek or a bomb crater to jump in. When the monsoon began and it started raining, many of us would jump out there with a bar of soap and lather up. You didn't take off your clothes; you'd wash your fatigues and yourself all at the same time. It would rain so hard it was just as good as a shower, but sometimes, it would stop raining when you were in the middle of getting soaped up; then you did have a problem. I guess we all stunk so bad that we didn't notice how bad.

Infantryman Richard Mengelkoch, an early arrival at Cu Chi, mentions the bizarre situation that could arise when the first rains hit the mound of dust that had accumulated over months:

The dust became a real problem. Everything was gravel. There was a lot of dust from the equipment. This fine powdery dust would pile up, almost like talcum powder. It would be inches deep in places, like around tents. It was funny when you first got into the monsoon season and it started raining. The rain would come down with driving force horizontally, and that's not an overstatement. But you would be standing getting soaking wet in the rain and get hit by a cloud of dust. If you've ever put water on talcum powder, it tends to repel it, so the dust was still swirling around in the rain until the rain finally beat it into submission.

Although the climate during the dry season was a serious burden, most soldiers probably preferred it to the monsoons. Combat slackened somewhat during the rainy season, something appreciated by all combat soldiers, but the tropical rains made life hell for men on operations. As C. W. Bowman recounts, the sheer ferocity of the storms astounded many Americans:

Some of the storms would really get violent. We were up north of Tay Ninh, near the Cambodian border. We had all of our claymores [mines—EMB] strung out. A storm came through, and lightning was so bad that it was setting off the claymores. They had an electric blasting cap, and the lightning set them off. Another time, we were outside of Trang Bang. We had dug in that night on perimeter, and it started raining. At the same time, the NVA or the VC started probing our perimeter, so my friend Gary and I stood in a foxhole all night. Our side was dropping illumination from Puff ["Puff the Magic Dragon" was the nickname given to an extraordinarily powerful ground support aircraft that, in this instance, was dropping flares in the search for a target.—EMB], but Charlie probed the perimeter all night. By the time daylight got there, Gary and I were up to our arms in water in the foxhole. That gives you an idea of how hard it can rain.

Those dry rice paddies that we walked through, we could swim through; they all filled up with water. It rained so hard that one day, the water was ankle deep, and the next day, it was up to your chest. One trouble we had was that the South Vietnamese built their wells level to the ground. Usually, they didn't build a wall around them or anything. I managed to fall in a well one night. Luckily, it wasn't that deep, and they were able to get me out, but it was a hell of an experience to take a step and have nothing under you all of a sudden.

Combat infantryman Kenneth Gosline, who went over with the 25th in 1966, was likewise struck by the weather, in particular the contrast between the fertility brought by the rain and the miserable impact this rain had on the men:

I can remember thinking how green and beautiful it was from the helicopters, but it was a little bit different when we got down on the ground. I really don't think the country was meant to be fought in by a bunch of young Americans not used to that kind of terrain. The thickness of the jungle, the heat, the rains. It's funny, I have in-laws that live in Florida, and when I go out jogging down there, it's almost like a flashback sometimes when I see some of these plants and trees common to the tropics.

The weather, at times, was terrible. The rains were so bad and we became so wet, I remember, at times, feeling like a prune. One time, we were building a base camp before we built our showers. We were so hot and sticky that when the monsoon rain came up, we all stripped down, soaped ourselves up. Wouldn't you know, it stopped. There we are, standing around with soap all over us. We had to take the water from the tops of the tents, which were dirty and dusty to begin with. Then we ended up just as dirty as we were before.

Although he was there two years later, helicopter pilot Gene Trask observed the same contrast that struck Gosline:

Depending on whether you were on the ground or in the air, Vietnam was both the beauty and the beast. From the air, it was sometimes absolutely breathtaking in its beauty. The symmetry of the rice paddies and rubber plantations could only be appreciated from the air. The beauty from the air hid the beast of being on the ground. During the dry season, it was so hot, it took your breath away; during the rainy season, nothing ever dried out and it was a constant state of dampness and mildew. The bugs were always there, regardless of the season. I remember seeing cockroaches the size of small field mice and rats the size of small dogs! Plus snakes and other assorted insects, and this wasn't the jungle, this was base camp.

When I was stationed at Tay Ninh base camp from May 1969 to September 1969 [the rainy season—EMB], the hooch we stayed in had a bunker dug out beneath it, supposedly so we could retreat into it during rocket and mortar attacks. The bunker was usually at least half full of water, with bugs, snakes, and rats swimming around. Never once did I use that bunker; I lay under my cot and prayed that our hooch would not take a direct hit with a rocket.

Kenneth Stumpf, later to become a sergeant major and Congressional Medal of Honor recipient, was sure that the monsoon was part of the eternal military idiocy encountered by every soldier in every army in history:

I was in Bien Hoa, waiting to be assigned to a unit. We had these details we had to go on. My first detail was chopping down bamboo. I was chopping that bamboo, and all of a sudden, a bunch of red ants seemed to fall out of the sky. Those big ants just bit the shit right out of me. They stung like crazy. I couldn't believe it. It was the monsoon season, too. Every time we had formation at 5:00 in the afternoon, people would be called up and told what unit they were going to and things like that. It seemed like every time we had the formation, it would rain. There would be hundreds of us in formation, and it would be raining like crazy. Exactly the time the guy said fall in, it started raining. It was so consistent. I couldn't believe that either.

Like many of the men serving under him, Lt. Col. Carl Neilson, commander of the 4/23d Mechanized Infantry Battalion during the summer of 1968, has some unpleasant memories of the local fauna:

During the rainy season, about 3:00 every afternoon, you'd get a real drenching, which varied from very heavy to extremely heavy to extraordinarily heavy. And then it was over, and it would dry off, and we would get to business. But there were lots of insects to bother you: stinging, creeping, crawling insects. I don't think we had trouble with poisonous insects, but there were a few dangerous snakes, cobras among them. I can remember very vividly a very large cobra that came to visit one of our bunkers in our firebase and became wedged between the top of the bunker and some clear plastic sheeting that had been used to waterproof the bunker. The soldiers were both terrified and amused at this very dangerous snake wriggling around, and eventually, they dispatched it. But it gave you some pause to think of what else might be crawling around there.

Tet veteran Jerry Liucci shares these fond memories:

Because of the rain, I'm sure some of the enemy tunnels flooded out. There were a lot of snakes. I saw a king cobra over there. I saw a bamboo viper. And a lot of bugs. It was funny—I had never seen a land leech before. But when you sleep on the ground a lot, you get to see all sorts of bugs. I remember having a scorpion on my helmet once. And having bites on my face from a very large centipede. They're healthy over there. We usually slept with a towel over our faces, or the mosquitoes would carry you away. The cocktail sauce they gave us for food wasn't edible but was great for leeches—you just squirt it on them, and they would drop off you.

Animal life, on occasion, posed genuine danger. There were rumors, likely true, of tigers in the jungle along the Cambodian border. In fact, tales of tigers dragging off the sick and wounded were a staple among the enemy soldiers that made the dangerous journey down the rugged and often lethal Ho Chi Minh Trail. Among Americans, there is no record of any injury due to wild predators. Water buffalo were another matter. American soldiers were convinced that the buffalo hated Americans in particular, and they were impressed by the ease with which Vietnamese children would handle these powerful and enormous beasts. Farmers know enough to treat any large animal with caution, especially a bull at any time or a cow caring for a calf. But, as previously noted, few Americans were from farms. Not always knowing what they were doing or due to freak confrontations (dikes and hedgerows could easily hide something the size of a water buffalo), several GIs had confrontations with these potentially hazardous creatures. Some attacks were fatal, and even lesser injuries to the men could be very serious. Gerry Schooler witnessed such an incident outside Tan Son Nhut air base during the violent first few days of the Tet Offensive:

We were going down the road. We'd follow blood trails and every now and then find a body of an NVA. We were sweeping one of the rice paddies that you find right outside of Saigon. All of sudden, out of the vegetation, a water buffalo charged our radioman, gored him badly in the leg, and threw him through the air. We had a track with us with a .50-caliber machine gun. That buffalo, like everything else on that road, was dead in an instant, just like that. The reason it did that was that it was a cow and it had a calf right beside it. The calf was still alive and came up to the mother, sniffing around. They dusted off our guy ["Dust off" is the term for the helicopter evacuation of wounded.—EMB]. I suppose he got a Purple Heart. He was hurt badly, and in reality, no one had any choice but to kill the cow, but it was just another sad thing on that odd day. We spread out in a line because we were going through the paddy. And I remember looking back, and at the very end of the line was the calf, following us. I have no idea what happened to it. A pitiful sight.

An inhospitable climate for men at war was the rule in Vietnam. Although the men of the 25th might dispute this, they did not have to face the worst terrain Vietnam had to offer. This dubious distinction might go to the soldiers of the 9th Division, who often operated deep in the Mekong Delta proper; because infantry frequently had to go over land and avoid the roads, that was like living in an ocean of mud. Or the soldiers in the rugged and sparsely populated Central Highlands area would perhaps lay claim to serving in the worst possible environment. Although spared some of the extreme heat found elsewhere, these soldiers had to fight and carry their loads over one exhausting hill after another and frequently found themselves in true jungle. As Sgt. Kenneth Stumpf, later a member of the 4th Division, quipped, "We always attacked uphill." Because the enemy normally chose the battlefield, Stumpf was no doubt literally correct.

The terrain in the 25th Division area of operations was less extreme. Whatever comfort this might have afforded was tempered by the frightening realization that the relative mildness of the terrain also attracted the enemy; consequently, this AO was among the most violent in Vietnam.

The land inhabited by the men of the Tropic Lightning Division was flat. Beyond that, it varied considerably because it was a geographical transition zone between the low, wet, and fertile Mekong Delta and the rugged mountains and jungles of the Central Highlands, Cambodia, and Laos. The French engineers who built Highway 1, the road leading from Saigon through Cu Chi and Trang Bang, chose the route because it lay on hard, flat ground. To the south was marsh, and to the north were the foothills of the Highlands. (In better days, Highway 1 went from Hanoi to Saigon, then west to Thailand.) As a result, American soldiers in this part of Vietnam might find themselves on marshlands, riverbanks, rice paddies, woods, rubber plantations, a bit of true jungle, or one very notable mountain.

In retrospect, the veterans had little to remark upon concerning the flat, somewhat densely populated agricultural areas in the southern and central portions of their AO. As just noted, the terrain there had an utterly different cast depending on the season. Beyond the dense swamps paralleling Highway 1 to the south and the Plain of Reeds west of the Vam Co Dong River, there was a certain monotony about much of it. James Gordon, a major at the time and the Division's paymaster when it first deployed to Cu Chi, remembers the area as it was before it developed into a small American city in exile:

The base camp area at Cu Chi was a large, flat plain. It was virtually treeless, with white or light gray soil on top, typically with very reddish, brown soil a few inches underneath. It was nearly the color of Georgia clay, possibly a little darker. It wasn't very hard. It was said to be an abandoned rice paddy.

Most of the hamlets and civilian villages were in areas like this. The 25th Division personnel operated in this zone from the beginning. Missions into hamlets themselves were common but brief. Ultimately, much of the populated area was utterly reshaped due to the war. This very important topic receives detailed treatment in a later chapter.

Most field operations, however, took place in broken terrain because, very simply, the enemy was there. In an overpopulated country like Vietnam, land was highly prized. And much of the wooded terrain that was the scene of extraordinary combat had once been farmland or plantations. But twenty years of disorder and war had caused much land to be abandoned, and in the tropics, abandoned land is reclaimed by nature very quickly. Therefore, there were several areas throughout the 25th Division's sector that were wooded and overgrown with dense brush. These areas resembled some of the dense woods of the American South more than true jungle. Interspersed with old canals, roads, and trails, these areas were longtime enemy redoubts, some of the oldest and most famous in Vietnam. The land north of Cu Chi, called the Ho Bo and Boi Loi woods by the Americans, was never controlled by Saigon (nor was the Plain of Reeds). As I will discuss, in these areas the Front constructed an incredible array of tunnels and field defenses. They were places to be feared.

They were also places that were extremely difficult to traverse. C. W. Bowman describes a typical portion of the Ho Bo Woods:

All of the rubber tree plantations around Cu Chi were overgrown and not kept up. Some of the plantations up north near Tay Ninh were in operation and were fairly clear of underbrush. But around Cu Chi, everything was overgrown with scrub, thorns, thickets, vines, and "wait a minute bushes." That was a joke among most GIs. The vines would reach out and grab you. They would grab your rifle, your legs, your ankles, and tell you, "Wait a minute, wait a minute." Trying to hump through this—and I walked point a lot—was hard. You could swing a machete all day, but you had to be careful doing that because there were an awful lot of booby traps in those areas. Over a period of time, if you were good, you developed a sixth sense that seemed to be more than sight or hearing. You could sense things before you saw them. It's kind of hard to explain, but you could feel things, feel vibrations, just sense things. That saved my butt several times.

The rubber plantations that were recently abandoned or still in operation were simultaneously eerie, dangerous, and beautiful and were quite unlike anything most Americans had ever seen. Richard Mengelkoch saw a recently abandoned plantation in the Boi Loi Woods early in 1966, before the systematic destruction of that area began:

We went through a big rubber tree plantation northwest of Cu Chi, and I was impressed with that. The trees were very neat and orderly. With everything laid out in rows, it was obviously a plantation. It seems incongruous that there was a war going on in such a serene setting. But it was eerie in the sense that the trees were so big and dense and it was so dark. It was easy to assume that there was somebody hiding behind every tree. And it was somebody who didn't have your best interest at heart.

In the northeastern part of the AO, the 25th Division had one of their three major camps at Dau Tieng. It bordered a large plantation, some of which had been owned by Michelin. For reasons that are not at all clear—

although GIs speculated about bribery and secret deals (with good reason, no doubt)—some of this plantation continued a semblance of operation throughout the war. It was a strange scene that struck everyone who saw it. Dan Breeding was there in 1969 and describes not only the terrain but an amusement that would be familiar to soldiers in many wars:

In Dau Tieng, where my battalion was headquartered, we had a village out on one corner of the compound, and on one portion, we had a portion of the Michelin rubber plantation, which was very pretty. The trees were planted in rows: I would never have thought something like that could have existed in Vietnam, but they were very well kept. Even as late as 1970. We were told not to shoot into them unless it was necessary: I guess the government had to pay for every tree that was damaged. I always enjoyed any operation we had in there; it was always cooler inside. It might have been safer, too. Dau Tieng was a small camp, and we always got mortared from the other side of the compound.

All in all, Dau Tieng was a pretty area. They had an air base there where the Air Force landed the C-130s and so forth. There were some old French buildings right at the edge of the runway, and they were very pretty from a distance. It was a very popular spot for picture-taking. Our officers always told us not to shoot into those buildings unless it was necessary because they didn't want them destroyed. But they were a good target, and we would always shoot at them anyway. We would zero our weapons in and see how close to certain windows we could get with our M79 grenade launchers. We riddled them at every opportunity. Whenever I was in the rear, they were always my primary target.

Mario Tarin was in the same area and describes the frustration felt by some of his comrades regarding the incongruity of the whole area:

There were big rubber plantations around our camp, and the more cynical guys were telling the rest of us that we were looking at the real reason we were over there: to protect the interests of the large rubber corporations. Sometimes, we would run over some of the trees in frustration. It's funny because they all had their little bowls attached to them with the rubber sap dripping into them, but I don't recall ever seeing anybody around them or collecting the rubber liquid. There were always papa-sans working the rice paddies but never around the rubber trees.

The plantations provided a dense cover and shade. They were fairly easy to move through and were cooler than surrounding areas. And, as their very existence testified, during much of the war, with bloody exceptions, they were relatively safe places to be. Yet, for some soldiers, none of this was worth it. Kenneth Gosline remembers loathing the plantations:

I liked working the jungles more than the rubber tree plantations. I hated the way those rubber trees were planted: It was like looking at tombstones at Arlington. If you were behind a tree, you were all right; but if you stepped out, they could see you diagonally and up and down about 2 miles straight.

One familiar, difficult, and very dangerous place for fighting men to be was along the large canals and riverbanks. Two major rivers flowed through the Division's turf. Going north to south, not far from the Cambodian border, was the Vam Co Dong. Meandering from the east to the northeast was the large Saigon River, which often served as a dividing line between the territory assigned to the 25th and that delegated to the famous 1st Division. Studded with secret hiding places, the rivers were natural transit points and often visited by GIs. As Gerry Schooler knew, working the rivers could be hazardous and unpleasant even if the day passed without violence:

We did a lot of work on the river, and that was different. Along the Vam Co and Saigon rivers, there weren't any villages. It was tougher because you were always walking in water up to your knees or waist. It was fatiguing and debilitating because there were organisms in the water that you would ingest and that would make you sick to your stomach. Being wet all of the time is very hard on your skin, and there was a lot of jungle rot, particularly around the river areas.
One thing about the Saigon River fascinated me and gives you an idea of how little we knew about Vietnam. When we first went in, there was this nice big grassy area behind this berm. [A berm is an earthen wall used for agricultural and military purposes. A heavily vegetated berm, generations old, could virtually hide a hamlet.—EMB] Normally, the berms we were used to were out in the paddies and were about 2 feet high and narrow, maybe 2 feet. There was a big berm on the river; someone must have built this centuries ago. It kept the whole area from becoming a lake when the tide came in. We didn't realize this. We thought the nice tall, soft grass behind the berm would be a good place to sleep. We were lying there the first night, poncho liners also on the ground to protect us from bugs. I remember waking up and feeling this poncho liner bubbling up a little bit. Someone said, "Water is coming in here." We sat on our steel pots, about 8 inches off the ground. It wasn't too long before they were submerged. We learned the first night to sleep on the berm, not the soft grass. The reason it was so soft was that it got a luxuri-

ous irrigation treatment every night. The tide would probably drop 6 or 7 feet. It would be a strong current going one way, then it would drop, and then a few hours later, there was a strong current going the other way. It was weird.

During the day, we'd go out and swim out there, pretty much horsing around. I remember once I was on an air mattress, feeling pretty good. I fell asleep. About that time, the tide started coming in, and when I woke up, my hand could feel motion. I had probably drifted a half or three-quarters of a mile upriver. That was kind of scary, getting separated from your unit, naked as a jaybird, no rifle, no nothing; if you had to get back, you'd have to go running through the jungle like Tarzan without a loincloth. It wasn't a nice situation. I remember paddling for my life, fearing getting stuck way upriver. Finally, I saw my unit around the bend: What a nice sight. I was so tired when I paddled up that I just lay on my belly. You just had to accept the fact that when you worked the river, you were going to be wet and tired from walking in it, it took so much energy.

The year in which an individual served also undoubtedly influenced his impressions of the land surrounding him. The men arriving very early in the war came to a land that had suffered much and had undergone a substantial redistribution of population due to fighting and the relocation policies of both sides. Yet, because the technology of the war was at a low level then, the land itself was largely untouched. In 1964, the 25th Division participated in a semisecret operation named SHOTGUN that provided American door gunners and other crewmen for Vietnamese helicopters. Sgt. Roberto Molinary, one of the men who volunteered for this duty, recalls the setting:

At that early stage, military actions were not at large scale. In the early part of 1964, South Vietnam was a beautiful country, green, very agricultural. The indigenous population seemed very friendly.

As time went by, the militarization of the conflict increased greatly. Leaving aside for the moment the debate concerning the loss of civilian life, there is no doubt that in hotly contested areas, American weapons, whether manned by U.S. troops or ARVN, did great—and let us hope temporary—damage to the land itself. Small and medium-sized enemy strongholds like the Ho Bo Woods were pulverized by artillery, air strikes, and defoliation. Many areas that were particularly sensitive received the most drastic treatment of all, delivered by the Rome Plow bulldozers that literally flattened everything in their path.

Descriptions from the later years often reflected this change in the landscape. Infantryman Robert Julian, one of the last of the 25th Division to serve in Vietnam, states bluntly that in 1971 "there were areas where fighting and bomb strikes had taken place. Agent Orange was used and Rome Plows went through. These areas were just devastated." Medic Lee Reynolds, who served in 1970, gives a similar description about the Ho Bo and Boi Loi woods: "We knew nothing about Agent Orange, but the general area around Cu Chi looked like a lunar landscape when you flew over it. Sometimes, you would see some God-forsaken, shriveled up thing that looked like a tree. But it was like the moon."

We must remember that soldiers looked at their world through a lens that was extraordinarily clouded. Sights and experiences that in other circumstances might have been pleasing or emotionally moving were obscured by fear and death. Yet, despite all of this, many of the men of the 25th Division found great beauty in the land. But the destruction was localized. If one wished to see it, the natural attraction of the tropics was always there. Robert Julian, who witnessed sights of destruction, also saw another side of the country:

I thought Vietnam had a beautiful countryside. So was the jungle. There were snakes, ants, mosquitoes, and other bugs. But we also saw all kinds of animals, like monkeys, parrots, deer, and even a leopard. Often at night, I would lie down on my poncho, look up through the trees, when we weren't in thick jungle, look at the stars, and just think how beautiful it was.

Todd Dexter was in the middle of the Tet Offensive near Saigon and had little time to appreciate his surroundings. When the action slowed, however, he took a chance to look around:

I volunteered to ride shotgun on a Tay Ninh convoy. This was my first good look at the Vietnamese countryside. Beauty was everywhere. Large palms and banana trees lined the roads and hamlets. The roads were a frightful mess, and I don't think we missed a single bump. Small children met each convoy that passed and begged for food, yelling, "Chop chop, you give me chop chop!" They also begged for cigarettes, and to see two- and three-year-old children puffing on cigarettes was not uncommon. I did not see many women smoke, though. Just the men, the boys, and the boom-boom girls.

Rifleman Bill Noyes arrived in October 1968. As he relates, the lushness of the terrain could make life difficult on a new soldier on one of his first patrols. Trained in the United States to keep a distance from the man ahead, Noyes got lost in the Vietnamese bush:

Vietnam is filled with many dazzling hues of green. The shrubs and bushes and the trees may have told an experienced tracker which way to go, but they said not a thing to me. I knew only that I stood where I stood, that I saw only the trees and the bright sky. Beyond this, all else seemed to have escaped me.

My first effort to find the others took me quickly into a thorny thicket, and then I backtracked to where I thought I'd been. It wouldn't do to yell, I assumed. Here I was, being new, with only four or five magazines and a rifle I'd never tried! "Well, I didn't want to be a part of this army anyway, so which way is home?"

It wasn't long before my nameless squad leader crashed through some bushes from a different direction. He told me to hurry, using some unflattering terms, and he didn't wait for my explanation. I stayed close to the man in front. Without any explanation offered, I was learning that real war happened in a different way than your training might cause you to expect.

One location struck virtually everyone as a unique and lovely place, although, as usual, it was also a place of violence. This was Nui Ba Den, the Black Virgin Mountain, which was easily the most significant landmark in the 25th Division's area of operations. Nui Ba Den was not a very high mountain, only about 3,000 feet, but it was utterly solitary and surrounded by nothing but flat, rugged terrain. On a clear day, if an individual was on the slightest rise, it was visible from almost anywhere within the AO. It was battle scarred, but mountains are not vulnerable to conventional weapons. Gerry Schooler remembers a short moment of deep delight:

Further northwest in our area, it wasn't mountainous, but there was the Black Virgin Mountain. It was very pretty, this perfectly shaped mountain coming up out of the jungle. A few places were kind of hilly, and some very high triple canopy forests and rubber plantations were up there. Some of the streams had clear water. Once, when we crossed one, it was like one of these old Bing Crosby and Bob Hope movies. Both sides of the stream were sandy and lined with big, tall palm trees. I used to study art, so I understood infinity and things of that sort. This stream was straight and went on to the horizon. But up one side, straight up this beautiful creek and past palm trees, was Nui Ba Den. That was the backdrop. That was the most beautiful scene I have ever seen. It was nice, in the eye of the storm, to see something that you could appreciate.

Many men of the 25th have expressed a desire to return to Vietnam. And one of the primary reasons why they want to return is to do what they could not properly do at the time—appreciate the countryside and people without a vulture on their shoulders.

The Works of Man

The men of the Tropic Lightning Division naturally spent much time at their bases of operation. Although South Vietnamese or old French facilities might be used for short periods, the men typically found a home of some sort in the web of a colossal system of encampments built by the American engineers or the soldiers themselves. This huge array ranged in size from small temporary perimeters, often called "hard spots," that would shield a small unit for a short time to the great base camp at Cu Chi, which resembled a small American city transplanted to the middle of Vietnam. In between these extremes were the two smaller permanent camps at Tay Ninh and Dau Tieng, a large number of fairly elaborate artillery firebases, and an ever-shifting number of large perimeters that might be home for a company or battalion for several weeks.

Whether large or small, encampments had both military and supply functions. The Army attempted to accomplish contradictory tasks with camps and perimeters of all sizes. On one hand, the commanders used perimeters as defensive points where men could rest and replace equipment in relative safety. On the other hand, the Army also employed perimeters as offensive bases for rapid thrusts and therefore located them in sensitive areas. If nothing else, officers believed, a properly situated perimeter, built on a known enemy transit route, would inhibit their opponent's movements. For example, the three permanent camps at Cu Chi, Tay Ninh, and Dau Tieng were situated astride the most important roads in their areas. Division units could simultaneously protect the approaches to Saigon (albeit barely, as the Tet Offensive of 1968 illustrated) or jump off for a rapid offensive. These factors, however, made the camps prime targets for enemy attack and bombardment. Obviously, this situation did not help officers attempting to rest and refit units. Later, I will examine the tactic of using field perimeters as "bait" intended to draw an enemy assault.

Vietnam has often and correctly been described as a war without fronts. This situation, however, did not eliminate the necessity for a rear. Any army at war devours supplies at an incredible rate. The U.S. Army, based on firepower and rightly or wrongly concerned with creature comforts for morale purposes, had a nearly insatiable hunger for everything from cigarettes to armored personnel carriers. In earlier wars, the rear had to be policed, guarded from theft by its own men. In Vietnam, however, because there were no lines between the contending sides and nothing was genuinely safe, the rear also had to be protected militarily. So did all of the lines of communication.

The system of supply and support fed on itself. In other words, every person conducting a support function—frequently absolutely necessary, frequently not—also had to be supported. So, too, did the people constructing the support facilities, as well as the elaborate medical apparatus. Because the lines of communication were vulnerable, it made a certain amount of sense to stockpile large amounts of supplies as near to the front as possible, where they could be distributed quickly. Thus was born the system of large base camps, of which Cu Chi was only one example.

It is extremely unclear how much forethought went into the selection of Cu Chi as the location for the Division headquarters. As noted earlier, everyone in the state of Hawaii knew that if any American contingent was slated for deployment to Vietnam, it would be the 25th. It was trained for jungle operations, had been practicing in mock Vietnamese hamlets for months, and was prepared to a fever pitch by late 1965. Yet the deployment of the 25th, when finally ordered, was characterized by a high degree of disorder, largely due to Gen. William Westmoreland's conviction in mid-1965 that the war might be lost imminently and that U.S. forces had to be thrown into the breach wherever needed, regardless of detailed plans and preparations.

Apparently, the site at Cu Chi was chosen in early December 1965 by members of a 25th advance party, operating under Westmoreland's directive. They naturally wanted a place on a major road and chose the intersection of Highway 1 and a smaller regional route running through the Filhol Plantation. The Army also wanted to be some distance from densely populated areas for defensive reasons and within firing range of enemy strongholds. Although the site was just some 20 miles from the Saigon suburbs, only the small, poor, and dingy district capital of Cu Chi was close by. Indeed, according to a member of the small Cu Chi advisory team there at the time, both advisers and South Vietnamese officials cautioned against the choice of Cu Chi. Whatever advantages the terrain offered, the advisers knew that the Army had chosen to put its major camp on the doorstep of the most heavily fortified enemy stronghold in the Saigon area. Furthermore, Cu Chi district and the entire surrounding area was controlled either totally or partially by the Front. This was not a small matter when the Army decided to hire large numbers of civilian workers for the base.

In early 1966, Dale Canter was one of the first to arrive, and he observed the transformation of Cu Chi from a desolate plot of land into a major military installation within months:

I flew to Cu Chi by helicopter to join the forward elements of the 25th Division, who were then clearing the area where we would build our base camp. The first couple of months were definitely the worst: no water, no jungle fatigues, constant patrols, very hot, no baths. The village of Cu Chi was very small and unquestionably sympathetic to the VC.

The area where our camp was actually built was dubbed "hell's half-acre" because of the difficulty of clearing that area and securing a foothold. There were snipers in the trees and spider holes and tunnels. The snipers and tunnels presented our biggest problems. The infantry battalions were formed in kind of a circle, and we would continually expand our perimeter, cutting down the jungle and clearing it away. The tunnel complexes were active under the base camp for the first three or four months. Snipers were constantly getting inside our perimeter and causing us a great deal of havoc, but as we cut down the vegetation, we discovered most of these tunnel entrances. Also, the engineers with their bulldozers would come through and scrape it out. So I don't believe any of these were active inside our perimeter after the first three or four months. Keep in mind, the whole district around Cu Chi was riddled with tunnel complexes outside the base camp that remained active throughout the war. It didn't take us long to discover that these tunnels existed, and we were really surprised to discover how elaborate some of them were. What we thought was a simple spider hole would turn out to be a large storage room or a hospital. We left some of them intact for display and training.

Cu Chi town had one main street, which was a dirt road, and a few huts. It grew to become a rather large city during my tour because of free enterprise; a lot of people moved there to be with the soldiers who were spending money. I do know that we never completely controlled the town. During the day, there was a lot of military traffic in and out, but at night, it still had a very ominous VC presence. Once we established our foothold there, I would make a laundry run into the village occasionally as part of the pacification program. I honestly believe that some of these people really liked us. It was kind of a strange mixture. They were VC, some of their family and friends were VC, but when they got to know us, they had a genuine affection. But they had no qualms about reporting our activities and setting us up for ambushes, which would result in the death of many GIs. In the village, you could smell the fish sauce. It was very primitive by our standards. I don't think our country was ever as primitive as that when the Pilgrims first landed. It was very backward. Vietnamese told us that Cu Chi had long been a rest area for the VC before we moved in. In my first pass through the village, you could readily see the hate in the people's eyes. That changed somewhat as time passed. I guess we must have looked as strange to them as they looked to us. [Canter was correct about Cu Chi. It was a Front stronghold in a Front area. Ironically, more hospitable, Christian hamlets were nearby.— EMB]

Unlike Canter, who was frequently on combat patrol, Paymaster James Gordon served in the camp permanently and was astounded by the speed with which the engineers created facilities:

The original base camp was about $^1/_2$ mile across. It was slowly enlarged over a two-month period to about a 1-mile circle. I couldn't believe how fast everything got going and we got to work. I was amazed at how fast the engineers built dirt roads, dug drainage ditches; at how all the support services got at their specialties, providing water for drinking and bathing; a post office was opened and operating—I don't remember when we first received mail, but it must have been within a few days. We had a fairly large tent city, with some improvements, within a matter of two or three days of arrival.

As Gordon's further testimony illustrates, the Army learned a hard lesson at Cu Chi. Whatever distinction later existed between combat and support personnel was very much blurred in those first months:

Initially, our military presence was tenuous. We didn't know what to expect from the enemy or where he was, at least not at my level. As everyone now knows, we set up camp nearly in the middle of a Viet Cong stronghold. And it didn't take very long before we found that out. Within a few days of arrival, the infantry began finding things they didn't like. The whole area was riddled with tunnels, where the Viet Cong and/or partisans could lie in wait until the troops passed them by. Then they would come out of their holes and do their dirty work. I never saw a tunnel; I never saw an "enemy" soldier; I never fired a shot in anger, as they say. But they *were there*. Whichever day it started, I can't say. Just one day, we were going about our business, and the firing started, not a long way away, but close by. You never saw finance clerks move so fast getting to "our hole," including one unnamed major. After that, it got progressively worse. We were really in combat, and we were shot at nearly daily for what seemed a long period of time. I do recall that it was around late March before we were allowed to go around the 2d Brigade base camp without our weapons, our steel helmets, and wearing our flak jackets. I was at a staff meeting at Brigade Headquarters one day when it got "shot up," with machine-gun fire, no less. Colonels and privates hit the dirt floor as one! The brigade commander's jeep outside the command post was slightly wounded, and the portable radio in the jeep was mortally wounded by a bullet in its side. Once again, no one was injured. We headquarters troops were uncommonly lucky during that particular period!

Richard Mengelkoch likewise remembers the dawning realization that the 25th Division's task, ill defined to begin with, was going to be a very hard one:

I arrived on 14 April 1966 and was assigned to the advance party at Cu Chi. It was like a steambath. Cu Chi was absolutely nothing. When I left, there were probably 30,000 troops there. When I got there, there were maybe 5,000. It was a wilderness. The roads were muddy when it started to rain. Everything was housed in general purpose tents. Later, tent kits, plywood frames with the tents put over, were installed. There was a dinky PX [post exchange—EMB], smaller than a 7-11, with a few canned goods and junk. I was assigned to a crew digging trenches. It wasn't so much that we needed trenches. We used a mechanical digger to get sand and soil to fill sandbags. We set up a strongpoint we named Ann-Margret in the northeast corner. [Ann-Margret, already famous, was one of the first of a stream of notables to visit Cu Chi. Conditions were not ideal for a concert, and the men, understandably, deeply appreciated her visit.—EMB] Later on, locals were hired—Vietnamese women, half of whom were probably VC, who sat around and filled the sandbags and relieved the GIs of this drudgery.

The work was hard, and it was hot. Everybody was miserable. I went to personnel constantly, trying to do one of two things: I tried to get out of the infantry, but that didn't work. Then I figured anything would be better than walking around here, so I volunteered to be a door gunner. That didn't work either. Cu Chi grew to about 4 by 2 miles. We slept in rough tents with cots in the mud. The first two weeks, we slept within 200 feet of an artillery battery. They were firing an almost constant barrage around the perimeter. There weren't many defenders there; if there would have been a concerted effort to overtake the place, it could have been done fairly easily. Fortunately, there were no North Vietnamese troops in the area, and the VC weren't that organized en masse. So the artillery was firing H & I fire. [Harassment and interdiction was an artillery tactic of firing blindly into an area that might logically have a target. It was expensive and controversial.—EMB] Anyway, I wasn't used to sleeping near an artillery battery before and didn't get a lot of sleep. But it was funny—maybe it took a week or two, but I never heard the suckers go off. I would sure hear one coming in. It's an old joke, but you can be dead asleep and immediately wake up when you hear a mortar round coming in.

By the time I left, conditions were very good. Tent kits kept you dry, and you could keep the floor clean, although there wasn't a lot of emphasis on housekeeping in our unit. We had a huge PX, many service clubs, theater, USO [United Services Organization—EMB]; it was a pretty decent base. This probably took six months.

Because the Cu Chi camp was located on the doorstep of one of the most prominent Front strongholds in Vietnam, the engineers continued to clear foliage well past the large perimeter. The decision to do so had some obvious merit. Any raid, sapper attack, or ground assault would have to come across several hundred yards of open ground, a dangerous complication for any potential attacker. Yet, the camp was never totally secure. Because the area was cleared, enemy mortar and rocket teams, who had a detailed knowledge of the interior of the base thanks to the help of hundreds of civilian workers there, had a perfect view of their target. With rugged terrain and the tunnel systems so close, probes of the perimeter at night were a common event. The northern portion on the edge of the Filhol Plantation and closest to the Ho Bo Woods and Iron Triangle was particularly dangerous, and the Ann-Margret strongpoint was the scene of frequent fighting. Mortar and rocket attacks varied in frequency, but they were always a threat. Scores of support personnel were killed or wounded throughout the war.

However, in Vietnam, danger was a relative concept. Compared to the field, Cu Chi was a haven of safety and comfort. As time went on, the permanent residents of the camp increased. Furthermore, every field unit had a permanent home in one of the three major camps, and all of them received short periods of rest at Cu Chi. Every combat soldier looked forward to a "stand down" at camp, even though it was usually very brief.

Only in wartime Vietnam, however, would Cu Chi have been considered a haven. In normal terms, even in normal stateside military terms, Cu Chi was a crude place. In particular, along with almost every camp or perimeter in the country regardless of size or place, Cu Chi possessed a hideous odor that all veterans recall with distaste. The primary cause of the dreadful smell was the disposal of human waste. Although the engineers worked hard at creating tolerable conditions at the larger facilities and the line soldiers did the best they could to make themselves comfortable in small field camps, it was impossible to create a proper sewer system: The time, expense, and difficulties caused by the water table ruled it out. Instead, the men constructed large outdoor latrines from canvas and wood. Dan Breeding's description is a good one:

The odor of the place: Around the base camps, there was always the pungent odor of kerosene burning human waste. It was a thick and heavy odor. Fifty-five gallon drums were cut in half, and after they were filled with waste, they were dragged out of the toilets and kerosene was poured on them, and they struck a match and kept stirring it until it was all gone. In the larger base camps, civilian workers had the responsibility of doing it. They cleaned the bathhouses and burned the waste. Around the bases, you would look up and see dark, billowing smoke, and nine times out of ten, that's what it was. It took place nearly 24 hours a day.

Although this disgusting duty was given to local Vietnamese at Cu Chi and their wages were among the highest at camp, in other locales soldiers were less fortunate. Gary Ernst, new to the country, remembers the delightful task:

My whole tour in the army was a snafu. When I was at Bien Hoa, our sergeant told us that the Vietnamese handled KP [kitchen patrol—EMB], and I thought, how great: The worst possible duty was done by them. Later, I found out there were worse duties in a combat zone. Then the sergeant assigned me to the shit-burning detail. There were latrines that all consisted of boards set up high enough to cover a 55-gallon drum cut down to about one-third its height and shoved under this little toilet seat. Shit-burning detail consisted of pulling these barrels out and pouring on gasoline and burning the waste that had piled up over the day. The smell was something you really wouldn't want to live with. When you got four or five of these barrels at once, the stench was just overpowering. By the end of the day, I wanted to get this over with in the worst way. Once, near the end of the duty, I wasn't satisfied with how one of the cans was burning. It was just sputtering, so I threw some more gasoline on it. Stupidly, I tried to throw it on the fire and caused a big fireball explosion that singed my arms and face. I was more embarrassed than hurt.

The comforts of Cu Chi varied, depending on how much time one spent there. Every unit was assigned an area in the camp where the men had their own "hooches" and could keep personal belongings. If a soldier's unit was normally in the bush, few of his comrades were left behind to look after things, and the area became rundown. Jerry Liucci, who spent 1968 with the *Wolfhounds,* rarely had the luxury of rest in camp. His little home in Cu Chi showed the results:

The *Wolfhound* compound at Cu Chi was no palace. Because everybody knew we were out in the field so often, no one really kept up the area. The line units' hooches looked pretty rotten. Mine got hit by a 122 rocket, and most of my effects in my locker box were burned. I had to wear penny loafers (with the pennies) with my khaki uniform when I finally returned from Vietnam. Being a grunt, you were like the bottom of the barrel.

Although many men echoed Liucci's observations concerning their individual dwellings at Cu Chi, most looked at the base camp with a kind of bemused awe. The irony of putting so much stateside comfort in the midst of a battlefield was not lost on soldiers accustomed to the harshness of the bush. Dan Vandenberg, who spent much of his tour in 1969 in a miserable perimeter near the large and extremely hazardous village of Trang Bang, expresses a representative view:

My God, base camps were incredible. They were the size of a big town. There were officers' clubs, PXs, enlisted men's clubs, and even dances. There was a sauna. I thought they were a joke until I tried one in Vietnam. You feel great for about 5 minutes. Then you step outside in the heat, and the sweat starts all over again. People were running around in civilian clothes, cooking steaks over barbecues. Everybody had a case of beer under his bunk. Some permanent hooches were air conditioned; they had maid service, with sheets and pillows. All of that stuff was totally unbelievable. Some of the guys had a life of luxury: They didn't have it that good back in the States. Every battalion had its own area, with bunkers and a place for the clerks. Each had its own little store for beer and sodas and such things. I'm not talking about the big PX here. It boggles my mind how much money it must have cost to set up each base camp. And then there were swimming pools. One guy I met recently had the job of lifeguard at a base camp swimming pool. It all depends on where you got stationed. Some people had the great life, and some people were treated worse than I'd treat a dog.

Vandenberg perhaps exaggerates somewhat. Cu Chi, the most elaborate camp in the Division's area, smelled like dung and was vulnerable to mortar attack at any moment. Yet, everything in his account was literally true. Civilian goods were everywhere. Food was hot and plentiful (although opinions concerning its quality varied, depending on individual taste). According to several accounts, the poultry industry of America did well at Cu Chi: The dinner menu often included "another fucking dead chicken." At least dessert was tolerable. The people of Hawaii donated an ice cream maker for Cu Chi. Ice itself, a luxury in the field, was made in huge quantities by machine. In some respects, the growth of Cu Chi showed the American soldier at his very best. Like their comrades from earlier wars, many GIs developed and refined the craft of scrounging into a high art. Indeed, much of the opulence described by Vandenberg and many others was the result of the efforts of the men on the spot, not due to policies dictated from above. Artilleryman Sidney Stone spent part of his tour in Cu Chi and gives an example of how this process worked:

Many of the longtime 25th Division people got the local Vietnamese to weave them straw roofs. They had these little straw sides you could prop up with bamboo, and they worked very well. Later, I was moved to a new billet, which I shared with another officer, and it had a straw roof. It was amazing how you could look up and see holes in the straw, but even during the heaviest monsoon, that roof would not leak. Of course, if one of our tents had the slightest abrasion, it would leak. Having the straw roof made it quite a lot cooler than a tent covering.

Our battalion commander decided it would be a good project for us to build an officers' club. We proceeded to send someone to Saigon to scrounge up building materials. We had an excess issue of heavy timber. We fixed up an old officers' billet and made our club. We built a bar and a patio with a roof over it, laid down a concrete floor, and put up a privacy fence around it all. We generally had parties every Saturday night. A few of our officers, especially the battalion surgeon, had made social liaison with some of the nurses over at 12th Evac hospital. We had some of the nurses over for Saturday night dinners. Since we were only 20 or 25 miles from Saigon, we would send someone to get a bunch of steaks from the commissary in Cholon. We would have a big cookout. We had an extra mess sergeant, and he was proud of the buffets he created for us. We had a lot of movies, and we would show them on the patio.

The presence of American women at Cu Chi obviously added to its unique character. There are larger issues involved concerning both medical care and morale that I shall examine in more detail. For the moment, however, it is sufficient to note that the men lucky enough to know the nurses socially considered themselves most fortunate and did not care for outside intruders. William McDill, a physical therapist for the 12th Evac during 1967, mentions a hazard faced by other officers visiting their club socially:

With the exception of the Red Cross workers, the only American women in our area were in the 12th Evac. Consequently, our club got a big play from any and all officer personnel on the base camp. As might be expected, this was a source of some friction between the medical officers and the "visitors," especially since the visitors occasionally left jeeps blocking the hooches or just generally in the way. And so the sport of jeep immersion was born. Jeep immersion consisted of releasing the brake on the offending vehicle and pushing it off the edge of the fill, into the "swamp," necessitating rescue by a tow vehicle. One night, one of our surgeons was caught in the act of depositing a jeep in the marshes, and the incident was duly reported by the offended party to the MPs [military police—EMB]. On the next day, the MPs came over to investigate the incident, and the surgeon in question told them that he had to be in surgery but would be happy to make himself available to them at 1100 the next day. At 0900 the next day, he, along with a large group of the original hospital complement, boarded a bus for Tan Son Nhut and a flight home.

The camp at Dau Tieng, although less elaborate, also became a haven of relative luxury, if one did not mind being mortared from any direction. In 1969, infantryman Dan Breeding was relieved of field duty and given a base camp assignment for the last few weeks of his tour, as was normally done. As luck would have it, Breeding became a bartender:

It was probably the happiest time of my life, getting out of the field and returning to the rear at Dau Tieng. I was a bartender at an enlisted men's club. It opened up at about 6:00 in the evening and stayed open until about 10:30–11:00. I just kept beer on ice. I got paid for it beyond my military pay. I gambled it all away, playing blackjack while sitting at the bar with the guys that came in.

While I was doing this, I realized how the Army worked, how a lot of your officers and high-ranking NCOs [noncommissioned officers—EMB] manipulated things. You scratch my back, I'll scratch yours. This included the allocation of supplies: not necessarily supplies that dealt directly with the war but supplies that were used in the rear, like an electric typewriter or, especially, booze. A lot of trading of that sort of thing went on. Each battalion was allocated so many cases of beer per month, and, naturally, at the end of the month, all of your better brands of beer were gone. So, you had to drink the rotgut, like Black Label or Falstaff. It was good if that was all you had. I found out from other NCOs how to get the popular beer. I managed to keep back maybe a couple of cases of Budweiser and Miller, the two top beers, just for our own use in their company area—a lot like stateside duty or regular civilian business.

In the rear, I found out that you could get a passport. Besides going to R & R [rest and recreation; a foreign leave granted everyone serving in Vietnam—EMB], I saved my money, got a passport, and went back on R & R. I just told the lieutenant in charge that I'd be gone for ten days, told him where I wanted to go, and he said, sure. I went back to Bangkok for the second time, this time traveling as a civilian, using my military ID as a visa, and had a great time.

Smaller camps sprouted up throughout the 25th Division's area of operations. These facilities were combat bases and were naturally quite different from the big camps. Some of the largest were the artillery firebases that
came to play a central role in the war. Some were temporary and could be
constructed in hours if the tactical situation demanded. Others were larger
and inhabited for long periods. Named after famous artillerymen, the
larger firebases also served as the field camps for other combat units. Lt.
Col. Carl Neilson, commander of the powerful 4/23d Mechanized Infantry
Battalion, guarded a large artillery base in Tay Ninh right after a furious
campaign during Tet and before another one the following fall in Tay Ninh
itself:

It was customary to locate artillery in the protection of combat infantry to
establish a network of bases with interlocking zones of fire. It was also customary to locate these firebases on infiltration routes. Firebase Rawlins was
my home for three or four months. Each night, it was the home of three rifle
companies, a 105mm battery, and a 155mm battery of artillery. But you
could never be sure if one or both of these batteries would be there because
they were frequently moved around.

We had taken a bulldozer and bermed up a perimeter around the firebase
that was about waist high. On top of it, we put barbed wire, and in front of
it, we put mines. We dug a ditch wide enough to put the armored personnel
carriers in "hull up," defilade position behind the berm: The only thing that
was exposed was the .50-caliber machine-gun mount. In the middle of the
camp were the support facilities: a mess hall, an aid station, command vehicles. Artillery was pretty much in the center, although there were provisions
to move them to the berm if it was necessary to fire direct. ["Direct fire" is
aimed at a visible, and thus close, target. Normally, artillery troops employ
"indirect fire" at targets they cannot see but are guided to by radio. Direct
fire from a berm would be a move of desperation and a sure sign that the
base was in danger of annihilation.—EMB] These camps were usually very
busy from 5:00 in the morning until about 7:00 P.M. when it was pitch-black.
At night, there really wasn't much going on, except that we were on guard
and anticipating attacks every night. There weren't any movies, there
weren't any lights, there wasn't any entertainment. There wasn't anything
for the troops to do, except sleep two hours and be on guard two hours.

Neilson viewed the war through the eyes of a mechanized battalion commander, and his men doubtlessly would have agreed with his description
of the firebase. The thousands of soldiers of the 25th, however, who served
as crewmen on the powerful armored personnel carriers would have said
that their real bases were the APCs—the "tracks"—themselves. Medic Lee

Reynolds served on one and found the life there preferable to that facing the infantry:

We lived in tracks and had it better than infantry. Infantrymen, they would tell you they wouldn't want to be in a track because it was a moving target for an RPG [rocket propelled grenade, a common and powerful antitank weapon used by the other side that resembled a bazooka—EMB]. Everyone likes to think the other guy has it worse. Living in a track is a little like touring the country in a Winnebago.

Bill Kestell, a track crewman during Tet 1968, has even fonder memories and shows the unlikely affection that many men had for their machines:

Living on a track was great! Tanks are mighty fine things: lots of armor, big main gun, but awfully short on room. Leg infantry has to carry every item they will need, and that means only the barest of essentials. When you live on a track or a Viper, as we called them in the unit, you have the best of both worlds. You have some armor protection against small arms. You have one .50-caliber machine gun and one 7.62-caliber machine gun, as well as a 90mm recoilless and an M79 grenade launcher for firepower, not to mention an assortment of small arms like M16s, M2 carbines, and M3 submachine guns. You have mobility without effort, and you have *room*. Room to carry the essentials and luxuries with the greatest of ease. Since we were RECON, we didn't have to transport troops, generally operating with 4- to 6-man crews. That left room for thousands of rounds of ammo, soda, beer, an ice cooler, and lots of C rations. You had a place to keep your personal possessions, a place to sleep in or under or on top of. It was like a compact camper! You were still a tempting target for the enemy but not so choice as a tank.

I lived with my Viper. I started driving in mid-February, transferring to #33, *Mellow Yellow*. [All tracks had numbers, but the crews gave them nicknames. I shall look more closely at them in the next chapter.—EMB] I liked driving a lot. I spent all my free time with her. When we would get into Cu Chi, RECON never stayed in their tents. We stayed with our chargers, in the motor pool. My favorite position for sleeping (dry season) was on top, with a blanket, over the radiator, under the M2 Browning. I have some very fond memories of track life. Like pulling the last guard before sunup, then making a big batch of steaming hot coffee for the crew (it was lousy coffee, but what the hell). When the situation was secure, the whole crew draped over her, sleeping up top, on the lowered ramp door, sitting, writing letters—oh, yes, it was a good life on a Viper.

Infantry troops also were at the firebases. Platoon leader Lt. Richard Blanks describes a rather different existence than that lived by Kestell:

Firebase Patton II was a perfect circle, with a berm 300 meters across, 24 bunkers in the berm, wire outside the berm. Usually, at any given time, three of the four companies were in Patton, along with some 155 self-propelled artillery. The fourth rifle company was usually out in a hard spot. My platoon was organized in three rifle squads: We didn't have a weapons squad; we assigned the machine-gun teams to the rifle squads. At any given time, I might have between 18 and 38 men, usually around 28. We were doing a lot of air missions during the day, about one every other day. My platoon was pulling about one ambush every third night. Sometimes, helicopters would take out the whole company about 5:00 P.M., and we would split up into platoon-sized ambushes.

Food was good at the firebase. We might have pancakes, bacon, orange juice, and a quart of milk. We had a change of fatigues every ten days or so. There were field showers. The trick was getting water. You'd take a bucket and go to the perimeter, where there were usually some Vietnamese kids. You'd pay one of the kids to fill the bucket at one of the Vietnamese wells in the paddies. One can of C rations was the going rate. During the afternoon, it was so hot we weren't usually hungry anyway, so maybe we'd eat a can of peaches. Had a subscription to *Atlanta Constitution Sunday*. It got there about eight days late. Somebody would have a radio. Radio Saigon played nonstop rock and roll, and it was on morning, noon, and night. Their call sign was "Radio Saigon, the beat goes on." The songs I remember best were "Sitting on the Dock of the Bay" and "Bad Moon Rising." The last one makes me think of ambushes.

Combat infantry troops were very often on extended field operations. They frequently constructed small temporary perimeters without names, referred to as "hard spots." They varied in size and permanence, but none was as large as a firebase. Jim Murphy had an unusual home, a small hard spot on top of Nui Ba Den, where he helped operate a strategically important observation and radio post. Relatively sedentary, Murphy found life tolerable:

As to the living conditions, we had a roof over our heads and hot meals. Nothing fancy, but when you have guys out in the bush chasing away mosquitoes and leeches in order to get a good night's sleep, one does not complain. I called it the Our Gang Club House, due to its architectural design. I spent six months in this five-star resort, sharing space with the rats, cockroaches, and snakes. There were 4 men in our hooch, a bit cramped, but we were not in there all at once. We kept some dogs that fared better than we did. These flea-bitten mutts didn't have to work, they ate well, and they enjoyed the companionship of the opposite sex. They were not champion stock, but we were very attached to them, and they kept the rats away.

Day-by-day life for infantrymen on operation was indistinguishable from their military existence, a subject for later chapters. Yet, even in the harsh and dangerous hinterlands, a type of domestic life-style developed. For instance, beyond coping with the rugged, hazardous conditions encountered in the field, many combat soldiers have strong memories of food and women for hire. C. W. Bowman, who spent the bulk of his tour in the bush, recalls the cuisine:

They would try to fly us a hot meal out to the field, but it didn't always get there. We ate mostly C rations. After a period of being there, if they issued us three meals of C rations, we'd sit down and eat all three and go the next day or so without eating. One of the favorites was to take your canteen cup, put in all of your coffee, sugar, and cocoa powder, and melt in the fudge bar you had with some rations; you'd end up with a canteen cup full of slurry. We'd drink that, and it had enough sugar and energy in it that you could go for a day or two without eating. Everybody had their own specialties. Guys would carry tabasco sauce to kill the taste of everything. Every now and then, if we were sweeping an area, we would rip off mama-san's cucumber patch or hot pepper patch and add that to our C rations. If you were back in camp, it wasn't so bad. You got to take a shower every day, you had three hot meals a day at the mess hall, and you had a roof over your head, with a cot to sleep on.

Morgan Sincock, a young combat officer, remembers relationships between the men and the local prostitutes:

Sex was for sale in many places in Vietnam. Prostitutes hung around fire support bases and even temporary tactical positions. I can recall setting up mortar tracks at a road intersection to support infantry searching an adjacent village. Kids and boom-boom girls showed up within minutes. Given the opportunity, some men would buy intercourse for less than $5. I recall one time when the battalion commander flew into one small base and spotted activity in a bombed-out building just outside the perimeter. We took a patrol to investigate and found a woman on her back on the floor servicing a line of GIs with $5 bills, waiting their turns in line outside the roofless room.

Like many of his fellow soldiers, Dan Breeding had experience dealing with both subjects:

The 25th Infantry was well known to keep the troops supplied, and they did. We were supplied quite often with water, C rations, and so forth. When you went out on a mission, you would, say, take two days' rations because it would be two days before you got resupplied. C rations weren't bad: When you were hungry, you could eat just about anything. You could usually have your choice of whatever you wanted. Everybody would go for the Beanie Weenies or turkey loaf, applesauce, fruit cocktail, or pound cake—that was a big item. You could swap off. There were lots of times we were resupplied with hot food. If we were in a place where there wasn't any contact, the mess sergeant would send out some hot food and cold milk: That was a treat. I've heard some guys from other divisions who said they never got anything like that. We were fortunate because we did get it occasionally.

Whenever we were around a village, the women would come out, the whores. I paid for a little nooky when I was there. I was the only one in my platoon who smoked Salems. When we got resupplied, there were always three or four packs of Salems or maybe a carton in our supply bag. As a whole, the Vietnamese girls preferred the menthol cigarettes. That's what I usually used for barter.

Dan Vandenberg no doubt expressed the feelings of almost all of his fellow infantrymen with his reflections on what was most prominent in his life in the field:

When you're over there, you sure appreciate the little things. Like when you got a can of Coke that was really cold, you didn't just open it and drink it. First, you rolled it up and down your arms, the back of your neck, along your forehead; you tried to cool yourself off, and when the can started to warm up, then you drank it. The first half of the can was just to get the dirt out of your throat, the last half you could enjoy. You dreamed about being cool again some day. You dreamed about taking a shower and not sticking a bucket down a well. You dreamed about lying in a clean bed with sheets and a pillow. Real simple things, but you think about it a lot. Think how nice it would be to have on clean clothes and not literally smell like a goat. All you wanted to do was get out of it in one piece, go home, and get a job. I can't say forget about it because you'll never forget about it but move on from it. Get on with the sort of life everybody else is living: normal life, where people aren't shooting or trying to blow you up.

Vandenberg got his wish, although it took a serious wound to achieve it. Many soldiers of the 25th Division did not. Regardless of how they lived, their existence was shaped above all by the violence encountered by each and every individual on or near the spearpoint of the U.S. Army in Vietnam. And the grim truth was that the soldier's fate often depended on the weapons used and how well he and his comrades employed them.

2

Tools of the Trade

O NE OF THE MOST PROMINENT characteristics of warfare since the introduction of gunpowder has been the increasing power and lethality of the
weapons used in battle. Not only have the weapons themselves become
more deadly, armed forces have also greatly increased in size, adding to the
number of increasingly effective armaments. The wealth of the state has
also increased, allowing the men using the weapons to expend a larger and
larger supply of ammunition and thereby greatly amplify the impact of the
weapons themselves. In the past, when battles were periodic and wars were
largely acts of maneuver or siege, ammunition was hoarded like gold for it
was expensive and difficult to transport and store. It might appear strange
that a fine general like Robert E. Lee would object to breech-loading and
repeating rifles on grounds that the soldiers would waste ammunition. Yet,
Lee knew very well that supplies were always short and had to be dispersed
carefully, often during battle itself. He also knew that if more ammunition
was available, the supply trains that were so difficult to defend and such a
drain on manpower would only become longer. And he realized that if a
weapon was easy to load behind cover, soldiers would use as much ammunition as they could lay their hands on. Artillery munitions were an even
larger problem. Frederick the Great had feared the consequences of an
"arms race" in the realm of artillery, knowing that this would greatly up the
ante on the financial costs of war and make his tactics, based on rapid maneuver with well-trained, closely packed infantry, ultimately obsolete. Yet,
nothing could retard the growth in knowledge and physical skills required
to create increasingly more lethal weapons. Although armies in the early
stages of conflicts often almost ran out of ammunition (as happened in
both world wars, for instance), modern industrial economies were perfectly suited to make the rapid transformation that produced today's killing machines.

All armies, to one degree or another, learned a horrid and bitter lesson as wars grew larger: Regardless of an army's training, skill, and leadership, if its opponent had the will to fight and was reasonably competent, there was almost no quick or easy way to bring a war to a conclusion on the battle-field. The military component of wars was always prominent, but it be-came only one part of the struggle between whole nations once political will, industrial capability, size, and resource base all became indispensable to the war effort. No longer could a king save his pfennigs, create a war chest, and hope to win a province with a quick thrust. Naturally, the devel-opment of great steel warships, the construction of hordes of vehicles, both combat and noncombat, and the introduction of aircraft in such numbers that during World War II they could blacken the skies represented further steps in this long process.

In one way, Vietnam fit very nicely into the developments just outlined. Like so many major conflicts of the past two centuries, it was a war of attri-tion, lasting years. Many commentators on the war have claimed that the Americans dropped several times more bombs in Southeast Asia than they did during all of World War II. Whether statistics like this can be genuine is questionable: Who would know how many tons of bombs and artillery were used during World War II? However, there is no question that U.S. aircraft dropped bombs in incalculable numbers during the Vietnam War. American ground forces and, to a lesser extent, their South Vietnamese allies used artillery whenever they wished, with little worry about short-ages. They also had technical resources such as radar, computer-guided ar-tillery, sensors, and "drone" aircraft. Helicopters and gunships are almost symbols of the war, just as the trenches were in World War I and tanks were during World War II. (Much information is still classified. The successes of the "smart weapons" late in the war were not something the Pentagon wanted to scream from the rooftops. And no air force likes to mention the word *drone:* It inevitably calls into question the ultimate role of pilots.) Compared with their opponents, allied forces in Vietnam had every tech-nical advantage imaginable. No wonder so many people have questioned how we could have lost.

Much of this paradox can be explained by examining the weapons em-ployed and the types of combat they were used in. For there was another dimension to the deadly game played by both sides in Vietnam. To an ex-tent that is rarely recognized, the nature of a war without fronts made it impossible for the United States to properly bring to bear its mighty arse-nal. Despite all the technological power in the hands of American commanders, the war in the bush usually was fought with infantry weapons in huge numbers of small, vicious, but lightning-quick exchanges of fire at very close range. This fact gave Vietnam a most unusual military character. It resembled, in an odd way, the adventure novels written years ago by Edgar Rice Burroughs about wars and adventures on Mars. His heroes and villains would ride around in spacecraft, fantastic weapons at their disposal, but, at the critical moment, they would fight it out, man to man, with swords and shields. In Vietnam, despite the artillery, B-52s, and gunships, the queen of the battlefield, amazingly, was the humble rifle and other weapons carried by combat infantrymen of both sides. The men of the 25th knew this and recognized the role played by the more powerful weapons. Indeed, weaponry was central to the soldiers' world. It is a good time to examine more closely the devices of death used in Vietnam.

Infantry Weapons

Infantrymen are a proud breed. In every war, ancient or modern, they have dealt with the worst conditions and done more than their share of the dying. For centuries, the infantry, particularly if properly coordinated with the other combat arms available, dominated the battlefield. However, despite the suffering faced by the "grunts" of all wars, the tactical role and importance of infantry has declined greatly in the twentieth century. Infantry traditionally performed three roles: It held ground, took ground, and conducted precise reconnaissance when on patrol. In recent times, only the last of these roles remained crucial during large wars. As best exemplified during World War II, the infantryman on defense served to protect the real queen of ground combat: the machine gun. One machine gun, properly concealed and protected by riflemen from infiltration by the opposing infantry, was capable of stopping an entire battalion of infantry in open terrain, as was shown time and again in the field. It is true that infantrymen took ground, but in many cases, they occupied it rather than seized it. The real work of destruction and psychological disorientation required to dislodge a determined defender was done by the other monarch of modern war: artillery. Ground-support aircraft, when used close to the front, had the same role as artillery. The lines manned by the infantry also served to protect the gunners and their lethal devices. When radio communications improved to the point where artillery fire could be used as an accurate and nearly instantaneous defensive instrument, the power of that artillery was amplified. And between machine guns and artillery, any infantry assault, no matter how skillfully conducted, ran the risk of instant annihilation. If tanks are properly defined as mobile machine guns or machine-gun killers (troops had to kill tanks to protect their machine guns), then the point is even more clear. In a later chapter, I will examine this lethal combination, which was very much in evidence on selected battlefields in Vietnam. It is a major reason why American ground forces were never defeated in a pitched battle—a record without precedent in past wars.

However, despite the astonishing power of modern weapons, only the infantry could patrol and probe. It was while conducting such missions that most infantrymen died, once it became clear to generals that massed infantry assault was suicidal. Military historians do not always do a good job of illustrating the obvious. How, for instance, do the lines that appear so neatly on maps get on these maps in the first place? There is a very accurate slogan in today's armed forces: What you can see, you can kill. This somber fact, however, has been true for a long time. No matter what the terrain, defenders have always taken extraordinary measures to remain hidden. If they did not, the artillery would kill them in short order. But, as already noted, a hidden machine gun, with infantry surrounding it, is ready and able to obliterate any small infantry unit in sight. (Indeed, if only small numbers of probing infantrymen were observed, riflemen would be given the job of shooting them so the machine gun's fire would not give away its position.) Therefore, good infantrymen advancing at the lead of any army move cautiously and remain alert. Yet, eventually, the defender will likely be the first to see and the first to kill. For example, if a commander during World War II wanted to know where a German position was, patrols were sent out. Where the men began to die in large numbers, the Germans could be found. It was then time to call for the gunners and pilots to dislodge the defenders and exact vengeance for dead comrades. Did the gunners and pilots do the job? The patrols again went forward and found out. If the answer was yes, the patrols went past the original killing ground, "mopped up" pockets of resistance, and continued on until the next batch of soldiers fell and a new enemy position was discovered. This is a capsule description of the modern killing machine that has made warfare so violent and wretched that it almost defies description or rational analysis.

In Vietnam, however, the chemistry of the conflict was quite different from that of the massive linear slaughters of earlier generations. As I will examine in the next chapter, the tactical momentum of combat in Vietnam had a unique character in comparison to what the U.S. Army was prepared and organized to do. For the moment, it is enough to note that during Vietnam, the patrol mission became the dominant mission for all the combat arms. Regardless of whether a fighter was on the ground, in a vehicle, or in an aircraft, the primary mission was to "find Charlie." "Search and destroy" aptly describes the bulk of operations during the war. When the enemy was found, usually the hard way, then the proper engines of death could be called upon. Finding the skilled opponents, however, proved very difficult. It also became a job best handled by the infantry. And if infantry is important, so are infantry weapons.

One reason that machine guns and artillery became so dominant in war was that they surpassed the power of rifles and other small arms by several magnitudes. The breech-loading rifles of the Franco-Prussian War in 1870, although single shot, were extremely formidable and not much inferior to the rifles carried by infantrymen during World War II. On the twentieth-century battlefield, the type of rifle carried did not mean much: Similarities among rifles far outweighed their differences. Nor were they very good weapons. Few soldiers are good marksmen in the heat of battle, and the rate of fire was low. At close range, ground soldiers became more dangerous. Mortars, the infantryman's own light artillery, would come into play first. If men closed further, accuracy became less important, and powerful grenades became extremely effective. Unescorted tanks attacked hidden infantry at their own peril. If, through luck or skill, attacking infantrymen succeeded in "killing" a machine gun, then hand-to-hand combat, the rarest form of fighting, became a very real possibility.

As World War II progressed, infantry weapons entered a renaissance. When it became evident that accuracy and marksmanship were the exception rather than the rule, more infantry troops were equipped with submachine guns of various types. These weapons lacked range and accuracy, but they could lay down a proper wall of lead. After the war, semi- and fully automatic rifles were developed. Rifles like the M14, developed for troops assigned to the North Atlantic Treaty Organization (NATO), were heavy but combined accuracy with a reasonably high rate of fire. They were complemented by light machine guns that could be handled by a single soldier in a pinch. Grenades, previously thrown by hand, were matched with several types of launching systems, in effect giving every squad one or more small mortars that were instantly available. Grenades themselves were redesigned and made much more powerful. And better communications made infantry forces on the ground the eyes for terrifying support weapons.

Americans have a long tradition of innovation in the realm of weaponry. Eli Whitney, famous for the cotton gin, also developed mass production techniques for muskets. We invented the submarine and were the first to purchase a military aircraft. During World War II, when the Germans had superior weaponry in general, American infantrymen carried the M1, a semiautomatic rifle still in use around the world today. Although not developed far enough, the bazooka was the first small infantry weapon that could kill a tank (if conditions were right, which they usually were not). Among infantry weapons, the M16 was a logical development and fit our ideas concerning war to perfection. It was the quintessential infantry weapon of the Vietnam War and the most controversial individual weapon since the crossbow.

On paper, the M16 was a work of art in the most grim of crafts. With a stock made of plastic, not wood, it was light, and a few pounds less to carry was much appreciated by an exhausted infantryman, particularly if the temperature was over 100 degrees. It fired a .223-caliber round, the smallest bullet ever used in war. There was an inevitable sacrifice in accuracy at long range; in return, however, came two huge advantages. First, there was the M16's incredible rate of fire. One reason why soldiers in Vietnam carried so much ammunition was because they could fire a great deal of it so quickly. Second, for complex reasons including its extraordinary velocity, the .223 bullet was far less likely than larger rounds to pass directly through a victim. Instead, it tended to deform or deflect on impact, creating a serious or lethal wound. However, this also meant that a very small obstacle could deflect the bullet in flight. It was a trade-off: The M16 was a superb weapon at laying down a wall of lead, but it was inferior if range and punch were required. This alone was enough to make it controversial. (This controversy has never stopped, although many armies today would like to adopt a similar weapon; Israel already has.) But another factor was at work, as well: The earliest models of the M16 were not reliable. It was the infantrymen serving in Vietnam who discovered the dual nature of their major weapon, which was slowly introduced in the early 1960s. And they did not always like the result.

Before examining the specific views of 25th Division veterans about the various weapons they employed, it is both important and interesting to note two characteristics of the relationship that existed between combat soldiers and their armaments. First, although some soldiers took a genuine interest in the technicalities of their arms and others did not, to a man they treated the subject with the utmost seriousness. It is the essence of the sad morality of battle that good weapons and good use of them can spell the difference between life and death. However combat soldiers felt about the subject of violence, it was a very rare individual who would not prefer to kill than be killed. In this regard, words are very important. For example, I never heard any combat veteran refer to his weapon as a "gun," unless, of course, he served in the artillery: The M16 or one of the others was invariably a "weapon" or a "rifle." Although many own guns in civilian life, several of the men openly expressed scorn for what one vet called the "civilian gun nut mentality." A .44-magnum pistol in the hands of Dirty Harry might impress film audiences, but to a combat soldier, it is a toy. This brings me to the second point: Combat soldiers were not only accustomed to state-of-the-art instruments of killing, they were also surrounded by them. This was especially true in Vietnam because the combat zone was almost unlimited. Weapons of all types were everywhere, and no soldier went anywhere without a lethal instrument within close reach. In the field, rifles accompanied men to the latrine and to their places of sleep. And even if one wielded the most basic of arms, larger and tremendously powerful weapon systems such as armored vehicles, helicopter gunships, and jet fighter bombers were a frequent sight. Artillery or mortars were so common that they blended into the landscape, unless, naturally, they were firing in a unit's support. The world of the 25th Division was a world overflowing with the instruments of war—and this was not at all unique in Vietnam. Veterans became so acclimated to this fact that many remarked that one of their most difficult transitions when joining civilian life was to stop instinctively looking for their rifles. No wonder this is a subject that veterans do not treat lightly. This is particularly true concerning the most common weapon in Vietnam—the M16.

Sgt. Charles Albridge, an early arrival at Cu Chi, participated in one of the tests conducted on the M16 immediately before the war began in earnest for U.S. ground forces. As he recalls, the weapon was not well received by the highly trained and often battle-experienced NCOs that put it through its paces:

In June 1965, CDEC [Combat Development and Experimentation Command—EMB] at Fort Ord was testing the M16 against the M14, the AK47, and the Stoner System that fired the same .223-caliber round that the M16 fired. All the feedback was negative. It had a tendency to jam, it was too temperamental, and the round itself wouldn't knock down a standard Army pop-up target. The original targets were made out of fiberboard, and their thickness and weight was based on the human body. If the round could knock down the target, it could knock down a man. Well, the .223 round would not knock down the targets, so they put some sheet metal behind them so they would fall down when we hit the darn things. They circulated a report among noncoms and officers (I was a sergeant at the time) so we would understand that our feedback had been taken into account. The report was negative. The recommendation was to keep the M14 rifle. You can imagine my surprise in June of 1966 when I was walking down a pier in Hawaii to get on a troop ship and they take my M14 away from me and give me an M16. I still wonder why, because the Army's own test units turned it down, and the Army bought it anyway.

Initially, the men liked it. They went from a rifle that weighed 9 pounds to one that weighed just over 5, and they liked it. Any time you give a soldier less weight to carry, he's happy. About the time they realized that a twig would deflect the bullet and 30 percent of your rounds fired into a jungle never got past the underbrush, you start mistrusting the weapon. The basic load was 200 rounds for each infantryman. The problem was that most of the guys were carrying 400, 500, or 600 rounds of ammunition with them if they could get it, simply because they knew they needed it.

They also started carrying cans of oil with them. When you stopped firing that weapon, if it was clean when you started, it wouldn't jam. But when you stopped firing and didn't clean it right away, you had a problem. Every weapon the Army has used that is semiautomatic—the M14, the M1, the old carbine, for that matter—was gas operated, and the gas was ported against a piston, which pushed a rod that activated the bolt. With the M16, that gas was ported straight into the bolt. The problem is that there is carbon in the gas. When the carbon gets in the bolt, as long as it's hot, there's no problem, and it will continue to fire. As soon as you quit firing and the weapon has a chance to cool down, the carbon solidifies and you end up with the weapon jamming. We found a stopgap. As soon as you stopped firing, you squirted oil into the bolt before you closed the dustcover over the bolt. You still had the jams, but it wasn't as bad. So most of the troops griped about the Tinkertoy.

As usual, Sgt. Maj. Kenneth Stumpf minces no words concerning this weapon:

The M16 sucked. Mine jammed four times under fire. I used to think, how can we be so far ahead of every other nation in the world and they can't give us a rifle that would shoot a fucking bullet? It was good in that it was light and the ammunition was light, a lot better than the M14 in that regard. But it lacked hitting power. There were times when I must have shot a guy twenty times and he kept on coming. You almost had to shoot the bastard in the head to knock him down. I wonder how many people died because of that weapon jamming. And I cleaned that weapon all the time. We should have had a better weapon. The later M16 was a better weapon. But how many soldiers died "testing" the weapon in Vietnam?

Although he served much later and received a newer model of the M16, Dan Vandenberg is also a critic:

I had an M16, which had a lot of bad raps. They say if you kept the thing clean, it worked just fine, which is great as long as you're operating on concrete. But out in the jungle, where it's nothing but dirt, it's totally impossible to keep them clean. Every time you had the chance, you were supposed to break them down and clean them. But you couldn't always get cleaning equipment, so that was a total waste. So every time the moment of truth came and you had to fire your weapon at somebody, you never knew if the damn thing was going to fire. And if it did fire, it would fire 5 rounds or 10 rounds. For jungle warfare, Charlie had much better weapons: the AK47. You could drive a truck over them, and you couldn't hurt those damn things; you could pour sand down their barrels and they would still fire. Ours would jam if you looked at them wrong.

Tet veteran Larry Fontana, although he wielded a redesigned model, pointed to a problem that went beyond reliability but resulted from the rate of fire, supposedly one of the advantages of the rifle. In a view that would have made sense to Robert E. Lee, he suggests that the M16 could be too much of a good thing:

My personal feeling was that the M16 rifle never needed an automatic cycle because of its extremely fast rate of fire. Most soldiers fought with it on semiautomatic. Autofire was just John Wayne stuff—impressive but not practical. [The M16 could be switched between semiautomatic fire, single shots as fast as one could pull the trigger, to fully automatic, which emptied a magazine simply by keeping the trigger depressed. The troops called automatic fire "full rock and roll."—EMB]

Jerry Liucci, who was in fierce combat throughout Tet, saw the old M16 replaced during his tour with a greatly improved model:

My first weapon was the old M16 with the open flash suppressor on the end. I found it to be a poor operating weapon. It would jam quite often. We had a light firefight in the Ho Bo Woods, and I had three jams. I removed the magazine, extracted the round that was in there, tried another magazine, then tried to clear the weapon and start over again. It seemed the weapon just didn't want to operate for me properly. It might fire a couple of rounds, then jam. I also thought it was poor because you could put only 18 rounds in the clip, not the full 20. The VC or the gooks had a weapon that fired 30 rounds at you. We were kind of outgunned by them. I thought it was the poorest weapon of its time.

Later, we were issued another M16, which I took on in my last sixty days. It seemed to be a completely new weapon. The chamber and bolt were chromed. Anything I put in there zipped right through with no problem. It fired flawlessly. But I still didn't have a banana clip. We used to tape our clips together to give us two 18-round clips. We usually carried between 16 and 25 clips, at least I did. [The "standard load," the military term for the expected amount of ammunition to be carried by infantrymen, was 10 clips with 20 rounds in each. Almost all riflemen carried more.—EMB]

Like Vandenberg and Liucci, Lt. Thomas Giltner, a platoon leader in 1966, had praise for the enemy's main weapon, the AK47:

I've handled the AK47 and fired it on a bunker line. It is a fine weapon. It has magazines of various capacities. There are very few moving parts because it is blow-back operated. It is not terribly accurate under field conditions but accurate enough. It has tremendous tolerances for terrain and climate. It is small and not too heavy.

The AK47 was a highly prized souvenir and frequently traded by frontline troops to those in the rear for choice booty. However, despite some books and movies to the contrary, no sane American would have used one in combat. The AK47 and the M16 make very different sounds. In addition, Americans employed red tracer shells at night, while the enemy used green. Because firefights were largely a matter of firing at sounds or anything that served as a visual clue to the enemy's location, a GI using an AK47, no matter how good the weapon, would have been in danger of being shot by either side. South Vietnamese militia units sometimes used captured weapons, but, in their case, the danger was minimal because they rarely fought at night until late in the war when they possessed M16s.

The M16 had its defenders. Roger McGill was one of the first soldiers of the 25th to arrive in Vietnam, and, because he had peacetime service under his belt, he was also familiar with the NATO-issue M14. This may be one area in which the extra training received by the first group of soldiers that went to Vietnam from the peacetime Army was helpful.

The M14 was very reliable and durable, single shot or auto. It had a 7.62mm, 20-round magazine, and I was trained with it before going to Vietnam. Before I left Hawaii, I was issued the M16. It also had a 20-round magazine but had a tendency to jam. The first issue had problems with the firing pin mechanism, but that was changed. I liked its light weight and ease of handling. It was simple to assemble and disassemble. You didn't have to put linseed oil on the stock because it wasn't wood but a very durable hard plastic. You did have to keep it clean and in good working order. The range of the M16 was adequate.

. Jim Ross was on the scene very late in the day, arriving in February 1970. Coming to Vietnam during the dry season was always an adventure, and Ross, serving with the 2/22d Mechanized Infantry Battalion, was in the middle of some very ugly fighting in April that led up to the Cambodian incursion. During this time, he got the chance to try out a number of weapons and had praise for the M16:

The M16 was the standard-issue rifle. It fired a 5.56mm shell with a very small bullet. At least, the lead portion was small. The shell casing, on the other hand, was about $1^{1}/_{2}$ inches and packed quite a bit of powder. The early models had a lot of problems, and some of our men were killed because their weapons wouldn't fire.

I read something called *Rules of Combat They Never Tell You.* The first item on the list was "Never Share a Foxhole with Somebody Braver Than You Are." Another item was "Your Weapon Was Made by the Lowest Bidder." And that's generally true. However, they revamped the M16. The government demanded satisfaction, and it was reissued.

In addition to its very light weight, it was very durable. It was almost impossible to tear one of those things up. The miracle is the wallop that the tiny bullet packs. The muzzle velocity of the bullet is 3,800 feet per second. That's how fast that bullet is traveling when it leaves the end of that barrel. That's about four-fifths of a mile in a second of flight. When you get hit with something traveling that speed, it's going to do all kinds of severe and ugly things. It was a very versatile weapon, and I really can't say anything bad about it. If there was a drawback, it was the rate of fire on fully automatic. It would fire so fast it was almost like taking a deck of cards and ruffling it with your thumb, then the clip was empty. It would just burp it out, and it was gone. You couldn't fire accurately on fully automatic, you just couldn't do it. Yet, it was a very good weapon and still standard-issue twenty years later. That tells you something about its durability and how well it fits into ground combat.

The M16 was the most notable weapon carried by the men of the 25th Division, but it was only one member of a lethal menagerie. Men that objected to the M16 were normally given the heavier but powerful M14. Some men, particularly if they were forward observers or if they filled other specialty roles, were allowed to carry more unusual weapons, sometimes at their own expense. A number of them carried short-barreled shotguns, which were good weapons in very dense terrain. There were more eccentric firearms also, as Dan Vandenberg recalls:

One of our men carried a sniper rifle, I have no idea to this day why. They sent him to sniper school, put a scope on his rifle, and that was the last of it. He just walked around like a dummy with the rest of us with an awkward scope on his rifle.

Humble weapons with long histories also played a very major role in Vietnam. For example, the men used variations on two World War I staples—sandbags and barbed wire. Although crude, these devices saved thousands of American lives: Sand is great protection from all types of weapons, and wire creates a tremendous obstacle for any attacker wanting to storm a position. Mickey Andrews describes their use:

We would only fill a sandbag about two-thirds full. That way, enough bag was left to use as a flap to hold in the dirt. We never had to tie a bag, and when we moved out, we simply picked the bag up and the dirt fell out. We reused our bags, and tearing down our bunkers was a relatively quick process.

After building bunkers, we stretched out strands of concertina wire. Sharp, razored edges were closely spaced along the wire. We used a stick or shovel to hit the wire and break the strands apart. We would reverse the process when leaving. The strands would be pushed together like a slinky and carried on the tracks for use at a new place. When laying out concertina wire, two rows were laid side by side, and a third row was laid on top of the other two for height. This job invariably resulted in cut hands, arms, and legs while handling the wire.

In addition, like their fathers and grandfathers, most men carried hand grenades. Normally, they were weapons, but some produced smoke and could serve as markers for artillery support or to help medical helicopters locate a unit requiring aid. Furthermore, the humble hand grenade was a little less humble in Vietnam than its predecessors had been in earlier wars. Thomas Giltner liked grenades a great deal:

Improvements were made in the hand grenade. I believe it was called the M26 A2. A very fine fragmentation grenade, with 13 ounces of composition B explosive. It weighs about 1 pound. It came with a $4^{1}/_{2}$-second fuse and possessed a killing range of several meters in all directions. It was a whole lot better than the old pineapple.

Kenneth Stumpf liked them even more:

I loved hand grenades. I carried a sandbag full of the things. I figured, if I can't kill the enemy, I'll scare the shit right out of them.

Because grenades were so valuable, it made sense to create weapons that could launch them much farther than a man could throw them. For most of the Vietnam War, until replaced by a model of the M16 with a special attachment, that weapon was the M79 grenade launcher. The M79 is almost unknown outside military circles. An odd-looking, short device, it looks almost like a toy rifle with a very short barrel. Looks can deceive, however. Although Hollywood has never included it properly in the fake renditions of Vietnam combat, it was one of the most commonly used and most admired weapons of the war. This was a reasonable assessment when one considers that this small weapon could easily kill within 5 meters of impact and wound within 15.

Medic Lee Reynolds, like most men in his job, realized that he was a prime target in a firefight: Medics rarely wore anything on their uniforms to distinguish themselves from other soldiers. Also, like most medics in combat, Reynolds believed in "preventive medicine"—in other words, he went out armed and would participate in combat unless his primary duty intruded, which often happened. Reynolds served with a mechanized unit, but like many crewmen, he fought on the ground more than once. The M79 was a favorite weapon:

The Duper is the M79 grenade launcher, which fires a 40mm explosive shell with a kill radius of about 5 meters. It was a pretty devastating weapon. If I killed anyone, it was with a Duper. It's known as a Duper because of the sound it makes when you fire it, which is different than any I have ever heard in a movie. When you fire, it makes a sound like "dupe."

Jim Ross was also a great admirer of the M79 and gives an accurate description of its odd nature:

The M79 grenade launcher is a fantastic weapon. The bore is 40mm, and the round is like a fat bullet, about as big around as a flashlight and half as long. It is shaped the same as a bullet you'd put in a revolver except it is almost the size of your fist. The M79 is short, like a sawed-off shotgun, and is hinged in the middle where it breaks open to load. There is no explosion when it fires, just a blooping sound, a little "punk, punk." It kicks some, and you have to

keep your thumb off the top of the stock to keep from getting cut by the hammer. I think its range is about 300 yards, and if your eye is quick, you can see the round as it flashes out and arcs through the air. You have to aim it upward, and it takes a lot of practice to get good with it. In Vietnam, a really proficient grenadier could get off a round probably every 3 or 4 seconds. There are a variety of rounds you can launch: high-explosive, flares, white phosphorous, smoke, etc. It you have a good fix on your enemy, you can bring a tremendous amount of chaos down on his head with just one M79 in nothing flat. It is very effective and deadly.

Like many men, Jerry Liucci at one time or another used several different weapons. During the early weeks of the 1968 Tet Offensive, the Duper was his weapon of choice. Liucci explains why:

After I got frustrated with the old M16, I took on an M79 grenade launcher. I felt it was as flawless a weapon as you could have. The only problem was, when you were out and walking point, the weapon wasn't good. There, you would need a shotgun round, and it only held one. Also, it had a high-explosive round that looked like a big bullet. You'd fire a single shot at a time. It had a thumb latch; you'd break it in half, and then you'd slip the round in and fire it. It made that "duping" sound. You'd reopen it, pull that spent shell out, and then go on. It had a nice range. It was fairly lightweight. The only thing that was heavy was the high-explosive [HE] rounds, and you had to carry a lot of them. I carried a claymore bag in the front, full of high-explosive, and my rucksack on my back was also full of HE rounds. During an ambush we sprung near Hoc Mon, I remember firing 25 to 30 rounds as fast as I could. That isn't real fast with an M79, but it's fast enough when you're firing hand grenades at people. During a large nighttime firefight outside of Cu Chi, I might have fired 50 rounds at a position I was aiming at. It worked very well. I think it really kept the enemy at bay. When you're tossing grenades at them, they tend to take off or get down. It was a good weapon. I carried it through Tet.

Dan Breeding also carried an M79 for a time. His observations parallel those of Liucci, although his experience proved a bit less dramatic:

I liked the M79, the grenade launcher. I used it mostly when guarding perimeter at the fire support bases. Sometimes, we would do free fire, with everyone firing at a point at a certain time. I carried it out in the field for a short while. The only trouble there was the weight of the ammo you had to carry. You had to carry mainly high-explosive rounds. But also, I carried a bandolier of the shotgun-type shells, white phosphorous, and smoke rounds. Once you had all of these, it contributed to the weight of your ruck-sack considerably.

Once, I remember, we were in a company-sized operation. I was out on the flank with my platoon, and to my right was some high elephant grass. I saw something moving in the grass. I couldn't tell what it was, but I could see the top of the grass moving. Me and another guy got everybody's attention and told them to be quiet because of what we were seeing. Naturally, I thought it was gooks crawling up to our position. We kept seeing the grass shaking and moving. It came closer, and it got within 10 feet, and you could hear the grass move. When it got to that distance, I just stuck up the M79 and fired off a shotgun shell. All it was was a wild pig or a domestic pig that just got lost in the jungle. It was a big occasion. Everybody said I had a KIA [killed in action—EMB] and that Walter Cronkite would announce it on the evening news.

Because the M79 was single shot and because point-blank combat in Vietnam was a very real possibility, grenadiers had the option of carrying a pistol, as well. Officers carried them as a sign of authority, and other specialty personnel also might use one. The standard pistol was the famous Colt .45-caliber automatic, in service for decades. Although some found it useful if one took the time to learn to shoot it with accuracy, Jerry Liucci's opinion of it is more typical:

Another weapon a gunner or Duper man would carry was the .45. I did not feel it was an accurate weapon. The enemy would have to be pretty close for you to get a decent round off. It was a heavy cannon. Accuracy came only through proper training, which I don't feel we got enough of. It usually was a rusting hulk on your hip, a poor weapon in the tropics because it rusted quite easily. Because the springs in the magazines would rust, chambering a round was difficult sometimes. It added to the weight we would carry, which was a lot if you were a gunner or a Duper man. It seemed like I was already bent over. Fortunately, I captured a .38 Smith and Wesson off a dead Viet Cong. They traced the serial numbers and found he had probably killed a military policeman. That was a good weapon.

Pistols might be secondary, even a hindrance. No soldier would say the same about the Pig, the M60 light machine gun. Like the M79, it never received publicity, but it was one of the most important weapons in the infantry arsenal and remains so today. All armies have the equivalent. There is good reason for this, as C. W. Bowman illustrates:

I carried an M60 machine gun for about a month. It had bipods on, and you could set it on a tripod, but nobody carried the tripod. We carried it on our shoulders. It was a good weapon. You could hold the weapon sideways, and the recoil would force the barrel left to right instead of up and down. You could fire a 100-round belt through it standing up. All you had to do when you fired as far to the right as you wanted was pull the gun back to the left with your hand. There was very little recoil to it. It had a quick change of barrel, but you had to be careful. They issued asbestos gloves, but we never carried them. Normally, if we had to change barrels, somebody would rip his shirt off, pull off the old barrel, and put the new one in. You could tell when the barrel was worn out. When you were shooting, the rounds would start going erratic, to the left and right, and the tracers would hit the dirt in front of you. Then you knew the barrel was burned out. And we burned out many a barrel.

Roger McGill had M60s on his armored personnel carrier. He was also a great admirer of the weapon:

The M60 was a real workhorse. We had two mounted on our track. It was easy to handle and fired 7.62 ammo and had the capability of using a belt of ammo. You could fire a lot of rounds in a short amount of time, and it was easy to assemble. The barrel could be changed easily, which sometimes had to be done because of the heat. At times, it would glow red from the rounds passing through the barrel. Every fifth round was a red tracer, so at night, you could see the direction of your fire. It was an excellent and reliable weapon. It was also used by helicopter door gunners. It weighed about 30 pounds.

Bowman recalls the weight to be somewhat less, but the M60 was a great burden. Carrying ammunition for it was a job shared by several men. But though no one liked to carry it, it was priceless in a fight. Consequently, as the war progressed, even leg infantry carried more and more of these powerful machines. Mickey Andrews served with a mechanized unit during late 1968. When on patrol, crewmen often walked, usually near the slowly moving APCs, and they, too, liked the Pig. As Andrews relates, soldiers altered the M60 to make it more effective:

The M60 was designed to carry a 100-round "assault pouch" to allow the gunner to open fire while standing. It either jammed or wasn't available. When we carried it on ambush, we used a 44-round belt the soldiers worked out. The weapon was loaded with one end of the belt, and the rest of it was wrapped around a frank-and-beans can attached to the side of the M60. The "beenie weenie" can came from our C rations and worked perfectly. There was no dangling belt to make noise or snag on something. You could fire while walking, and the gun never jammed.

The Army included virtually everything in its bag of tricks for the infantry in Vietnam, whether the weapon suited the war or not. Two specialized weapons, designed primarily for antitank warfare, were quite common, although they often stayed in camp. One was the LAW (light antitank weapon)—a small, disposable rocket launcher. Because American troops encountered enemy tanks on only a handful of occasions (the 25th never did), the LAW's primary role was moot. And as the following remarks from Dan Vandenberg show, soldiers had little patience with weapons that were not useful:

Sometimes, we'd take a LAW along. It's disposable. Leave it to the good old United States of America to come up with disposable weapons. They're a one-shot deal, a minibazooka. After you fire, you just break the damn thing against a tree. It's more or less made out of cardboard. I heard stories that the reason we broke them after firing is that Charlie could convert them into mortar tubes.

Yet, as Tet veteran Jerry Liucci recalls, there is a time and a place for everything, including generally ill-suited weaponry:

The LAW looked like an olive-drab tube. You popped off the end caps and extended it. It had pop-up, clear plastic sights and a rubber trigger on the top. So, when you held it, it looked like a toy bazooka. It had a rocket with a warhead inside, and when it did fire, it was effective, but you had to be careful because of its backblast. Unfortunately, we were in a lot of water, and after a while, that damaged the firing mechanism inside the rocket. I did fire it once and hit a bamboo clump from where the enemy was firing at us. And, boy, it must have rung his clock because it was quite powerful when it did go off. I also had a misfire. I crawled away from it at a perpendicular angle and wasn't hurt.

Other men gave secondhand accounts of the 25th Division infantry using LAWs against enemy bunkers, which was their purported role in Vietnam. More men griped about the 90mm recoilless rifle, which was sent to Vietnam in large numbers. It is among the heaviest infantry weapons and is almost never used in the field. Firing powerful shells of various types, it had a very dangerous backblast. Because of its weight, it was used almost exclusively as a defensive weapon in a fixed position. Various vehicles carried it, with ad hoc devices frequently attached. As Bill Kestell remembers, the recoilless rifle was the star player in a choice tale of military idiocy:

One time, we noticed that the front band had loosened and the handle of the recoilless rifle had fallen off somewhere in the Ho Bo Woods. When we went to the armorer for a replacement, they told us that we would have to hand over the original part before they would issue a replacement. We explained that we needed a new part because the original one was lost, but the armorer was not moved: no old part, no new part. To make a long story short, this went through three levels of maintenance, all with the same result. However, without the front handle, the 90mm was inoperable. In desperation, we took the recoilless rifle back to the motor pool and placed it on the ground in front of a track. We drove over it, squashing it like a tin can. Then we took it back to the first armorer, who accepted it as a damaged item and issued a new one, complete with missing handle.

A very simple but extraordinarily deadly device gave new life to the recoilless rifle and added to the power of several other weapons. The item in question was called the fléchette, a very small and sharp projectile that resembled a dart, complete with fins. It found its way into everything from shotgun shells to bombs. Although obviously limited in range, the fléchette gave any weapon great power at close range. Jerry Liucci, who found a use for the LAW, also saw the frequently scorned recoilless rifle employed with lethal results during a major North Vietnamese night assault on a well-prepared and reinforced *Wolfhound* perimeter during Tet:

Charlie rolled up a .51-caliber heavy machine gun with airplane sights and wheels on one of our positions. Hours before, our guys had flown a 90mm recoilless rifle out to the field. It was loaded with a fléchette round. One of our men fired it at the advancing machine gun and pinned the enemy crewmen against a tree. There were little marks all over that gun where the darts had bounced off it. The wheels were wood and were all torn up by the darts. That enemy was silenced.

C. W. Bowman occasionally carried a shotgun. The Army developed a 12-gauge shotgun shell with fléchettes instead of buckshot. Bowman describes the result:

The shotgun was a Remington pump that held 5 rounds and carried buckshot. Later in the war, they came out with a new type of cartridge that held the same fléchettes in it that artillery used for antipersonnel rounds. It was a little miniature steel dart with fins on it, and the penetration of these things was unbelievable. We test-fired the shotgun one day. We took an ammo crate made of $1/2$-inch boards on both back and front and set a shrapnel vest on it. We fired at it, and the fléchettes went through the front of the vest, through the box, and out through the back of the vest. It was quite frightening.

Another widely used and extremely powerful weapon, the claymore mine, was a variation on the same theme as the fléchette. In the next chapter, I will examine the havoc that enemy mines caused for the men of the 25th Division. But American soldiers, in this regard, were forced by circumstances to use such weapons sparingly. It was a serious disadvantage. Although they, like some other weapons, are not widely understood outside military circles, mines are among the most powerful and useful of all killing devices. In linear warfare, they have been used in the millions. NATO and Warsaw Pact forces, until recent events changed the political situation, both planned to use mines in countless numbers and great variety in case of conflict. And no doubt, some of the sophisticated means of employing small mines were tried in action during the Persian Gulf hostilities. However, in Vietnam, Americans and their allies wanted to keep roads and lines of communication open. Mines, by their very nature, are designed to close zones or exact a heavy price from any unit entering a mined area. Consequently, we rarely used powerful, permanently emplaced mines. Instead, American soldiers made do with smaller antipersonnel mines placed on the surface of the ground for ambush or point defense. Afterward, if these mines were not detonated, soldiers would retrieve them at daylight. Foremost among these devices was the claymore. Although small and cheap, it was one of our best weapons and certainly ended the lives of thousands of our opponents. C. W. Bowman was very familiar with the claymore:

Another nasty little weapon was the claymore mine. It was about 12 inches wide and 7 or 8 inches high, and it had little legs you could stand it up on. On the back, it had a pound of plastic explosive, and on the front, it had approximately 250 steel ball bearings. Once fired, the blast would fire the ball bearings out toward the enemy and covered quite an area. It had one hell of a noise, too, if you were close to it. It also had a backblast, so you had to set it about 40 meters away from you. We were in the rice paddies a lot on ambush though, and sometimes, we'd just set them on the other side of the dike and move down the dike a little way and get down. The backblast would actually blow the dike away in that spot.

As Bowman also illustrates, the men of the 25th, like soldiers in all good armies, were extremely inventive when it came to killing someone who wanted to kill them. In this case, Bowman and his mates created a home-made version of military-issue fougasse, a relative of napalm:

Sometimes, we couldn't get claymores, so we'd make our own. We'd take an ammo box, made of steel, and punch a hole in the bottom of it. Then, we would line the bottom with plastic explosive, about 2 pounds or better. Next, we would visit the motor pool and scrape together everything they had on the work benches: spark plugs, pistons, pushrods, whatever was there. All of that stuff went into the box. Then, we'd lock the lid on it, and that square box would shape the charge. Finally, we'd put a blasting cap on the bottom of it and set it out on the perimeter. On other occasions, we took a 5-gallon can of gas and poured powdered soap into it, which thickened the gas. We called it FU gas. Back in the bunker, we'd set a charge, place the 5-gallon can at an angle, put a sandbag under it, and, underneath that, put about a 2-pound charge of plastic explosive. We would then run the wire back to the bunker. If we got hit, you could wire up the FU gas to the field telephone. When it blew, it would just light up the whole night. Then, if you saw the enemy coming through the wire, you'd set off the homemade claymore. It was quite effective. A couple of times, we were hit at night and used our inventions. The next morning, we went out and found bodies with spark plugs and valve lifters and anything that was in the box stuck in them. Some bodies were actually blown in half by it. Quite a nasty weapon. When you blew the FU gas, it would turn into a jelly and stick to anything it hit, almost like a napalm.

The plastic explosive that Bowman refers to was an all-purpose substance that was put to all sorts of uses. As Jim Ross notes, the unusual chemical composition of the plastic explosive made it valuable for nondestructive uses:

We used a lot of C4 plastic explosive, which is shaped like a little brick and wrapped with green cellophane. Inside is a white brick of plastic explosive, which was kind of like putty. It was great stuff. You could tear off little pieces and light it, and it would burn. You could use it to heat your coffee. The beauty of C4 is that you can apply pressure or heat and it will not detonate. It takes pressure and heat combined to make it explode. So, in other words, you could burn it all day long or stomp on it all day long, just as long as you didn't apply heat and pressure at the same time, such as you would do when you stuck a blasting cap in it.

Combat engineer Michael Butash used C4 on a frequent basis. As he remembers, it was in great demand. He also gives a fine example of the dangerous tendency for the soldiers to grow lax around things they were accustomed to, no matter how deadly:

We used a lot of C4 plastic explosive. It made great cooking fuel for C rations. Cut off a little piece and light it, it would heat up anything you wanted. It made great trading material. We were demolition guys, and we got all we wanted. You could trade it for beer, for extra Cs, almost anything. We used to set charges all the time. We used crimpers, a tool very similar to a pair of pliers with two holes, one for cutting and one for crimping. We would take a blasting cap and open one end, which would be recessed $^{3}/_{8}$ of an inch or so, and put a time fuse in. Then, you would crimp the blasting cap onto the time fuse. I remember many times being so tired and using the wrong hole and cutting the blasting cap right in half. Frequently, you didn't have crimpers because they would get lost. So, we would use our teeth. Just think, we were nineteen-year-old kids crimping blasting caps with our teeth.

Infantry officer Thomas Giltner also found C4 extremely useful. His description is short but very much to the point:

Composition C4 is the greatest stuff I've ever seen. You could wad it up into a ball with your fingers, light it, and heat your coffee. Put a blasting cap in it, and it will blow your house right off its foundation.

Obviously, the combat soldiers of the 25th had great firepower. However, it is essential to realize that their opponents had the equivalents of virtually every device or weapon described here. In some cases, our varieties were superior; in some cases, the enemy's were. In terms of weapons, short engagements were even affairs, but the fact that the infantry could use such great firepower actually worked greatly to the other side's advantage because, as I will examine in detail, the enemy normally made the decision on whether to fight. As good as the American infantry was when decently led, there is no doubt that the enemy would have been delighted to have the entire war fought with ground soldiers. One can appreciate the particular hell the French troops faced in their phase of the war because, lacking our resources, they had to rely far more on infantry. Americans did not. The infantryman in Vietnam was at center stage, but our supporting players had very major roles.

Armored Vehicles

The use of armored vehicles in Vietnam is an excellent example of the best laid plans going awry. Regardless of their size and type, such vehicles have some common characteristics that led fine military men to believe that they would play only a limited role in Vietnam. First of all, even a very "light" fighting vehicle like the armored personnel carrier is a heavy thing. Vietnam's roads were poor, bridges were weak, and much of the terrain was too soft for the large-scale use of armor. In addition, all armor is fickle and requires constant maintenance. The APCs given to ARVN in earlier years had not done well, nor had French half-tracks. Moreover, the Army believed that surprise and maneuver would be crucial in tactical operations against a foe who would disappear if the odds were not good. But armored vehicles make an unmistakable and loud noise. Bound to the roads, a drain on maintenance, and of little use at night, so the reasoning went, armor would have only specialized use, such as in convoy escort and the protection of fixed positions. All of these views were widely held at General Westmoreland's headquarters.

Ironically, it was Gen. Frederick Weyand, the first commander of the 25th and arguably the best American general of the war, who insisted that Westmoreland's staff was wrong. The 25th did not have as many vehicles as armored divisions did, but Weyand believed such vehicles would be tremendously valuable. To say the least, he was correct. Officers and men quickly realized that the Vietnamese terrain allowed for a considerable degree of cross-country movement in the areas where Westmoreland deployed American troops. Furthermore, the largely unanticipated growth of the base camps, firebases, and smaller positions made the defensive capabilities of APCs very important. The convoys and related road security became major military endeavors and in these assignments, armor was indispensable.

As so frequently occurs in warfare, the earliest engagements proved to be unreliable indicators of what was to follow. Westmoreland's planners were seriously misled by the large and perilous battle in the Ia Drang Valley, during which huge numbers of helicopters were used in war for the first time. Although the battle had been close to a catastrophe for U.S. troops, the Americans ultimately prevailed. The engagement provided evidence for what Westmoreland wanted to believe—that the enemy forces would accept battle in dense terrain where helicopter-borne U.S. infantry, backed by artillery and air power, could find them, force them to battle, and defeat them.

The Ia Drang, however, proved to be an exception to the rule in Vietnam. Large enemy units would fight, but as the war progressed, *they* chose the place and time, not the Americans. The bloody frontier battles of 1966 and 1967 were battles of attrition, pure and simple, and took place in areas where the other side had prepared a lethal welcome. Although it is not easy to read the minds of the military leaders in Hanoi and in the South, it is reasonable to assume that these battles were fought to inflict losses on the Americans while simultaneously providing time for both the North Vietnamese and the Front Main Force military units to increase in size, improve in training, and receive more sophisticated weaponry. So, for the first two years of war, enemy battle objectives in the hinterlands alternated between defensive engagements that inflicted casualties on Americans and occasional attacks on isolated U.S. bases. It was never their intention to win the war outright in this period. They were not ready and undoubtedly feared a larger and more aggressive U.S. effort that would include a ground attack against the North. However, sometime in 1967, after fierce debate in Hanoi, the Front military leaders persuaded the North that a general offensive would win the war. The eighteen-month bloodbath that ensued took place in inhabited areas, not in the hinterlands. And in each situation, armored vehicles proved a great asset.

In truth, the great promise of helicopter operations, touted by their advocates, was never realized. The elaborate nets thrown out by air proved far too porous to trap major enemy units. The only way to produce serious combat, as events showed, was to wait for the other side to attack and then slug it out. In these conditions, the helicopter proved capable of splendid service. But if push came to shove, the infantry wanted tracks in the vicinity. And the infantrymen got their wish. Whatever the Army believed early in the war, its troops soon had a huge supply of APCs. Tracks had always been given a major role in a theoretical battle with the Soviet Union in Europe, and it proved simple enough to ship them to Vietnam by the thousands and produce them in commensurate numbers. The Army sent fewer tanks, but they, too, proved valuable at critical times. Americans learned that no weapon alone was decisive. All had weaknesses and vulnerabilities, and each had unique strengths. If the situation called for the punch and power wielded by an APC or a tank, nothing else would do.

The thousands of armored personnel carriers the military deployed to Vietnam were all based on the same M113 track, which looked remarkably like a large metal shoebox with Caterpillar treads. Nevertheless, probably no two were exactly alike. The crews made on-the-spot modifications to increase protection, firepower, or creature comforts. They all had one thing in common: None was used as envisioned by its designers. The M113 was created for Europe where, officers believed, enclosed APCs would bring infantry through much of the killing zone near the front lines. At the proper place, the infantrymen would disembark and rush to their positions, and the APC would either retreat or take up a defensive position if the terrain was suitable. On a European battlefield, where monstrous tanks, hundreds of armored self-propelled artillery vehicles, and clouds of aircraft were expected to dominate a (hopefully) nonnuclear battlefield, the APC was small potatoes in the realm of firepower. But none of this was true in Vietnam. There, the tracks were given to the mechanized infantry and powerful armored cavalry units. Regardless of their configurations, tracks played the role of offensive fighting machines. On a battlefield where tanks were rare, the humble APC, frequently made even more lethal by its crew, was a very important weapon. Jerry Headley, a lieutenant in the 3/4th Armored Cavalry Battalion—the 25th's most powerful unit—describes his mount:

The M113 ACAV [armored cavalry assault vehicle—EMB] was the M113 vehicle with modification. To make room for more ammunition, they removed all of the seats in the vehicle except for the driver's. The vehicles were supposed to be able to swim, but we carried so much ammo and equipment that it was impossible. They removed the track shrouds. You had a .50-caliber machine gun and an M60 mounted on the rear of the vehicle to cover your rear. The threat could come from anywhere, so you wanted 360-degree protection. Some guys mounted extended laterals, extended driving sticks. Mines were the number one enemy weapon next to RPGs to armored vehicles in Vietnam. If you were sitting inside a vehicle and a mine went off, the damage resulted in a killed or extremely badly wounded soldier. As a result, the guys rode on top. Very seldom did you ride inside the vehicle. As track and troop commander, I had one of the fellows borrow a jeep seat from a jeep that had been destroyed, and I sat on top of the jeep seat on top of my track. You might find pictures of some tracks with little metal fighting positions mounted on top. They didn't last long in the jungle and got knocked off quickly and were almost never replaced.

Lt. Col. Carl Neilson, who commanded a mech battalion during 1968, speaks about the vehicles under his command:

The main vehicle was the M113 diesel. Each company was authorized fourteen, including the command vehicle. Most had been converted either officially or unofficially by adding additional M60 machine-gun mounts on the top and were commonly referred to as AFV [armored fighting vehicle—EMB]. They were not used by us in the manner the planners had ever envisioned for the use of an M113 on the plains of central Europe. Rather than an APC, they were more an open-top truck. We never closed the tops unless it was raining. The troops rode with their heads out. It was terribly hot and dusty. There was the fear that if a mine went off or if a rocket propelled grenade launcher hit the vehicle, it would cause more damage if the vehicle were buttoned up than if it were not. Consequently, the normal mode of operation was with the top open. Of the fourteen authorized, typically they would have nine to eleven. Invariably, they would have one or two that had been damaged beyond repair and not replaced and one or two that never seemed to get out of position because of maintenance troubles. Since we were so short of infantrymen, the balance was about right, so it really wasn't a big deal. In addition to rifle companies, I had four gasoline-powered M113s that carried flamethrowers. There was some very exotic plumbing necessary to propel flaming napalm 75 yards or so. It was very delicate and prone to break down. It was difficult, time-consuming, and somewhat dangerous to replenish the napalm supplies. They were used very infrequently and, in my estimation, very ineffectively except on one occasion when we used them to burn some NVA out of some bunkers in the woods. I don't think they were worthwhile, considering the amount of time, money, and effort invested in them.

In addition, the reconnaissance platoon in the HQ [headquarters—EMB] platoon was organized much like an armored infantry company. It operated much the same way. I had some 4.2 mortar carriers that didn't work very well because the light hull of the 113 was not made for the abuse coming from a 4.2 and frequently cracked, making it inoperable. So, we used the 4.2 in a dismounted mode, when we used it at all. We had the usual accompaniment of jeeps and trucks and armored wreckers. We usually had one or two platoons of M48 tanks attached, tanks that belonged to 25th Division. The tanks and APCs were generally reliable, considering the state of training of the average soldiers and their willingness or unwillingness to maintain them, the general lack of appreciation for mechanical things then current with the average soldier, and the climate with the dust and dirt. It's a wonder the vehicles ran as well as they did.

Lee Reynolds notes that his vehicle sported an even more unusual contraption:

Our track was equipped with two M60 machine guns, one .50-caliber machine gun, and a minigun. That meant that our track had more firepower than a walking infantry company. It took a while to get it cranked up, but when it was cranked up, it was devastating. The enemy did not want to get into contact with us because of our firepower. The other tracks were similarly equipped. Every track had at least two M60s and a .50-caliber. At least one track in a company had a minigun; also, one would have a Super Duper. A Super Duper is based on an M79 grenade launcher, which fires a 40mm explosive shell with a kill radius of about 5 meters: a pretty devastating weapon by itself. The Super Duper was an advanced version that fired the same shell automatically, with the shells fed with a belt like a machine gun. Every line company had 81mm mortars, and our headquarters company had a 4.2-inch mortar. We also had flamethrowers, which were tracks with an 800-gallon napalm tank inside. We had one hit with mines and incoming rounds, but we never had one explode, even when pressurized. That would have been really something if it did, but it never happened. We also had an M42 tank equipped with a dual 40mm cannon that fired automatically. These are similar to the 40mm antiaircraft gun used by the Navy in World War II. Of course, in training, I'd never seen anything like it. At night, it was very impressive. Sometimes at night, when we were in the boonies away from everybody, we would have a "mad minute," which was announced on the radio. Everybody would count down from 10 and fire everything we had. We put out so much firepower that you could read by the light of the tracers. It was a lot of firepower, really helpful, and gave you real peace of mind. [The minigun referred to was an extremely powerful multibarreled machine gun, normally mounted on aircraft and helicopters. I will cover them directly.—EMB]

Despite all the clever modifications that turned a lightly armored bus into an ominous weapons carrier, the originally mounted .50-caliber machine gun was the track's most fearsome weapon. Too heavy for mobile field use by the infantry, the .50 was a good match for the APC. As Roger McGill recalls, his track, dangerously powered by gasoline in 1966 instead of the diesel fuel that was used later, derived its power to kill from the .50, with its great range and fierce punch:

The real weapon of honor was the .50-caliber machine gun mounted on the M113 APC. This was a very powerful and awesome weapon. It could cut a tree in half if it was two or three football fields away. What it would do to humans was unbelievable. Every fifth round was a tracer. It was very powerful. It could be carried and used on a tripod mounted on the ground. It was very durable and easy to take apart and clean, and the barrel could also be changed when it got overheated.

One characteristic of the APC that made it effective was the room inside, which allowed the vehicle to carry great amounts of ammunition. Automatic weapons are all excellent killing devices if they have unlimited ammunition at their disposal. When this is the case, the vehicles and men carried by them could create an intensely lethal killing zone in any area within range of their weapons. "Wall of lead" is not a cliché but expresses something very close to literal truth if enough automatic weapons are in place and there is plenty of ammunition to fire. The problem in Vietnam, of course, was finding a target at which to fire. The lack of well-defined targets during a firefight made firepower all the more important. If one is being shot at, destroying the opponent is a splendid idea because dead men cannot harm you. In reality, however, it was almost as good to drive off the enemy: They may get another shot at you tomorrow, but for today, you have made it through.

Track crewman Eddie Madaris, who was in Vietnam in late 1967 through Tet, saw the war turn more violent and the demand for his weapon grow. He does not boast in his analysis of the APC's usefulness:

The use of tracks was outstanding strategy. They did quite well in jungles, rice paddies (especially in the dry season), and on the roads. You could move the troops quite rapidly, and you had firepower with the .50s and the grenade launchers and all of the ammo. They afforded comfort to the troops: Sometimes, you were able to sleep in them. There were times when you didn't want to sleep in them because you were exposed to the profile of the ground. They were excellent for securing villages and guarding convoys. They were one of the supreme weapons, along with the artillery.

Jim Ross served on a relatively unmodified track in 1970 and recalls the great amount of ammunition they carried for the infantrymen that accompanied them:

In addition to our own ammo, we carried maybe 15,000 rounds of M16 rifle ammunition, boxes of C4 stick explosive, boxes of hand grenades, and boxes of flares. We had a lot of everything on each of those APCs. If we had to, we could dig in and go the long term.

There were countless times in the war when the ability of the APC to, as Ross puts it, "go the long term" saved 25th Division units from annihilation. However, the APC was also vulnerable to a number of problems. First of all, as critics had foreseen, any armored vehicle is hard to maintain. Dennis Casola joined his track in January 1968, just in time for the Tet Offensive, during which the APCs had unusual importance and were used with desperate abandon. As he remembers: "Operations never quit. We'd drive the tracks into the motor pool and tell them what was wrong with them. And there was always something wrong with them. They were pieces of shit, always breaking down."

Mines were a continual danger for APCs. Moreover, because the APC was very lightly armored, an enemy heavy machine gun firing at close range could pierce the side armor. But the track's great nemesis was the enemy's hand-held rocket launchers, direct descendants of the American bazooka and German Panzerfaust of World War II fame. Jerry Headley describes the situation:

In the field, we were a lot better off having tracked vehicles than were the leg infantry. When they slept at night, they slept in a hole that they dug, if they could without getting into too much water. But we had the tracks, so we could sleep on them or near them, plus it was easy to heat your C rations. While these things offered more protection than was available to a leg infantryman hiding behind a tree, they also were like magnets. The enemy had a very good weapon called the RPG, rocket propelled grenade, and he made very good and liberal use of it firing at the tracks and tanks.

Bill Kestell, who received a serious wound when his track was overrun during a ruthless battle near Trang Bang during Tet, outlines the evolution of the track's vulnerability when conditions were wrong:

Up until February 1968, I would guess that we had lost most of our tracks to mines and booby traps. However, that changed when the enemy started using RPGs in large numbers. Our unit got hit very hard in the months following my wound. I don't think there were too many people I knew that escaped without at least being wounded, and too many I knew were not even that lucky. I think that since we carried such large quantities of ammo, if you managed to get a shot in that would cause a fire, you lost the vehicle. The RPG was certainly a great equalizer, and making an assault on a bunker line was certain to result in casualties for us. For all our arsenal of deadly, sophisticated weaponry, Charlie always managed to keep inflicting casualties on us, always draining us, always keeping up the pressure and the tension.

Despite these deadly weaknesses, the APCs played a vital role in beating back the Front's great year-long General Offensive during 1968–1969. Larry Fontana served in the infantry during the nearly forgotten but bitter battle pitting the 25th Division and ARVN Ranger units against a large NVA offensive directed at the city of Tay Ninh. Frightened that it was a feint aimed at drawing U.S. units away from Saigon, Fontana and his comrades, though seriously outnumbered, fought a desperate battle. It proved to be one of the classic conventional military campaigns of the war, and when the smoke had cleared, the 25th had stood their ground and smashed their well-trained and highly motivated opposition. APCs played a pivotal role, and infantryman Fontana describes operating with them:

I found being in a rifle company was different than being with a mechanized unit. You're relatively bullet-shy when all you've got between the enemy and yourself are the buttons on your shirt. We worked with a company of armored personnel carriers for two weeks around Trang Bang. These guys were confident and aggressive, and after a while, I could see why. Their type of fighting was so different from ours. When fired on, the tracks and infantry wheeled toward the enemy and charged right into them, machine guns blazing. If we tried that, we'd get murdered! Those APCs were real confidence builders. Unlike us "legs," these guys had plenty of water and food in their tracks. After we split up two weeks later, I never felt so naked and humble in my life. I would have accepted a transfer, no questions asked, in less than a second, to be with a mech outfit.

Tanks were also with the 25th Division, although in much smaller numbers. And they, more than APCs, were the focus of the disagreement between Weyand and Westmoreland. Tanks, to a greater degree than APCs, embodied the strengths and weaknesses of armored vehicles. They were much heavier and harder to maintain than tracks but also possessed much stouter defensive armor and greater firepower. When Weyand was given permission to bring his tanks, he did not see them often. Every unit in the Saigon area pleaded for their services. It is true that they were more limited by conditions than APCs, but it is also true that, when the conditions were right, tanks, more than APCs, were irreplaceable.

The most widely used tank in Vietnam was the old M48 Patton medium tank. On a European battlefield, it would have been considered an inferior vehicle, but in Vietnam, it was extremely powerful. Jerry Headley's armored cavalry battalion had some, and he discusses their features:

The M48 A3 was a diesel vehicle. Initially, when we got to Vietnam, they were gasoline powered, as were the APCs. Obviously, when these vehicles took an RPG hit, there were a lot of traumatic injuries, mostly burns. Probably the biggest fear of anybody working in armor or tracked vehicles is the fear of fire. Later on, over time, diesel engines lessened this possibility. A vehicle might still catch fire, but it took a little longer to get out of control and wasn't so explosive.

The M48 had a 90mm gun, and the primary round was a canister filled with hundreds of big buckshot: a terrific antipersonnel weapon. It carried a .50-caliber machine gun. Normally, it would be mounted inside, but in Vietnam, to allow the commander to see, it was taken out and put on top of the cupola. This allowed the commander better ability to apply an area of fire. In addition, the GIs were always good at inventing things, and they figured out ways to link hundreds of rounds of ammunition. The disadvantage was that the commander was more exposed. You also had a 7.62mm machine gun, which was mounted coaxially with the 90mm gun. The loader also had a 7.62 machine gun. The fellows made other modifications. The 7.62 coaxially mounted machine gun was often replaced with a .50-caliber. Also, you had a telescope primarily used for fighting other tanks, which was irrelevant, so it was often removed and another machine gun placed in there. Some tanks had a cutter bar mounted in front to improve their ability to move through jungle.

Although it suffered even worse maintenance problems than the APC because of its weight (getting a tank out of the mud takes some doing), the M48 served well. In early 1969, it was partially replaced by another vehicle, the Sheridan light tank. Like the M16 rifle, the Sheridan was perfect on paper. Light and nimble, it was better suited to the terrain. It carried a monstrous 152mm gun and was capable of firing an antitank missile. Yet, there was a heavy sacrifice involved. Despite its firepower, it was far lighter because it had an aluminum hull, like the APC. Thus, it traded utility for protection, and the crewmen did not like the idea at all. Also, like the M16, the "field testing" was done by the combat soldiers, a situation that should be avoided whenever possible. Lieutenant Headley describes the situation:

We had a 50-ton tank, and when it hit a mine, very seldom was a crew member injured because it usually just blew a track off. Sometimes it was catastrophic, but very seldom. Then we got the Sheridan, a light-skinned armored vehicle, 16 tons. It was almost like the APC but mounted a very large gun. We had the first casualty with these things in Vietnam as a result of one hitting a mine. The driver was killed, and the Sheridan was almost totally destroyed. Others, when they later took RPG hits, caught fire and just melted down to the tracks. As a result, the troops were not confident in this vehicle.

The men also knew it was a new vehicle, so new that we had civilian contract teams that would fly out after firefights and go over all the Sheridans, interview the crews, and make on-the-spot fixes. It was amazing. What we did was what was called development testing: Normally, you did that before a vehicle is fielded. We did it in Vietnam. The Sheridan was "validated" as to its reliability and survivability in Vietnam. It also had engine problems. Parts were aluminum and wouldn't hold up. Over time, they fixed these problems, but the troops were not fond of them. As a result, their confidence in the vehicle dwindled. The good old initiative of the GI helped. We let the troops do anything they wanted to the vehicles for their morale. They would paint different names and all. But they would also make an RPG screen, which was nothing but cyclone fencing. On the front slope of the tank, they built a makeshift stand-off screen so when the rocket hit, it would detonate early. I don't recall any RPGs hitting those screens, but the troops really liked them. If it made them feel good, we didn't care. The cyclone fencing was effective for our night positions and worked as a stand-off protection.

During a night attack, when you received several RPGs, this was very effective protection.

It was not unheard of in Vietnam for a state-of-the-art, high-technology weapon to fail and something as simple as intelligently used cyclone fencing to cause problems for the other side. Yet, in other areas, the technical resources of the military were put to far more productive uses. Although commanders confronted the frustrating fact that it was often difficult to use the Army's most powerful weapons, their very availability shaped the nature of battle in Vietnam. Furthermore, when conditions allowed the officers of the 25th Division to call on their most lethal arms and use them as they were designed to be employed, the result was almost always a catastrophe for the enemy.

Supporting Arms: Ground

In modern war, the infantry serves as the eyes for more potent weapons of destruction. That was the plan for Vietnam, and, indeed, it often proved the case. The enemy naturally realized this fully and took great pains to avoid the consequences. The simplest way to avoid what was called the "storm of steel" by Ernst Junger, the famous German author and veteran of the World War I trenches, was to keep exchanges brief. American ground units had tremendous power behind them, but even the quickest response—whether from the unit's own mortars, from artillery, or from helicopter gunships—took several minutes to come into play. Furthermore, the eyes in Vietnam were rarely sharp: The terrain and enemy tactics saw to that. The method by which support was called to the scene varied in particulars but was similar in concept. Ground units all had forward observers capable of reaching support via radio. In fact, radiomen and observers were probably the most important individuals in any unit and were normally kept near the officer in charge. There were also observers in the air, in helicopters or specially designed aircraft. This treatment was reserved for large operations, but any fight that lasted a few minutes and appeared to involve a decent-sized enemy force would bring observation aircraft to the scene in short order.

Yet, it was the mortars assigned to the infantry battalion and the nearby artillery positions that normally were the first to come into play. If gunships were nearby, they might appear even more rapidly, but the odds did not favor that. Mortars and artillery, however, were always there, regardless of time and weather. Charles Albridge was one of the well-trained NCOs who accompanied the first contingent of the 25th to Vietnam. It was his job to act as forward observer, and he addresses the difficulties of his assignment, particularly in the early part of the war:

The 81mm mortars were the best high-angle weapon we had when I was there. It would do the job if you were in its range, and that was about 4,000 meters. We had a couple of different high-explosive rounds for it, plus the illumination round and then the white phosphorus.

Being a forward observer in combat was a real pain in the ass. You couldn't see more than a couple of hundred feet sometimes. You worked on the basis of sound. One example was a company-sized sweep supposedly into a secure area. We were only a few thousand meters outside the camp. We went out the gate and did the basic training maneuver of spreading out as we swept through the banana plantation, which contained a lot of thick underbrush. This type of operation just was supposed to get us acclimated to Vietnam and get us used to moving through this type of brushy terrain. We thought Charlie was not that close to the camp. We got hit about 3 hours after we left camp. We were walking parallel with a tree line and started taking fire. The platoon I was with reacted well. It was the only one I could see because of the terrain. You must understand that in 1966–1967, when I was over there, we didn't have a lot of green troops. They lacked actual combat experience but were well-trained soldiers. It wasn't till later that you got replacements that had been put through eight weeks of basic training and just sent over there cold. We had plenty of training and knew how to react in certain situations. My platoon acted well, particularly when you consider it was the first time any of us had ever been shot at.

We were so close to our own area that we had support from our own mortars still back at base camp. I called in for a white phosphorous round to mark the center of Charlie's firing area because there was no way I could tell where that was without it. The beautiful thing about white phosphorous is that it puts out white smoke that you can see through almost anything. I was able to call in a few adjustments, and some shells started landing pretty close to where the enemy was firing from. I made one final adjustment for range and called for 10 rounds of fire for effect, and Charlie played his game. He could hear the guns firing as well as we could, so he just faded back into the bush. So, by the time the mortar rounds got there, he was already gone. That was typical of the early years. I have heard since of the pitched battles later, but early on, it was mostly hit-and-run guerrilla attacks. You seldom saw them, and even less often did you come into really close contact with them. That's where I got nailed on 5 May. I guess I didn't get down fast enough, and I wasn't able to sit down for about a month or so. I guess that tells you where I caught it. It was a small piece of shrapnel, but it did a number on the left cheek of my hind end.

Mortars are very good weapons, and they were used often. The enemy relied upon them far more than we did because they were portable and capable of doing very serious damage. However, as American units increased in number, so did the number of artillery batteries, and artillery is far more powerful than mortar fire. Soon, the firebases could cover almost the entire area of operations. Portions not covered could be brought within range within hours if helicopters were used to deploy a battery in support of a rapid operation. Frequently, infantry units dispensed with their own mortars altogether and used the mortar teams as an additional rifle squad. Artillery support was complicated and called for very good training; artilleryman Sidney Stone reviews some of the ways in which the guns operated in support of the 25th:

In a day, we would probably fire about 60 percent preparation fires, about 20 percent H & I, and about 20 percent on targets of opportunity. [Prep fire was used to shell an area where infantry was about to enter if it appeared dangerous: This was almost always done if helicopters were employed to drop off troops. H & I was random fire at areas that might serve as transit points for the enemy. Targets of opportunity were points called in from observers and fired upon because enemy activity—or something observers thought might be enemy activity—was seen directly.—EMB] We also fired registration missions. We had data on our fire tables showing where our shells should land. To find out if we were correct, we would fire and find out where the shells hit. You would make a mark on your firing table, showing the results. Maybe you're firing at a registration point at 10,00 meters. When you fire registration, you find out that, due to the condition of your guns, the weather, and the condition of your ammunition, you would hit at maybe 10,400 meters. We would make a 400-meter adjustment. That way, when you had a fire mission, you would read this 400-meter change on your plastic cursor. Hardly a day went by when we didn't register one or two batteries. We generally fired H & I at night. The crews believed that was just a way to keep them from getting a good night's rest. Of course, we had radar, and we had other instruments where we could pick up VC movements. Also, they moved in certain patterns. We would get these targets down as H & I fire from Division artillery.

We fired prep fire before helicopters would bring troops in the landing zone. We would fire around the landing zone to hopefully seal off any NVA trying to deploy for an attack on the troops and helicopters coming in. Prep fire was usually planned at night with the infantry. Our unit was a general support artillery battalion. They tried to marry up one artillery battalion with one maneuver battalion. We had three liaison officers. Usually, the liaison officer would be with the maneuver battalion commander. Each liaison officer had three FOs [forward observers—EMB], and generally, one of these FOs would be with one of the company commanders on the ground. That was what we called our fire support channel. We were very careful to speak correct artillery lingo over the radio so as not to confuse ourselves or the men we were supporting.

We had targets of opportunity when the forward observer ran into something. Of course, the battalion commander with his artillery liaison officer was usually flying overhead. Of course, we learned to react damn quick. We were real good. The LO [liaison officer—EMB] would identify the target, like a VC machine-gun nest, and if he wanted any special fuse or adjustments, he would tell us. Before he had that last digit out, we already had the pen on the firing chart. Of course, we had a vertical control operator who determined the site based on the right angle and decided how much we had to add or subtract, depending on whether the guns were above or below the targets. This was all done simultaneously. If we didn't have to wait for clearance, we'd have already shot out two sets of adjustment volleys. That was how quick we could react. The chart operator gave the range, the vertical control operator gave the site, and as soon as you gave them the fire mission, we were already hollering down to the guns battery to adjust. Commands would go something like "Shell A chief, fuse quick, center right," and you already had your two center pieces ready to start firing the adjustment phase. The four guns on the flank were ready to give one round or two registration rounds and then fire for effect. This is all done very quickly. You can see projectiles as they go out the tubes. As they come out, you'd swear they cross, but they don't. You can see them when they're landing. When they go overhead, they kind of make a whoosh-like sound. You won't hear them if they hit on top of you. If you hear them, you're all right because they have already gone on.

During my tour, we were beginning to use the FDAC computers [to control artillery fire—EMB]. They were real nice. Instead of using a firing chart and all the graphical firing tables, all you had to do was just punch in the grid. We had six in our general support battalion. There was only one thing wrong. After about 50 hours, the generators would break down. We never had any problems with FDAC. If something went wrong with FDAC, you'd find one of the components, put in a new one, and you were back in business, no problem. In a few weeks, we had all six of our computers stacked because we only had one generator that would operate. We cannibalized the parts off of the other five generators. If they could have figured out how to run off of one of the big generators we used for lights, that would have been great.

Although it does not fit the stereotype of an army possessing unlimited weaponry, American ground forces were not supported by a large number of "tubes" during Vietnam. Nevertheless, the guns that were there had ample supplies of ammunition and could fire more or less at will. Hoarding ammunition, a common occurrence in World War II, rarely was necessary. And the numbers of rounds fired was, indeed, large. For instance, according to Division records, the 25th artillery fired 122,000 rounds in direct support and another 85,000 rounds for harassment and interdiction in the first quarter of 1967 alone. For this expenditure, intelligence estimated that 231 enemy fighters were killed. Even if true—and damage estimates *were* only estimates—it is quite clear that the Army was willing and able to expend enormous numbers of shells to kill and maim a relatively small number of opponents. Obviously, these totals, on both sides of the ledger, mounted up. Yet, it was a rich man's war and one that required a very large "tail" to keep the "teeth" in operation.

Supporting Arms: Air

I hesitate to describe helicopters as support weapons. As noted earlier, just as the extremist tank exponents before World War II found their theories fail in the face of operational realities, the prophets of helicopter warfare also had cause to be disappointed. The extreme mobility and intricate tactics that seemed to be possible rarely led to the expected result of trapping large units of antagonists. Instead, helicopters exhibited great versatility and served in nearly every conceivable military capacity. They were airborne transport, killing machines, medical evacuation vehicles, command-and-control devices, reconnaissance instruments, carriers of exotic technologies, and delivery trucks, sometimes bringing mail, hot meals, and ice cream to troops in the field.

Although not well appreciated by the public, two of military aviation's most important roles are reconnaissance and, with sophisticated electronics, the closely related task of command and control. It was French aircraft in 1914 that allowed generals in Paris to prepare for the great battle on the Marne. More recently, radar-carrying AWACS aircraft have received a great deal of well-earned publicity. And the U.S. president possesses a specially equipped Boeing 747 that, in theory, would allow him to conduct a thermonuclear war from the air.

The reconnaissance application of air power was much in evidence in Vietnam. For ground units, helicopters were ideal. They were available in large numbers, they could fly low, and they were tremendously maneuverable and very versatile. But whether it was a good thing to have a high-ranking officer overhead conducting the larger engagement depended significantly on whether that officer was a good one. Indeed, more than one ground commander rued the day the helicopter was invented. On occasion, the command situation bordered on the ridiculous. An engagement might begin on the ground and thus beckon helicopters carrying the battalion commander, then the brigade commander, then the division commander, and even a Field Force commander if he was in an inquisitive mood. With all this brass flying overhead, conflicting orders were a real possibility. Fortunately, such occasions were the exceptions, not the rule.

Gene Trask explains the odd position that he and other helicopter pilots held in Vietnam. Unlike Air Force pilots, who were all commissioned officers, helicopter pilots were warrant officers. Yet, their prestige was very great. The troops depended on their "birds" for so much, and all veterans had witnessed acts of great bravery on the part of pilots, particularly during the Medevac (medical evacuation) flights that were so essential to morale. Both the troops and high-ranking officers respected the helicopter pilots, as Trask relates:

Being an aviator was a unique position in the normal Army hierarchy. As a warrant officer/aviator, I had all the privileges of rank as an officer and maybe even more so because aviators were held in such high regard by the grunts, whereas commissioned line officers were not usually granted that level of respect. Most grunts I talked to did not have much use for officers but thought warrant pilots were the coolest dudes in the war. Personally, I thought that a lot of the military structure was pure bullshit. As an aircraft commander for over 900 hours out of my 1,397 hours of combat flight, I found that I was treated with a great amount of respect by both enlisted men and high-ranking officers. Understand that while our helicopter was in flight, the final decision concerning the flight rested on my shoulders, despite the fact that I usually had a full bird colonel and sometimes a general on board. Naturally, I certainly tried to accommodate their wishes, but the final decision was mine to make. More than once, I refused to land, even after being requested to do so, not because of enemy fire but because I thought the terrain was unsafe to attempt a landing. The officers respected my decision.

The mountain Nui Ba Den was a singular feature in my area of operation and a good example of hazardous terrain. We used to land on top of that mountain on a regular basis while I was the pilot for the first brigade command-and-control ship. That was an interesting experience in itself. Never mind the possible sniper fire; landing on Nui Ba Den was a risky business, indeed. Wind currents and cloud cover always played havoc with our helicopters. If you weren't paying attention, you could get sucked into the side of the mountain on approach.

Commanders naturally depended greatly on their helicopters. A battalion commander—and especially a brigade commander—had units spread out over an extremely large area. Trask continues his account and gives a fine example of the multitude of tasks conducted by even a specialized command-and-control helicopter:

A typical operation from the aviator point of view consisted of several stages of aviation assistance to the grunts on the ground. First off, if intelligence had information concerning an enemy location, either the troops arrived overland by armored personnel carriers or they were airlifted by either the 25th's own helicopters (the *Little Bears*) or the 116th Assault helicopters (*Hornets*) into a chosen landing zone. Usually, our command-and-control helicopter was over the landing zone (LZ) prior to the insertion, coordinating artillery, gunship support, and, if need be, fighter bomber support. We had a seven-radio console situated in the cargo area behind and between the two pilot seats. In this way, the colonel or general and his assistants could be monitoring all pertinent frequencies. The brigade commander was able to assess the situation and take proper courses of action. It was sort of like a command central. During almost any contact with enemy forces, we could be found circling overhead and, on many occasions, landing for Medevacs or other reasons. We also landed daily at the different firebases so the commander could talk strategy with his subordinates. Basically, we continually covered the brigade area of operation on a daily basis.

Do not think that a command-and-control vehicle in the air was just a flying radio. Like their counterparts on the ground, the command APCs, helicopters like Trask's were armed to the teeth. This was, after all, Vietnam:

I was assigned the same helicopter for several weeks at a time unless we had mechanical problems, in which case we switched to a temporary replacement. The other platoons were assigned a different helicopter each day. My arrangement was good because I got to know the individual characteristics of my helicopter since I flew it day after day. After a while, it fit like a glove, and I became comfortable with it.

As a C & C (command-and-control) helicopter, we were equipped with two M60 machine guns, a grenade launcher, a case of hand grenades, and a case of smoke grenades. We usually had a couple of M16s with us. I carried a .38-caliber pistol in a shoulder holster. As you can see, we were well armed.

Glenn Jeffers was a helicopter crewman throughout 1968, one of the worst times to serve with a combat division. His recollections impart an excellent picture of the range of missions that faced Army airmen:

The Division's 25th Aviation Battalion had A Company, the *Little Bears,* and B Company, the *Diamond Heads.* A company flew UH-1 Huey helicopters that were all-purpose and called "slicks." B Company flew Huey gunships for ground support. We also had six command-and-control ships—three for colonels, three for generals—and an extra for an artillery colonel.

On command-and-control missions, we would fly over troops and control operations from the air. When I first got there, these C & C flights were some of the hottest numbers going. Officers used their helicopters when there was a contact, so when we went up, there was almost certainly action. A lot of commanders flying these missions liked to get real close to get a good look. They also wanted to show their troops that they were part of the battle and supported the ground troops with our firepower. Many times, we would be in an area before the artillery zeroed in or jets arrived, or the gunships would have to leave when they ran out of fuel. If it was a long-standing fight, the C & C ship would do a lot of air backup, which meant you did a lot of shooting and did a lot of getting shot at. It was irrelevant whether it was a colonel or general in the aircraft. Some were just more active at it than others.

As Jeffers points out, even resupply missions, though often tranquil and relatively easy, could also be extremely hazardous for the helicopter crew:

We flew resupply missions night and day, delivering food and ammo to units in hot contacts that needed to be rearmed that instant. And you can't just fly in and push supplies out because you might kill one of your own people. Supply packets weighed 20 to 50 pounds an item, and if you drop that from 40 feet, you kill people. You might do that five or six times in a night and use three different helicopters doing it because each time you went in, the helicopter got all shot up.

The company I was in was extremely fortunate. We had nobody killed flying in the year and a half I was there, and the only person we had killed was a sergeant who stepped into the commander's helicopter blade and was killed by accident.

Fire support missions were dangerous for the crews and, if badly done, dangerous for the ground troops, as well. They also came in great variety. As Jeffers relates, sometimes both high technology and GI ingenuity left something to be desired:

We flew "sniffer" missions. The sniffer device looked like a big vacuum cleaner. You were supposed to try and pick up odors of stinky people or animals. It was a volatile mission because you flew low and slow and flew over the same area over and over again. They would track hot spots, and if they thought there was a concentration of enemy around, they would use the intelligence for a B-52 bombing. One day, I remember, we were over an area and getting all sorts of hot spots. I punched the chemical guy in the shoulder and said the thing was picking up flowers because it was springtime and the smell of the flowers was so strong you could pick it up with your nose in the helicopter. Yet, I am not saying this technique didn't work. Numerous times we'd fly in an area, find a hot spot, and get shot at. [According to Division records, the "people sniffer" was so plagued by false readings that it eventually was used for a different purpose. If an area was read "clean," it probably was: Knowing where the enemy was *not* could be very useful if the information was current.—EMB]

We also tried countermortar missions. In War Zone C, we parked our helicopter at a compound in the middle of the night and sat and waited for Charlie to shoot mortars. As soon as they started shooting, we'd start the helicopter, take off during this barrage of mortar fire, and try to see where it was coming from. That was probably the most dangerous operation we had, beyond a doubt. One pilot would sit and sleep in a helicopter at night, and everyone else would just sleep around the edges; you'd stay there until things got hot, and you jumped in real quick when the stuff started blowing off. Personally, I made the mistake of taking $100 from a guy to take his duty for a night because he was getting short and wasn't much interested in doing it. It was the last time. It wasn't worth the money.

And then there were the "fire-bear" missions. We loaded the aircraft up with incendiary grenades and white phosphorus and flew over places like the Iron Triangle and the Ho Bo Woods and attempted to destroy the ground cover and make a nuisance of ourselves, I guess. Basically, we tried to burn down the woods. We flew low and level through the area with the helicopter stuffed with these grenades, and two people did nothing but pull pins and shove grenades out of the aircraft. We started fires all over the place. And of course, that would draw the attention of whoever was on the ground because they didn't much care for all of these grenades dropping out of the air on top of them. Another bizarre idea thought up by a general was dropping mortar shells from a helicopter. You'd fly along and make a guess where to drop these things, and supposedly, the people on the ground would direct us. But helicopters were not set up or calibrated to do this, so the ground troops were very leery when we were around. Aside from that, only about three-quarters of the rounds detonated, and the rest could be used against us by the enemy.

Jeffers points out that some of the missions were designed with little regard for the safety of the valuable helicopters and crews:

One time, they had us dropping napalm out of these helicopters, which was really ridiculous and dangerous to our own ships. It was stupid and something I refused to do after the second or third time. We sprayed Agent Orange all the time I was there. It was another mission that I refused to do after a few times because you flew at low level back and forth. Also, you'd get this spray on you, and it would stick to your skin. The first time I did it, I didn't know what it was and didn't have any extra clothes on. It would stick to your skin, and you might have it on all day before you got into a shower. It made you sick to your stomach. Plus, it was dangerous because you did it without any sort of support. It was like the incendiary grenade missions, except that it didn't start a fire. It would just slowly kill all of the woods. Maybe the bad guys on the ground thought we were giving them a bath or something. But whatever they thought, they caught on because they started shooting at the helicopter doing it. [Front forces in that area were accustomed to chemical warfare. It had been going on since 1963 and was continued despite the fact that dead trees proved to be very effective cover. Ground spraying of likely ambush spots was another matter. In any case, herbicides broke down quickly and were probably more hazardous to the crews delivering them than to anyone else. This remains a point of great controversy. Specially outfitted bulldozers, called Rome Plows, also flattened huge areas of rough terrain.—EMB]

However, as Jeffers also points out, ground support was a lethal threat to the enemy:

We also flew a mission at night that was quite effective. We flew at night with a minigun set up on the doors of the aircraft and a starlight scope. We would work the areas like the Ho Bo Woods, the Iron Triangle, and the supply line areas. You could actually see what was going on. We had a lot of contacts.

[The starlight scope was a passive infrared telescope that allowed decent visibility at night. The deadly combination of the starlight, the helicopter, and the minigun was another invention of the 25th Division's crewmen and not developed stateside.—EMB]

Ground soldiers knew the value of helicopters. Choppers brought soldiers much-wanted things, but more important, they added greatly to the combat power of the ground units. They also saved American lives. Junior officer Jerry Headley of the 3/4th Armored Cavalry Battalion stresses the importance of the helicopters to ground operations:

The ground troop that I was assigned to as a platoon leader and troop commander would be quite helpless without information on the enemy. We had a Delta Troop, which was the airborne eyes and ears of the squadron. [Delta Troop was the helicopter-borne unit that was an organic part of an armored cavalry battalion.—EMB] We had OH-6 scout aircraft, a light observation helicopter that kind of looked like an egg with a propeller. They were a lot of fun to fly in. The pilots that flew them were highly qualified because they did dangerous, low-level contour flying in search of the enemy. But reconnaissance was only part of Delta Troop's mission. They had Huey gunships, which were UH-1s with machine guns and rockets mounted on them, and Cobra gunships. The Cobras could fly at a higher altitude and had massive firepower. So they lay back. The scouts or the ground troops would find the enemy or be in contact. Instantly, the gunships could fly in support of any of the fighting units of the Division. On the Cobra gunships, you had 3.5-inch rockets, antipersonnel rockets primarily filled with fléchettes, and an M79 launcher in the belly that fired automatically, and you also had machine guns. They had a lot of firepower and, on more than one day, saved our fannies out in the bush. D Troop also had its own infantry platoon, referred to as aero rifles or the "blues." The squadron could conduct limited ground action of its own. You might insert the blues in a night position to prepare an ambush: Pop the ambush, and the rest of the squadron would react to it. The speed with which infantry could be inserted and extracted made it a tremendously effective fighting force.

As the war progressed, helicopter gunships became more common. Initially, gunships were modified and heavily armed Hueys, but lethal Cobra gunships soon took over much of the ground support mission. The Cobra was a dedicated killing device, with no other role. The pilot sat behind the gunner, offering a very small forward profile. They carried many weapons, but the minigun was the most feared. The minigun appeared in several guises in Vietnam because of its extraordinary firepower. A multibarreled Gatling gun, it fired so quickly that it made a distinctive rumble rather than the normal staccato of an automatic weapon. One veteran recalled that a minigun sounded like a "chainsaw at maximum RPM." Jerry Liucci saw the famous *Puff the Magic Dragon,* an ancient C-47 aircraft armed with miniguns, at work at night during Tet, acting in support of his unit's perimeter, which was under massed assault by North Vietnamese regulars:

We could see tracers and hear explosions. We were ordered in. On the way in, the battalion commander called in *Puff the Magic Dragon.* This antique plane just lumbered around, but when he opened up with those Gatling guns from his windows, it was quite impressive. *Puff* was taking machine-gun fire from the enemy, but he silenced them. The noise and the sound were unbelievable.

The minigun was a natural weapon for the helicopter gunships. Robert Julian saw them in action often in 1971:

Gunships were pretty frightening. I was more afraid of them than I was of the enemy. They had the minigun, the grenade launchers, and the rockets, and they would usually fire all three. We popped smoke right in the middle of where we were and told them just to shoot on either side. They did an excellent job. You could literally see the jungle on either side of us being torn up where they were blasting with miniguns. Shrapnel was getting all over us, from their grenades and rockets.

Potentially the most powerful of support weapons were Air Force and Navy jets. But the use of aircraft in Vietnam has not always been well portrayed. Although it is true that they were there in large numbers and that a great many sorties were flown, much of this effort was directed at fixed targets like the Ho Chi Minh Trail or used in the campaign against the North. Tactical air support was certainly available, but it was not normally employed unless a substantial contact was taking place. And because of their great power, jets were very tricky weapons to use, as Lieutenant Colonel Neilson recalls:

It was a major challenge coordinating the competing combat support, which was usually mutually exclusive. By that I mean you could not fire artillery into an area if you had jets ready to attack or if you intended to use helicopters. You had to make your choice and, when the weapon in question was expended, move to the next one. The Air Force jets had a maximum loiter time of 10 to 15 minutes over a target, so when they arrived, you had to use them or you knew you would lose them. So, I had a number of occasions when I had to stop artillery, bring in the air support, and start the artillery again, and about that time, the helicopter gunships would arrive and tell me they were there to support me, and then again, I would stop the artillery and use the gunships. It is just a commentary on the amount of fire support we had available.

The enemy was accustomed to dealing with aircraft. Normally, an air strike, for all of its apparent fury, accomplished little or nothing. However, if the time and place were right, aircraft had power that stuns the imagination. Lieutenant Colonel Neilson's mech battalion was attacked close to Saigon during Tet. Neilson consequently had occasion to use jets in the manner for which they were designed and for which the pilots were trained. He watched as the jets pounded a North Vietnamese battalion:

The Air Force began to send sorties off the runway at Bien Hoa, which was just east of Tan Son Nhut. We were so close that the fighters would barely clear the runway at Bien Hoa and gain altitude to about 1,000 feet, then they were ready to descend and drop bombs. Their forward air controller could see the North Vietnamese out in the ricefields quite close to our forces. The first thing we had to do was to agree that the fighter bombers would drop bombs closer than the normal distance, which was typically 500 meters for a 500-pound bomb or 1,000 meters for a 1,000-pound bomb. It was quite a sight to see fighter bombers come up over the horizon from the east, over our heads, and swoop down. Each released two bombs that would be slowed by fins so the bomber could make its escape without suffering any damage. The soldiers would stand there and watch. Just at the last possible moment, just before the bomb hit, everybody would hit the ground, and there would be a tremendous pair of explosions with tremendous concussions through-out our laager area. There was God-awful shrapnel flying through the air, cutting off antennas and crashing into APCs. I can recall that my command tent was ripped to shreds. But we were all flat on the ground, so we were safe. As soon as the shrapnel flew by, we would immediately jump up. Where the bombs had landed would be great clouds of dust. And you could see the North Vietnamese who were suffering terribly from these concussions get up, probably in great confusion. Now, the jets were attacking only 100 to 150 meters from us. Every person that I had who could lay his hands on a weapon would fire very intensively for 40 seconds, at which time the next fighter bomber would come over and drop a set of bombs. Again, we'd all hit the deck and repeat the procedure. This went on from 6:30 in the morning until 10:00 A.M., when I ran out of ammunition. The North Vietnamese couldn't leave, they couldn't attack, there wasn't anything they could do. They were being decimated.

Large, sustained attacks like the one Neilson describes were very rare. Dan Vandenberg witnessed jets in a more typical role. The events occurred on a smaller scale, but the results were similar:

Well, one day, we were out on a company-sized patrol, which is pretty rare, and we got sniper fire, so we pulled back. In cases like that, if possible you'd pull back and bring in some artillery or gunships and, if need be, jets. So, we pulled back and sat outside of rifle range and watched the gunships work over this small forest. Then they came with the jets, and those are awesome to watch. They come in at treetop level and drop these bombs. Jesus, they tore up that area something fierce. And all of a sudden, there's a thump next to me and there's a piece of shrapnel about 4 inches long and about 1 inch wide or so, and like a fool, I went and picked it up. Of course, it was hot, and I burned my hand. But just picking it up I cut my hand: It's incredible how sharp that stuff is.

Last in the repertoire were the B-52 heavy bombers. B-52s did not fly in close ground support. Their bomb load was so great and dangerous that the slightest error would have been suicidal. Most runs were preplanned area missions against enemy strongholds or infiltration routes. Heavy bombers were not sent to the North until 1972. Ultimately, they almost destroyed enemy positions in the Ho Bo, although that took over a year of sustained attack. Most soldiers saw the B-52s in action at one time or another, or, rather, they saw the results as one could rarely see the planes themselves. As Morgan Sincock puts it, "The initial reaction to being in any proximity to a B-52 strike is the certain belief that the end of the world is at hand."

But most B-52 strikes came up empty, and the havoc they created actually made ideal terrain for ambush. The 25th Division infantry units, frequently sent into an area that was bombed to assess damage, often found wrecked trees and a very active enemy. However, it is impossible to say how often these attacks did succeed at killing or burying alive enemy troops hiding in even the deepest of tunnels. No effective defense was possible against a direct hit.

Some remarkable testimony concerning the results of a B-52 strike comes from Jim Ross. During the Cambodian invasion, his mechanized unit was sent into a known enemy redoubt after a very intense bombing attack. As we now know, the border areas were attacked by B-52s for months during 1969. And as we also know today, the U.S. invasion of Cambodia in 1970, an operation in which the 25th Division played a leading role, very nearly succeeded in capturing the Front's leadership and several large enemy units. Caught without the normal period of advanced warning, the enemy's retreat was a rapid, helter-skelter affair.

One North Vietnamese unit in the area was obviously caught in the open by a B-52 strike. Given the startling nature of the account that follows, I checked it against the Divisional records, which validate the fact that Ross's unit was, indeed, on a reconnaissance mission into a longtime enemy haven in Cambodia. The hellish scene that Ross recounts was undoubtedly uncommon, but almost any American soldier in the Vietnam War would have seen something like it, albeit on a smaller scale. Although the term "carnage of war" is a cliché, Jim Ross describes the reality:

It's been said that the sense of smell is one of the strongest links with something in your past. That is why what I will describe for you sticks up so powerfully in my memory. It wasn't a firefight, but it was so eerie that it is unforgettable. The event took place when we went in to reconnoiter the site of a B-52 bomb strike near Krek. The B-52s had pinpointed and taken out a combination NVA base camp, hospital, training center, and food distribution center. It was a very large complex, and it was deep in the Cambodian jungle. B-52s came through there and wiped out about 400 NVA. We were the first element to enter through there on the ground. This had happened three to five days earlier, but nobody had been in there yet. We were ordered to police up what we might find, reconnoiter the area, and take any prisoners that might be there. It was a gruesome task. The area we were in was triple-canopy jungle, with very thick, huge trees. It was close to the noon hour when we got in there. When we were about 100 yards away from the outer edges of the base camp, the odor—the stink of decomposing, rotting human flesh—was almost unbearable: We were already wrapping towels around our faces. A dead body smells exactly the same as a dead animal.

We got in there, and the first thing we noticed were the bomb craters. There were these huge cone-shaped pits in the ground, maybe 25 feet in diameter and maybe 12 feet deep. Going down to a cone-shaped point, there were maybe only 50 to 60 feet separating the craters, that's how tightly the bombs struck. Huge trees, trees maybe 2 to 3 feet in diameter, were just bent over and splintered like broken twigs or matchsticks. Trees had fallen everywhere: Little beams of sunlight were coming in through the canopy, where the holes were left. Then we started finding the bodies. They were scattered everywhere. Trees had fallen on some and crushed them; some didn't have any marks on them and had probably been killed simply by concussion. We found one body that had been hurled up against a tree head first, and a piece of his skull had been taken off: We actually found his body first and wondered where the saucer-sized piece of his head had gone. It was as though somebody had taken a knife and just lopped off a little round piece of his skull at the back of his head. Later on, we found this gooey, hairy mess stuck to a tree about 20 to 30 feet away. Others had been hit by pieces of trees or bomb fragments and blown apart. Pretty ugly stuff. All of the bodies were swelled up and turning black. Literally bursting at the seams, eyeballs bugging out, tongues pointing straight out, vermin crawling in and out of body cavities—you get the idea. We had to go through there and cut the rucksacks off these people, go through their belongings, and collect any documents or valuables that might have some intelligence purposes. We spent all day there doing that. By the time we were through, we had stockpiled quite a bit. An underground hospital there was collapsed. They actually dragged out a survivor. Talk about hard luck: Apparently, this guy had been injured; he had splints on, and he was also delirious with malaria. He was dehydrated and looked like a skeleton. To make matters worse, while he's trying to survive this, the bombs come along and brought the hospital down right on top of him. He was barely alive and was evacuated. I don't know if he lived or not, but at least he lived to see the sunshine again. Almost all of the guys had pictures of Ho Chi Minh on them. The flies swarming around the bodies were unbelievable. They didn't want to get out of your way. You had to try to work with one hand and shoo with the other.

The violence that caused the episode Ross describes was relentless in Vietnam. However, B-52 strikes rarely obliterated enemy units, and the task faced by most infantrymen was far more perilous than picking up the pieces, however repulsive a job that was. Most fighting was quite different. It was shaped by a very strange blend of geography, military structure, politics, and the Front's style of military-political warfare. For the men of the 25th Division, this usually meant finding Charlie—an incredibly difficult and dangerous task. We are now ready to examine the flow of warfare on the Vietnamese battlefield.

3

Around in Circles: Warfare in 360 Degrees

THE CONFLICT in Vietnam had several dimensions. The one most commonly associated with it in the public's mind is the high-technology war of B-52s, fighter bombers, helicopters, and large search and destroy missions. The high-tech war's mirror image is likewise a part of public lore. In this largely mythical world, the war was fought by Green Berets, CIA agents, and others with similarly mysterious backgrounds, in an exotic setting inhabited by a collection of trained killers, mercenaries, drug dealers, and other colorful heroes and villains. Some Americans think of Vietnam as a gigantic My Lai massacre—a bloodbath largely directed toward the civilian population and a natural reflection of a malignant Western society. To be sure, elements of all of these interpretations existed in Vietnam. But to emphasize them is to miss the essence of warfare in Vietnam. For the men of the 25th Division and for their comrades on the spearpoint elsewhere in Vietnam, combat was, above all, the arduous, frustrating, and dangerous job of finding Charlie. Whether soldiers were beating the bush or "humping the boonies," it was their job to find the enemy—hopefully in large enough numbers to make the ensuing combat worthwhile.

Like any war, Vietnam was shaped by the political objectives of the antagonists. Unquestionably, the single most salient characteristic of combat south of the demilitarized zone (DMZ) was the lack of a front line. Although this fact can hardly be news to anyone remotely aware of the course of events in Vietnam, few observers have tried to explain why this was so. Yet, finding an explanation for this is important, and it will do much to explain why the daily grind of Vietnam developed into the military equivalent of the Chinese water torture.

Most wars in contemporary history have been linear, characterized by an often fluid but recognizable line, with one set of combatants inhabiting one side and their opponents holding the other. Two closely linked factors produced this result. First, one or both sides had objects of value that, for psychological or economic reasons, they considered indispensable to the war effort and thus worth the risk of guarding with their armies. During World War I, for example, if the French thought Paris was worth defending with an army, the only way for the Germans to seize it was to defeat this army. The Germans, for their part, wished to seize Paris, but they also wanted to defend the Rhineland. Moreover, they were forced to deploy an army for both attack and defense. And the armies had to form lines. Obviously, if troops were in position and a 100-mile hole was left wide open on either flank, they were inviting their opponent to move by them and seize what had value. Or something else, just as bad, could happen. Armies require supplies, and their supply lines must be kept open and reasonably secure or their ability to sustain combat will be seriously compromised. Here is the second reason for linear war. If ground forces do not deploy in line, this offers the opponent the chance to get behind them, sever their communications, and perform the most feared maneuver in ground war: encirclement. Encirclement is rare, but when it takes place, catastrophe follows. The trapped forces use up their supplies, and the attacker can strike from all directions. The French found this out in 1870, and the Germans faced the same predicament at Stalingrad. But encirclement is not the only tactic possible. If a front can be penetrated and a breakthrough accomplished, the defenders face either a rapid retreat or doom.

There is nothing inherently Western or European about this type of war. It can take place any time there is something of value that a nation believes it can and must defend. World War II in China and Southeast Asia was linear. The island defensive perimeter established by Japan, although it relied on air and naval forces (protected by large land garrisons), was designed to serve the same purpose against the United States. The Korean conflict was a linear one, as well. U.S. intelligence long believed that any Sino-Soviet war, an event that once seemed so likely, would be a linear conflict. And had the United States invaded North Vietnam and pushed toward the Red River and Hanoi, a linear conflict would almost certainly have taken place.

But in South Vietnam, the two preconditions for linear war were absent. The Front and the NVA were willing to yield any particular square yard in the entire country to allied forces—if we were willing to pay the price to take it. Retreat, therefore, was always an option for revolutionary forces.

Furthermore, ARVN had to defend Saigon and other cities, and American forces had to defend their base camps and lines of communication. The other side did not have a similar burden. And because the Vietnam conflict was the archetypal civil war, where brother fought brother (though rarely face to face), the supply situation was also different from that of traditional linear war. Both sides did have lines of supply and lines of communication. Our power was sufficient to defend allied lines, especially because it was complemented by air supply, but the effort was a constant drain. The other side's situation stood in marked contrast. Lacking vehicles and aircraft, if the North wanted to launch a major attack, its forces were forced to undertake a long, risky, and arduous process they called "preparing the battlefield." Both men and supplies had to be prepositioned. The supplies were slowly collected into strategically placed caches, and the men were deployed much more rapidly through carefully planned night maneuvers. Attacks required surprise, and if the North's troops did not succeed quickly, U.S. power would soon be brought to bear. This happened frequently enough to warrant fuller discussion in a separate chapter. But, again, retreat was always possible for the NVA.

Except during the general offensive, lasting from late 1967 until May of 1969, the enemy relied on different tactics. The classic Maoist technique of "people's war" was made a religion by Vietnamese military and political thinkers. And it was on this battlefield that most Americans fought. The difficulties for the NVA were extraordinary. Supply lines were elusive. Foodstuffs had to be locally grown and gathered in almost every hamlet in the country, with a small reserve kept available for the Front's regular fighting units that were passing through. The local guerrillas, who called themselves the Vietnamese equivalent of the maquis, either lived right in villages that were under Front control or stayed extremely close by and came in at night. Only a small amount of military supplies were required for "shoot-and-scoot" fighting. Here, the other side was helped greatly by the great power of modern light infantry weapons. In one portion of the military arena, after all, the respective relationship between the two sides was precisely the opposite. The enemy's precise location was usually a mystery to American forces, but the Front had no trouble finding men of the 25th Division. The bases and the well-traveled supply routes that kept them running were as obvious as Nui Ba Den. The enemy, therefore, almost always struck first. Six guerrillas with a command-detonated mine and AK47s could cause terrible grief in a lightning exchange, and a few hundred rounds—a hopelessly inadequate supply for Americans—could do serious damage if one had a visible target. The enemy was thus able to rely on one of the oldest and most important military principles: economy of force.

I do not want to give the impression that the Front and the NVA were scattered evenly across the landscape. The truth was very different. Small military operations could be launched from almost anywhere. This was especially true as local guerrillas received more and better arms through 1966 and 1967. Yet, the enemy did intend to win the war militarily. Hanoi and its subordinates leading the Front's military forces always assumed that the war would end with large revolutionary military units playing a major or central role. It was also in the enemy's interest to keep our forces off balance. This meant that there had to be a component of the Front/NVA armed forces that was professionally trained, moderately well supplied, and capable of concentrating quickly. It was here that the geographic facts of life dealt a very bad hand to the 25th Division.

When the Americans arrived, the North began a major effort to improve the Ho Chi Minh Trail and solidify its supply lines running from the port of Shihanoukville in Cambodia up to the border between Cambodia and Tay Ninh and Hau Nghia provinces, part of the 25th Division's AO. Furthermore, in early fighting (much of it taking place before U.S. intervention), many pro-Front civilians had fled endangered hamlets and created "villages in exile" across the border. By 1967, Cambodia was well on its way to becoming an all-purpose rear area, complete with supply depots, training facilities, hospitals, and places where hard-pressed fighters could rest in relative safety. Why President Lyndon Johnson considered Cambodia a neutral nation must remain a mystery.

But Cambodia was only one piece of the puzzle. As previously noted, the 25th Division's area of operations encompassed several longtime Front redoubts. These areas were rugged and filled with observation points and thus capable of being mined in an instant by enemy forces; frequently, they were home to very large enemy units. North of Highway 1, where the terrain allowed it, there was an astounding array of tunnels that had been under construction since the time of the French war and were never controlled by Saigon. Other redoubts were not so elaborate, but all had well-concealed hiding places and supply caches, and all were in the enemy's backyard. Every large enemy attack came from one of these areas, and unfortunately for the Americans, there were many areas like this. Smaller ones might not have presented the same level of danger, but they were lethal nonetheless, and enemy forces on the move might encounter one anywhere.

In reality, the situation was even worse than this suggests. The Front had prepared a very powerful and sophisticated political apparatus throughout South Vietnam. Drawing on the Chinese experience in the 1930s and the Vietnamese experience against the French, they attempted to create "liberated zones" wherever possible. A liberated zone was an area controlled day and night by the Front. Invariably, at least at the beginning, the liberated zones were near the redoubts: It lifted the spirits of the revolution's supporters and struck fear into their opponents' hearts to know that the revolutionary fist was close by.

American-supplied air power and U.S. ground intervention prevented the development of the large liberated zones the Front had hoped to establish. Yet, many hamlets were controlled totally by the revolutionary forces and had to be physically seized before the Saigon government could establish any sort of presence. Many areas that were on their way to becoming liberated zones instead became "contested." By day, the South's government had a presence, although often precarious, but at night, government officials abandoned the hamlets or slept behind barbed wire in one of the countless little forts that existed in almost every village. And they had good reason to position themselves behind barbed wire because they were potential targets of "revolutionary justice" at any time. An efficient, honest, and zealously anti-Communist government official was in desperate danger of assassination. Therefore, in many areas, Front cadres operated with varying degrees of freedom at night. Large Front rallies, for instance, were routinely held within shouting distance of the government fort.

The organizational apparatus patiently constructed by the Front cadres throughout South Vietnam was termed the "Viet Cong infrastructure" by the allied forces. It was the political heart of the revolution until at least 1970, and it played a major role in the conflict until the bitter end. The village and hamlet political organizations had military units at their disposal, and in 1966, the men and women in these groups were almost all locally recruited, serving in or close to their homes. Naturally, they had an intimate knowledge of the terrain. And though poorly equipped in the beginning, the local revolutionary "citizen soldier," like everyone involved in the conflict, progressively received more and better weapons. Unfortunately for the men of the Tropic Lightning Division, their area of operations, with the exception of a few Catholic hamlets, was a longtime Front stronghold, and the revolutionary apparatus there was particularly well entrenched.

Thus, the size and the range of terrain presented a great challenge for a 25th Division soldier. Danger could come from any direction. Yet, action was required. The main targets for U.S. troops were the largest of the enemy's military units. However, if the United States ruled out an attack against North Vietnam, as the White House did for some very good reasons, the battlefield would be confined to the South. And here, whether they knew it or not, the U.S. soldiers faced political fact number one of the revolution in the South: Regardless of how they felt in their hearts about the revolution—and there *was* substantial opposition—most South Vietnamese believed that the enemy would prevail. This belief was like a ball and chain for the allied war effort. The only way out, or so it seemed, was to find the enemy and pound him into the dust. Then, hopefully, the people would see that the South Vietnamese government had a genuine chance of victory, and opponents of the revolution could rally behind it. Americans in Saigon hoped to hasten this process by cajoling leaders there into a series of political and economic reforms. Yet, reforms by the weak mean nothing. And in the first two years of war, Saigon was very weak, indeed. Thus, on smaller operations directed toward rebuilding Saigon's basic presence in many rural areas, some sort of security for the local inhabitants had to be provided if the political struggle was even to begin again. But the United States believed that struggle could only be conducted if the enemy was physically weakened and progressively kept at bay. This mission, too, required force.

For all of these reasons, American commanders believed it was imperative that the men of the 25th Division and their comrades elsewhere in Vietnam destroy the enemy. This task naturally required finding Charlie. Unfortunately for American plans, Charlie rarely wanted to be found. And when we did find him, the hidden enemy usually got off the first shot, as had happened with patrolling forces in all past wars. Beyond that, the 25th Division fought in the same general area for the entire war. Therefore, it pursued the enemy in the same areas, over and over again. Our soldiers would sweep, patrol, and sometimes fight. Always, they would leave, and nearly always, they would go back to repeat the process. Sensitive locations within the 25th's sector were visited literally hundreds of times over the four years the Division served in Vietnam. What I am describing in outline here is a world enveloped by a military nightmare. More than anything else, this was the world of the 25th Division.

Preparations for War

It is difficult to generalize about the training received by the soldiers of the 25th. It obviously varied with the individual; it also varied with the period in which the soldier was trained. At the beginning of the war, the 25th Division was, in some ways, at the peak of its efficiency. Its men had months or years of training, many officers were combat experienced, and its NCOs were tough and practiced. Yet, in another sense, they were very poorly prepared. Despite the claims of some officers that the U.S. Army possessed guerrilla war expertise coming from old campaigns in the American West or the Philippines, the Army of 1965 was organized and prepared to fight a massive linear war, precisely the opposite of what it encountered in Vietnam. Thomas Giltner, then a junior combat officer, describes his training:

I completed my training at Fort Benning Officers' Candidate School on 13 May 1965. My training for combat in Vietnam was nonexistent. I fired one magazine of an M16 rifle; I took one helicopter ride on one afternoon counterinsurgency problem. The only thing I remember was being carried from one area to another on a simulated airmobile mission and hauling an M60 machine gun around to secure some obscure objective. Our training was conventional—it was Monte Casino, North Africa, the Battle of the Bulge. Mostly, we prepared for mass tactical deployment of large infantry and armor formations. The training of 1944 and 1964 had little apparent change, and that's how I was prepared for my assignment as a rifle platoon leader. In all honesty, it was probably not thought that Vietnam would ever expand beyond an advisory effort, and I'm not talking about training from a critical point of view. I'm just saying that's the way it was. We were more concerned with fighting the Red Chinese or the Soviet Union.

Finally, in that nine-month period of time when I was at Fort Polk, Louisiana, when the buildup began in late 1965, especially in the advanced infantry circles, they started running problems dealing with moving through VC villages, moving through rice paddies, search-and-destroy-type operations, and the use of more jungle-type weapons, such as the M16 rifle. That came long after U.S. forces were actually deployed to Vietnam. Previously, the only thing some officers received was an assignment to Panama for two weeks of intensive training there before Vietnam. So training and indoctrination, in my experience, followed at least a year behind events.

Yet, some of the early veterans watched with dismay the decline in tactical effectiveness and discipline that inevitably occurred as the original group of 25th soldiers rotated and were replaced by new men who lacked the peacetime preparation that the earliest group had received. Robert Conner, an eighteen-year-old enlisted man, went through the 25th Division's unique training program in Hawaii, intended to acclimate men to war in the tropical villages:

The jungle warfare training in Hawaii helped tremendously. But the replacements came in with a different attitude. They were more belligerent and didn't care as much. They didn't have enough time to train and become soldiers. They lacked the desire, dedication, and obedience, the two or three years that's required to become the best possible soldier before entering battle. By 1969–1970, American soldiers just didn't have it.

Conner's views are echoed by Carl Quickmire, then a captain and a commander of a squadron of the 3/4th Armored Cavalry Battalion in 1966, who returned to the 25th in 1969 for a second tour. He was not pleased with what he found:

The 25th Infantry Division was an entirely different unit this time, some two years later, as I am sure that all other units were. We were well into the replacement cycle. Some things struck me immediately. One was the lack of career NCOs, the men we called "hard-core" NCOs, and the prevalence of the "instant Jack" or instant NCO, the young kid who did well in basic training and then was given accelerated training and commissioned a sergeant E5 and sergeant E6 with less than a year in service. Don't get me wrong, some of these fellows turned out to be excellent leaders in combat. But it was appalling to me to see the lack of career NCOs out in the front lines. It seemed that we had more NCOs dodging duty back in Cu Chi than we did in the front lines.

The process that Quickmire describes began very early. As I shall examine directly, field units were badly understrength from the beginning. There were never enough NCOs to go around. In addition, because the existing NCOs knew the ropes well, they were in a very good position to heed what one soldier called the "call of the rear." Obviously, there were many fine professional NCOs in Vietnam, and many of them were rotated to train the large army that was arriving. Yet, Quickmire's opinion was shared by others. Kenneth Stumpf's standards were high, but his comments have the ring of truth:

They always talk about the NCO corps being the backbone of the Army. In Vietnam, they weren't worth a shit. In my three times in Vietnam, I couldn't count on one hand the career NCOs that were in the field. It was always us young draftees. And we needed that leadership from soldiers that were thirty to thirty-five years old. I found out when I went back on the second tour where most of them were. Most of them were sitting back at the damn base camps, working in clubs and things like that. Then the Army went to the "shake-and-bake" thing around 1968. How stupid. You go through training, and you go to this "instant NCO" school, and you come out of there, and you're an E5 buck sergeant or E6 staff sergeant, and you're going to Vietnam in combat arms. That caused problems after 1968. Now, not only do you have a green lieutenant, but you also have green NCOs. My first tour, I took over a squad after three months in-country, a little experience anyway. But now, you have four shake-and-bakes and a green platoon leader. And then you had guys that were there for seven or eight months, being led by those who didn't have any experience. Why not promote the guys from the field? We had one real live NCO during my first tour, a black sergeant with seventeen years in the Army. He was one of my idols and a great leader. When he was wounded, it hurt us all.

Ironically, Robert Conner, the soldier who expressed dismay at the decline of professional standards in the 25th, became one of the first of a legion of remarkably young NCOs. His promotion came from the field, and his experience was sobering:

In the next five months, I led twenty-eight ambush patrols. You know, that's a lot of responsibility put on a kid. Back in the world, you'd never think of putting that kind of responsibility on a kid. A kid should have the responsibility of buying a car and making payments. Imagine an eighteen-year-old kid reading the map coordinates, saying, "You go out here at dusk, go out 300 meters, and set up an ambush patrol." In that group of people, you might have some transfers who have been in the service for five years. I took out sergeants just into Vietnam who had been in the service for fifteen years. I don't want that kind of responsibility again. When I look back, God, I was scared. I was so stupid and naive I could hate myself. Today, I have a son and two daughters. I would never dream of letting them go off and fight. Especially under the supervision of an eighteen-year-old.

Other viewpoints reflected a different reality. As time went on, the stern lessons of war began to filter back to the United States. As a result, though the training may have been less intensive, it was probably more realistic. Richard Blanks arrived in 1969 and considered his preparation as a junior officer good:

I had Infantry OCS [Officer Candidate School—EMB] at Fort Benning, starting in February 1968, and I was commissioned a lieutenant in September of 1968. I've always been proud of attending Fort Benning. We started with a class of 212 and ended up with 98. We thought the main purpose of OCS was to make you quit. If you were going to quit, it was better to quit in there than in Vietnam with people depending on you. It was a rough program; they worked you hard. The usual pattern was assignment stateside for six months and then on to Vietnam. I spent three weeks in Panama at jungle training school. And then on to Vietnam. Incidentally, in defense of lieutenants, grunts fucked up all the time and folded. If I did, it was a lot more visible. We were held to higher standards.

When men arrived at Cu Chi, they received a week or so of additional training. Some men called it "charm school." Whether it was effective depended, again, on the individual and on the time period. Dan Vandenberg was not impressed by the Army's methods of getting him ready for a deadly challenge:

Everybody spends a week at jungle warfare school. The name is a lot more impressive than the school itself. What happens is that one day you go out and sight in the rifle they gave you, if you could get the rifle to work. Most of the stuff was rusted and had to be cleaned before you could get it to fire. Next day, they'd take you around and show you a bunch of booby traps, which is kind of nice but does absolutely no good in the field because nobody is going to point them out to you then. The only way you find them is the hard way: by tripping them. Then they show you some tunnels that somebody had dug. Actually, it's like a walk through Disneyland. But at least after that week, the brass could say they gave us a week of jungle training. At least, it was a good way to get acclimated to the climate. Believe me, it is quite a shock. Twelve hours before we landed in Vietnam, we had stopped at Anchorage, Alaska, in January, and the next thing you know, you're in Vietnam. It's quite a difference.

Lee Reynolds served late in the war. Despite problems at camp, the field army had learned a great deal by then, much of it the hard way. Reynolds was impressed with what he saw:

I was drafted and didn't want to go but volunteered to be a medic and volunteered for Vietnam. The 25th was a good organization. The troops were very knowledgeable and impressed me with their actions. One of the reasons the 25th Division was more successful was because we had better in-country training. From time to time, we had additional training. Out in the field, we would have occasional stand downs and use the time to do some additional training. They had other schools: They had a combat marksman school they were always trying to recruit people into; they had a tunnel rat school that they had trouble recruiting people into. We thought they tricked people into tunnel rat school by advertising it as demolition school, knowing the little guys always wanted to make the biggest bang. LCLC [lightning combat leadership course—EMB] training was popular and led to better-trained soldiers even if they didn't pass. It was very effective and led to some good squad leaders. People were real bushwise. They were highly professional and very skillful. It bothers me that the media portrays the Vietnam soldier as an idiot. We got out of a lot of situations when the odds were against us because the people were good; they really were.

Intelligence

The 25th Division's AO might appear to cover a small area on a map, but it was, in fact, an extremely large area. Again, the lack of a front line worked against the U.S. war effort. Had the combat battalions been able to concentrate their forces, their story would have unfolded very differently. As it was, however, units were spread out across the entire area of operations. Danger could come from any direction, and the enemy might be found in any corner. Thus, the concentration of force, so beloved by officers, was impossible to achieve.

With the combat units dispersed and the opposition extremely difficult to locate, good and timely intelligence was at a premium. Unfortunately for the men of the 25th, operational intelligence often left much to be desired. This situation was never resolved, despite a growing experience with the terrain, improved fighting techniques, and an ever-increasing number of technological devices. At the outset, as Carl Quickmire recalls, intelligence gathering was not much of an issue. Finding the enemy was no trouble because at least some were inside the fledgling camp at Cu Chi itself:

At that time, we thought there were more Viet Cong inside the perimeter than outside. The camp at Cu Chi was built over the most extensive tunnel complex that the Viet Cong had in South Vietnam. It was not uncommon for them to pop up from inside the perimeter as well as outside and start sniping at us.

Although the immediate situation stabilized in short order, the basic problem—poor intelligence—definitely remained. Thomas Ferguson was deployed with the first wave as the signals officer for the Division. His job of monitoring the movements of all units gave him an excellent insight into the difficulty. Obviously, the problem itself was a hard one, but according to Ferguson, the Army made a bad situation worse by its own techniques of "safeguarding" intelligence, which often meant denying it to the men who needed it most:

A million words would be necessary to discuss intelligence. My impression was that it ran from nonexistent to unsatisfactory. Not that the effort was not made within the Division, but we were forced too often to rely on the higher command indicators from their extensive intelligence network under their control. While there was no doubt that they were acquiring solid information from their agents, and I had every reason to believe that they had good ones in Hau Nghia and Tay Ninh, the time lag in distributing the "sanitized" product was such that the NVA or VC units had simply moved away. With the number of men we had in the field, which was generally less than 50 percent of our combat troops at any given time, the NVA/VC units, which were often small to begin with, only had to move half a mile or so and we would miss them. I had the feeling that the NVA/VC in our area were very widely dispersed and would assemble only for a specific operation. We had a low-level radio intercept company with us from the Army Security Agency. But like the other agents under MACV [Military Assistance Command, Vietnam—EMB] control, all of the information they collected first had to be processed through Saigon before coming back down to us. MACV didn't want to compromise their sources. But old information is no information. On the whole, I was not impressed with our intelligence network.

The situation at Cu Chi did not improve greatly over time. Maj. Gen. Ellis Williamson, who commanded the 25th during part of 1968 and 1969, addresses the problem as it appeared at high echelons:

The Army at that time was designed and equipped for the European battlefield of massed tanks and artillery operating on European terrain. Its target acquisition and intelligence sensors were conceived, designed, and produced with that in mind. The enemy in Vietnam, however, was different. He was foot mobile, operated from jungle sanctuaries, and was more often than not a "night" creature. None of the U.S. Army organic sensors were designed to consistently detect, classify, identify, track, or project these forces. Consequently, there was a continual battle to modify existing sensors for the immediate purpose or to beg, borrow, or steal items still in the research-and-development cycle. The 25th G-2 [intelligence officer—EMB] has told many times his experience, i.e., "General Williamson would often come in and say, 'Just give me an address! I know what to do, if you can just tell me where.'"

A lack of decent intelligence always caused serious difficulties. At the battalion level, operating in the dark meant dead soldiers. Battalion commander Carl Neilson, who led his mechanized troopers through Tet, reflects on the situation with bitterness:

I thought we had a terrible lack of timely, accurate tactical intelligence. Literally nobody ever told me accurately before an attack was going to be made. I was told many times to be especially watchful tonight in a given area because indications were that an attack was going to occur. The only thing I could be sure of then was that it wasn't going to happen. Conversely, when attack came, it frequently came at a time and place we did not expect.

The 25th Division, naturally, did its best to gather its own local intelligence. Helicopters, small aircraft, various sensors, and, above all, actual sightings by units on the ground or in the air all served the purpose. Yet, what one unit saw was not always communicated to another. And though this would vary depending on the commander, junior officers were not always told how their task fit into a larger design.

Part of this was certainly just poor communication. In 1969, Capt. Henry Bergson, an experienced field officer, was assigned to be 3d Brigade night duty officer. As he describes the situation, the night war, frequently so important, was largely run by men of surprisingly low rank considering the stakes:

In mid-March, I was reassigned to be the night duty officer in the tactical operations headquarters of the 3d Brigade. There, I had one of my revelations of the war: After 6:00 p.m., the entire war in Vietnam was controlled by a bunch of captains, majors, lieutenants, and sergeants sitting around at various tactical operations centers. They were the only link with the people in the field. All of the colonels, generals, and anybody else who could get away with it had long since gone to bed. It was here that I first started to get a closer feel for what the military operations were.

If something hot started, officers would wake quickly, but Bergson's point is valid. Because some intelligence was gathered haphazardly and some was jealously guarded by higher command echelons, junior officers in the field frequently had to operate with little of this precious commodity. Troop commander Jerry Headley recalls the general lack of information:

Although you got periodic briefings from the squadron intelligence officer, I generally felt, even looking back on it years later, that while intelligence on the enemy and his movements was probably well known and documented on the higher level, it never seemed to filter down to the people who needed it at the company level, where they could execute or plan your day's activities.

Headley also illustrates what could happen if operational intelligence was rapidly gathered and acted upon. In January 1969, Headley's troop of the 3/4th Armored Cavalry had a small contact in a village near Cambodia. A North Vietnamese unit was cornered close by, and combat was certain:

Moving into a village where we knew some NVA were trapped, we had received some small-arms fire and had captured a very young prisoner, maybe about sixteen years old. You could tell he was a new recruit. He was scared to death, and his head was almost shaved like new recruits in armies the world over. Our troops wanted to go ahead and kill him, but we told them no, that was not the thing to do. We needed to question him and see if he had information, which, indeed, he did. We airlifted him out, and we were later informed that he said there would be an attack that night to take pressure off the troops that were surrounded in the town so they could escape into Cambodia. Indeed, at midnight that night, right on the dot, we were attacked by rocket fire and mortar fire, followed by a ground assault. Fortunately, we had brought in an infantry company and two 105mm howitzers, so with the additional fire power, after an all-night fight, we were able to sustain our fighting position. Unfortunately, an ARVN unit that was blocking to our north bugged out. The advisers with them called us on the radio and most apologetically said, "Sorry, we've got to because ARVN's bugging out. I've got to go with them or I'll be left behind." This opened up the door, and the NVA went through it and slipped into Cambodia.

It is a strange aspect of warfare that enlisted men, who by sheer numbers do most of the fighting, almost always know the least about what is going on around them. The Department of the Army wrote the various official histories of recent wars, in part, to help the common soldier—who, at the time, was totally ignorant of what was taking place beyond the next hill— see how his work contributed to the war effort. Vietnam was no different, even though small-unit actions cannot be counted. Jim Ross explains the relationships between soldier and higher authority on operations:

As far as intelligence gathering, we had very little knowledge of that as infantrymen. From the level of captain on down, the captain would be the one who would have most of the knowledge about where we were going, why we were going, and what we were supposed to be doing. On the front lines, the infantrymen were not privy to the intelligence part of the missions that we went on. We might be given a briefing where we were told what our basic mission was and what we might expect when we got there, but they did not see fit to inform us of the nitty-gritty of the intelligence part, like the names of the North Viet units who we might run into and why we were going to this place exactly. Most of the time, we didn't know what other friendly units were going to be involved in the operation and how the thing was going to be coordinated and structured. We were pretty well left in the dark. It was pretty much on a need-to-know basis. In the eyes of the brass, the peons, such as the enlisted men, didn't need to know.

Lee Reynolds, who was serving when the intelligence apparatus was at its peak later in the war, still had reservations about its effectiveness:

We had a saying that military intelligence was a contradiction in terms. I'm sure we must have had excellent intelligence. I'm sure we did because without good intelligence, we wouldn't have been as successful as we were. But everything that came down to us that we knew about and checked out would turn out to be wrong. For example, late in my tour, we were down south. Some guys from the 9th Division had been transferred to us when the 9th went home, and we were in their AO. We were out on an airmobile mission, working off of intelligence. We were patrolling down there in what they called the Nuk, the Vietnamese word for water. It was a real wet area with canals running through. We patrolled this island and slogged around in the mud for a while. When we were sitting waiting for the helicopters to come and pick us up, the guys from the 9th Division were telling us—and this was confirmed by our Kit Carson scouts—that we were on the wrong island. [Kit Carson scouts were Vietnamese, sometimes enemy defectors, who helped guide American forces through unfamiliar terrain. ARVN liaison personnel were more prevalent and acted as interpreters on large operations.—EMB] We could see that across the canal, there was a structure they called the "death hooch," and that's where the VC were. So our intelligence was wrong, and we were on the wrong island, but the guys were not going to tell anyone any different because you don't get in trouble if you stay out of contact. We were all getting pretty short [close to the end of their tours—EMB] and didn't want to take any more chances than we absolutely had to.

Ironically, the enlisted troops sometimes received information from a most unlikely source—Vietnamese civilians. This situation, though it seems bizarre, was really quite explicable. All American camps had large numbers of civilian employees, many of whom spoke English of one sort or another. Everyone knew that many of the people were enemy agents or sympathizers; others, however, were not, and they might take an interest in the men they were cleaning up after. The Vietnamese naturally talked with each other, and by simple observation and camp gossip, they could pick things up very quickly. Many men believed, whether rightly or wrongly, that the locals could find out about operations before they themselves did.

Another situation also came up. It was common for Vietnamese civilians to gather around the most meager of American perimeters, hoping to sell things or collect scrap. Obviously, the civilians would frequently (but not always) know if there was danger in the area. Thus, their absence put the troops on edge, as Dan Vandenberg remembers:

As soon as they wouldn't go any further, we got uneasy real fast, I'll tell you. If we wanted to know what we were going to do next day, we'd ask the civilians. They'd know before our commander knew.

It is not at all unusual during wartime for leaders to withhold military information with the men in the grass. However, the 25th Division was part of the best-educated army in history and one made up of individuals not accustomed to the stricter hierarchies of the past. Gerry Schooler, a Tet veteran with the *Wolfhounds,* expresses a widely held belief that the Army made a serious error and underestimated its own soldiers in this regard:

I always had the feeling, and it's a cliché, that the blind were leading the blind. One of the most frustrating things for me was not ever knowing what we were doing. We were never told the names and objectives of big operations: Some I found out years later while reading through an old yearbook. I don't understand why they did that. All we were ever told was what we were to do that day, which was usually to take seven guys down this trail and try to make contact or check out some hooches. So, I feel the military failed terribly in the area. If people are dying and especially for the friends of the people that are dying, you ought to give them some really good reasons why they're doing it. We were never given any objective and told that some people would get hurt but this would lead to this and so on. I think the guys should have known something. I think there was some paranoia about what was going on in the States. The generals had TVs, and we didn't. Maybe they wanted us in the dark because of the trouble in the States and hoped that our mind-set, due to our training, would be to follow orders. It worked in some cases, but in some cases, it didn't. If just once they would have come up to my platoon and said, "Look, here's what's going to happen," it might have helped. Maybe not, maybe it's never been that way in war. I don't think they thought of us as thinking people. Maybe they should have.

None of the above is meant as an indictment of military intelligence in Vietnam. It is a murky field at best, and the practical difficulties in the Vietnamese environment were daunting. Yet, it is also true that the Army was not able to rise above itself and create new and faster methods of obtaining and distributing information to those who needed to know it the most, the junior officers leading the men in the bush or the tracks on patrol. Whether more could have been done is difficult to say. Regardless, in most cases, the men of the 25th operated blindly.

Objectives, Tempo, and Terrain

In most wars, factors concerning the objectives of military operations, the tempo or pace with which they were conducted, and the military terrain where they took place would be treated separately. But in Vietnam, these points became so interwoven that they constituted the core of the military experience for most combat soldiers in the 25th Division. Unraveling the weave is difficult but essential if we hope to understand why warfare in Vietnam took the form that it did.

As already noted, geographic points had a very different meaning in Vietnam than they did in linear wars. If an American unit was sent to a given place, it was not to hold and exploit a valuable objective but rather to seek the enemy forces that the American commanders hoped might be there. The troops would arrive, search, and then leave. If the fortunes of war favored the 25th Division—from the command's point of view, at any rate—the soldiers would find a worthwhile quarry, and a large firefight or battle would ensue. Normally, however, that was not the case, and contacts, if they took place at all, were small and incredibly quick. In addition, because it was rarely possible to identify the location of an enemy formation, combat units of the 25th were constantly in motion, casting their net as widely as prudence allowed.

For the men involved, this meant an incalculable number of medium or small operations, day and night, over terrain visited again and again. The other side could be anywhere, so American soldiers tried to go everywhere. Moreover, because there was no concrete objective, it was not possible for the brass at Cu Chi to control the pace of operations. For instance, commanders prefer to rest their forces before a battle, knowing the fierce rigors that will come. But this opportunity was lacking in Vietnam because a large firefight or battle might come at any moment and at almost any place. Periodically, a unit might be withdrawn for a short stand down at a base camp, but normally, the men were ordered to maintain a frantic pace of activity.

Although the tempo of activity was intense, the men themselves rarely understood what they were doing or why they were doing it, beyond "finding Charlie." Of more immediate concern to them was the appalling reality that the nature and tempo of operations engendered. Under the best of circumstances, continuously driving the very limited number of men actually in the field so hard would have guaranteed intense fatigue and physical exhaustion. In the Vietnamese climate and terrain, this situation inflicted an extreme physical and psychological toll on the men on the spearpoint. It also brought them face to face, at almost all times, with two of the most feared threats on their battlefield: mines and lightning ambushes.

Concerning the military objectives or lack thereof in the typical operation in Vietnam, troop commander Carl Quickmire gives an excellent and concise description:

It essentially amounted to going out and beating the jungle every day and every night looking for the enemy. There were all kinds of fancy names given to the "tactics": search and destroy, cordon and search, sweep and search, anvil and hammer, etc. and etc. But it all amounted at the tactical unit level to going out, looking for the enemy, and trying to kill him. Despite all of the highfalutin gadgets, intelligence for the most part was extremely poor. We did not know who we were looking for or where to look, in most cases. We frequently were ambushed, sometimes due to our own stupidity, for taking the same route or setting a daily schedule or setting a certain established routine.

Platoon leader Thomas Giltner, another officer and thus privy to more information than the average soldier, agrees with Quickmire:

It was a war without fronts. We would literally go off on operation and go around in a circle. In fact, most of our operations were in circles, particularly if they were ground to ground. We'd leave the wire, go someplace, and sweep around a circle and come right on back. The perimeter security operations were always in a circle. We'd try to vary these, so sometimes we went clockwise and sometimes we went counterclockwise. When we were running search and destroy missions and penetrating an area in a helicopter, we wouldn't necessarily be going around in a circle. Instead, we'd go from point A to point B, then be picked up and taken to point C. If we weren't going around in circles, we were leapfrogging, like pieces moving around a chessboard. One day, we'd be north of Trang Bang; one day, we'd be south of Bao Trai; one day, we'd be outside Tay Ninh. Sometimes, we were in several of those places in one day. So where is the front line in a war like that? The answer is, it doesn't exist: It's everywhere. The only place you go back to for support and relative safety is whatever perimeter you've got going, whether it's a base camp or a small compound or a foxhole at night.

Infantryman Larry Fontana served from mid-1968 to mid-1969, probably the worst twelve months imaginable for a 25th Division veteran. Although he started green, he soon received a field promotion to NCO and thus was in an excellent position to assess the daily pace of operations:

I'll never forget the feeling of putting a loaded magazine in my M16 before my first patrol. I can still remember feeling sort of numb, realizing that when the round slammed into the chamber of the rifle, it wouldn't be for the rifle range anymore; I wondered as I strapped on the grenades if I'd have to throw one. I almost felt embarrassed as we patrolled through villages because my equipment was so new that everybody and their cousins would know I was a new guy. The old-timers' fatigues and helmet covers were faded to the extreme. Every chance I had, I would rub my helmet in the dirt so that I could change the new into veteran ugly.

Fontana did not have to put on an act for long:

Patrols and operations were daily. You either patrolled an area close by or you were flown by helicopter to the more remote places. Every night, listening posts would go out a short distance, and several squad-sized ambushes would fan out from 400 to 800 meters. During daytime, these were not long distances; however, at night, they may as well have been 4 to 8 miles. The night patrol would consist of a squad sergeant, medic, forward observer from our heavy weapons platoon, a machine-gun crew, radio operator, and five other infantrymen. We pretty much carried a standard day patrol complement of equipment, plus several claymore mines each and poncho liners. A compass was used for direction, and a man with a good pace counted out the meters of the patrol. This was standard for the majority of all patrols, day or night. It was imperative that the sergeant reach the ambush site with some degree of accuracy since our own mortars had preplotted firing zones around the ambush site. Ambush patrols at night were always in single file, with no point or flank security. Upon reaching a site, the patrol would break into 3 groups of 4 men. This was the standard night ambush formation, and we called it the triangular ambush. After the men were down, soldiers from each position would lay out claymore mines. When this was done, the patrol would literally have 360 degrees of explosive protection outside of the perimeter. Groups were usually no farther than 30 feet from each other, our feet pretty much pointing at each other. Our night patrols left after dark, except for rare exceptions. The ambush would leave its position the next morning, at first light, to return. I disliked night patrols. After I became a sergeant, I hated them. I understood the importance of having patrols out at night, but I always felt a squad of 12 men was somehow wrong. I always felt that 4 men going out no more than 400 meters would be quieter and less conspicuous. Also, they could move faster, if need be. They would be great for night observation. If they wanted to go out further, I felt that the whole platoon should go: 30 men in trouble more than a half mile from help at night had a lot better chance than 12.

Our daylight patrols were usually company sized, a little over 100 men. Our standard patrol formation was column. Whichever platoon was picked for the point platoon also supplied the point team, which usually consisted of 3 men, a sergeant who usually did the compass work, a pace man, and the actual point man. The distance a point team was from the formation depended, of course, on terrain. The point team would be much closer in a jungle than in open rice paddies or fields. The platoons would patrol in two parallel columns, and like the point, the distance between platoons depended on terrain. Each column had a machine-gun team. To the outside of each column were 2 soldiers. These were the flanks. Their job, which I always considered the most dangerous, was to protect the vulnerable sides of the patrol. Prepared ambushes were almost always triggered from the flanks. There was no such thing as a typical operation. Sometimes, our patrol might be made from choppers to the uninhabited Ho Bo Woods for one day. The next day, it might be searching specific villages in the middle of rice country. Another day, it would be road security patrols for the resupply convoys. They could be platoon, company, battalion, and multibattalion sized.

In retrospect, Dan Vandenberg is not impressed with the efficiency of military tactics in Vietnam, and he shares Fontana's ugly memories of night operations:

They took us out by convoy to Trang Bang for the first week to ten days. Our job was to pull security on the bridge at Trang Bang, which was kind of a joke because nobody wanted to blow it up. Charlie was using it as much as we were, so it was the safest bridge in Vietnam. One day, we'd direct traffic around the bridge, fill sandbags, and pretend we're guarding the thing. It was incredible, pulling duty on the bridge, because you'd get these Vietnamese on their mopeds and three-wheel vehicles and they'd take on a tank head to head. Only one vehicle can go across the bridge at a time, and you'd get these tanks and APCs, and damned if the Vietnamese on these mopeds would back off. They were perfectly willing to have a convoy 2 miles long wait while they pedaled across these bridges.

The next day, we'd rotate with another platoon and go with the engineers and pull security while they swept for mines, which was also a good job because it was rare for there to be sniper fire or anything. About once a week, the engineers would recover a mine. This was the road to Tay Ninh, so every day, it had to be swept before the convoys came through. We'd walk about 100 yards to the side of the road, get about 100 yards ahead of the engineers, and then wait for them to catch up. Then we'd go another 100 yards further. In theory, we were providing security. Anyway, it would take us until about 2:00 to get to the end of the road where the engineers quit sweeping. At that time, we'd take a break and wait for the convoy to come back from Tay Ninh. We'd catch a ride back down to Trang Bang. After supper, such as it was, there was mail call. You were also supposed to clean your weapon, which wasn't all that easy because the materials you needed weren't always available. You could go to town and buy them off the black market, but getting them from your supply sergeant was another story.

Then we'd pull ambush, generally squad size, which would be about 6 or maybe 7 guys in our case. We'd wait until an hour before dark, and then we'd head out 3 or 4 clicks or something like that to someplace known only by the squad leader and CO [commanding officer—EMB]. The rest of us didn't know or care. We just plodded along like a bunch of sheep. We'd set up our claymores and had 2-men positions—two hours on, two hours off, each guy rotating in each position. Come daybreak, we'd pick up our gear and head back to camp. We'd eat breakfast, refill canteens, and then go out and do the same damn thing we did before: road security or go stand down by the bridge and eat dust as the convoys went through.

The thing I hated most over there was the nighttime. During the day, you could act kind of cocky, walk around like you knew what you were doing. Once it got dark, it got dark. It's nothing like here, where you have street-lights that can illuminate things. There were many times you were out on patrol and literally couldn't see your hand in front of your face. You'd have to put your hand on the shoulder of the guy in front of you so you didn't get lost or separated. You're walking around through these paddies, and you never know if you're going to step into a well, which were usually dried up and full of snakes. You sure couldn't see any booby traps: You couldn't find your feet, much less a booby trap. You're just out there playing blindman's bluff, but you're making enough noise so that it sounded like a damn parade. On the other hand, Charlie just thrived on nighttime. He could move through the dark and never make a sound. He knew exactly where he was going; he was good. It was always such a relief when you saw the sun come up: You made it through another night, and Charlie didn't do much during the daytime. He pretty much lay low and did most of his damage and nastiness at night. So, if you made it through the night, you could say, "Ah, another 12 hours" when the odds were in your favor for a change. When nighttime came again, everybody's ass puckered up, and you just held your breath until it got light again. If Charlie did attack at night, you could never see what you were shooting back at. You could see the muzzle blasts, but you didn't know what you were going to hit or what you were aiming at. The main thing is just to see how many rounds you can fire in the shortest amount of time.

The military situation had changed dramatically for the better by 1970, largely due to the Front's suicidal offensive of 1968–1969. Yet, according to Dan Breeding, the essence of operations had not changed from the first day Americans arrived in Cu Chi:

There was never a front. I can recall operating in the same area three or four different times. I even knew where we would sit down for half a day. We'd be back in the very same places, and that always bugged me. Not the fact that we weren't getting into contact but the mere fact that we never accomplished anything. We weren't taking over any land, we were just trying to beat the enemy from it. From that aspect, we weren't doing a damn thing if we had to come back to the same place a week later. Even if we had been in contact, we'd be back there again. It was stupid. But I don't know any other way to do it. The VC just infiltrated; they went where they wanted to go. It always bugged me, going on the same patrol, going on the same hill, setting up the same ambush. The enemy must have known what we'd be doing a week from now because I am sure every unit operated the same way.

As Gary Ernst recalls, the seemingly aimless wandering that was typical of infantry operations had its parallel in mechanized units:

A major duty was convoy escorting, and it got monotonous. You had to watch the boredom and monotony because, especially near Dau Tieng, you were subject to ambush at all times. We also guarded the laterite pit and rock pile at Nui Ba Den. We also went on search and destroy operations, which meant going smashing through the jungles looking for the VC that intelligence said were in the area. We would sometimes have regular straight-leg infantry, and if they saw a tunnel complex or something, they'd check it out. I was there six months and a day, and I think, except for the spare mortar attack, I only saw actual combat maybe ten days. You'd go along for weeks at a time, with a lot of boredom, escorting convoys by day, guarding areas or building our camps at night, and maintaining your vehicles. It got extremely boring. Then something would happen, and all hell would break loose, and the level of intensity rose tremendously. Consequently, you were always a little on edge. On some of these search and destroy missions, we often seemed to be right behind Charlie, probably because of the noise our tracks made. We came upon base camps and tunnel complexes: Once, rice was still cooking. But they could always just get away. And they wanted to because of our firepower. We had ten APCs, and each of them had a .50-caliber machine gun and two M60 machine guns. You're talking thirty machine guns, which could put out an awful lot of firepower.

Jerry Headley, an often-decorated officer of the elite 3/4th Armored Cavalry Battalion, also remembers hours and hours of purposeless activity:

At night, we'd sweep the roads. We'd have engineer units with us, and they would just go down the roads, and we would follow them, the floodlights on our tanks on and the rest of the men, the infantrymen and scouts, dismounted on the sides of the road, trying to prevent ambushes. The engineers would sweep the road, trying to prevent the enemy from putting in mines that would stop or destroy vehicles in the convoys that would be running the next day. The bad part of this, obviously, was that, at night, we were very susceptible to ambush, and Charlie was very good at putting out booby traps. They could be anything from punji sticks [sharpened wood sticks buried beneath leaves and branches—EMB] in the ground to grenades and tripwires. We lost several men doing these sweeps, mostly due to grenades going off. This was very hard on everybody. The men didn't like it—nobody liked it—because they knew they couldn't see the enemy, so we couldn't fight back, and we were having people wounded almost daily. During the day, you'd try to get some rest, but you had to maintain your vehicles and outpost the roads, usually a couple of tracks together in a supporting role. And if the convoy was ambushed, you would react. It was very hard and stressful. It was almost impossible to get some rest.

Headley's last comment highlights a crucial point and one remembered by every combat veteran of the 25th Division. Because operations were practically endless, the men were tormented by severe fatigue, made worse by the fierce climate and terrain. Colonel Ferguson recalls that this situation arose immediately upon deployment and doubts that the Army properly appreciated its impact on both men and operations:

Lack of sleep was an important physiological experience. All that's been written in novels about problems with sleeping is quite true. We learned to sleep through tremendous noises, such as outgoing mortar or artillery or machine-gun fire. But the moment we heard something unusual, such as an incoming round or a distinctive sound of the AK47s, boy, we were up in a matter of seconds. We all developed this sensitivity toward sound. Few of us enjoyed more than two hours of uninterrupted sleep in a day. This left us physically exhausted much of the time. I feel I have never recovered from this to this day. My sleep patterns follow those I experienced in Vietnam. During the daylight, I can fall asleep if the opportunity presents itself very easily, like I used to do waiting for a helicopter lift and then falling asleep on the lift to the landing zone. The need for sleep is not always considered by higher commanders, even though it does influence performance.

Kenneth Gosline was an early arrival and among the first to experience the realities of warfare in Vietnam:

It was funny. My mother saved all of the letters I wrote her. And I read them a couple of years after I came back. And I never realized how tired I was. I must have spent the whole year going through in just a stupor. I guess we must have got three, three and a half, at most four hours of sleep a night. Then you bust your buns through the boonies all day long, sweating, just soaking wet. Then you try it again at night. Every letter I wrote her, I just kept telling her how tired I was. I guess we were all like that.

C. W. Bowman gives a detailed, vivid, and frightening account of what it meant to "hump the boonies" in Vietnam. He also points out the connection between the extreme pounding suffered by the men in the field and the lack of manpower where it counted, in the bush:

We were always understrength. People always say you had 500,000 men over there. But out of those 500,000, maybe 20,000 were doing the actual fighting. Everybody else was back in the rear echelon. [Bowman is on shaky ground here. His point, strictly speaking, is correct. Considering the low field strength of units and the small number of them, his figure of 20,000 soldiers "in the grass" is defensible. If one looks at people at risk, however, the number was far higher. Pilots, helicopter crews, engineers, artillerymen, patrol boat crews, training teams working with ARVN, and many others were under the gun: Add the people in some sort of danger, and the number is far higher yet. Neverthless, the best way to get killed in Vietnam was to be part of a combat battalion.—EMB] Because we were so understrength, we heavily depended on our firepower, the artillery, and air strikes. Because there were so few of us, we carried a very heavy load of ammunition. I carried an M14 with 22 loaded magazines. In my rucksack, I sometimes carried 10, 15, or even up to 50 pounds of C4 plastic explosive because I also ran tunnels. We also used it to blow up bunkers and similar things. Along with that, you had to carry extra ammo for the machine gun, which was usually 200 rounds. Then you had your grenades, claymores, maybe a 60mm mortar round stuck in your hip pocket, smoke grenades, CS grenades, and anything you thought you might need. That wasn't counting your C rations.

You didn't carry anything you thought you didn't need, that was for sure; mostly just ammunition and a change of socks. Nobody wore underwear:

That was one thing you learned real quick. With the heat and the moisture and being wet all of the time, underwear would eat you alive. A lot of guys didn't wear socks either. We had a company commander that made us wear our flak vests, and that thing was heavy. Most of us just wore that and a T-shirt or no shirt at all. You carried your poncho liner: That was probably the best piece of equipment you had. The thing kept you warm at night. Even though it only got down to 80 or 90 at night, after a while, that was cold over there. They were worth their weight in gold.

We were pretty wrung out in the later part of the year because we were constantly on patrol, sweeping the jungle, on night observation, whatever. It was constant. You averaged three or, if you were lucky, four hours of sleep a night. I've got photos of all of my friends, and you can see, especially in the black-and-white photos, our eyes are sunk back in our heads; we have dark circles around our eyes from lack of sleep, like somebody punched us in the eyes. All of us were skin and bones. It was a joke among all of us that if we wanted a strong guy to carry the machine gun, what we needed to do was crawl back to base camp and get one of the clerks because every time we went there, we saw guys from muscle city trying to punch keys on the type-writers. Out in the field, we looked like a bunch of drowned rats. . . . It's amazing how fear can keep you awake all night and keep you going the next day, but it reaches a point where you have to try to get your buddy to stay awake for you because you're saying, "I have to sleep. I don't care if they come up and slit my throat or shoot me in the head, I just can't take it any-more."

GIs carried many pounds of gear in their rucksacks, mostly ammunition. So when they said you humped the boonies, that's exactly what you did, you humped the boonies. I would sweat so hard that my shirt collar turned white from the salt leached out from my body. I saw people suddenly pass out, just have all of their energy drain out of them from the heat. We'd be so tired that when we stopped along the trail somewhere, just to take a 5-minute break, 2 or 3 guys would just fall asleep or pass out, it was hard to tell which. Guys would pass out from heatstroke. It just got to the point that when you did move through the jungle, it was one foot in front of the other. It was all you could do just to keep going. If you did come into contact, you'd forget about all of the humping and strain and stress: A couple quarts of adrenalin pump-ing through your heart gives you the strength to do what you need to do.

We did a mission near Trang Bang in the middle of the night. It was rain-ing so hard that you had to grab the web gear of the guy in front of you so you didn't lose contact. Anyway, it was raining so hard we were up to our knees in water. We stopped for a minute. All of a sudden, I heard a terrific splash, I turned around, and my friend Mike was down on the ground, rolling around. I thought he had stepped on a punji stake. He was cussing and mumbling. I said, "What happened, Mike?" and he told me he had fallen asleep. That gives you an idea how tired we were some of the time.

Do not think for a minute that Bowman is only describing a case of fatigue. The experience was far worse than that. Combat soldiers on operations—and the infantry certainly had it the worst—suffered a serious assault on their general health. Only a handful of civilians have gone through the sustained physical abuse that was routine for combat soldiers searching for Charlie. Bowman continues:

During the monsoon, everything would rot. Your clothes would rot off you, sandbags would rot, everything was wet and would mildew. Water was full of leeches. After a while, if you acclimatized yourself well to the heat, you could get by with just two canteens of water a day, but a lot of guys carried four. But sometimes, we sweated so hard that the supply of fresh water ran out. If they couldn't resupply us with fresh water right away, we would drink anything that was wet and would go down. Sometimes, it was like a yellow mud, and you had to keep swallowing or you'd puke it back out. But we were thirsty enough to drink anything.

That's when everyone started getting ringworms. Guys would have chunks of hair fall out of their heads from ringworms; one time, Gary and I counted over 170 ringworms on my body. I finally had to write home to get some medication: The ringworms seemed to thrive on the stuff the medic gave me. You couldn't work out in the paddies more than three or four days before your feet would start rotting. There was trench foot, and guys couldn't walk because of the plantar warts on their feet. Most of us had immersion foot, ringworms, leech bites, and hepatitis. Some guys got malaria.

We went through thirty days once without bathing. We humped every day and went on ambush patrol at night. We didn't bathe or shave or take off our boots or clothes or anything else. When we did come back for a stand down, I took off my boots, and from the top of my boots to my toes, I probably pulled off a whole layer of skin. It smelled like a cesspool and was blood red down to my toes. We were a pretty ragged and sorry group. The sad thing about it was that most of us felt more at home out in the field than in base camp. In base camp, we were the animals and the outcasts.

Bowman's point about his unit being understrength is a vital one and vindicated by much similar testimony. It is also important to note that this state of affairs had nothing to do with the overall strength of the Division. I have read almost every quarterly report from the 25th, and divisional strength was one of the first items covered. It was very rare for the Division to be under 95 percent of its paper strength, and it was often over 100 percent. Yet, out in the field, the situation was very different, indeed. Lieutenant Colonel Neilson gives a very good analysis of how this circumstance came about:

The battalion was organized with a headquarters company with an assigned strength of 194, a service company with a paper strength of 149, and three rifle companies, A, B, C [All line companies were code-named Alpha, Bravo, and Charlie.—EMB], with an assigned strength of 188. That is a total of 907. This number bore little resemblance to what we actually had in the field. Typically, infantry replacements were sent to Cu Chi for seven days of intensive training. The new man was then sent to his battalion in the field, where he would spend some time at the base camp the unit operated from. Halfway through his tour, he got R & R leave for ten to twelve days. We were not free from the peacetime practice of allocating personnel to take care of battalion and company administration and run the administrative side of the base camps. We also provided the Division with standing details of various and sundry types. Invariably, the people who bore these duties were the infantrymen, thereby stripping the infantry companies of the very resources that they needed. According to my records, although the rifle company was authorized 188 personnel, it rarely had more than 120 available at any one time. And when we left the base camp, we always had to leave some of the remainder behind for perimeter defense. So, when we actually got out in the field with our company, we were lucky to have 100. And I can recall making several air assaults where the guiding factor determining the number of infantrymen on the ground was the number of transport helicopters available, each of which could take 10 men. We would rarely have more than 8 or 9, so now you're down to 80 to 90 people actually engaged in combat, that out of an authorized strength of 188. Looking at my records, I find that rarely in a combat situation operating out of a firebase was our strength more than 350 out of a total of 907.

As a savvy professional officer, Lieutenant Colonel Neilson no doubt realized that there was something else at work—what one soldier earlier described as the "call of the rear." Some of the men that came to Cu Chi were either mentally or psychologically not ready for the trial of combat. Later, I shall examine the group dynamics of fighting units, but for the time being, it is sufficient to note that a platoon or squad in combat was not a good place for someone who could not or would not fill his arduous role in the group. A mentally deficient or unstable individual was not wanted on the line, even if there was a shortage of men. Good men were at enough risk as it was. And bad ones made mistakes. They caused lethal accidents, made noises at the wrong time, and froze when action was required. Clearly, many men were not up to the challenge. Others were terrified. I throw no stones at either, but the reality existed, nevertheless.

A good combat soldier knew very well that he was far better off with a smaller group that he could trust than a larger one that included individuals who desperately wanted to be elsewhere. Robert Conner, who was an eighteen-year-old sergeant at the time, describes the process by which unsuitable individuals were weeded out of combat units, which took place over and over again. In this case, the cause for the action was tragic:

We fought in small units. A squad is supposed to have 11 or 12 men. If you had 5 or 6, you were full strength. So, if you took a squad out on ambush patrol, you took out 5 men. We learned to depend on each other. We fought small and learned to see what each other could do. I remember one guy named Chambers. We were in the Delta. We had been fighting hard that day, and all of us were very low on ammunition. We were heading for the landing zone and could even see a chopper coming toward us. Then Charlie hit us from the wood line. We had a couple of guys shot. And we were trying to call in artillery, but for some stupid reason, our artillery couldn't hit anything that day. Chambers had the M60 machine gun. His ammo bearer was a Puerto Rican, a nice kid. We were pinned down behind the dikes, with bullets zipping all around. The ammo bearer lifted his head above the dike to help call in artillery. He caught a bullet right in the forehead, and it blew the back of his head off. White stuff comes flowing out, and he flew back into the water. Chambers panicked and buried himself and the machine gun in the stupid rice paddy. We tried our best to get it from him. We finally took it from him and opened up with the rounds we had to show the Viet Cong that we had a little firepower. I believe with all my heart that we were about to be overrun. But just in a matter of a few minutes, they called in the Navy. Praise the Lord for the Navy. You know, I'd rather have the Navy support us in a firefight than the Air Force anytime. That Navy jet came in, drew the fire from us, and let the wood line have it. The men tried to reach the Puerto Rican's body to keep the Viet Cong from riddling it to pieces. Chambers was relieved and moved out. I guess that's what you had to do to get out of combat: Act like an idiot or freeze. But he was no good after that anymore. They put him in a trucking company and made him a mechanic. Happened around Christmas.

In short, if an individual was determined to avoid combat and was willing to disregard peer pressure or risk disciplinary measures (people with serious discipline problems did not stay in the field long, if they got there at all), that individual would get his wish. The U.S. Army has never had the sort of discipline that seeks to instill in recruits a blind fear of their own officers. In many armies, shirkers would be shot or imprisoned for long periods; in Vietnam, they probably wound up washing bottles at Cu Chi.

More testimony on the state of affairs described by Conner comes from company commander Henry Bergson. Bergson's company served in southern Hau Nghia province during late 1969 at a time when the tide of battle was running, for the moment, in favor of the 25th. It was also a period when discipline problems were appearing in the rear and were widely reported in the press. According to Bergson, however, the field was a different world:

I had an excellent infantry company. A lot of the negative stuff that you read about are things that annoyed me at the time. We regularly fielded from 95 to 110 men. By the time we were out in the field, we were well rid of all of the shirkers, those that didn't want to play, and others that did not fit in. When you got outside the base camp, you had the finest bunch of young Americans you could want.

Understrength and overtaxed combat units of the 25th were extremely vulnerable to enemy hit-and-run tactics in all their guises. Because of the great number of missions, large and small, the men were frequently at risk. In every war, contact means casualties, and in Vietnam, American units led with their chins. The fact that the units lacked field strength and that the men were normally either tired or exhausted made the situation all the more perilous.

It is often said that American soldiers never saw their enemy in Vietnam. That was true enough, but this had less to do with Vietnam than with the fact that, on most missions, the GIs were on the offensive and the enemy was on the defensive. And, it is rare to see defenders in any war. (Famous poet Robert Graves spent nearly four years in the trenches during World War I and never got a clear view of a German soldier.) Just as it is true that attackers rarely see defenders, it is also true that attackers are more vulnerable to indirect forms of violence. American units, continually on the move in Vietnam, soon found that movement was hazardous, whether their enemy was in the direct vicinity or not.

Mines and booby traps were continuous plagues to every combat element of the Tropic Lightning Division. In many respects, they were the perfect weapons to use against the Americans or their South Vietnamese allies. Although mines and booby traps are often lumped together and share a lethal simplicity, they are actually very different weapons. The mines used in Vietnam were generally much larger and were frequently buried in the roads. It is a sad irony that the American stress on random firepower came back to haunt U.S. infantry. A certain percentage of the bombs that were dropped and the artillery shells that were fired failed to detonate, and properly modified, they were natural raw materials for mines. A bomb, in particular, could be made into a mine of great power and fully capable of destroying a tank. APCs were vulnerable to smaller mines, and trucks or jeeps were obviously in even more danger. Truck drivers would weld armor on the floorboards and sit on sandbags, but a proper mine would still send them to oblivion. Nor was it necessary to destroy a vehicle. Even a relatively small mine could do very serious damage to the treads and suspensions of an APC and put it out of action temporarily or send it to the scrap heap. During battle, this would accomplish as much as destroying the vehicle. Large claymore-style mines were mounted on the surface for use against infantry, frequently with deadly effect.

Depending upon what was available and the local situation, mines were detonated by fuse or command. Many mines that were produced in the North or in China were a bit more sophisticated: They were made of wood to make them difficult to detect with metal detectors and had fuses that would detonate when a certain weight passed over them. The advantage, of course, was that a fused mine, once laid, could do its deadly work at any time and with no risk to those installing it. But fuses had disadvantages, as well. They were not always reliable and often blew up the wrong targets. Frequently, for purposes of creating fear, the civilian vehicles that clogged Vietnam's few roads were destroyed on purpose. Often, however, it was accidental. Consequently, large mines were often command detonated; in other words, a wire connected to the mine ran back to a concealed position, where a guerrilla waited with an electrical switch. When a choice target came by, the enemy detonated the charge and, if all worked well, shattered his victim and ran off.

Like all APC crewmen, Lee Reynolds feared mines. One day, he saw the devastation caused by a large mine on an unlucky track with 8 men aboard:

We did a lot of road security. We'd go out looking for signs of the enemy and "bus" the road, which is, in effect, a stupid minesweeper technique of driving down the road and seeing if you can run over a mine and blow something up. We got a lot of people hurt and killed unnecessarily doing that. I remember writing my girlfriend and telling her about that, and she wrote me back and said that she didn't know what an armored personnel carrier was but thought it was something like a tank. That isn't quite true, but for a civilian, it is pretty close. She did know it was a kind of tracked vehicle. She said if you know the roads are mined, why don't you stay off the roads? It was brutal logic but initially too overpowering for our colonel. One day, one of our tracks was demolished by a huge mine. Eight of our people were blown to bits. Shreds of their tissue hung from the trees, and birds came to feed on it. After that happened, we stayed off the roads.

As Richard Mengelkoch, who served in 1966, recalls, it was not necessary to go far from base to find instant extinction:

I was made radio operator for the company commander. Being the radio operator is not the most desirable thing in the world because you're a target; you've got that antenna sticking up. And you're always close to an officer. One of our first operations was just a general sweep right outside of Cu Chi, almost a training mission. We didn't expect enemy contact, and in fact, there weren't many enemy around then. We set out, and the road tapered off into a trail. The captain wanted some clearing done so we could move some equipment through. Engineers brought in a big bulldozer. He told the other radio operator and me that we could go sit down and take a rest because we had these heavy radios that weighed 25 to 30 pounds. We sat behind a berm and took off our radios while still listening to them. All of a sudden, the whole earth shook. There was a tremendous explosion. Gravel and rocks came down along with what we later discovered were pieces of bone and flesh. We didn't know what the hell had happened, and everyone was excited. Then it became clear. Our company commander and some other people were standing beside the bulldozer. The driver let the blade down and detonated a land mine. There wasn't enough of that captain left to put in a body bag. All of a sudden, he and about three others were just gone like that. It blew a chunk of the blade out. Everybody was shook but especially the other radio operator and myself. Normally, we would have been right by his side if he hadn't told us, for whatever reason, just to go take a break, being a nice guy, in effect. It was a sobering experience. This was just a practice mission to get the troops used to going out in the jungle.

Gary Ernst was on a track that hit a mine. Fortunately, unlike many of his comrades who suffered a similar fate, he lived to relate the terrifying experience:

For whatever reason, the mine-detecting equipment and the operators, probably through a lack of experience, didn't seem to operate very well. Some mines were plastic, and some very deep. On one of my first operations, near Nui Ba Den, all of a sudden there was a huge explosion. We thought we were under attack, but the mortar track had hit a mine in an area that the engineers had just cleared. We only had one man slightly wounded. We called for the engineers to reclear the area. We had to wait for a tank to tow the heavily damaged track off the road anyway. While we were waiting, my platoon leader ordered my track to mount a little patrol; I guess he was afraid that Charlie might be around. About the fourth circle around the column, there was a tremendous explosion, far louder than the first. It wasn't until I was flying through the air, out of the cupola, and falling back into the body of the track that I figured out that we had hit a mine. Charlie mixed in some tear gas with the mine. The gunner next to me had been knocked out by his own gun hitting him in the head and was bleeding. He was on top of me. The driver was saved by two cases of C rations he was sitting on, but he couldn't see or breathe because of the tear gas. The only one who kept calm was the commander, who helped me and the others out, fearing a secondary explosion. We took a look, and it was really a mess. It was a miracle none of us was seriously hurt. I was thinking, "Oh, sweet Jesus, thank you Lord."

When I'm upset, I like to go off alone. I also was shell-shocked and started walking off. Then I realized I had walked off several hundred yards, around the bend toward the mountain, without my rifle in an area filled with VC. I had a sinking feeling that Charlie was looking down at this stupid GI, trying to figure out whether to take me prisoner or just shoot me. A definite number 10 situation. I decided to act calm and started to walk back toward my platoon. I even started to whistle. Finally, all pretense disappeared, and I started sprinting. The guys all grabbed their weapons, thinking that a whole VC battalion must have been on my heels. But I was just scared.

Jim Ross suffered a similar experience during the Cambodian invasion, a harrowing period that abounded with fighting of all types:

On the third day, we were traversing a tree line; actually, we were on our way back to Vietnam. We were moving down this little sandy road, kind of like a trail through some fields, and at one stage, this road followed the edge of a tree line. Why we were on this road instead of off it in the fields I've never figured out. There was a danger of mines. The sun was very hot, about noon; a lot of dust. We weren't too worried about mines because of our position. Well, that's when the mine went off and spoiled everybody's day. The force of the blast lifted the APC off the ground, threw everybody in the air, tossed us around, then we came back down and hit the dirt. I was the only one who didn't hit the ground: I hit the top of the APC and came to rest on its deck. We were all stunned from the explosion. The explosion was extremely painful. It was as if ice picks had been driven into my ear. There was this tremendous clap, and the shock of the explosion, the jolt, scrambled my brains up; I was confused, as was everybody. I sat up and looked around. There was dust everywhere and dirt falling, sifting down. I couldn't hear anything; there was a tremendous ringing in my ears and a numbness inside of my skull. Everything was muffled and muted. I could barely hear. I looked around and tried to get my senses and figure out what had happened. About this time, my friend Dennis was climbing back on the APC, his glasses kind of cockeyed on his face; he came up over the top of the APC and stood up. The cobwebs started to go away, and it became obvious there wasn't going to be a firefight.

A dust-off was called: Everybody in the squad was given the option of being dusted off to Cu Chi with perforated eardrums, concussions, etc. We were only three days into the mission: It was probably going to be one of the most successful or remembered missions of the war. A couple of years down the road, I didn't want to be one of those people who wasn't there when the action took place. I knew I was going to stay. Everybody else chose to go back to Cu Chi. The truth of it was, as miserable as things were, I just wanted to say I had been there.

Mines were intended primarily for vehicles, but infantrymen also fell victim to them. Platoon leader Richard Blanks recalls a catastrophic afternoon for his unit:

Three of the four men in my platoon that were killed during my tour died in June. We were on a company-sized heliborne mission. Our firebase had been taking mortar fire from a wooded area some distance away. The entire company was flown out early one morning, with air support overhead. The entire company moved across a rice paddy in echelon formation. My platoon was the lead platoon on the extreme right. We were the first to hit the wooded area. Three of my men entered the woods, and we heard an extremely loud explosion. The sergeant yelled stop, and everyone froze. Our medic entered the wooded area. The point man had stepped on an antitank mine. It blew him in two and destroyed him completely. The second man was severely wounded. We took out the point man's body in a poncho. Air support came and strafed and bombed the wood line, trying to detonate any more mines. Early afternoon, we reentered the woods, my platoon still in the lead. This time, I was up on the wooded area myself, and we heard a loud explosion behind us. I turned around and saw my machine gunner flying through the air. He had also stepped on a mine. He was the sixth or seventh man in the column. Apparently, everyone else, myself included, had stepped over this mine without detonating it. He was killed instantly, and two others were wounded. They pulled us back again. It was getting late in the day. It started to rain. The company commander was still flying overhead and told us we had to go in one more time. It was getting late, and we had lost our air support and would have to walk back in, so they canceled the mission. It was a pretty dejected lot, 24 men in the platoon, walking back with 16 men, everyone else either dead or wounded. Most of the survivors were carrying extra rifles and equipment that had belonged to the killed and wounded, and the rain was pouring down on us. One more man died of his wounds later.

The very presence of the mines necessitated a large allocation of precious manpower to keep the roads open. It also frequently slowed movement, as Tet veteran Bill Kestell mentions:

Round a bend—there's a barricade—flankers out—herringbone formation—clear the road for the engineers to get by to check for mines and booby traps. Then either blow them or push them out of the way with the articulated scraper. Then pull in your flankers—mount up and take the point to the next barricade. Sometimes, you could see two or three beyond the one you were working on. And always the questions—how many eyes are watching you? Be careful not to get careless or let your guard down just because nothing has happened yet—or yesterday—or last week. To cover 20 miles or less might take the better part of a day!

For the infantry, however, a more common nemesis was the booby trap. Booby traps were usually small and frequently made out of a grenade, with a simple tripwire attached. They wounded more often than they killed, accounting for the unusual number of amputees that returned from Vietnam. Enemy redoubts were strewn with booby traps as a matter of course. But they were used in another manner, as well, that caused much grief for everyone involved. When American ground troops approached a hamlet or were seen heading in an obvious direction, local guerrillas would sneak out and lay fresh traps directly in their path. No matter how many of these devices were laid, pure chance never could have explained the large number of casualties that resulted from these devices. Unfortunately, soldiers knew this very well, and the belief that villagers either set the booby traps or, at the minimum, knew they were there and did not warn GIs was a major cause for the poisonous atmosphere that existed in rural Vietnam. In a later chapter, I will examine this problem more fully.

One of platoon leader Del Plonka's men triggered a large booby trap, capable of damaging a vehicle, right outside the Cu Chi perimeter. Plonka recounts events:

There were these things called stick mines. It's nothing more than taking a dead piece of wood attached to a mine with a trigger device: You knock the stick over, and it goes. Needless to say, when this young man tripped this stick mine and it went off, he lost both legs immediately. He was more or less split open from the groin area up to his neck. The best I could do was put him in a poncho. It was a very sickening sight seeing all that blood and seeing that poor young man with that face just looking at you with those bewildered eyes, and, well, it stays in your mind.

Dan Vandenberg, who later developed an even more intimate knowledge of enemy booby traps, recalls the havoc that ensued when an American unit stumbled into an area filled with these nasty devices. In this particular case, Vandenberg's company was almost certainly in the feared Ho Bo Woods, not far from their home base at Trang Bang:

We were on a company patrol in an area full of tunnels and took 3 prisoners. We had some bulldozers, and they tried to dig out the tunnels. But pretty soon, we lost the tunnels completely in the debris, so we gave up and moved to another area. The next part of the woods we entered had skull-and-crossbones signs, indicating that the area had been mined and booby-trapped: Charlie had put the signs up. We never believed anything we saw and had to find out the hard way. Within the first 10 minutes, we had 6 guys wounded from different booby traps, mainly hand grenades. So one of the guys driving a bulldozer said he wasn't going to move it until he had a couple of guys up next to him riding shotgun. A guy from our squad got on the right side, and I got on the left side. We must have moved all of a foot and a half before we hit a booby trap. The guy on the right side lost the better part of his face and was all messed up; I ended up with ringing ears. So I lucked out again.

Just as Bill Kestell noted earlier concerning tracks, the indirect effect of booby traps on infantry movement was serious. It slowed troops down, forced them to traverse ugly terrain that was unlikely to have booby traps, and added immensely to the already heavy psychological strain of living in a war zone. Michael Call describes the impact vividly:

We begin to walk with our eyes fixed on the ground, looking for some telltale sign we should avoid. I ask myself: "Is that little thing ahead the three prongs of a Bouncing Betty [a mine that springs up to about waist height before going off—EMB] or just three blades of grass?" As my right foot moves in front of my left foot, I carry on a debate within my mind if I should place it down on that rock just ahead, or behind it . . . or in front of it . . . or to the side of it. But now I face another dilemma. If I choose to step to the side of the rock, which side do I choose?

These gooks are very clever. They must figure that I will want to place my foot on hard ground, so maybe they put the mine under the rock. Maybe I shouldn't place my right foot anywhere near that rock. Maybe I should move over to the left a little or to the right. Then again, why not place my foot in the step of the guy ahead of me? But he is already too far ahead. And if you walk too close to him, he will get pissed off because if I trip a mine, he'll get blown away, too.

What to do with my right foot? I say: "I can't stand on my left foot forever." I finally put my right foot down and nothing happens. My next decision is what to do with my left foot, which, in the act of walking, comes up when the right foot goes down.

Mines and booby traps were only a part of the problem. Because the enemy normally was hidden and had the choice to initiate contact or not, the quick ambush and mortar attack were perpetual threats.

Lt. Richard Blanks learned about these dangers in very short order when he took over his platoon in 1969:

I reported to Company B on 19 May. They were at some little hard spot out in the field, I didn't record the name. I was assigned 2d Platoon leader. I managed to get a shot almost the minute I got off the helicopter. It was about 1800 hours, and my radioman told me to leave my gear and he'd show me where the water truck was and we'd fill our canteens. We were walking across the hard spot when we heard the mortar round hit the tube out in the woods somewhere, and my radioman threw me to the ground. The VC walked 5 rounds right across the hard spot. Two men had minor wounds, but the shrapnel cut up my radio gear. So the first round had hit just where we had been sitting.

Combat engineer Michael Butash suffered through a far more violent incident:

It was like *Lord of the Flies*. We were all kids. I don't say that facetiously; it was true. I was nineteen, and I was a sergeant. The captain was twenty-six. It was just incredible. The tempo of operations was fast, impressive. I came to the Nam from Germany, where I thought the military was just a big fuck-up, a big bureaucratic mess. Well, Vietnam with the 25th Infantry was impressive, very impressive. It moved fast, disciplined, like the end of the God-damn world.

I remember being ambushed up by Tay Ninh. We had hitched a ride with an armored unit, 6 Patton tanks. I thought, who's going to fuck with us, we're on 6 Patton tanks. The earth shook when they rolled by, their fire-power was awesome. So, hey, kick back. Damn if they didn't command-detonate a mine on the first tank. Then they sprang an ambush on us. That's when I first realized how indoctrinating our training had been. We were infantry trained. We were off the tanks in no time. Our first instinct was to hit the dirt. Hitting the dirt, behind the tanks, under the tanks. Meanwhile, the tankers did neutral steers and were just blasting with their guns. A good deal of the time, we were trying to get out of the way of those tracks as they were spinning around. A good friend of mine was wounded; there were a bunch of people hurt. It just happened so quick.

Jim Ross relates that ambushes were an unavoidable part of life for the men on tracks:

Being mechanized infantry, our firepower was so superior to a straight leg infantry unit that we didn't think the enemy to be much competition as far as a toe-to-toe battle. Naturally, we didn't have many toe-to-toe battles. When we did, the enemy almost always had the opportunity of striking the first blow. That's one of the main disadvantages of mechanized forces. You move around a lot, you make a terrific target, you can be seen from quite a distance, and you can be heard from even a farther distance, so they had ample time to interdict us if they chose to do so. And very often, they could get away with that without paying any price at all. All they would do was simply set up a 2- or 3-man RPG ambush, attack the lead APC or maybe the tail APC, and either damage or destroy the track. They might kill or injure a few American soldiers and scoot off into the woods before anybody could react. They did have the luxury of hit and run. Many times when we were set up in our wagon wheels out in the bush somewhere, we would receive mortar fire. They could attack us without too much in the way of reprisal. On the other hand, the times when we were able to encounter them when they couldn't hit and run or were in a number large enough to slug it out with us for a little while, they would suffer greatly.

Gary Ernst was in exactly the situation just described by Ross in November 1967. Although Ernst did not realize it, the enemy's unexpected decision to fight it out was undoubtedly related to the decision made by Hanoi and the Front to launch the Tet Offensive. In the weeks preceding it, several ugly battles took place involving American forces. It is reasonable to surmise that this was part of an effort to keep U.S. ground forces in the hinterlands and away from the cities where the major blow was aimed. Whatever the case, Ernst's mechanized unit stumbled into a lethal situation. Note that the outline of the engagement was largely shaped by the desire of American forces to aid a stricken track and its crew:

Charlie normally avoided us. There was an exception in November 1967 near Dau Tieng. Intelligence said that there was a VC base camp in the area. Our platoon was designated as a blockading force and was spread out on a picket line along the northern edge of the jungle. We were supposed to move slowly, with at most 25 to 50 meters between our tracks. The problem was, the brush was so thick that if you got more than 10 or 12 yards from your neighboring track, you'd lose sight of him. Therefore, we got strung out.

One of our tracks on the left end of the picket line happened upon the VC base camp. Immediately, he was hit by RPG and machine-gun fire. We didn't know it, but we had found the target, and for some reason, they weren't going to run. They were dug in and fighting. We were ordered to make a circular maneuver to bring us toward the engaged track. A mass tangle ensued. You could hear the firing; ours was slowing down, and the enemy's was picking up. It seemed like it took forever to reach our track. Finally, a second track found the first one, and it also was immediately struck by machine guns and RPGs. Now, we had two tracks in trouble. All 8 crewman were wounded, and 1 was killed. We were plowing through the bush to help, and it was a wild ride. We were ordered to prepare a dust-off area for the Medevac helicopters while the rest of the platoon surrounded the VC base camp. When we decided we had them pinned down, they called in an air strike. Some F-4s came in, and it looked like they were hitting the target pretty good; we sure hoped so. They called in all sorts of reinforcements, including tanks and mech infantry and infantry. They decided to launch an assault after the bombardment, with my platoon in reserve. The VC were waiting. The area was a narrow, fortified front. Basically, they had to move straight in on this fortified position. All we could do was listen to these frantic messages on the radio: "Man down, watch your right flank, just took an RPG, four men down—request permission to pull back, a track is burning." We lost three tanks and many infantry. That night, we attacked with artillery. The next morning, we mounted another operation. By this time, there were only 2 VC left to offer token resistance. Even though we had them surrounded, many had gotten into those damned tunnel complexes that were throughout the area. We didn't feel too good about that operation. We lost two of our tracks and 8 out of 40 men, three tanks, and God knows how many infantry. All we got out of it were 2 VC prisoners and a good portion of rice and matériel. Not much to show for it.

Naturally, infantrymen were even more vulnerable to ambush, as Dan Breeding's brutal experience during the Cambodian operation proved:

Our platoon was lead platoon. We walked into this uncovered base camp. We apparently had surprised them because there were still smoking pots with food in them. The base camp area was in a valley in some thick bamboo. They had it covered over so they couldn't be seen from the air. It was very sophisticated. We knew we were in some deep shit at that time. Everybody was given instructions not to touch anything because of booby traps, but we had surprised them and they didn't have the time to set any booby traps. Our platoon was lead, and as we walked out of this base camp, we walked into an ambush. We started receiving mortar. That was probably the most frightened I had been. When being mortared, you are just helpless. The mortar rounds are coming in, and I was surprised how much of your body you can get inside a hard hat: It felt like you were crawling up inside your steel helmet. Everybody was just lying on the ground, praying the next round wouldn't get them. Luckily, none of the rounds hit. It was just terrifying. Then we started receiving machine-gun fire. Out of 22 men, 5 minutes later there were 11 left. I was carrying extra ammunition for the machine gunner, and one of the rounds hit close to the gunner and assistant gunner. I was behind him to the right. Once the mortar rounds started falling, I jumped behind an anthill with my legs exposed. This one mortar round took out our machine-gun team, and I received some shrapnel. I didn't realize at the time that I was hit. All we were concerned with was getting the injured out of there. We managed to fire into some bunkers where we were receiving fire, but there were so many of us hurt, we just started pulling back the wounded. Our forward observer and company commander came up and called in some helicopter gunships. We found out that half of our platoon was gone. Eleven of us were put on the Medevac chopper. Only 1 of us was killed: A boy had a mortar round fall right on him.

It was just shortly before the choppers came that I realized I was hit. I was feeling nauseous from heat exhaustion and had sort of passed out. When I came to, I thought I had water in my boot, but it was blood. We were all pitched on a helicopter and flown to Tay Ninh. Everything happened so quick. I was passed out part of the time, and I remember coming to on the operating table; they had cut the boot off of me. I didn't know the extent of the injuries, and it turned out to be minor flesh wounds. Some general came and pinned a Purple Heart on my pillow. I had a guilty feeling for several years because my wounds weren't very bad. Myself and another guy were the only ones able to come back and join the company. Anyway, we were glad to come back to South Vietnam. I never thought I would be, but we were. We got back to Tay Ninh for a three-day stand down. I got the drunkest of my whole life there.

Robert Conner recalls his first combat in Vietnam, which resulted from a large ambush. Note his reference to an interesting factor that was very typical of any engagement that lasted more than a few seconds: The fight itself revolved around a wounded man and the attempt to help him. And there is something else worthy of attention in Conner's description. His retreat almost turned into a catastrophe because of an accidental encounter with friendly fire, another menace facing combat soldiers.

We were on a search and destroy mission. I was fire team leader. We were going through this wood line. I was third or fourth man back. We went into this jungle. Things sound strange in the jungle; there's an echo. Next thing you know, rounds go off, and we had a guy hit. We got our cherry popped that day, and my platoon was in the lead. That's the first fire we got in. Rounds were going off everywhere, people were screaming and hollering, directing mortars in and everything else. I had a man hit up front. In my stupidity—or whatever you want to call it—I tried to move around to his left. The sergeant was barking orders out, and I was trying to get to this man who was shot and pinned down: to try to draw fire or flank them and find out where the fire was coming from. As I moved to the left, I ran right into a big old anthill. I stopped and fired a few rounds. I called for help. The "wait-a-minute bushes" were grabbing me, and they were hugging, and the ants were all over the place. My adrenalin was flowing, and I didn't know what to do. I was firing and shooting, and then I stopped for a second because my helmet had slipped down over my eyes. I kind of threw my head back so my helmet would get out of my eyes, and at that split second, two rounds hit right in front of my nose, 2 or maybe 3 inches away. I backed up as far as I could, but I was hung up in the bushes and couldn't move. I didn't know what to do. And there was firing and screaming and hollering at the same time. And I remember our machine gunner; he moved up as close as he could to me, and he was over the top of me. He was firing his M60 for everything it was worth. The spent casings were hitting the back of me, and the concussion was pushing my head down. It was so hot. The noise blew my eardrums out, and they started bleeding. I heard our lieutenant, who was our forward observer, in the background hollering, "Drop five zero: fire for effect; Drop five zero: fire for effect!" And he kept walking the rounds in, and finally, he told us to pull back, pull back. The machine gun was still firing, and he was trying to help me get loose from the bushes. We had one man hit, and we were trying to get him out. I have never been in a situation where I was so scared in all my life. But I didn't run: I was no hero, but I considered myself a soldier. We finally rescued our wounded, and, with the artillery still pounding, we called in for an air strike. All they could get was a local Vietnamese air force. And they came in an old prop plane. We pulled back from the wood line, and the artillery ceased for the air strike.

We saw the plane and heard the bombs falling to earth. I guess we were maybe 100 yards off the wood line, walking double abreast, with our platoons maybe 100 feet apart. We heard a whoosh, and we looked back: The plane had missed its target, and this napalm was coming right at us. We all scattered. Fortunately, the napalm hit right between our platoon and the one next to us. For a split second, it took the oxygen out of the air. That smell of burning soap or whatever it is—gasoline, kerosene—the fumes and everything were all up your nose, and your eyes were running. And just for a few moments, you're gasping for breath, and you're hollering and screaming. The smoke took your breath away. The whole thing, from the initial attack to almost being burned up by napalm, took less than 30 minutes. But it felt like eternity. It's like you miss part of your life.

In 1967, newly arrived trooper Gerald Kolb was with the 3/4th Armored Cavalry on night patrol moving down a road, with the tanks using their powerful xenon searchlights to illuminate the roadside. It was an unpopular tactic, obviously designed to trigger an ambush. On one night, it did. Kolb experienced the ambush, and because of bad luck, he also experienced the awesome power of American supporting arms:

One particular night, they ambushed us pretty good from one side of the road. They told us later it was about 30 VC, but of course, we didn't know that because it was about midnight when it happened. They opened up with machine guns, rocket launchers, RPGs, whatever. Our tanks and tracks kept going a little bit and stopped to return fire immediately. One of the tanks was firing beehive rounds point-blank. That tank caught on fire, but the guys kept on pumping out the M60 and the 90mm: Finally, the stuff got so hot and was popping so much, they had to jump out. I got into this ditch I was walking next to with 2 other green guys. We covered our heads and our butts pretty good, and we started to return fire at the tree line about a quarter of a mile away. I dropped my M16 into the mud and was out of action for a few minutes. About this time, the column started to withdraw. We didn't dare get up because their side was firing, our side was firing, and tracers were going about 3 or 4 feet over our heads. We were just scared shitless. They withdrew. We were left behind, 3 green guys who had been there about a week or ten days.

About 5 to 8 minutes later, miniguns come in on Hueys. The bull moose was on the loose. What I mean by that is that the minigun was firing away up in the sky: There was this real low roar, right over us. We didn't dare get up because at that distance, they would think we were gooks. So, we stayed there and waited for the bullets to rip through our backs. That was done in about 10 minutes. Then we heard some artillery come up and some 90mm tank guns fire. There were explosions all around us. That went on 5 or 10 minutes. From our own guys; they thought we were dead, they told us later. About half an hour later, the tracks and tanks returned. We were waving our arms and yelling. You never saw anybody jump up on an APC so fast in your life—that's about 6 feet off the ground. We found out later that they just about shot us, thinking we were VC. No one had been killed. And the only guy hurt cut his hand opening an ammo can. The VC took it pretty bad.

Conner and Kolb were extremely fortunate to escape both the enemy and fire from their own side. It is well known in military circles, although not widely discussed in public, that at least 5 percent of all casualties are due to accidents and friendly fire. In Vietnam, nearly 10,000 of the men and women who died perished due to noncombat causes, such as accidents or illnesses. (Anyone in the entire Southeast Asian theater who died for any reason was considered a Vietnam casualty. When one considers that 3.5 million men and women circulated through the area in the course of nearly ten years, the number is not surprising. Friendly fire deaths, even if one knew with certainty what happened, were listed as KIA: killed in action.) Young men driving trucks and jeeps fast often got into wrecks. Moreover, tracked vehicles are inherently hazardous, and explosives were everywhere. But above all, tired, fearful troops under great stress were often tricked into tragedy by their own self-defense mechanisms.

Robert Julian, who was one of the last to serve in Vietnam, was in a medium-sized engagement with tragic consequences:

I hadn't been in the field more than a week when I was in my first real action. We were in an area of an old rubber plantation near Xuan Loc, within sight of Highway 1, the main highway in Vietnam. Normally, we just hoofed it everywhere we went. But there were three or four APCs around, and the guys offered to give us a ride. So we hopped on and were going through this old, overgrown rubber plantation. Several Viet Cong appeared and ran right between two of the APCs. A fight ensued, with shots right and left. Although I didn't realize it until the next day, while the shooting was going on, there was an American tank nearby. He heard the action and decided he wanted to get into it. He fired 2 fléchette rounds. Unfortunately, 1 of the rounds went right into my platoon, and 11 were wounded, a couple very seriously. Several of the wounded were back in the field a few days later. Myself and one other escaped. That was quite frightening. I believe I was more afraid of our own firepower than the enemy's.

I can remember just how unreal this all was. During all of this, the excitement and smoke, I can remember looking 200 yards off the left and seeing the traffic going up and down Highway 1 as though nothing were taking place. Everybody was just ignoring it. Of course, when it was over, the Medevacs came for the wounded and landed right on Highway 1, and we had to block traffic. The whole situation was very unusual and not quite what I expected it to be.

Dan Vandenberg gives a powerful description of a situation that would be familiar to thousands of combat veterans:

When I first got to Vietnam, Marsh and Sanchez had been there the longest and I believed everything they said as gospel. They could tell me the most bizarre stories and I took it as truth. They had the walk, they had the talk, they had the cool: They looked like vets and were able to carry it off. I thought, nothing ever scares these guys. Well, one day, we were out on a company-sized patrol, which was pretty rare, and we got sniper fire. We pulled back in cases like that if possible and let artillery, gunships, or even jets hit the area. When the big stuff is done working over the area, it's time for us to get up and sweep through, looking for bodies or anybody still foolish enough to be in there.

So we walk up to this woods. Marsh and I were walking parallel to each other as we entered the woods. You're all pretty jittery because you know Charlie is in there someplace, and instead of staying 10 to 15 yards apart, we started coming closer together without knowing it because you couldn't really see through the thick terrain. All of a sudden, we came to a break in the woods, and out of the corner of my eye, I saw something. I turned and started to pull the trigger, and I was looking right at Marsh, and he was pulling his trigger. If a fly would have sneezed, that's all it would have taken for each of us to have ripped off a magazine at each other. That's when I saw the ultimate look of fear. When I looked at his eyes, all I saw was white: I couldn't see any pupils. I imagine my face looked the same.

That shook me, when I finally saw the look of fear on Mr. Cool's face. Then I realized everybody over there was pulling an act. Everybody was walking around with a puckered up asshole. It shook me to think how close we came to emptying a magazine into each other. And it happened so damn quick: You just see out of the corner of your eye, and all of the slack is taken up. It makes your knees weak for quite a while after that.

We continued through the sweep and found a few huts and found no bodies whatsoever. I saw a bag but because of my training warning of booby traps didn't pick it up; but the guy behind me did, and it was full of Vietnamese currency, worth about 50 bucks. If I would have picked it up, it would have blown up: He picks it up and gets 50 bucks. Got a little farther into the woods, and they wanted us to check out some tunnels. My idea of checking out a tunnel is throwing a hand grenade down it. They talked me into going down into one, and I got about 10 feet and couldn't think of a single reason why I would want to go any farther. I backed out, and told them it looked clear all the way. I may be dumb, but I ain't a total fool.

The ambush was the enemy's game. He was skilled at it and had decades of practice. Yet, to keep the record straight, not all of the night ambush patrols sent out by officers of the 25th Division came back empty-handed. It is the nature of war that the tables can turn easily. Pure happenstance and luck had much to do with life and death on both sides. As Richard Blanks remembers, Americans, too, pulled off ambushes:

On the night of 14 August, we had an ambush patrol. It was company sized, outside our hard spot. My platoon was lead platoon, and we went out 3 or 4 kilometers. My platoon went deepest into the wooded area we were going into to set up an ambush patrol. It was a very dark night, it was foggy, there was dense underbrush, and you really couldn't see more than 4 or 5 meters in front of you if you were lucky. We set up on an old trail and put out our claymores. About 5:00 A.M., 3 NVA walked into our position. They were within 5 meters before we even saw them. Fearing an accident, we challenged them, and they opened fire. We opened fire immediately after that. It was incredible. I remember our red tracers going out, their green tracers coming in. Everything was lit up by tracers going every which way at once. Claymore mines went off. RPGs farther back were opening up at our position. The entire thing was over in maybe 20 seconds. I called in mortar illumination rounds and then requested that the mortar team fire high-explosive rounds in front of us. An NVA platoon had stumbled into our ambush. Their 3-man point element had walked right into us. Other elements were further back, and they started firing. Normal procedure after a contact is to pick up and move your ambush at once. But since it was extremely dark and nearly dawn, we stayed put. After light, we could see what had happened. At first, we didn't see anything. Then we swept the area in front of us, and there were 2 dead NVA within 5 meters of our position. The brush was so thick you couldn't see them until you walked right up to them.

Firefights

Mines and quick ambushes were not the only forms of combat encountered by the men of the 25th Division. Any combat soldier who lived through a good portion of his tour experienced one or more proper firefights. Admittedly, the distinction between an ambush and a firefight is not an easy one to make. Yet, a difference existed. A firefight might well begin as an ambush but, for many different reasons, develop into combat that was larger and lasted longer than a typical ambush. Major firefights often resulted from large offensive sweeps that either forced the enemy to battle or seemed to offer an opportunity to inflict casualties on American units in exchange for acceptable losses. In these bloody affairs, American firepower was much more in evidence. Although the other side got the better of American units in many firefights, the larger the battle, the greater the advantage for the 25th Division. If the enemy usually benefited from an ambush, he was more likely to regret a proper slugfest.

Not that anything was ever easy. In most cases, it was the other side's option to accept and initiate battle. Many firefights resulted when 25th Division units located enemy fortified zones. Indeed, a very large percentage of them took place during U.S. sweeps through enemy redoubt areas. When dug in, our opponents in Vietnam were rarely easy to dislodge.

Two points must be made concerning firefights—one military, the other psychological. In the military realm, a sizable engagement fought by Americans normally exemplified the guiding doctrine of the U.S. Army: Spend bullets, not bodies. In other words, when contact was made, especially if it was made by American infantry, our forces would pull back and allow their powerful supporting arms to have a shot at the other side. It was a controversial tactic then and still is today. The most highly skilled soldiers advocated rapid maneuver and quick assault when contact was made. Any delay, they believed, allowed the enemy to withdraw or wait out the storm in his field fortifications. On the other side of the coin, most soldiers believed there was no such thing as too much firepower. Skilled and experienced fighting men are always a rare commodity, and the normal citizen soldier, regardless of personal fortitude, did not have the split-second timing required for fire and movement to work as planned. In addition, even members of an elite unit, if luck was against them, could advance on a position oblivious to the location of a hidden machine gun. A slaughter would follow, regardless of how good the men were. Elite combat units, in past wars, tended not to remain elite for long. Whatever the merits of the argument, firepower was the order of the day, and most soldiers of the Tropic Lightning Division heartily agreed with their leaders on that point.

A profound psychological reality must also be appreciated if a civilian, safe in time and place, hopes to grasp even a small part of the experience of combat. Although there were exceptions, most men did not like fighting. They did their duty and would frequently risk their lives to save a comrade.

But in Vietnam, at any rate, there was a notable lack of any desire to grab the flag and charge a machine-gun nest. The men killed because they had to. It was not something they enjoyed or normally sought out. Field soldiers loved to complain about the idiot duties the Army would dream up and the boredom that accompanied much of their life. But almost all of them preferred that to combat.

Del Plonka, a junior officer with much combat experience, expresses this sentiment vividly:

In *Apocalypse Now,* some idiot says, "Ah, the smell of napalm in the morning." That's baloney. You smell death one time, you won't like it, I guarantee it.

Fellow combat officer Larry Fontana voices similar sentiments:

When you are fighting a war like Vietnam, you have no idea if you're doing anything useful militarily or not. You know you killed and wounded more of them than you, and that is it. Nothing would have made me happier than to never have gotten into a fight. Only the crazies hoped to get into a fight while on patrol. Luckily, we had few crazies.

Combat infantryman C. W. Bowman shared these sentiments; he watched his best friend get mutilated when a new officer, not realizing what was at stake, took over:

Toward the end of my tour, our morale did drop because we got a new CO. Officers only spent 6 months in the field before they were moved back to the rear. We got a new captain in, and he was Gung Ho John Wayne. But it wasn't the place to play John Wayne because Charlie was real good at suckering people into ambushes. He'd snipe at you and get you to chase him and lead you into a minefield or booby trap area or ambush. This officer thought he was John Wayne, and that's when Gary was hurt real bad. Charlie tried his trick one day, and we tried to tell the CO what was going on. But he didn't want to hear it, so we were suckered into a minefield. Gary stepped on a Bouncing Betty. It blew his left leg off. His left arm was shredded— there was just bone, and all the muscle and skin were just lying in one spot. Gary's arm was lying in another spot. He had a hole in his side and another one behind his ear. But he lived: They sewed his leg back on, and he's still walking around with a brace and a cane. But if the CO had listened to us, Gary wouldn't be in the shape he is now. Neither would the several other guys who were wounded because of his stupidity. That was the place to be cautious and watch what was going on. And we got John Wayne.

None of this means that combat soldiers of the 25th Division were unwilling fighters. A sense of duty, combined with an almost fatalistic realization that they had a job to do, sustained field operations for five long years. Furthermore, what the men express echoes the sentiments of soldiers in wars throughout history. Generals and political leaders might lust for personal or national glory, but it is a rare fighting soldier who looks forward to combat. They might be justly proud of their comrades and their units, but if some other formation is tagged for a shot at glory, the soldiers guarding an inactive flank are not usually quick to complain.

Exceptions arose when a fellow American unit was in peril. This was particularly likely if the two units involved were organically connected—for example, two companies in the same battalion. It is one of the greatest ironies of human behavior that soldiers, whose business entails killing, perform at their best and bravest when they are trying to save the lives of their comrades. This is true in a small-unit action, and it is also true in a larger campaign. Note in the descriptions of combat that follow how frequently a wounded soldier or stricken vehicle will be the nexus of the battle. Certainly, this also held true on the other side. And it unmistakably brings to mind the descriptions of battles in Homer, where whole engagements revolved around the attempt to seize or recover the body of a fallen hero. The anomalies of war are endless.

Firefights resulted from a multitude of causes. Some, however, stand out. The enemy redoubts that existed throughout the 25th Division's AO were constantly watched and probed. On occasion, a defector or prisoner would reveal the location of a weapons cache or a strongpoint. Better yet, from the point of view of headquarters, was intelligence revealing the general whereabouts of an enemy unit. Conditions like these would likely trigger a rapid reaction. Frequently, several of the different arms available were employed. It was the helicopter, however, that was prominent. A genuine target meant a very strong likelihood of a fight. It also might mean a helicopter assault into something that struck terror into the hearts of all infantry: a "hot LZ" (landing zone).

A few notes concerning helicopters are in order here. As useful and versatile as they were, helicopters in the process of landing and taking off were extremely vulnerable and made splendid targets. Frequently, the choppers were heavily laden. Consequently, helicopters spent as little time as possible on the ground. Unless the terrain was hard or the situation demanded it, helicopters sometimes did not really land at all but hovered at very low altitudes while the men jumped out, hopefully into dense grass, mud, or something soft. The door gunners were firing all the time, but other weapons were far better designed for support. Helicopter crews, naturally, wanted to survive and did not like crashing. But if the choppers took a pounding, the ground troops also suffered. The 25th Division rarely had the helicopters on hand to bring in an entire unit in a single wave. Instead, they flew in one wave after another. If the helicopters took heavy losses, fewer ground troops made it to the battlefield—most unwelcome news to those that did. So caution was the order of day. Robert Julian gives a good example of a landing in Vietnam, even though there was no enemy action on the day he describes:

I was almost immediately sent to the field; I had maybe been in-country only three or four days. I caught a supply chopper out to my platoon, which was already in the field. I can remember seeing on TV the pictures of the choppers and the soldiers sitting on the side, and I always thought that would be a pretty thrilling thing to do. But the first time I did it, I was scared half to death. Once you got up in the air, it looked like it was quite a long fall, and I was hanging on for dear life. The more we did it, I guess, the braver I got. My unit was in a large field covered mostly with elephant grass. They had popped smoke for the helicopter to identify them. I remember the gunner telling me that the chopper couldn't land because of the grass and that they would hover just a few feet above. I was to jump off, and they would throw the supplies off with me. I did just that. When I hit the elephant grass, I just kept going. That elephant grass must have been 5 or 6 feet tall. I thought I was going to break my neck before I ever hit the ground. Then a ton of C rations and ammunition and whatnot came down on top of me. I was wondering what in the world I was doing and where in the world I was.

C. W. Bowman served in 1967, which was the period when large and medium-sized helicopter operations were most in favor. Like the majority of infantrymen of that period, he spent much time flying aimlessly from one spot to another. On two occasions, however, he was in the middle of classic Vietnam firefights. The first took place in southern Hau Nghia province, a densely populated area filled with canals, berms, hedgerows, and streams. It was a natural transport point for enemy supply lines into the Mekong Delta proper. It was also Front territory and had been for years. Bowman's unit picked a tough objective that day. The result, as Bowman recalls, was a military victory that nearly ended his life:

We were put into a pineapple plantation, somewhere close to Cu Chi down around Bao Trai. We flew in, the first chopper ride I ever had, and it was a hot LZ: We were receiving fire when we went in. I kept thinking I was going to fall and slide out of the chopper, so I had a deathgrip on the edge of the seat. We bailed out, they took off, and I was lying in the mud. We could see bunkers built along some of the canals in the plantation. Charlie broke contact with us, and we started searching bunkers. At that time, I did see movement off to my right, and there was Charlie running through the pineapple plantation. I opened fire, and the captain hollered at me because I was a new guy and he didn't think I knew what I was doing—and he was probably right. Then the rest of the company saw Charlie, and everybody opened up on him. He ran like a deer: I don't know if we hit him or not because we started receiving fire again, and the captain told us to get on line and start sweeping the field in front of us.

We had to cross a small canal. John, the machine gunner, who must have had 300 to 400 rounds of M60 ammo linked together, turned around and looked at me and said, "This is it." He scared me to death: I didn't know what the hell he meant with "this is it." We crossed the canal and spread out. At that time, Charlie opened on us with a machine gun. He shot my helmet off my head and knocked me for a backflip back down into the water. Our medic was carrying an M16 rifle. A machine-gun round blew his thumb off and ricocheted off the rifle, hit him in the shoulder, and then came out the back of his shoulder and hit another guy in the chest. They dragged those two to the other end of the field and threw them over the dike into the water. They told me later they thought I was dead. I was about 30 yards from the bunker where Charlie was shooting from when I woke up. I had blood over the side of my face and found my helmet had one bullet hole in the top and one ripped through the side of it. I don't know why I still have a head on my shoulders; I guess somebody was watching after me. Needless to say, I was scared to death, and nobody was around. I was alone, lying in water up against a dike. Every time I hollered, Charlie would start shooting and I kept trying to get further and further below the dike, which was only 2 or 3 feet high. But then I heard someone hollering at me, telling me to get the hell out of there. I asked him why, and he said they'd called in an air strike. So I didn't have much choice. I either had to get out or get blown up with Charlie.

I waited a few minutes, and I got up and ran, and I fell and crawled and had tears in my eyes. I don't know if Charlie hesitated at first, but he began shooting at me. I could hear the rounds hitting close and going by me. It sounds like a dry stick being broken in half close to your ear, a snap. I could see the rounds hitting the water close to me, and everything went in slow motion. It felt like the harder I tried to run, the slower I was going. I was trying to zigzag and I'd fall and get up. I knew I was going to die. Somehow, I made it to the dike, dove over the dike, and there was my whole squad. They destroyed the bunker and killed Charlie. After a while, they dusted me off to base camp; I had a concussion and couldn't walk straight.

Shortly thereafter, Bowman was in a larger and more violent attack on enemy positions along the Vam Co Dong River. The 25th had another victory, but like so many, it was a Pyrrhic one. Bowman's description emphasizes the fact that there were many ways to die in Vietnam:

They were supposed to bring us in at the edge of the wood line, and we were supposed to sweep through the horseshoe bend near the river. Instead, they started out with twenty-three choppers and took Alpha Company in first, and twenty choppers came back. I was on the second lift with Bravo Company. As we were coming in, I could see and hear the rounds hitting the chopper. They were tearing holes inside the door. The guy next to me got shot in the neck on the way in. Just prior to our assault, they had fired 6,000 rounds of artillery and bombed it all morning. But you could see two choppers burning on the ground anyway. They dropped us off in the middle of the horseshoe, and when we jumped out, we immediately sank up to our hips in the mud of the rice paddies. I was stuck in the mud, and so was everybody else, and we were trying to get out. Gary kept hollering, "Watch out, watch out." I didn't know what he was talking about until I turned around and saw the chopper trying to take off and saw the tail rotor coming for me. Right then, I thought I was going to die, and I just kind of fell forward in the mud, and the tail rotor missed me by about 2 feet. After the chopper took off, Charlie was still shooting at us, and we had to crawl through the mud until we got behind a dike. Then they brought Delta Company in. Out of twenty choppers, they only had fifteen or sixteen left, and they dropped Delta Company off. Charlie Company never even got in there because by the time they got back, they had thirteen choppers, and seven or eight of them were so shot up they couldn't get back off the ground.

We were pinned down there all that day. They called in air strikes all around us. They called in artillery. We assaulted the wood line three times, and we got run out three times. One time, we were assaulted by our own gunships. They opened up on us and killed and wounded a bunch of guys. We lay there all night in the mud and water. We couldn't get any of the wounded out that day or night. You could hear them moaning back in the rear area. Charlie was probing the perimeter all night. The next day, most of us were soaking wet and wrinkled and covered with leeches from lying in the water all night. The battlefield was covered in smoke, like a fog. The next day, our officers said they were going to walk artillery in front of us as we assaulted the wood line. When we attacked the wood line, I watched the artillery throw mud and trees up in the air, and the only thing I could think of was, "Damn, this is just like the movies." It was like I stepped out of my body and walked around me and then stepped back in myself and then continued the assault. We fought for the rest of the day and swept the horseshoe. We blew up the trenches and the bunkers and did a body count. Everyone wanted a body count. Next day, they brought Chinooks in and pulled us out.

There was another way to get into a firefight—a technique that, as time went on, became a hallmark of 25th Division tactics. It was simple, and, re-markably, it worked every time the enemy obliged with an assault. The command at Cu Chi would order a unit into a sensitive enemy redoubt, have the men establish a perimeter, and hope the other side attacked, thus allowing American supporting arms to go into action and shatter the ene-my's strike. This tactic was employed throughout the AO with units of dif-ferent sizes. A favorite place was the infamous Ho Bo Woods, close to Cu Chi but a powerful enemy stronghold. Going to the Ho Bo was always cause for alarm for American infantrymen, as Jerry Liucci relates:

Helicopters took us to an area that will always bring a certain amount of fear to me, a place called the Ho Bo Woods. Quite extensive, this area was filled with thick brush and trees. There were small trails that wound off to who knows where. It was there that I saw my first American killed by Charlie with a Chinese carbine. It was kind of a look at the old part of the war with the VC, kind of crude weapons compared to what, a month or two later, would be more sophisticated soldiers. This VC and his buddy were killed in a spider hole. . . . This area was definitely Charlie's stronghold. He had a net-work of tunnels there. We found caches of weapons. He had underground hospitals, spider holes, booby traps, you name it. It definitely gave you that eerie feeling every time you went there because the VC that you fought in the Ho Bo Woods were hard-core, fight-to-the-death kinds of characters. It gave you a lot of respect for these guys: They were definitely hard and sea-soned. We spent through Christmas in the Ho Bo. It was definitely a free fire area. If you ran into anybody, he was the enemy. The enemy in the tunnels was a tough fighter. I give them credit. I don't think I could have lived down in a hole like that.

Dan Vandenberg's company was sent to the Ho Bo in 1969 and suc-ceeded in triggering the hoped-for assault. As one might imagine, those under attack did not enjoy the experience, even though they were scoring another victory:

We went out on a company patrol, and, as usual, we set up in the middle of a rice paddy in broad daylight so Charlie knew exactly where we were in case he wanted to hit us that night. The reasoning behind that is that once Charlie hits us, we can call in artillery and everything else on his ass. So that night, I guess it was about 2 or 3 in the morning, Sir Charles hit us with everything: mortars, machine guns. I mean, you couldn't move. It was incredible. It was just like you see in the war movies: It sounded like hornets coming over your head. I, personally, at the time, wondered why the army put buttons on my shirt because I wanted to get much closer to the ground. I had a reasonable foxhole at the start, but when it was all over, I had dug a hole that I needed a ladder to get out of. It sounded to me at the time—I couldn't really turn around and look—that they were dropping mortars within 15 yards of my position all the way around me. You sit there and wonder when they are going to drop one in your hole.

My squad leader was in the hole next to me and yelled for me to stick my head up and see if Charles was coming up at us under the barrage they had laid down. I told him I looked last time and it was his turn to look, and we argued back and forth. I brought up the point that since he's the sergeant and getting the big bucks, he can stick his head up and look. Neither of us was that crazy about finding out whether Charlie was coming or not, so we took our M16s, put them on full automatic, held them above our heads, and sprayed the area in front of us as fast as we could change magazines. Probably won't hit nothing, but you'd sure discourage anybody coming up on you. And doing it that way, the worst that's going to happen is that you get your hand shot off: You keep the rest of your head and body behind the dike. It was a pretty common practice in the infantry when things got hairy—stick the gun up and keep your head down. I got through that night, too, and I'm not too damn sure how.

Sometimes, American units did not come out well despite their firepower. No combat unit, regardless of how powerful or skilled, can survive unscathed with poor commanders. Jim Ross was in a wicked firefight in Cambodia. According to his account, verified by divisional records, an incompetent leader used mechanized vehicles in a place where they did not belong. One can guess who paid the price:

On Memorial Day in Cambodia, we were ordered to reconnoiter an NVA base camp that was supposedly guarded by a securing force of some type that had been ordered to stay there and defend this camp at all costs. Whether our colonel volunteered us for this or not I don't know, but I do know he was gung ho for the mission. What was wrong was that it should never have been conducted by mechanized infantry. It should have been conducted by straight leg infantry almost exclusively because of the denseness of the jungle. The jungle area we had to go into was so thick, the APCs

25th Division Huey helicopters flying out of Trang Bang carry infantry on a small "search and destroy" mission into the Ho Bo Woods. Although the Army placed much faith in such missions early in the war, most were futile. (Photo by C. W. Bowman)

The light M551 Sheridan tank, deployed to Vietnam in 1969, was not popular with the crews. With an aluminum hull, it was vulnerable to rocket grenades. The turret of this stricken Sheridan melted into the hull. (Photo by Jerry A. Headley)

(Top) A track prepares to tow a truck damaged by a mine in Tay Ninh during 1969. Nui Ba Den is visible many miles away. (Photo by William E. Noyes) *(Center)* 25th combat engineers await the dangerous job of clearing terrain near Nui Ba Den in 1969. Although chemical herbicides were widely used, bulldozers were more effective at clearing terrain. (Photo by William E. Noyes) *(Bottom)* Nui Ba Den Mountain. Called the Black Virgin by Americans, the top and bottom were controlled by U.S. forces, and the enemy ruled the slopes. It dominated the horizon of the 25th Division area of operations. (Photo by Morgan J. Sincock)

(Left) C. W. Bowman is helped out of a tunnel found in the Ho Bo Woods during 1967. In this period, the huge enemy tunnel complex near Cu Chi was operating at maximum efficiency. (Photo courtesy of C. W. Bowman) *(Below)* Some tents in the mud constituted Cu Chi base camp in the early stages of U.S. involvement. (Photo by Dale Canter)

(Left) Close to Saigon, Cu Chi received many visits by VIPs. Ann-Margret was a favorite because she came in 1966 when Cu Chi was ugly and hazardous. The men named the most dangerous spot on the perimeter in her honor. She returned in 1968 with Bob Hope. (Photo by R. H. Broyles) (Below) 25th Division Headquarters at Cu Chi in late 1968. At this stage of the war, Cu Chi had become a large American town. (Photo by R. F. Broyles)

(*Top*) A 25th Division mechanized unit rests at Dau Tieng base camp in 1969. (Photo by William E. Noyes) (*Bottom*) The crew of a 25th Division track prepares to embark from Dau Tieng base camp in 1969. Note that, because of the fear of mines and RPGs, soldiers rode on the top instead of inside, as intended by the vehicle's designers. (Photo by William E. Noyes)

These infantrymen are resting on the shady side of a track on a hot day. Sleep was a precious commodity in Vietnam. (Photo by William E. Noyes)

A combat soldier writes a Christmas letter. Mail was critical for field morale.
(Photo by William E. Noyes)

(Top) A track escorts a convoy on Highway 1 toward Cu Chi. Supplying the base camps was a serious drain on manpower and very dangerous. Highway 1 was the best and most traveled road in the 25th Division's area. Nevertheless, mines and ambushes were commonplace. (Photo by Thomas A. Giltner) *(Bottom)* A track stands solitary guard along a road as a storm approaches. (Photo by William E. Noyes)

An infantryman rests after the attack on Firebase Gold. He wears a helmet captured from one of the attackers. (Photo by Bradford D. Bromley, courtesy of Gary Silva)

A Vietnamese soldier who died at Firebase Gold. Note the grenade launcher behind him. GIs were astounded that their enemies, even in elite Front assault units, were frequently so young. (Photo by Bradford D. Bromley, courtesy of Gary Silva)

Firebase Gold under attack during March 1967. The American defenders were close to annihilation in this engagement but were saved at the last moment by an armored relief column. (Photo by Bradford D. Bromley, courtesy of Gary Silva)

This soldier is on patrol near the Ho Bo Woods in 1967. Chasing Charlie on foot, the principal vocation of combat infantrymen, was exhausting and dangerous. (Photo by C. W. Bowman)

(Above) At the beginning of what developed into a large firefight, a platoon leader calls in artillery support. The 25th Division's area of operations had much wooded terrain like this; often, visibility was limited and fighting was at very close range. (Photo by Todd Dexter)

(Left) Infantryman Jerry Liucci carries his M60 machine gun during the fierce fighting around the Saigon suburb of Hoc Mon in the Tet Offensive of 1968. (Photo courtesy of Jerry A. Liucci)

Anxious *Wolfhounds* wait to board their helicopters, bound for Saigon on the first day of the Tet Offensive of 1968. With fighting all around them, the soldiers knew that a major battle was under way. (Photo by Gerry S. Schooler)

American troops move cautiously into an area pounded by air strikes and artillery during a large battle in Tay Ninh during 1969. Moments later, fighting began again when hidden enemy soldiers attacked this unit. (Photo by William E. Noyes)

Two monks walk down a provincial road near Dau Tieng. American soldiers would not have been so serene in this dangerous area. (Photo by William E. Noyes)

(Top, left) Prisoners, ages nine and sixteen, captured along the Vam Co Dong River. (Photo by Morgan J. Sincock) *(Bottom, left)* The captured boys were carrying powerful RPGs (rocket propelled grenade launchers), capable of destroying an armored personnel carrier or tank. (Photo by Morgan J. Sincock)

Opposite page:

(Top) The town of Trang Bang, the scene of several large battles, was in the middle of a longtime Front stronghold. The densely populated areas nearby were heavily contested. (Photo by William E. Noyes) *(Bottom, left)* A child scavenges through an American garbage dump at a temporary perimeter in Tay Ninh province. American wealth astounded Vietnamese villagers. (Photo by William E. Noyes) *(Bottom, right)* A pair of local "fun girls" are told to move away from a small 25th Division hard spot in the Michelin Plantation. (Photo by William E. Noyes)

(Above) Unless a unit was in the "boonies," Vietnamese children were regular visitors. The men of the 25th served in a land with a very high birthrate. (Photo by William E. Noyes) (Below) Two infantrymen negotiate prices for beer and soda with the local merchants that traveled to American outposts. (Photo by William E. Noyes)

could only travel single file. There was no way to maneuver, even to turn around and get out if we had to. We virtually trapped ourselves trying to get into this place.

When we reached the outer perimeter of the base camp, we were ambushed by dug-in NVA. They had lots of ammunition and lots of desire. When the enemy attack occurred, only the first two or three APCs were involved in the firefight. The others strung out single file behind were impotent. They couldn't do anything. The tracks in front were the target of heavy fire. The reason I'm so intense about this is because it was my platoon in there. Track 13 was point, and my Track 14 was next. We were pinned down and taking a real hammering. We couldn't turn around; we couldn't go forward. We couldn't do anything except sit there and slug it out. It was, without a doubt, the worst firefight we had in Cambodia. Ahead of us was an element of Bravo Company that had gone in dismounted. We were inching along this pathway that was nothing more than a tiny tunnel through the vegetation. I heard a large whoosh and a tremendous explosion right in front of me. At that point, small arms and automatic weapons opened up. The roar was incredibly loud because of the thickness of the jungle and because it was so close. As always, mass confusion ensued. The infantrymen were leaping off the APCs. I recall 3d Squad's track in front of us being in flames. We were returning fire.

I was the .50-caliber machine gunner at the time, firing at 2 o'clock. I was firing away, incredibly scared, terrified, almost frozen in place. My mind was numb. I just knew I was going to die because the volume of the small arms coming in was so heavy and the RPGs were so intense. There was a lot of noise on the radio, a lot of people yelling, and the staccato of the .50-caliber going off like automatic. And we couldn't move. Track 13 in front was out of commission, with its people on the ground, prone, in firing positions. I couldn't even be certain whether the attack was coming from the right side of the trail or the left side. For all I knew, I was firing on the wrong side of the trail. I didn't know, couldn't know. There were bullets and tracers flying every which way. Track 11, maybe 50 yards back, couldn't even get into action. We got hammered for 10 or 15 minutes. Finally, the firing tapered off; we didn't know why.

Track 13 was in flames: They had taken a pretty heavy hit from an RPG. They were maybe 20 feet up the trail from us. We had 1 or 2 guys slightly wounded. One of the guys from 3d Squad came walking on down toward us, walking away from the burning APC. I was feeling a little bit of the rush you get when a firefight is over and the optimism that comes with it. I leaned out of my turret and asked if anybody up there was hurt. He just looked up and said, "Dave's dead." Dave was probably my best friend I had over there, the

.50 gunner on Track 13. He was killed instantly, a direct hit. I was stunned, and my mind locked up on me, and I didn't want to believe it. I just stared at the guy, trying to think of something that I could say to make him take it back. But I knew it was true, and there was nothing to say.

So we stayed in position for maybe 5 minutes until some of the other tracks backed up and turned around and we figured a way to get the hell out of there. While all this was taking place, Bravo's straight legs were filtering back. They had been in a firefight also in the woods ahead of us. They had some guys injured and 1 guy killed. They carried this guy right by my APC on a stretcher. He was a tall guy, I remember that. He was covered with a poncho on a litter. He was lying on his back, and his right leg from about the knee down was hanging off the edge of the litter. I could see his boot, and his fatigue pants were pulled up just enough so I could see some of his skin: It was real white and hairy. As the litter was being jostled around, his foot was flopping around, real loose, totally lifeless. For some reason, that struck me, that image burned itself into my memory. To make it worse, we were told a little later that he had been killed by a .50-caliber round from one of our own machine guns. Either I killed him or the APC behind me did. They were the only two .50s that were in the action. I like to think it wasn't me because of the direction I was firing in relation to the firefight, but I'll never know. We had no idea whether we had done any damage to the NVA or not.

When we withdrew, a tactical air strike was called, and they were directed to drop their bombs around the burning track. The strike came in, and they unloaded 250-pound bombs and napalm and really pounded that area for maybe 45 minutes. About 3 o'clock in the afternoon, we were ordered back in. We were going to go in there and police the area, pick up the bodies, get that track out of there, and recover Dave's body. We go back in. On this trip, yours truly gets to be point gunner. Understandably, despite the air strike, which I didn't trust a bit, I was scared to death. We go back in a creepy crawl up the trail, same scenario. We didn't have straight leg guys in ahead of us this time. We finally got to the last bend of the trail before the burning APC. Everybody had fingers on triggers, and nobody knew what was going to happen. What happened was the NVA ambushed us in exactly the same position with exactly the same intensity. They fired an RPG, which, to my fortune, was not well aimed. I heard the whoosh, and it exploded to our left. Once again, we opened fire. I was virtually petrified this time. The thing went on for I don't know how long. They say you lose track of time after a while, and I think that's true. Eventually, firing ceased. At this point, we still had not seen a dead NVA. We had not seen the base camp; we had not recovered David's body. We hadn't done anything.

So we backed out of the jungle and called in another air strike. Bashed up the woods again pretty good. Then we went in again, by now it's 4:30 P.M. It was the same scenario, with us on point. For some reason, the fear subsided. We arrived at the ruined APC, and nothing happened. We went around it, traveled another 30 yards, and came upon the base camp. What we found was an abandoned base camp. There were underground bunkers with thatched roofs, but no weapons, no food, no caches, no prisoners, no nothing. The place was a little ghost town. We got nothing for our efforts. To top it off, no effort was made to go after these guys. No effort was made to reconnoiter the area for bodies—nothing at all was done. We collected a few bullets and, most of all, stood around scratching our heads, thinking, "Why did all of this happen?" We retreated again and set up to spend the night. That night, we could hear the ammunition in the burning APC go off all night: It was faint little popping sounds. Dave's body was being melted into the APC. The next day, the colonel decided we would go in again.

As Larry Blanks relates, incompetence in the field on the part of an officer was always dangerous:

By late July, we had built a hard spot outside Firebase Patton in Hau Nghia, near the Ho Bo. It was supposed to be temporary, but we used it for many months. On the night of 27 July, we had another one of these disasters that seemed to keep happening in Vietnam. My platoon and another lieutenant's platoon were assigned night ambush. I took my platoon 300 meters east, the other lieutenant—let's call him Smith—was supposed to go 300 meters west and set up. We went out right after dark and set up. There was very little cover. We were pretty much lying there in the open. Right after dark, we heard firing, and over the radio, both the hard spot and Smith's platoon were in contact. Everyone inside the hard spot was firing in all directions; rounds were flying over us and hitting in the middle of our position. We were all hugging the ground just hoping and praying to stay alive. We knew there were casualties because Medevac helicopters were coming in. When we went in the next morning, we found out what had happened. Smith's platoon had not gone out on ambush: He had attempted to hide them outside the berm. One of the men inside the hard spot on guard duty who didn't know what Smith was up to saw figures moving in the dark and opened fire. Two or three men were killed, and five were wounded. It was quite a disaster. Smith was court-martialed a few months later.

As Larry Fontana also remembers, negligence on the part of enlisted personnel was also very dangerous—for themselves, if not so much for others. Good soldiers in Vietnam often died; bad ones faced even bleaker odds:

I found that the quest for creature comforts over safe discomfort was a dangerous game to play. The gooks would booby-trap heavily traveled areas. If an old abandoned hooch was next to a roadway that is patrolled daily, stay away! If it isn't booby-trapped, it should be. It never ceased to amaze me to watch soldiers head right for these places. You can find their names carved on marble in Washington, D.C. Shortly before I left to go home, I was ordered to build a bunker for a team of medics who would be working in the villages and staying in our patrol base at Trang Bang at night. I picked 3 men, and we dug the hole, filled sandbags, and, I have to admit, built a hell of a bunker for these guys. Trang Bang got hit with incoming all the time, and I even added an extra layer of sandbags on top. Near the bunker was a small, wood-framed building with a corrugated roof on it. It was used to house supplies. After dark, the gooks fired a recoilless rifle into the firebase. The shell hit the roof of the building and made a mess of the inside of the building. Part of the mess were 2 dead medics who were sleeping on cots in the building. I guess they didn't care to sleep on the dirt floor of a fortified bunker. They died for their quest for comfort in a hostile environment. To this day, I still feel no remorse for these men. They were given the choice and chose wrongly. Four men worked hard all day to give them safety, and they spurned it.

Soldiers in all armies find ways to deal with bad officers. C. W. Bowman describes the sort of ruse that no doubt happened more than once:

We got a new lieutenant in, and he really didn't know what was going on. We had just set up in a company perimeter, and it was starting to get dark, and we were getting ready to go on ambush patrol. Then Charlie started firing mortar rounds. We all scrambled for our foxholes, and when the mortar rounds started hitting, Charlie opened up with AK47s and RPGs. Then everything got quiet. I asked our sergeant if we were still going out on ambush patrol, and he said yes, as far as he knew. So I said, "Wait a minute, get down." I took a grenade, threw it out there, and hollered, "Incoming." When that thing blew, the whole perimeter opened up, and they called in more artillery and dropped flares around the perimeter. I think, all in all, we did that about three times that night, and finally, they called off the ambush patrol. Hell, we knew if Charlie hit our perimeter before we even left it, he was out there waiting for us. We wouldn't have gotten by the perimeter, but the lieutenant kept insisting that we were going out. He was gung ho; he was going to get Charlie. We probably wasted $300,000 worth of artillery that night to keep us from going on ambush patrol. But, then again, it probably saved us.

Although most soldiers accepted combat, few relished the thought. However, the aftermath of the experience—doubtless a reflection of a maximum dose of adrenalin—belied this fact, at least for a short time. Michael Call, like all men in the line units during 1968, saw more than his share of combat. Yet, his recollections of the experience show an ambivalence I found in nearly every veteran I have spoken with, regardless of the war they were part of:

I find it really difficult to define combat; I think it is something a person has to experience firsthand, to really gain an insight on how fragile and precious life is. Combat brings to mind a monster with two heads. On one hand, I am absolutely terrified. I mean screaming, pissing in my pants, and fighting for my life in some ungodly part of a jungle I never heard of. The sounds and sights encountered at these times will remain etched in my memory forever. Rifle fire, grenades, RPGs, machine guns, mortars, explosions, screaming, the cry "Medic," and the blood and gore that was once my friend will be something I will never be able to shut out of my mind. However, on the other hand, I remember the feeling of possessing the latest high-tech inventions in my hands, or as close as a radio call, to send the enemy to hell in a handbag, which gave me a feeling of being somewhat invulnerable.

There was not a doubt in my mind that I could and would blow that little gook SOB away if he gave me the opportunity. I felt much more confident in myself during a firefight as compared to being mortared or receiving a rocket attack; I felt I had more control of the outcome if we were only exchanging small-arms fire. And of course, that little shit has no right to try and ambush me or get me with a booby trap! After my first combat encounter with the VC, I felt very sad and depressed but, at the same time, extremely wound up, with a hell of an adrenalin surge. I was acutely aware that there was some little bastard out in the jungle trying his best to kill my young ass. I also was doing all I could to send his to hell. Now, I am going through a real struggle with my emotions and beliefs at this time. I was raised in a somewhat religious regime and found myself searching for justification in the tug-of-war going on inside me concerning the idea that I had probably killed someone. However, it did not take a whole lot of time to qualify my actions. I only had to watch the Medevacs taking the dead and wounded guys from our unit back to base camp.

The guys in my outfit all talked and recounted the firefight after we secured the area. I think we did this to try and relieve some of the fear and to reinforce the fact that *we* were still alive and unhurt, at least physically—but not necessarily mentally. I only brought up the fact of our casualties briefly while we are sitting around in a group; however, some of the guys broke down and needed to get off by themselves or to cling to a close friend, myself included. We all grieved in our own way, but whenever we lost someone in action, it seemed to draw the rest of us very much closer, which in turn made the next operation with casualties even that more difficult. Perhaps it was a "catch-22."

Platoon leader Fontana has similar recollections:

Combat always came in degrees. You can be in the worst of it by walking into the kill zone of a prepared enemy ambush or be on the edge of a fight that another unit was fighting. There were times that you were literally fighting for your life in close combat or trading shots at 200 yards at a fleeing enemy. Once you were in Vietnam, after a while, if you bothered to learn and listen, you could usually tell after the first 1 or 2 minutes if you were going to be in a bad fight or not. Combat is awful, and there is no denying it, but to be able to walk out of the smoke of combat and still be fairly unscratched is a feeling that is unique. It was almost narcotic. I would never repeat it, but I do understand the guys that went back for more with second and third tours. Once was enough for me.

Combat engineer Michael Butash remembers the strange mental effects that combat had on the men involved:

Combat was pure confusion, very fast, and it happened when you least expected it. Everything was in slow motion. Then afterwards, you'd get the shakes. It happened so fast. You remembered everything you were thinking. You were thinking so rationally, like being in an automobile accident where you can see everything happening to you; you know what your options are, you know what you're doing. Your training took over. You knew what you were trained to do and what you were trained not to do. Just fast. And then it would be done, and there would be nothing but silence. And then you'd hear the choking sobs of the guys that were hit. The smell of gunpowder, cordite in the air—it was just sweet smelling, like a haze everywhere. It would just start and stop so fast. Then you'd get the shakes.

According to Jim Ross, the switch from adrenalin rush to fear and stress was rapid and could take unusual forms:

While the shit is going on, you don't have time to be afraid. All you do is react, and then your adrenalin starts flowing, and you're yelling and cussing like a madman! Seems like you get "high" on it, and maybe just for a few seconds or minutes, you feel indestructible. Anyway, after one fight was all over, I turned around and saw that in the APC behind us, the track commander had been hit bad. He had been knocked off the track, and in addition to being wounded, his leg must have been broken because it was twisted around. Well, after it was all over and the chopper came and he was dusted off, along with the other casualties, all of a sudden I got this incredible urge to take a leak. I almost wet in my pants before I got off the track to relieve myself. The funny thing about it was that absolutely nothing came out. It was nothing but fear! I guess the adrenalin had already left my body, and I was left only with the realization that it could have been me in the next track, especially considering where I had been sitting! You kind of get the shakes, fumble for a cigarette, and make God all sorts of promises about what you're going to do for him when you come back.

The world of combat for the men of the 25th Division was one of fear, frustration, and death. The horrid reality that, in most cases, it was Americans that would receive the first shot and that that shot might come at any time was stressful enough. No wonder many of the experienced soldiers burned with frustration and wanted desperately to effectively use the power that they had and knew how to wield. Skilled artilleryman Sidney Stone speaks for many on this subject:

We were terribly frustrated because we were sitting in fire support bases and we were getting mortared periodically. In the ten months I was with 13th Artillery, we had about 3 killed and 25 wounded. That was enough for you to get really frustrated when you had all this firepower and didn't really have anything to release it on, and you couldn't really cut loose on someone. We were just firing in the dark too much, just shooting off our guns. We didn't know where to shoot or where to go. We had the punch but never really could throw it.

In some places and at some times, the 25th Division could fight the way it was trained and structured to fight. When it did so, the enemy paid dearly. When the combat soldiers of the other side took the offensive, be they North Vietnamese or followers of the Front, they, too, learned the dreadful lesson of modern war: Fire kills. When in their element, the 25th Division was invincible.

In a deep sense, however, it was during the day-by-day agony I have tried to portray that the men of the Tropic Lightning Division showed their true mettle. Their opponents were skilled and courageous and possessed many advantages in low-level warfare. The American combat soldiers, on the other hand, were not ideally trained, were operating in a viciously hostile environment, and had to face a daily dose of stress that still knots the stomach of any sensitive student of the war. Despite these handicaps, the men acquitted themselves well. Mistakes were made, as in all wars. But the men of the Tropic Lightning Division were formidable opponents on the battlefield and, by and large, their conduct showed them to be decent and honorable men.

In the long run, the row proved too long to hoe. It is arguable that America's defeat in Vietnam was highly predictable given the desperate nature of the situation and the social realities of the times. But when the chips were down, the men of the 25th did not go quietly.

4

The Shifting Battlefields of Vietnam

Aₛ I HAVE TRIED to illustrate, the lack of a front line created a tempo of fighting in Vietnam that imposed a serious physical and psychological toll on the soldiers and the American public alike. Yet, not all of the fighting was part of the continual exchange of low-level, seemingly aimless violence. In fact, large engagements in Vietnam often took place. They were never as big as a major World War II battle, although the 1972 Easter Offensive came close. During the American phase of the war, any battle that involved more than 2,000 men was a big one. Those involving several hundred men were more common. Frequently, however, these battles came bunched together. When Front or North Vietnamese forces launched a local or general offensive, many medium-sized clashes took place instead of one massive bloodbath. That is why no single battle is associated with the Vietnam War. The Tet Offensive achieved great notoriety, but as I shall show, it was not a tightly organized battle in the conventional meaning of the term. In addition, American soldiers had to face other military challenges that were unique to Vietnam. Their efforts in response to these challenges contributed to the overall attrition, which is typical of modern wars, but they took forms that no previous American soldiers had ever confronted. The chase for Charlie dominated the daily operations of the 25th Division, but the Division was there for many days. If we hope to understand the military experience of the soldiers of the Tropic Lightning Division, we must look, if only briefly, at the great variety of battlefields on which they struggled.

The Tethered Goat

One battle in Vietnam was world famous before it was over: the Viet Minh's great victory over the French in 1954 at Dien Bien Phu. American generals and intelligence experts studied it closely, and it is good that they did because Dien Bien Phu, in the hearts of Vietnamese revolutionaries, was the greatest moment in their nation's history. It was also a source of considerable pride to many opponents of the Front in the South who were anti-Communist but had borne no love for France. It is important to remember that almost every Front and NVA commander in the Vietnam War had been at Dien Bien Phu. Gen. Nguyen Vo Giap, the military architect of the battle, was still in command of NVA ground forces, and military writing from North Vietnam concentrated on the subject to an extraordinary degree. Dien Bien Phu, to our enemies in Vietnam, was not a historical moment but a religious one. Moreover, this military revelation had not occurred in the distant past, like some of the other great victories that gave confidence to our opponents, but a mere twelve years before the 25th Division set up camp at Cu Chi. And as Communist military writings and prisoner interrogations by American intelligence showed, enemy leaders continually promised to deliver a similar blow to the Americans.

An extraordinary convergence of military goals for both sides took place thanks to the ghost of Dien Bien Phu. There was a great debate within Communist ranks concerning the best way to deal with the Americans. The makeup of their various military coalitions is not always easy to follow. But it is evident that some revolutionary leaders wanted to slug it out with U.S. forces when favorable opportunities presented themselves. They believed that superior knowledge of the terrain, superior spirit, greater battlefield experience, and clever tactics could compensate for the greater firepower of U.S. forces if an advantage of numbers was gained at the local level. Other revolutionary commanders, particularly within the NVA, urged caution and argued for a more sustained people's war. These officers wanted large engagements with the Americans when defensive terrain was ideal. Inflicting American casualties, rather than outright victory, was the goal for this group. In addition, they believed selective large battles would keep American forces concentrated and off balance. But the voices of caution were more eager to inflict pain on American forces than to take large risks. They feared tactical defeats due to U.S. firepower. They also feared the consequences that a large battlefield victory might have for the revolution. That, they knew, carried with it great risks early in the war. If their powerful enemies were humiliated, they might react in exactly the way no one in Hanoi wanted: They could mobilize, declare war, and attack the North directly. Not surprisingly, Hanoi decided to greatly increase the size and power of the NVA in this period. And Moscow and Beijing were glad to assist.

Ultimately, the advocates of risk won the day, and the Tet Offensive resulted. On one subject, everyone on the enemy side agreed: A medium-sized military victory would be a tremendous gain for the revolution. The United States might react violently if a large force were entrapped, but that was far less likely if a smaller base was annihilated in a lightning assault. Meanwhile, the propaganda gains of a victory would be great. American forces would be more cautious than ever, leading them to project their power into fewer areas. And the North's supporters around the world could use any military victory as prime ammunition in the propaganda war. Inside Vietnam, the view already held by many Vietnamese—that a Front victory was inevitable—would become accepted by almost everyone. All of these calculations reinforced another point agreed upon by all in the Communist camp: A great effort should be made to increase the Main Force military units, both Front and NVA, in size, armaments, and professional skill. The more cautious opponents wanted to do this so victory would come quickly once America lost its will. The more aggressive wanted to use the great army they were building to "kick in the door" as soon as possible.

Paradoxically, the enemy was playing into American hands. U.S. commanders were desperate for large battles that would enable their forces to use their firepower and training as intended. More importantly, however, it soon became very obvious to military men in Vietnam that the United States would accomplish nothing as long as the enemy continued to build strength. Westmoreland and others believed that only defeats in the field could weaken the other side and give our South Vietnamese allies the confidence to join the struggle more vigorously. Considering the political restrictions that Lyndon Johnson imposed, it is hard to see what other card the Army had to play.

Westmoreland more or less got his wish in 1966. There were several ugly battles against enemy forces in the hinterlands, and the American side claimed great body counts. But the results were, at best, inconclusive. Many of these engagements highlighted American attack on North Vietnamese prepared positions, an experience soldiers of the 25th Division grew to loathe when it happened to them. Yet, the outcome of these battles was not satisfactory. Enemy units were never encircled and wiped out in large numbers, and our casualties were painfully high. A good "kill ratio" did not sound like victory to the American people.

However, these engagements were not totally satisfactory to the other side either. America was building its force and obviously settling in for a long stay. And though the rhetoric and logic of a people's war was most compelling, the prospect of a protracted conflict was not appetizing, particularly when the people involved sincerely believed that they were trying to oust a foreign invader from their homeland. The length of the French phase of the war had been inevitable because the Viet Minh were so weak militarily. When massive Chinese aid changed the equation in the early 1950s, the war turned decisively against France. One can imagine how many Front officers and men wanted to annihilate an American unit as their military strength built. Hit and run might be a marvelous strategy, but running takes a psychological toll when one's comrades die. Inevitably, the Front, which had proved itself a great matador, chased a foolish illusion and became the bull.

Geography and some very wise leadership at Cu Chi spared the 25th Division many of the vicious Hamburger Hill–type battles that other divisions faced. Although Front leaders deployed their Main Force units throughout the Division's AO, they were not eager to face battle in the first year. In fact, North Vietnamese forces were rarely encountered until late in 1967. The 25th Division, however, eventually became a prime target for lightning Communist assaults aimed at the complete destruction of an American perimeter. Ultimately, the enemy hit elements of the Tropic Lightning Division dozens of times. Each time, the opponents possessed a numerical superiority in men, frequently a very large one. Yet, each time, when the smoke had cleared, the enemy was smashed. In the process, though, the American soldiers flirted with catastrophe on several occasions, and Division veterans are quick to recognize the incredible bravery shown by the men trying to kill them. No doubt, firepower played a role in the outcome of these battles, but almost all took place at night, and American advantages in firepower were far less striking than they appeared on paper. In the final analysis, only soldiers possessing skill and bravery could have survived this long series of harrowing encounters without suffering a single defeat.

There were so many of these lightning assaults on isolated American perimeters that a historian could easily write an entire book charting them all. The first major battle the Division fought, in April 1966, was an attack on an isolated company by a reinforced Front battalion. The green American troops made many tactical errors, and a shortage of ammunition on their enemy's part probably saved them just before dawn. Several civilian employees at Cu Chi were later found dead in the barbed wire set out around the perimeter. It was an ugly preview of what was to come.

The largest, most frightening, and probably most violent of these bitter battles was the enemy attack on Firebase Gold, sometimes called the Battle of Soui Tre, on 21 March 1967. Westmoreland himself indirectly caused this vicious battle. In 1967, MACV ordered a series of multidivisional operations into enemy safe zones, aimed at trapping and destroying large Main Force units. MACV still suffered from illusions concerning the opportunities for surprise that helicopter assaults offered American units. The 25th Division participated in the first of these early in the year, code-named Operation CEDAR FALLS, which entailed a huge sweep through the Iron Triangle. Americans captured much material but failed in their prime objective of destroying Front military units when enemy forces dispersed and declined to fight. MACV consequently aimed one of the biggest operations of the war at War Zone C. Several elements of the 25th Division took part in this massive exercise in futility. C. W. Bowman remembers that the number of helicopters used reminded him of a "swarm of gnats." Yet, despite attempting sophisticated maneuvers that looked impressive on paper, American forces were swinging at air. Then several elements of the 9th Front Division, the enemy's most powerful ground force in the area, decided to counterattack.

Although the exact location and intentions of the enemy were unknown, American intelligence picked up enough signs to identify an area where the enemy was clearly present in force. Elements of 25th Division artillery, infantry, and armor were sent in pursuit, right in the middle of War Zone C. Infantry battalion commander Jack Bender recalls events that led him to expect a rough time:

I was told there would be direct support from two batteries of artillery—one battery firing west to east, and one battery firing south to north. This was a phenomenal amount of fire support, and I knew we were in trouble and something big was on. I also learned that we had priority for air support for the duration. I hoped we wouldn't be killed by too much kindness: We now had maximum artillery support, maximum air support, and just about our desire on anything we needed. That only happens when you are in a serious situation.

Infantryman Kenneth Gosline's suspicion that something ugly was ahead came earlier. In retrospect, he does not like what he learned:

We all know we were used for the whole war. I can remember, before we left Dau Tieng before going out to LZ Gold, standing in formation while the colonel told us that if a smaller U.S. force can hold off a superior force of NVA or Viet Cong, then we would be rewarded and decorated. At the time, I couldn't figure out what he was talking about. After the whole mess was over, it made sense. We were kind of used for bait. Elements of mechanized battalions were held in reserve, kind of like the cavalry. Supposedly, they were going to come to our rescue. The problem was that the Vietnamese were a little smarter than our bosses, and they held them up.

It is not clear whether Gosline was correct in his assessment that commanders were anticipating what was going to happen at Firebase Gold. Later in the war, they openly admitted that perimeters were used as bait. In this instance, however, it is possible that the 25th Division officer was alerting his men to a very obvious eventuality. Considering the course of events, though, it is quite understandable why Gosline and many other soldiers believed that American commanders foresaw the attack on Gold.

Whatever the case, American commanders ordered the bulk of an infantry battalion to secure a landing zone and prepare it for the aerial insertion of an artillery battalion. Officers chose an area made barren by chemical defoliation, and U.S. artillery bombarded the area. Evidently, however, the landing zone was too obvious, and the enemy was prepared. Colonel Bender was in his command helicopter and watched the first huge wave of lift choppers arrive with his infantry:

We started our insert into Gold, and all heck broke lose. The VC had placed large antitank demolitions in the rice paddy edges around the landing area, all aimed inward. They detonated from a distance and timed it to make sure they would get the maximum effect. I was flying in the helicopter battalion commander's chopper. Approximately half of the ships were so badly destroyed going into that first lift that the chopper commander did not want to continue the mission for fear he would lose more ships. But it was too late to turn back, with troops on the ground. We finally landed the rest of the battalion, less C Company, cleared the hot landing zone, and set up a defensive perimeter.

Sgt. Bill Riggs was waiting for his lift back at base, and he watched the first group fly off in the biggest operation he had experienced in Vietnam:

It was quite a sight to behold, all of the helicopters taking off at once. At that point, we had never been on an operation that big. We usually worked on company- or battalion-sized operations, but this was huge, and everyone was involved. The first wave took off, and the sky just became alive with helicopters. When they returned for the second wave, there were probably only about three-quarters of them left. Some of them were wobbling all over the sky because they were so shot up they couldn't fly straight. They landed and moved off to the side because they weren't going to use them again. That kind of really sets the mood. The second wave took off. We were in the third wave, and by the time we took off and landed, the first two waves had gotten it secured. When we came in over the tree line, all you could see was smoldering fires of crashed helicopters. Some had crashed in the trees. The enemy had homemade claymore mines maybe 6 feet apart aimed straight up, so when you came down low over the tree line, they'd be detonated and blow the helicopter out of the sky. We got on the ground and set up a perimeter. Everything was pretty quiet that night.

Sgt. Jack Wood describes the initial debacle:

The LZ had been a rice paddy at one time or another. At this time, it was dry, and grass had grown up in parts, some of it 3, 4, 5 feet in height. There was no water, but the old levies marking the rice paddies were still in existence. The VC had a bunker in the east end of the landing zone. The VC had taken 175 artillery rounds, propped them up on their base, and clustered 81mm mortar rounds around them and run wires back to this bunker where they could be command-detonated. The artillery prep had not destroyed most of these rounds. As A and B Company were lifted into the landing zone, the Viet Cong detonated these artillery rounds. I don't know exactly how many men and choppers were lost, but there were a considerable number. Several fires started in the tall grass on the initial assault. I remember a helicopter pilot lying on the ground with everything missing from his rib cage down; the fire had evidently burned over him, causing his skin to take on a color similar to an Oriental. He also had a fresh crew cut, which added to the unreal appearance of the scene. After we established a perimeter, Firebase Gold was about 500 meters east to west and 400 meters north to south.

For the next two days, the artillerymen at Firebase Gold feverishly prepared defenses. The guarding infantry probed the area but encountered nothing. The men at Gold had some reason to be confident, for a mechanized infantry battalion was based close by, and Gold was within artillery range of another firebase. But the perimeter was small and surrounded by forest. American commanders assigned the defenders two "quad-50s," an old but powerful weapon. Originally designed for close air support, the quad-50 was simply four .50-caliber machine guns mounted together. It was a frightful antipersonnel weapon at close range.

Not realizing their peril, men from different units began the petty bickering typical of military life. Sergeant Riggs notes that his infantrymen had some nasty words with the gunners:

It was kind of interesting. When we'd come in from patrol, we'd go past the artillery men. They had their water trucks there. We'd go up to get water, and they'd holler at us, "Get out of here, straight legs; that's ours, get your own. Stay away from artillery water." That attitude would soon change.

In retrospect, one realizes that the Americans at Gold were in terrible danger. They were in the enemy's backyard. And despite the presence of reconnaissance from the air and several ground units, Front strike forces showed, not for the first or last time, their uncanny ability to concentrate their dispersed units for a surprise assault. While the men at Gold prepared their defenses, Front commanders prepared a massive, coordinated ground assault on the firebase. Furthermore, this assault began later than was normal for the enemy. Large attacks typically began around 4:00 a.m. or earlier, but in this case, perhaps because the numbers were so large, the attackers were unable to complete their preparations on time. It is also quite possible that the Front decided to strike just before dawn in the hope that the culminating phase of battle would take place at first light. Daylight brought American firepower, but it also made operations far easier. No Army, no matter how well trained, can possibly fight as well at night as it can during the day. But this equation, as Front officers were to learn, worked both ways.

Jack Wood recalls the opening stage of the battle:

I remember I was awake on the morning of 21 March at about 5:30 A.M. It was still dark, and I didn't have my boots on. When I heard the ping of the sound of a round leaving a mortar tube, I yelled, "Mortar!" and dove for my foxhole. The round had not landed before small-arms fire broke out all around the perimeter. B Company had a small patrol out to the east, and these men were all killed and later recovered. The enemy directed heavy mortar fire at the artillery positions while an assault was launched on all sides of the perimeter. Firing was so heavy that you could not hear the person next to you. The perimeter was manned on the northeast by B Company and the reconnaissance platoon and on the south and west by A Company. B Company had already sustained heavy casualties from the landing and the patrol lost. Our entire force consisted of about 450 men.

The fighting continued to grow in intensity, and as morning came, air strikes began, one after another, on the edge of the timber. We could see the VC near the perimeter on the tree line. Some that had been hit would reap-

pear later with bandages on. The air was filled with smoke and dust, making visibility extremely difficult.

American battalion commanders in Vietnam rarely awoke to see their units facing oblivion. Lt. Col. Jack Bender, the infantry commander at Gold, was an exception:

That night, security was 100 percent, and I hit the sack for forty winks. One of the first mortar rounds hit under my hammock, and if I had not been wearing some protective clothes, i.e., my pistol harness, the war would have been over for me right then. It was immediately apparent that we were being hit from both sides of the perimeter where we had placed the quad-50s. We had also placed squads about 100 to 300 yards in front of our position. These forces were fighting their way back to friendly positions, but most did not make it. Then we saw the advancing line of enemy soldiers bobbing up and down as they approached our position. I also realized these were not VC guerrillas but an organized force wearing uniforms and under strict control. Snipers began firing from the trees at an elevation of about 40 feet and about 300 yards away and had a field day on my forces. Because the M16 lacked long-range accuracy, it was necessary to round up all of the World War II M1s to give us the range necessary to counter this problem. I was glad that I had carried an M1 throughout most of my tour to add to that cause. At this point, the "in-house" artillery was firing point-blank range at the attacking troops with maximum results. The artillery was coordinated with air cover to ensure that we had maximum air support on all flanks of our perimeter. At this moment, the air controller was shot down. This was a severe blow because we needed him desperately.

Battles rarely go according to plan. One company of American infantry had left Gold the day before on a short-range sweep. Although these men were totally exposed, the enemy did not pick up their position. Sgt. Bill Riggs describes the result:

We wandered around out in the jungle the whole day, and about dusk, we set up our perimeter for the night. Just about daylight, we heard mortars in the distance. Then we heard a lot of small-arms fire, which sounded close, so we weren't that far away. At first, we thought, that's the mech unit having a "mad minute." Often, before mechanized units moved out in the morning, they would have free fire for about 1 minute. That way, if any VC were waiting near their perimeter, they might get them. But it lasted too long.

Our radio really started popping with reports of what was going on. The company commander said, "They're being overrun, and we're going back for support." So the distance that took us all day to travel on the way out, we covered back to base in just over an hour. We broke through the tree line from the north. Off to our left, we could see the artillery pieces. At that point, they were fighting hand to hand. The gunners had to blow up some of their own artillery pieces to keep them from being turned on themselves. The artillerymen kept falling back and had the 105mm howitzers lined up at point-blank range with the barrels level at the ground, firing beehive rounds that would turn the howitzer into a 105mm shotgun.

As soon as our company was in the open, the whole tree line to our right just opened up with muzzle flashes. They knew where we were and which direction we were coming from, and they were waiting in ambush. Our whole company was pinned down. We just dropped to the ground. We were in the open and couldn't move. There was no place to hide. I was a 90mm gunner, and I had two 90mm rounds on my back, one HE, and one beehive round. I crawled out from underneath my rucksack, looking for something to hide behind because I wanted to get away from those two 90mm rounds, but we were in the open, so I crawled back behind them. Finally, we started returning fire, and at that point, the mech unit finally got there. They broke through the tree line to the southeast, I believe. We had our backs to them because we had turned to face the direction where the enemy was firing at us from. The mech unit, because they were behind us, got hit from some stray rounds from our firefight. Assuming they were being ambushed, they opened up on the tree line. There we were in the middle of it, with no place to go and nothing we could do. So we just lay there and just watched what was going on. We could hear bugles blowing in the background from the Vietnamese human wave attacks, just like in Korea. Just a mass of people charging.

The arrival of Riggs's company undoubtedly blunted some of the enemy's drive. Any Vietnamese attackers who were forced to deal with the reinforcements were also kept away from the assault on the artillery just a few yards distant. And finally, the arrival of the mechanized infantry and armored units at the eleventh hour turned a potential catastrophe into a smashing victory. But that was not obvious inside the perimeter when the enemy assault reached its peak. Sergeant Wood gives his account:

When daylight came, the VC brought up 75mm recoilless rifles and continued to try to knock out the artillery. The artillery was firing at low elevation and was practically out of high-explosive ammo. We were also helped by artillery from another base. Soon, there were several VC inside the perimeter. One VC was close enough that I could hear the 2-shot sequence of his AK47, although in the tall grass, I never saw him. I remember thinking he might get to the aid station. It was already filled with wounded, but someone killed him before he made it to there.

Colonel Bender had lost contact with B Company's commander, who was about 100 meters from the battalion command group. He started to go in that direction, but as he neared my foxhole, I told him that I would find out what the situation was. I found the B Company commander and 2 or 3 other men there. He had lost communication with his platoon leaders and stated that the last he had heard, everyone was running short of ammunition. On returning to my foxhole, I found it occupied by the 3d Platoon of B Company. I told them that the battalion commander wanted them to regain their original positions, and this they were able to do by crawling under covering fire.

A day or two before, several cases of beer had been brought in and stacked by my foxhole so I could control their issue. I gave no thought to this until heavy mortar fire began to hit extremely close. It occurred to me that the VC probably thought the cases contained ammo. A mortar round landed about 10 feet from my foxhole, and a sergeant who was in the hole with me at the time was hit in the left side of his face. I put his first aid bandage on and remember thinking how funny he looked with this big pink bandage around his head. About the same time, I looked over to the foxhole where the artillery forward observer and his assistant were and noticed that the assistant had set a can of Budweiser up on the edge of his foxhole. I remember thinking he was either the coolest man around or was so damn scared that he had to have some alcohol.

Both quad-50s had been overrun, and the VC were attempting to turn them around but could not because of heavy fire from the perimeter. Many snipers had taken positions in the tall trees at the edge of the clearing and were keeping up a pretty good rate of fire. At the northwest edge of the clearing, a large tree with a fork in it stood out from the tree line, and a sniper had managed to reach this fork and was able to see into the command bunker, which had no roof, only sandbags. Members of the engineer demolition team had taken a position on the northwest corner of the command group and were armed with M14 rifles. One of them killed the sniper and probably saved some of the command group.

By 10:00, the situation was precarious at best, and ammunition was extremely low. The artillery began firing beehive rounds, which I had never seen before at minimum elevation. It appeared to be extremely effective, although the first few rounds detonated behind our perimeter and may have possibly hit some of our own men. At about 10:30 A.M., elements of the 2/3d 34th Armored appeared from the east and broke the encirclement. Had they been 10 or 15 minutes later, I believe we would have been completely overrun.

Kenneth Gosline was also inside the perimeter and speaks of the chaos and peril of the morning:

It's hard to describe that day. It was total and utter confusion. The end of the movie *Platoon* was close. You were too scared to be scared. It was almost like an out-of-body experience. Like you weren't really there. But you were experiencing total chaos and confusion. As the VC were charging, you would shoot one and see him fall. And then his guys would drag him back. A little while later, you'd be shooting the same guy, who was all wrapped up. I guess they must have taken them back and shot them up with opium or something. It was unbelievable. The chopper pilots were great. Choppers were dropping ammo boxes inside the perimeter. They didn't even set down—just flew over and kicked the stuff out. The VC broke through the lines. They were shooting behind you; they were shooting in front of you. When the artillery guys lowered their guns, they were firing these beehive rounds point-blank at the charging Vietnamese. They were opening the breech, sighting down the bore, slamming in a beehive round, and just firing. Our sergeant ran in front of an artillery piece, and the beehive round cut him to pieces.

After at least 3 hours of bloody combat, which included sustained artillery fire, many air strikes, and small-arms fire from inside the perimeter, the attackers were hit in the flank by American APCs and tanks. A slaughter ensued. Sergeant Riggs remembers the conclusion of the battle:

We could see the gunners on their artillery pieces holding their M14s like baseball bats, just swinging at the enemy. Then the APCs arrived. A friend of mine was on one and told me that they would just find a Vietnamese, chase him around with the track, chuck hand grenades out of the top hatches, and just run him down. The mech unit and the tanks saved everything. We finally got radio communication with the mech unit, and when they found out where we were, they made a sweep around us and got in between us and the tree line, then laid down fire so we could maneuver. After several hours, everything quieted down, and we set up a perimeter again. We started digging in, waiting for a counterattack that never happened.

William McDill was a physical therapist back at the 12th Evac Hospital at Cu Chi. For the first time, waves of casualties appeared, and the medical personnel went into high gear:

In late March 1967, an artillery battery was overrun at a place called Soui Tre. Naturally, the speculation was that they had been left there as bait to draw Charlie into a real battle. If that was the case, it certainly worked. A company commander who was there told me that they had counted 647 dead VC in and around the battle area. The hospital had just finished a fairly full surgical schedule in late morning when the casualties began to arrive. It is my recollection that the 12th Evac received 109 wounded and 31 KIA from the battle. It was the first mass casualty situation we had, and we set up a triage station in a Quonset hut, where you sort battle victims according to severity of wounds. This is something also done in case of natural disaster.

I interviewed a young grunt who was filthy dirty, had some bruises across his back, and was obviously in the throes of near hysteria. This is what he told me: "They had closed our perimeter down to about 25 percent of where it had started out. The tubes were on zero elevation, and we were firing beehives. I thought that it was just a matter of time. All of a sudden, the mech came out of the jungle in line, did a flanking movement, and came straight at us. It was great. Here came the tracks with their .50s firing. The troops and I stood up and cheered. There was a track coming straight at me. And I was cheering. And the track kept coming straight at me, until I realized that the driver didn't see me. I barely had time to fall into a little depression, and the track ran over me. That's how I got the bruises on my back. They came from the tracks that ran over me."

The aftermath of battle is a strange time for all concerned. With many men under extreme physical and psychological stress, unusual sights and occurrences are common. In addition, the survivors are inevitably surrounded with the painful and grotesque reminders of the recent violence. Sergeant Wood describes the moments after battle at Gold:

As mopping up commenced, we were able to view the area, which was littered with dead bodies, VC as well as some Americans. I observed 3 or 4 GIs with a prisoner who appeared unwilling to move, although he showed no evidence of being wounded. I told them to get a medic, which they did. The VC died shortly thereafter as he had been hit in the abdomen by one of the beehive projectiles, which resemble a small arrow about an inch long. Internal bleeding had killed him with only a drop of blood showing. Another prisoner appeared to be an Oriental of some type. He was extremely arrogant and had a brand-new Chinese radio. I took him to be some type of adviser to the local VC force. He would spit on people and resist in every way he could. Division informed us that they wanted him back in Cu Chi, and I never heard what his actual situation was after that.

Tank dozers were brought up, and several mass graves were dug for the VC. They were buried by the time we left the area a couple days later and emitted quite an odor. General Westmoreland came in that afternoon and congratulated the men who participated in the engagement.

One incident that has always stuck in my mind was when I dove for my foxhole at the opening mortar round. I only took my M16 and several bandoliers of ammo, leaving my boots and web gear with my canteens outside. When everything was over, my boots were full of holes, and all of my canteens had been punctured with shrapnel.

Sergeant Riggs's infantry stayed in the area longer and learned that the gunners had undergone a change of heart toward their colleagues in the infantry. They were also given the grim task of tabulating the level of victory:

We went over to the artillery trucks to get water, and the artillery people would say, "Here, have some water. Hey, I got some cookies in the mail, you want a cookie?" Their whole attitude toward us changed when we came in and saved them. We stayed in that area several more days, taking late patrols out around the perimeter, going out a little further, trying to get a bigger body count because that's all the higher-ups were interested in, body counts. We had a tank with a bulldozer blade that dug a trench, and we were chucking the bodies into the trench; it looked just like one of those photographs from the concentration camps in Germany after World War II, with bodies just dumped in a big long trench. With the heat and humidity, it didn't take long for the stench to really get to you. There's no way to describe it, just the smell of rotting flesh. A day or so afterward, a chopper flew into Gold, and an officer on board said that wasn't the proper thing to do, that they were human beings, too, and deserved proper burial. I don't know how that turned out, but I know it was quite an incident. We continued with the patrols, and you could just tell when you were coming up on a body after a couple of days. At about 100 yards, you were hit with the smell of rotting flesh and the burned napalm that was dropped around the perimeter. I think we stayed for about a week just trying to get more and more of a body count. That's about it.

A phenomenon takes place in many wars that is very common but extremely difficult to explain. I call it the Stalingrad complex. It is the tendency for one side, through misunderstanding or self-deception, to misread battlefield realities and reinforce defeat. Something like this apparently happened to the commanders of Communist Main Force units that confronted the 25th Division. Perhaps they believed that bad fortune denied them success; an enemy commander might well have made that argument after the battle at Gold. Perhaps they believed that the consequences of just one victory would justify all of the losses they had sustained. If this were so, we will never know because victory never came. Perhaps a succession of new local commanders believed they could succeed where others had failed. Or perhaps they were trapped by their own past and the memories of French paratroopers helpless under Viet Minh guns.

Whatever the case, the events at Firebase Gold were a preview of what would come in the following two years. Time and time again, Front and North Vietnamese forces stormed isolated American perimeters. Many— perhaps most—of these assaults were happy conclusions to preplanned enterprises on the part of the 25th Division's command. The men, as one might imagine, were not so happy with the tactic. Three or four individuals likened the technique to the use of a tethered goat in a tiger hunt. Yet, in defense of the command, it was a technique that appeared to work. The enemy units that bore the brunt of these attacks would be out of action for weeks or longer: Those were enemy soldiers the men of the 25th did not have to face under more adverse circumstances.

Clearly, most men would prefer that battles pass them by completely. Yet, if they are in one, most men want to come out on top. It is safer and an excellent way to express your feelings toward the enemies that are trying to kill you. Although undoubtedly unexpected, one result of the increasingly frequent attacks on American units was extremely unfortunate from the Front's point of view: They were building the tactical confidence of many American commanders. Although there were harrowing moments aplenty, the American troops began to believe that when fighting toe to toe, they would win, even if the numerical odds were heavily against them. It was a confidence grounded in reality. It was also a confidence that they would need when confronted with the greatest test faced by the Tropic Lightning Division in Vietnam, the Tet Offensive of 1968.

Tet

No major military campaign in recent history is as poorly understood by the public as the Tet Offensive of 1968. The image associated with Tet is one of a vicious but relatively short battle highlighted by the sapper attacks in Saigon, the NVA's seizure of much of Hue, and the siege of Khe Sanh. Some people are also aware that fighting extended on a lesser level throughout much of the country. And most know the result of the battle: a great political victory for the Front that destroyed a U.S. president and ended forever any thought of an American victory in Vietnam. The military losses suffered by the Front were assumed to be acceptable sacrifices, considering the magnitude of the psychological triumph.

In reality, there is only a kernel of truth in this scenario. This is not the place to assess the political importance of Tet in the United States, but the fact is that the American public was clearly not united behind a confident administration in early 1968, only to find out the ugly truth because of Tet. Nor am I totally convinced that replacing Lyndon Johnson, the worst war leader in U.S. history, with Richard Nixon and Henry Kissinger was a good exchange from Hanoi's perspective. Furthermore, the other side had to wait seven years for victory, making Tet a rather delayed "turning point." Instead, I would suggest that the other side won in spite of Tet, not because of it. In any case, it is certainly odd that Communist writers have been almost silent concerning Tet over the past two decades. Perhaps they were too concerned with the wreckage of their own forces to notice the great victory.

To understand Tet and the crucial role played by the 25th Division, we must first look at what the Front wanted to accomplish. As usual when dealing with events that took place within the Communist leadership structure, an element of uncertainty persists: Candor and truthfulness have never been characteristic of the government in Hanoi. Yet, between intelligence gathered by the Americans and South Vietnamese after the event and a large volume of postwar writings from Hanoi, there is enough evidence to draw some basic conclusions concerning the Tet Offensive.

The first and probably most important point is that the Front intended to win the war in short order with a great military and political offensive in 1968. Front political cadres in contested territory and within the huge urban shantytowns reported hatred toward both Saigon and the United States. Furthermore, revolutionary military leaders had contempt for ARVN and believed that a stunning hammer blow could shatter it; no doubt, undercover cadres within ARVN and the South Vietnamese militia reported bad morale caused by inept and corrupt officers. If ARVN could be humiliated and the armed revolution brought to the cities, then the prospect of a general uprising against the Saigon government appeared very feasible.

Along with Dien Bien Phu, another moment from the recent past had taken on an almost religious significance for revolutionaries in Vietnam. This was the remarkable series of events in Hanoi during 1945 that left Ho Chi Minh momentarily in control of the country. If the people rose against their oppressors once, surely they would do so again when it was clear that the revolution would protect them.

In retrospect, we can see the Front leaders were lying to themselves. Yet, at the time, their views appeared to have some foundation. In addition, despite Washington's bogus claims, the strength of the Front military forces peaked in late 1967. They had at their disposal a very powerful light infantry army with experienced officers and very high morale. Although there were still voices of caution raised in Hanoi, even the conservative leaders had reasons to hope. By 1968, an American mobilization and attack on the North seemed far less likely than it had in 1966. And more than their subordinate forces in the Front, Hanoi's army had grown greatly in size and power. It was time, Hanoi decided, to take some chances.

Anyone with a passing knowledge of the military history of the Vietnamese is struck with the great importance of ruse and stratagem in their long and illustrious string of victories over foreign armies. The Tet Offensive followed this tradition. The attack was timed to coincide with the Tet holiday and its traditional truce. Hanoi knew that South Vietnamese commanders, if the past were any guide, would give short leaves to huge numbers of men and that government leaders in Saigon would be tending to family affairs. The fact that many Vietnamese were repulsed by the idea of launching a vast military offensive on the holiest day of the year does not seem to have concerned Hanoi.

Communist commanders counted, however, on a far more important ruse than attacking on a holiday. When Hanoi assented to the offensive in July of 1967, Communist commanders believed that Westmoreland would follow his policy of the first two years and seek battle in the hinterlands. This would be especially true, the Communists believed, if NVA forces appeared in great strength in the far north sector of the country and near the Cambodian border elsewhere. Surely, judging by their past actions, the Americans would take the bait and deploy their army far from the real locus of attack. This would give Front strike forces, reinforced by strategically placed North Vietnamese regulars, the opportunity to smash the South Vietnamese apparatus without American intervention. By the time the Americans could regroup and intervene, the Communists hoped, the Saigon government and its military would be crippled or mortally wounded.

Although the Tet Offensive was aimed at achieving a quick end to the war, Hanoi never believed it could accomplish this goal in the first hours of battle. Instead, the enemy planned for a multiphase attack that would last several weeks or months. Apparently, the plan of action after the opening gunfire was subject to revision. It is unclear, for instance, whether the NVA intended to attack Khe Sanh if the offensive went well. What resulted, of course, was not what Hanoi or the Front command had in mind. Their forces were turned back time and again, but the battlefield defeats apparently raised the North's ante greatly. Perhaps the Front could not admit to itself that its assumptions were wrong. Perhaps the disruptions in the United States came as a welcome surprise. Whatever the reasons, the enemy kept up the pressure, with very few lulls, for over a year. Finally, after a year and a half of fighting and countless defeats, the enemy bowed to reality and ceased attacking. When the smoke had cleared, the southern revolutionary movement found itself seriously weakened and virtually disarmed, its troops becoming totally subordinate to Hanoi. The 25th Division played a crucial role in every phase of this violent period. Indeed, no division in Vietnam did more to crush the Front's General Offensive. And no unit paid a higher price to do so.

The 25th Division was one of the first units to feel the effects of the change in the war's direction. Beginning in the fall of 1967, sharp engagements in Tay Ninh were common, and for the first time, the Tropic Lightning Division faced North Vietnamese regulars. On 1 January 1968, a large North Vietnamese force attacked Firebase Burt near the Cambodian border. After some perilous moments, American defenders defeated the attack. (The attack on Burt has been portrayed twice in fiction. It is a highlight of Larry Heinemann's great novel *Close Quarters*. It also inspired the battle at the conclusion of the movie *Platoon*.)

Throughout Vietnam at the beginning of 1968, American divisions were deploying toward the frontiers. The siege at Khe Sanh began, and it must have seemed to Hanoi that the hoped-for deception was working perfectly. But within a week, Hanoi's plans were in ruins. The individual most responsible for defeating the Tet Offensive was Gen. Frederick Weyand, commander of Army ground forces in the provinces around Saigon. Weyand, who had commanded the 25th when it was deployed to Cu Chi, was greatly admired by his officers, and he led the Division well. As previously noted, he was one of the men responsible for introducing armored vehicles to Vietnam. Promoted when he left the 25th, he moved to Saigon where, having climbed one additional step up the ladder of rank, he once again led the 25th, as part of the broader command he assumed. (Eventually, Weyand became Army chief of staff and was the last head of MACV, in 1975.) A former intelligence officer, he listened with great interest to an increasing flood of reports from across the country indicating that the enemy was up to something very big. Westmoreland was also growing concerned and wisely took Weyand's warnings seriously. In the middle of January, Westmoreland ordered a major redeployment of American ground forces in central Vietnam. Half the battalions in the hinterlands were brought back closer to base. Several of these battalions were with the 25th, and all were soon needed very close to base, indeed.

Fate dealt another bad card to the Front. One commander in the northern part of the country committed a major blunder and launched an attack hours before the country erupted in violence. The South's intelligence was also concerned, and President Nguyen Van Thieu canceled all leaves and ordered ARVN soldiers back to their units. Many did not obey, but most were close by when the storm hit. At that point, rather than deserting or changing sides, most ARVN soldiers returned to their units to face the worst battle they had ever confronted.

The last twist of fortune took place at Cu Chi. After weeks of hard operations, the 3/4th Armored Cavalry was brought back for a rest. Two troops deployed nearby to the west, awaiting a short stay at camp. C Troop returned to Cu Chi itself. Instead of a rest, however, the men of C Troop were destined for a death ride that had momentous consequences.

Despite all the activity and the phones ringing off the wall in intelligence headquarters at MACV, the officers and men at Cu Chi were not ready for what hit them. This is not at all surprising. The Division was not privy to all the information being collected in Saigon, and its own intelligence had been picking up signs of enemy activities for weeks. For most people at Cu Chi, the traditional Tet truce was anticipated as a welcome respite. There was little sign at the moment that anything particularly unusual was afoot; in Vietnam, let us remember, something unusual was always afoot. It was the nature of combat in Vietnam that American units always had their guard up. Nonetheless, no one expected the timing or the scope of events that began on 31 January 1968.

Sidney Stone, after rotating from his position with the artillery, was the 25th Division's historian and worked closely with Division intelligence. He recounts the shock of the opening hours of Tet and the speed with which the 3/4th Armored Cavalry reacted to the crisis growing outside Saigon:

I shared a Quonset hut with Division intelligence, and no one around me knew anything. There was just speculation all the time about when we were going to get mortared again. We knew there was an NVA regiment around Dau Tieng, but nobody had an inkling about attacks in our direct area. I was awakened about 3:00 A.M. by a real large boom. It was the first time that we had those large rockets coming in. We were surrounded by the better part of a Main Force regiment. We were cut off from Saigon by another regiment. I am sure there was at least one regiment attacking Tan Son Nhut. We didn't have any artillery because it was forward for the dry season operation north in Dau Tieng. We just didn't know. They have a saying in armor: "Re-gas, bypass, haul ass," and that's what the 3/4th did. They took off like a bat out of hell for Tan Son Nhut.

The orders sent to Cu Chi were simple, on paper. The Division was to dispatch the 3/4th Armored Cavalry immediately and have it meet representatives of the capital military district at Hoc Mon, a large suburban village of Saigon. At that point, higher command would take control of the unit. In the early morning hours of 31 January, however, the order posed great difficulties. Front units of all types were attacking targets throughout the Division's AO, and Cu Chi itself received a sustained bombardment of rockets and heavy mortars for days. Highway 1 was cut at several places. The Front also captured the village of Cu Chi, and an NVA unit seized the large village of Tan Phu Trung between Cu Chi and Hoc Mon. Because it was obviously a prime objective to sever Highway 1 and prevent units of the 25th from reaching Saigon, the entire area was swarming with smaller guerrilla units waiting in ambush.

In addition, armored units did not normally operate at night in Vietnam; because they were so noisy, vehicles were very vulnerable to ambush after dark. But the orders received by the 3/4th Armored Cavalry were urgent, and it was not a time for caution. Wisely, the battalion commander, Glenn Otis, instructed his men to make the trip using back trails and cross-country movement. Otis flew over the column, dropping flares to help the nearly blind tanks and APCs navigate the rough terrain. Before dawn, they arrived at Hoc Mon and, now under command of the capital military district, proceeded at once to Tan Son Nhut.

The men of C Troop were heading toward the most important single location in Vietnam. Although reporters were mesmerized by the sapper attack on the U.S. Embassy, the Front Main Force attacks on the nerve centers in and near the capital were far more crucial. The great bases at Bien Hoa and Long Binh were hit hard. So were all the major South Vietnamese government and military headquarters. But Tan Son Nhut was the greatest prize for the North. It was an enormous air base, with great intrinsic importance. Even more important, both MACV and the South Vietnamese Joint General Staff had their headquarters there. The destruction of MACV alone would have been an astounding victory for the North. Realizing this, the Front cleverly assembled a huge force that night, using a textile factory directly across Highway 1 from the base perimeter as a staging area. At 3:30 A.M., an enemy regiment attacked, quickly stormed through a gate, and headed for the base's defenses. Once inside, they encountered some ARVN troops and a makeshift unit of U.S. Air Force personnel, civilians, and South Vietnamese police. The enemy's initial attack was slowed down in the chaotic night fighting, but the advance went relentlessly forward.

C Troop smashed into the enemy's open flank some time around dawn, near the textile factory. Supported by some of their own helicopter gunships, American armor did great damage. At the crucial moment, they turned the locus of the battle from inside the base to outside, along Highway 1 near the textile mill. Armored vehicles fighting infantry in the open can do frightful damage, and C Troop did. But they were in over their heads. Their opponents were armed to the teeth with antitank weapons, and they greatly outnumbered the Americans. After fierce fighting, C Troop was nearly destroyed.

Back at Cu Chi, Colonel Otis was monitoring the battle over the radio. Hearing the beginning of what was obviously a crucial conflict, he alerted the rest of the cavalry to prepare to move and took off for Tan Son Nhut in his helicopter. Unfortunately for the Americans, an NVA unit hit A Troop, stationed near the Vam Co Dong, and tied it down. Otis soon ordered B Troop at Trang Bang, now operating in early light, to hustle down Highway 1 and use its speed and firepower to punch through the opposition. In the meantime, Otis, flying toward the battle, heard serious news:

En route to Tan Son Nhut, I monitored C Troop radio frequency. It turned out that the radio was keyed continuously, and the only voice was a single trooper crying for help. Obviously seriously wounded, he had keyed the set so he and he alone could speak, and it was not coherent. It was clear that C Troop was in dire trouble.

Upon arrival, the scene was one of complete disarray. C Troop had obviously been hit from its right flank while it was in column on the main road, right near the gate of Tan Son Nhut. Several vehicles were burning and destroyed. The few left that were operational were deployed along the road, and some were just inside the wire of the base. Very little fire was being returned by C Troop when I arrived because there were very few survivors able to do that. Meanwhile, heavy fighting was going on in and around Tan Son Nhut. Later, we were to find out the extent of the attack. C Troop, in effect, split that attack but did so at great sacrifice to itself.

Meanwhile, there was much activity in the C Troop area, with aircraft from various units trying to interdict the attack of the remaining North Vietnamese regiment. All during this period, some of the casualties from C Troop were evacuated, including the troop commander, who had received a life-threatening head wound. There were no officers left in C Troop to provide command and control, and very few people were left to fight. A few survivors had managed to get some dismounted weapons to use in ground support. In fact, one of C Troop's tanks was actually occupied by the enemy, but before it could be brought into action, one of our men was able to get back to the tank and put some hand grenades in the turret and effectively silence it.

Back near Trang Bang, B Troop was spread out over several miles of Highway 1, guarding bridges. Dave Garrod recalls that the men of his track were unprepared for the events that unfolded. The evening before, they had befriended a local family and had received a Tet dinner. The men had gone to bed in a rare mood of good cheer but were abruptly awakened in the early morning hours. As Garrod's description makes clear, the Front used every possible resource during the Tet Offensive:

Our sleep was abruptly interrupted by the sounds of a firefight near the bridge on Highway 1. A small unit of Viet Cong soldiers had crept in under the cover of darkness to within 10 yards of the bridge and would have blown it up had it not been for a well-placed trip flare that illuminated it, allowing our men to bring effective fire. When the firing stopped and we walked up onto the bridge to observe the aftermath, I was surprised to find the Viet Cong dead were elderly men, probably in their fifties. The vivid memory of an old man spread-eagle, naked except for a loin cloth, lying on his back in a tangle of wire will always be with me.

While waiting for B Troop, Otis and his pilot were kept busy. Otis lost the first of his two helicopters that morning and crash-landed at Tan Son Nhut. With a new helicopter, he ran a supply of much-needed ammunition to the unusual Air Force battle group holding the line inside the base. Losing another helicopter, Otis was back in the air just in time to issue orders to B Troop as it arrived at about 10:00 A.M. Otis's account, fully corroborated by II Field Force reports of the action, presents the development of a classic military maneuver with unusual clarity:

Visualize the main highway, with C Troop and its remnants scattered along the highway and inside the fence at Tan Son Nhut and its weapons facing to the west. B Troop was coming from north to south down Highway 1. When B Troop got to the vicinity of a big factory just to the north of Tan Son Nhut, I had the lead tank make a column right, with all the other combat vehicles of B Troop following that lead tank at 90 degrees to Highway 1. Once the last vehicle of B Troop had cleared off Highway 1 heading west, I had the lead tank and the entire column stop. At that point, I ordered them to do a left flank. This brought B Troop on line on the left flank of this entire enemy regiment, at a distance of about 2,500 meters. I told the B Troop commander to attack on line. His attack to the south would bring him right across the remnants of C Troop, facing to the west. The troop commander carried out this entire maneuver with superb reactions. With B Troop attacking the flank of the regiment and D Troop and other air assets attacking from over-head, the Vietnamese regiment was caught in a tremendous trap. They could not move to the east because of Charlie Troop and its remnants defending the air base. They were being attacked from the north by B Troop, and they were effectively in a complete box. The attack was a complete success. Many of the Vietnamese that could escape to the west did so, leaving behind weapons and equipment in great numbers.

The factory on Highway 1, it turned out, was loaded with enemy troops and was a storehouse of enemy equipment. Our first indication of this took place when B Troop took fire from the upper windows of the factory and had to divert some of its tanks to bring that factory under fire. As soon as possible, I asked for Air Force support to attack that factory. They did ex-actly that and silenced it with several sorties of fighter bombers. Although the bombing was effective at silencing the enemy, I was surprised how little damage was actually done to the factory. Later on, in the next two days, an-other battalion cleared the factory and found it loaded with weapons and large stockpiles of ammo. It had obviously been used as a staging area for the North Vietnamese attack.

An individual on the battlefield can rarely see a large portion of what is taking place. And events close by, naturally, are of the greatest importance to anyone at risk. To Dave Garrod and the men on his track, the advance possessed a more episodic nature than their commander was able to wit-ness. As Garrod relates, no one knew what to expect:

We really had no idea what size of an enemy unit we were coming up against, and we could only guess what we were in for. It was extremely difficult to keep our concentration focused while listening to one of the survivors from Troop C, who had his radio key open, pleading for help.

We advanced across a recently harvested rice paddy that was now dry and still had shocks of rice stalks randomly stacked around the field. After some time, it became apparent that the source of some of the small-arms fire was from these shocks of rice stalks, or "haystacks." Evidently, we had surprised the enemy when we entered the field, and some of them took cover inside these haystacks. In short order, we had five or six bonfires going, and not long after that, 8 to 10 enemy soldiers came running out of their hiding places with hands up. Remaining stacks were blown away with tank fire.

Periodically during the day, we received fire from a large factory to our north. This was one of the "no-fire zones" around Saigon. Finally, in the afternoon, we received permission to return fire and handed the task over to Troop D, our air support company of helicopters. By the time we left the area that evening, the factory had been reduced to a pile of twisted metal siding and roofing.

The 3/4th Armored Cavalry's brilliant victory at Tan Son Nhut was the 25th Division's finest single hour during its tour in Vietnam. At the most critical moment faced by the Division's forces, these men performed magnificently. We can see, in retrospect, that the first day's actions, repeated by other U.S. and South Vietnamese units around Saigon, doomed the Front's attack on the capital. But at the time, of course, this was not at all clear. The Division had passed the most crucial test. Most of the fighting, however, was still to come.

In the next few days, elements of the 25th Division streamed toward the suburbs of Saigon. The first to get out were several companies of infantry from the *Wolfhounds*. Already in combat near Cu Chi, Gerry Schooler witnessed the exhausted men's hurried departure:

We went into Cu Chi for a stand down. We were in for about an hour or two. I remember sitting there eating, and some courier came, and all the officers jumped up and headed for a meeting. We hadn't changed clothes or taken a shower. Normally, a stand down would last three days or so. But the word came back within 30 minutes for us to saddle up. This was the beginning of Tet. Everybody was bummed out because we thought we were going to have a little time off, but we didn't know what was going on. But when we got in the choppers, we could see that something was different this time, that it wasn't just another eagle flight.

It was dark by the time we took off. Everywhere you looked, you could see firefights. Every little ARVN compound, everywhere, there were firefights. You could see the tracers everywhere. Every American unit out in the boonies was engaged: It was a remarkable sight to see that much going on. When you're up at that level, about 2,000 feet I think, you could see firefights many miles away because of the tracers. And it was tremendous, like looking at the Milky Way galaxy. And below were all of these embers from the napalm: During the dry season, everything tended to catch on fire. The ground was lit up by glowing embers, with all the smoke. We realized that something big was going on.

The lucky thing for us was that we landed right next to MACV headquarters or right beside it. It was a nice thing. We got to go into an air-conditioned building and watch a movie while all hell was breaking loose outside. I saw Westmoreland about 50 meters away, so we were close to the big shots. Rumor had it we were transferred after a day or two because we weren't clean enough. Tell you the truth, I think they just needed us outside in the field. Any Air Force guy in starched fatigues could have done what we were doing. One thing is for sure: Nobody knew that this Tet thing was going to happen. When our officers jumped up in the middle of their meal, we could see there wasn't any warning.

The Cu Chi–Saigon corridor was not the only area the enemy attacked. It was part of Front strategy to attack everywhere possible at once to maximize the shock value and hopefully tie down American forces. Ron Hart was at Tay Ninh with his mechanized unit on the eve of Tet:

We all knew when we returned from the field in late January that things were going to be quiet in Tay Ninh base camp. After all, this was Tet, the Vietnamese new year celebration. We were wrong. Midmorning, we got the word that we were ordered to go to the perimeter and fire anything we had; it appeared we were being overrun. Ammo dumps were being detonated by incoming mortars and rockets, and all hell was breaking loose. VC were found the next day tangled up in the concertina wire, dead. Nobody knows whether these guys were drugged to attack without concern for themselves or just desperate to attack. We knew now no place was safe and we could be attacked at any time, even in a "secure" base camp like Tay Ninh. When I returned to Cu Chi later, I saw the same devastation, just on a larger scale.

The *Wolfhounds* back at Tan Son Nhut had a short lull before the furious fighting around Hoc Mon began. Gerry Schooler paints an eerie portrait of the battleground outside the base perimeter:

Our job that morning was to sweep our area of the perimeter, I think the west, and we started going down Highway 1. The thing I remember is that there was not one thing alive there. Chickens, ducks, people, nothing: Not one thing was alive. Nothing could survive in that small area. It was right outside the wire where they had made their attempt to breach the perimeter. There were VC sappers strung up along the wire, so you could see what they were trying to do. They couldn't do it, just too much firepower. I still remember there was some type of enemy soldier lying in the road. A truck had run over his head. He was already dead, no doubt. But the truck pushed his skull right out of his face: The teeth and the bone were separated from his head. But his hair was still there, and you could still see his eyes and ears. He was just lying in the road, looking straight up. I remember the road was full of these lovely Vietnamese girls, many part French, in their white dresses,

riding their bikes to college with their books under their arms. I don't know
how you could have class while this was going on. My friend and I were
standing next to this crushed guy on the road, after this horrid battle, and
there were these hundreds of people riding by on their mopeds, bikes, and
Lambrettas. The battle had ended maybe three or four hours before. We
watched the people riding by and looking at this guy lying right in the middle of the road. They would take a long look. It was a bizarre sight, with the
guy's eyes still open. You should have seen the people's expressions. Like us,
none of them had ever seen anything like that.

   We continued down the road. Me and another guy were assigned to go
down this row of houses, not really hooches, made out of stucco and all connected. We were going door to door, making sure there wasn't anybody hiding out. We heard a little racket in one, and it was wind or something, but it
was spooky, like an episode in the show we used to watch called "Twilight
Zone." There wasn't any life anywhere. Everything was dead. It was so quiet,
and then you heard a tapping or something. Anyway, we went into this
house, and everything had been messed up. The roof was hit by something,
and the place was torn up. We didn't find any adults, but in the very back,
under this table, we found these two kids, obviously brother and sister,
about five, embraced, no doubt because they were so frightened. They were
dead, of course. Who knows who killed them. It's another thing I will always
remember. This was a day after Tet. Things did not feel like a movie anymore. It was the horror that you read about when you grow up. If my mind
could be transposed to film, I could remember probably about thirty good
or really meaningful shots. That was one of them.

   Dennis Hackin had joined his mechanized unit in October. Luckily, he
had seen very little heavy fighting. That changed abruptly in early February:

My tour of duty in Nam can be divided in two: life before Tet and life after
Tet. We had been brought down from Nui Ba Din to the outskirts of Saigon.
I remember it was a night drive, and everybody was on full alert. Running
the roads at night wasn't a fun cruise. And then, as we neared the Hoc Mon
Bridge, somebody pointed up and yelled, "Look!" We all looked up and noticed a Red Star flag hanging over the road on a telephone line. The NVA was
near, and they were telling us they were ready.

Hoc Mon had already been hit. For the first time, Vietnam really looked
like the documentary war footage I grew up watching on television. Up a
road on both sides was a burned-out village. Tanks, tracks, trucks, jeeps were
burned and destroyed. We spent days searching the area for the NVA, but we
couldn't find them—only NVA bodies. Also, I found an American soldier

buried. I remember his name because when I was going through basic training at Fort Bliss, we had a sergeant with that name. I don't know to this day if it was the same man. His face had been shot off.

On 14 February 1968, we were given orders to pull out. Second Platoon (my platoon) was in the rear guard. We were doing some last-minute sweeping of the area. We broke for lunch. My squad was at the far end. We were all eating C rations when we heard the firefight start. We rushed over to an area where the rest of the platoon was pinned downed, and then we got pinned down. What we found out immediately was that Lieutenant Williams and his squad were hit inside the village area. (We later found out they walked right into an NVA battalion's perimeter.) Well, the war finally happened.

February 14 is my parents' wedding anniversary. I'm not the most religious guy, but I remember asking God not to take me on that day because it wouldn't be good for my folks. Not a whole lot of logic; when the man's ready to take you, it don't matter what holiday it is. But, at the time, when you're sucking the ground with your buddies, a little prayer goes a long way. Later in the day, we were pulled out. We had to leave Lieutenant Williams and his squad. Some of the guys who saw them go down didn't think they were alive. I remember all night hoping they had found cover and were just waiting for us to go back in and get them. It was not to be.

We spent the next five days maneuvering around Hoc Mon, confronting the NVA. By 19 February, Charlie Company, 1/5th Mechanized, was inoperable. What had started out as a full company on the 14th (183 guys) wound up with less than 50 men still on the ground. I was very lucky. I was one of 3 guys who didn't get wounded in 2d Platoon. My platoon turned out to be the hard-luck platoon. We took the most casualties. Besides losing Lieutenant Williams's squad, we had another lieutenant come out to take over, and he was seriously wounded. For the next five months, except for a brief period, our platoon was run by Sergeant Polk. During the brief period I spoke of, we had a second lieutenant take over the platoon. I don't even remember his name. I do remember he was stubborn and wouldn't listen to the old-timers and got himself killed. He didn't last three weeks.

Jerry Liucci was with the *Wolfhounds* during the bitter fighting around Hoc Mon. As he points out, the enemy, for once, was not fighting in his backyard. Most of the enemy Main Force soldiers were ignorant of the terrain, and American ambush patrols, normally futile, scored several major successes. Large engagements were almost always American victories. Liucci recounts the result of a bungled night attack on his unit's perimeter:

One night, we could smell a lot of pot through the woods; probably some of it was our own. We heard a lot of noise, yelling and screaming, and we even heard "Take Five" by Dave Brubeck as dusk was coming on. We just had this gut feeling it was going to be heavy. The medic looked at me and said, "I got this bad feeling: I think we're going to get hit tonight." We dug in a lot better than usual. We had triple concertina wire set up, claymores, and tripwires, and we even cut some fields of fire.

Our platoon went out on night ambush about 2 clicks away. About 0200, we heard lots of fire from the perimeter. There was squawking on the radio between our companies. There was penetration on the bunker line, and the enemy was repulsed. It got really heavy. It was very dark, and from the distance, we could see tracers and hear explosions. We were ordered in. We humped in just before dawn, and fighting was still going on. There were over 100 bodies. Later that day, we found more surface graves. To give you an idea of how steadfast the people were that we were fighting: I found a dead VC medic who had tied himself to a bamboo clump, with a morphine syringe stuck in his arm. He had a large wound in the leg and a large wound in the arm and had bled to death. He had an RPG at the ready, with the safety off. He had mortified. We had him blown up because he was like a booby trap himself. Another guy was clutching one of our claymores when we shot him: He was going to try to command-detonate himself on our perimeter. That impressed me. When a person is willing to do that, he must have a pretty strong will. When we were sweeping the perimeter, a VC jumped up and killed one of our guys. We killed him, but that really got the better of us. Amazing.

Not everything went well for the soldiers of the Tropic Lightning Division. On 2 March, they suffered their worst defeat of the war outside of Saigon. Despite heavy fighting in the area, the enemy ambushed and destroyed a company of the 4/9th Infantry (*Manchus*). The company had 49 men killed and 29 wounded during a very short exchange. Todd Dexter was serving in another *Manchu* company nearby and describes what happened:

Artillery hit the area hard throughout the night, and in the morning, Charlie Company—the lead element for the battalion—moved down the blacktop road. Being in the area for a week now, they relaxed to the point where they had no flank security—a very dangerous move. When they got two canals down and saw the pedestrians turn and pedal away on their bicycles, they should have suspected something, but they continued to march into a quarter-of-a-mile-long, sudden death ambush that snuffed out 48 lives, wounded 30 others, and left 11 unaccounted for, all before anyone knew what happened.

All communication was lost between Charlie Company and the rest of the battalion. It was thought that the command group had been wiped out. We found their commander later. He was wounded but all right. He said that gooks were running all over the place, grabbing our weapons and shooting. He called the artillery so close that he was injured himself. While all that was going on, we were called up. After 5 hours, all of the bodies were collected. A ³/₄-ton truck was lifted in to help haul the bodies.

The battalion commander had been having a conflict with Division over how he ran the battalion. The battalion commander was crying and kept saying, over and over, "I've got *Manchus* lying all over the road down there." He was up in his helicopter, and I heard the whole thing on the radio. It was really sad. The day was too much, and the battalion commander requested to be relieved of his duty. He was replaced by a hard-core sonofabitch whose first statement was, "We will never break contact with the enemy." Our old commander loved this battalion, I know. He used to make the hump with us whenever possible. Believe it or not, he knew most of the short-timers by name.

Before we set up for the night, we made a sweep of the entire area. The road where the ambush took place was catacombed with trenches and bunkers, and they were stocked with medical supplies and food. The enemy, patient once again, was waiting for us to use that road.

Although initially defeated around Saigon, the enemy had carefully reserved a large force for the anticipated second and third stages of the attack. Westmoreland assigned much of Tay Ninh province to other American units and ordered the bulk of the 25th Division pulled to the Trang Bang–Cu Chi–Saigon area. In March, the NVA smashed across the Cambodian border and attacked Trang Bang. The NVA forces were turned back with terrible losses, but several 25th Division units were, in turn, ambushed until the NVA was finally routed.

In May, the Front sent its remaining reserves against Saigon once more. On the alert, ARVN forces turned them away inside the city. Just as in February, however, ugly fighting erupted as the Front forces tried to get close to Saigon and then again as they tried to flee. Lt. Col. Carl Neilson's 4/23d Mechanized Infantry Battalion established three company-sized perimeters within firing distance of each other. Expecting enemy activity, security was high. At about 10:30 P.M., an NVA regiment, one of the enemy units that had attacked Tan Son Nhut three months before, attacked the battalion. His troops badly outnumbered, Neilson had some very anxious moments:

I had been sweeping that day, looking unsuccessfully in the rice paddies, and had come back into a three-company laager, a laager being a formation where we would circle our wagons just like the pioneers did with the Indians. They were usually arrayed on a north/south aspect, linked like a necklace with interlocking zones of fire between the companies. We were located in a rice field area, and most of the vehicles (but not all of them) were behind berms. About 10:30 that night, the first attack occurred on the north perimeter. In what later turned out to be a battalion-sized attack, the 1st Battalion of the 271 NVA Regiment threw itself at A Company. Not being able to penetrate, it bounced back, moved south, and resumed the attack against the middle company. In the meantime, the 2d Battalion of the 271 Regiment, moving forward in a column, engaged the northernmost company. I had two companies engaged by two battalions and the third company waiting patiently. The first Vietnamese battalion attempted to disengage again and move farther south and flank the laager position, and it ran into the third company. The second enemy battalion also attempted to move south. By this time, the third NVA unit ran into my company on the north. I then had three companies engaged fully with three battalions of the North Vietnamese. I was being supported by a U.S. Air Force gunship, which was dropping flares and firing around my perimeter. I had the brigade commander overhead offering me encouragement over the radio. He was shortly joined by the division commander, who offered me more encouragement. Eventually, the field force commander joined in, all of them offering encouragement. It was perhaps comforting, but there really wasn't much for them to do.

We fought on through most of the night, and when first dawn broke, we were still fully engaged. This was very unusual because the NVA typically broke off an engagement when dawn broke and fell back so they could regroup. They didn't ever want to be caught out in the open. Apparently, something went wrong, and when daylight came, the three enemy battalions were out in the rice fields with no place to go. And there I was. Perhaps fortunately for the North Viets, I was virtually out of ammunition. The Air Force began to send sorties of jets. This went on from 6:30 in the morning until 10:00, when I ran out of ammunition. The North Vietnamese couldn't leave, they couldn't attack, there wasn't anything they could do. They were being decimated. I was ordered to saddle up and make some sort of attack, but I pointed out that I was out of ammunition and that I had a number of casualties. Luckily, a chopper got through, and we were resupplied with ammunition.

All of a sudden, here came Glenn Otis at the head of the 3/4 horse [3/4th Armored Cavalry—EMB]. He had heard about our battle, and the Division commander had sent him to my aid. He came overland for 2 or 3 hours and galloped up, much like the U.S. Cavalry did in the movies. He formed up a line of APCs and tanks on either side of my position. I gathered my troops together. By this time, we had ammunition, and we were loaded up. We swept forward, and as we did, there was just an absolute scene of carnage like I have never experienced. There were bodies and parts of bodies and weapons and equipment all over the area. We drove through that, and it was at this time that we captured 15 to 20 POWs and lots of equipment. It was in that period that Glenn Otis was shot off the top of his tank by a North Vietnamese RPG and very seriously wounded in the hand, was evacuated, and never returned to his battalion. He did recover, however, and went on to become a four-star general and retired as commander of U.S. Army Forces, Europe. At the end of that day, we had a terrible accident where a box of claymore mines went off in an armored personnel carrier and killed 5 soldiers. We had fought all night and all day, had swept the battlefield, had suffered 5 or so men killed and about 10 men wounded, and had inflicted 400 casualties, and then, right at the very end, 5 guys were killed through the carelessness of somebody who had left a set of detonators in with the claymore mines. I guess that is kind of the story of Vietnam combat. There were moments of sheer terror and high exhilaration, feelings of triumph, and then feelings of sheer loss and desperation and worthlessness—great swings of emotion.

The fighting in May was a catastrophe for the Front, and they were forced to regroup. A welcome lull set in. The respite was only momentary, however. The 25th Division was ordered to keep a large force near the capital. MACV, well aware of the turmoil in the States, no doubt was eager to avoid a repeat of Tet. This left one brigade of the 25th guarding much of Tay Ninh province. In mid-August, the NVA attacked Tay Ninh with a very large force. MACV feared it was a feint and refused reinforcements to the 25th units. But MACV was very much in error: Tay Ninh was the objective, not a feint. Curiously, Westmoreland had frequently worried that the enemy might try to seize Tay Ninh City and set up a provisional capital. Obviously, Gen. Creighton Abrams did not. For ten days, American units engaged in a running battle that saw examples of every kind of large-scale combat experienced in Vietnam. There were painful ambushes, battles of maneuver, and NVA assaults on firebases. In retrospect, the brigade commander, Col. Duke Wolf, believes that the enemy forces could have seized Dau Tieng had they realized how weak defenses had become. Nevertheless, the 25th again showed its superiority in conventional combat and forced the battered NVA to retreat.

At this time, the Front and Hanoi made one of their worst mistakes of the war. The fighting during 1968 had cost them dearly. Naturally, Hanoi heralded the bombing halt and the peace talks in Paris as great victories. It also claimed that Lyndon Johnson's demise was a step toward triumph. Inside Vietnam, however, the scene was radically different. Every peasant in the country knew what had happened. The Front had promised victory and had raised taxes to pay for it. Yet, at the end of the year, the U.S. Army controlled the battlefield, and the Saigon "puppet forces" were stronger than ever. Instead of going back to the very successful mix of a people's war punctuated with large defensive battles, Hanoi decided to go on the offensive once more. This time, however, American units were the target. No doubt, this decision was influenced by another event of the recent past, the Geneva Convention in 1954. During the Geneva negotiations, the Viet Minh followed the strategy of "talk-talk, fight-fight." Events in the United States fourteen years later showed how sensitive the country was to American casualties. An offensive that emphasized sharp attacks by elite sapper units and large ambushes along the long road network used by the Americans therefore seemed to offer Hanoi the opportunity to maintain the diplomatic pressure, keep the military initiative, and weaken American morale. What resulted, however, was a bloodbath that nearly destroyed the Front and left the NVA reeling.

The 1969 Tet Offensive is best seen as part of a larger, sustained enemy campaign that began in January 1968. In this phase of the offensive, the allied forces had no need to charge off at top speed to attack communist forces. Instead, the Front and NVA came to the soldiers of the Tropic Lightning Division, for the 25th was the primary objective of the opening attacks. Exactly as had happened the year before, the major offensive was preceded by a significant upswing in fighting. Mickey Andrews had been in the field with his mechanized platoon for forty-five days. He was already on the way to being considered an old-timer when his unit confronted catastrophe:

Our medic, Steve, who we called "Doc," like every other medic in Vietnam, became one of my best buddies. He had already been decorated for bravery. I had studied pharmacy in college; he was in premed. So we became good friends because of our similar interests and education. We also shared a couple of close encounters with danger. Our platoon leader was a lieutenant who was very well liked and respected. He had a sense of humor. While I was there, he became a new father.

On 8 January 1969, while operating in the Boi Loi, my platoon was ambushed by a recon platoon of NVA regulars. After moving through thick jungle, we reached a clearing. One of our men spotted a freshly dug fighting position. Our lieutenant ordered it checked out. A Puerto Rican soldier walked up to the hole. A grenade was tossed at him from behind, and the ambush was triggered. The soldier up front ran a few feet and fell flat: The grenade missed him. Everyone began jumping off the tracks. Just as I was about to jump, the driver hit the gas and lurched forward, throwing me off. I managed to land on all fours and started to run for cover. It was total confusion. The tracks began turning around to face the enemy fire. The Puerto Rican soldier ran up to me, speaking only in Spanish: He was too excited for English. I saw my buddy Steve and another friend out front. I ran forward out of one of the closest instincts in combat—to be near my buddies. I ran to join them and raised my rifle to fire a burst for cover as they ran past me. I never got off a single round. A RPG hit almost at Steve's feet and killed him instantly. My other buddy was also hit and died shortly after in a half-sitting position, propped up by his arm, eyes fixed. The same blast threw me in the air. My hearing was gone momentarily, and everything seemed to be in slow motion. I landed in a heap on the ground and never saw either my helmet or rifle again. Shaken and dazed, I foolishly tried to run but could not move. A second RPG slammed into my track, and I received a neck wound from another piece of shrapnel.

This time, I stayed down and started crawling. I crawled by my buddy and watched him draw his last breath. I made a feeble gesture to dress his wound but realized he was dead. I saw our lieutenant run toward me, holding his chest with both hands. He looked as if he knew he was dying but could not believe it. He ran another few yards and fell. Two other wounded men and myself started crawling farther. We were still very close to the enemy. I finally rolled into a small shell hole, and the other two continued crawling. That was when I started praying out loud. The only thing I could say was "Oh, God, let me make it," over and over. I expected to be shot or bayoneted soon. My prayers were answered in those anxious minutes but not as you might think. I strongly felt as if I would die, but I was not afraid. The answer to my prayer was not the assurance of continued life but, rather, peace and calmness in the face of death. It changed my attitude about a lot of things.

Our second platoon came to the rescue, guns blazing. One of their medics found me and said the magic words: "You're okay, everything's intact. Looks like the million-dollar wound!" I had been hit in eight places. On the helicopter, the pain really started. They gave me a morphine shot and flew toward the 12th Evac at Cu Chi.

The major offensive began with large but futile assaults on Tay Ninh and Dau Tieng in late February. Cu Chi had already been visited from the inside. In January, a "hooch maid" planted a bomb in an engineer mess hall that killed 15 men when it detonated. On 26 February, the NVA launched a large sapper assault on Cu Chi. It was a chaotic and embarrassing moment for the Division. Jim Murphy witnessed the disorder:

I remember the sapper attack on the base camp quite well. I was assigned as a battalion guard, which normally is a piece of cake; but this time, I was in for a rude awakening. Around 3:00 A.M., we were awakened by a large racket and went outside to see what was causing the commotion. Our sector on the perimeter was lit up like a Christmas tree, and we were concerned with our buddies out there who we had been bullshitting with a few short hours ago. The sirens went off, and we were loaded into trucks and told we were going out there as a reaction force. On our way, we drove straight into an ambush that can only be described as a light-and-sound show. It's like being a few feet away from fireworks going off. I became separated from my group and stumbled toward the command post. Needless to say, the rising of the sun was a welcome sight. On a sad note, troops manning the sector by the airstrip dozed off on watch and were found the next morning with their throats slit. Although I didn't know these guys, their fate has stayed with me to this day. Had those poor fools stayed awake, they would have been partying in Washington in November 1982, instead of having their names chiseled on a black wall.

The sappers succeeded in getting onto Cu Chi air base and destroyed several helicopters. The assault, except for the small number of casualties, was more of an embarrassment than a defeat. The people at Cu Chi had grown used to attacks, and the mortar and rocket attacks that started in earnest during Tet 1968 continued sporadically through the 1969 offensive. Maj. Robert Broyles served there throughout 1968 and describes the working conditions caused by regular bombardment:

There was an intensity about Cu Chi that was unusual during Tet because Tet signaled throughout Vietnam a new level of activity, which, after the initial shock and flurry of activity in those areas most affected, remained at a very high level all the time I was there. The tension was there, even in the center of the camp. With the shelling mostly during the night but occasionally during the day, you had a routine that was anything but that. Things were not frantic. People were professionals. New people become accustomed, to the extent that one can, to that sort of tension in your daily activities. But you developed a routine of doing your job and absorbed the rocket attacks and alerts into your job and didn't dwell on it. I am reminded of one young man working with us who was killed during a daytime rocket attack. Outside our offices, we had sandbagged bunkers. Everyone was trained, like a fire drill, to tell the rhythm of these attacks: There would be an initial barrage, then a lull as they reloaded, and then another barrage when they re-loaded. We were very carefully instructed as to what to do. The young man killed was not new and had been through these before. We'll never know his reasoning, but during a barrage, he went to his bunker as he was supposed to do and then went to another bunker. A rocket landed nearby, shrapnel severed a vein in his leg, and he bled to death almost instantly before anyone could do anything for him.

Whatever plans the enemy had to keep casualties down through the use of elite troops were disbanded very quickly. In some ways, the quality of Communist forces was declining, and heavy casualties do not improve morale in any army. Front forces, in particular, lost a very high percentage of their best men in 1968. They were forced to rely more and more upon North Vietnamese replacements. These new men, however well trained, did not know the area, and they could not fit into the village landscape the way earlier Front guerrillas did. American troops had also become extremely wise to the methods of the enemy. Bill Noyes witnessed a sapper attack in late February against the perimeter held by his mechanized unit. As Noyes relates, catastrophe awaited the enemy on that occasion:

As the second group of sappers regrouped and began their slow, final advance, our ambush patrol outside the wire detected some movement. The word spread by the company radio net, and, as we listened, the 6 men outside received permission to reenter the wire. They moved quickly without blowing their claymore mines. The perimeter was alerted, and most were awake. Each bunker guard strained intently at the night shadows before him. Finally, word spread that the main starlight scope at the command bunker had again spotted movement and fixed the position of the second group of sappers. Rounds were chambered, and the mortar positions prepared to fire. The camp waited, and more minutes slowly passed.

Far away, artillery and helicopter units were alerted by higher command. The sappers crept a little closer, past the vacated ambush site. Then the other group was spotted by the bunker to my left. Their yells were enough to notify the command bunker, but their radio report was being monitored at each track.

Shortly, they received permission to fire, and with their beginning shots, the rest of the bunker line began machine-gun and .50-caliber fire. Though the smaller group of sappers was between us and the village, direct fire toward the village was sparse. Only when the attackers answered with some desultory fire did we know for certain that they were there, and we directed our fire at those sure targets. Soon, our mortar platoon was putting flares up.

As the outgunned enemy tried to fire back, our fire became less random. His few RPGs were answered by long bursts from our .50s, while our other guns pecked away everywhere. The two hapless groups of men now mostly hid, endured, and awaited their opportunity to fire back or escape.

Artillery began to crash into the tree lines, and artillery flares fell, as well. The enemy were still hard to see apart from the clumps of grass and the wavy ground. Then flareships and gunships began to arrive. The gunship would circle like a ghost, its machine guns stitching a merciless staccato into the enemy ground. Later, when all was quiet, my platoon mounted up and made a sweep of the area.

There lay the enemy dead. Our tension was intense as we maneuvered our tracks in the dull, shifting flare light between the small clusters of poorly seen and motionless shadows. A machine gunner was ordered to dismount and search for prisoners. There were none to be taken, and he dispatched a couple of the living dead. Back inside the wire, the gunner told of his anguish, and we all agreed that it had to be done. No one would have wanted to do the job in his stead.

In the morning, there were 28 dead accounted for. They lay in small clusters and alone. One group of 3 was pressed into the same small rocket crater where they had sought shelter. It seemed not so much grisly as extremely sad. Our casualties were slight, with 1 wounded in our squad.

The change in the tactical momentum was evident in the nonstop combat during the spring of 1969. Several times, sweeps through rough terrain, which had previously yielded nothing, resulted in the discovery of enemy units. Usually, discovery meant catastrophe. The enemy tried dozens of large ambushes during the period. Some succeeded in wreaking havoc on 25th Division tracks and infantrymen, but more often, the ambushers themselves ended up the quarry. Stymied on every front, the enemy fell back on frequent assaults on American perimeters. All were horrible failures.

In April, 25th Division commanders pulled off their greatest success using the tethered goat tactic. In the morning, elements of the *Manchus* and engineers were taken by helicopter to a place right on the Cambodian border. They built a firebase called Frontier City in less than a day. That night, the NVA attacked and were crushed, with the Americans suffering only 1 wounded.

Gene Trask flew his helicopter in support of two of these assaults in June. He describes the scene from both air and ground:

I was there, over Firebase Crook on 6, 7, and 8 June 1969 when the enemy tried a mass attack. It was a sight to behold! Our ship was circling at around

3,000 feet, trying to stay out of the way of gunships, jets, and a "spooky" gunship that was constantly firing its several miniguns around the perimeter of the firebase. There were several enemy .51-caliber machine guns firing up at us. Around 3:00 A.M., all of a sudden, our cockpit lit up with an orange glow, as tracer rounds from a .51-caliber surrounded our helicopter. We took four hits, and immediately, we went into a rapid descent to elude the machine guns. Our transmission and fuel gauges showed a rapid drop in fluids, so we low-leveled at treetop height back to Tay Ninh base camp. We made it back to base camp, but the machine ran out of fluids just moments after we touched down.

I remember one time landing at Firebase Washington near the base of Nui Ba Den after a vicious battle the night before. We landed just after dawn. Enemy soldiers were lying everywhere. As I stepped out of the helicopter, I had to step over a dying Viet Cong whose guts were cupped in his hands as he lay on his back. His eyes met mine, and I quickly turned away. The smell of death was overpowering. I felt so bad for this human being lying there in the grass with his life ebbing from him. I wondered if he also had a wife and children waiting at home for him. I was also aware that he would probably kill me in an instant if he could.

Trask saw one of the last enemy assaults of the campaign. In July, enemy activity fell off greatly and never returned to an intense level in the Division's AO while it was in Vietnam. But the 25th Division paid a high price. In the year-and-a-half General Offensive that began in January 1968, killed and wounded levels were at their highest of the war. The battle casualties of the combat units were nearly as bad as those on World War II battlefields. Nor was the pain over. Vietnam was dangerous from first to last. The Main Force war never returned, except for the foray into Cambodia, but the daily "chase for Charlie" was always fraught with hazard.

Yet, the 25th Division was a combat unit. It is not unreasonable to judge it as one. Despite many sad hours, many tactical reverses, and many mistakes, when all was said and done, the Tropic Lightning Division fought a fierce and brave enemy for a year and a half and ultimately crushed him. I can think of no better compliment to pay the 25th Division as a fighting unit than to state this obvious truth.

Above the Earth and Below

Most large military campaigns are marked by some unique factor—perhaps geographical, like the sands of North Africa, perhaps tactical, like the trench lines of World War I—with which the men involved come to identify their experience. I have already discussed the overall terrain and the climate of Vietnam and the strong impression they made on the men there, as well as their great influence on operations. There were, however, two battlefields that the 25th Division troops fought on that were uniquely theirs in Vietnam: the Black Virgin Mountain, a freak of nature, and the labyrinthine tunnels created by the men they fought.

Nui Ba Den—the Black Virgin Mountain—was one of the oddest battlefields in American military history. It was a 3,000-foot granite slab, rising in total isolation from a flat plain. The Black Virgin had sister mountains farther south but none where American troops were stationed. Perfectly shaped, it was a thing of rare beauty. Men could see it on a clear day from anywhere within the area of operations if their view was not blocked by a tree line. Right on the southern edge of War Zone C, the peak of the mountain was a natural location for an observation post. U.S. Special Forces established one on the top before the 25th arrived. Soon after deployment, the Division assumed responsibility for guarding the signal station, and the rough terrain at the base of the mountain was also more or less controlled by the 25th Division. In between, however, entrenched in nearly invulnerable granite caves, was the enemy. It is hard to say how many from the other side inhabited the mountain. Americans claimed that rockets were hidden in the caves and fired at 25th Division positions. U.S. troops made sporadic patrols—sometimes from the bottom up, sometimes from the top down—and frequently, these patrols ended in deadly ambush. The enemy periodically attacked the Americans at the top but never dislodged them. So an uneasy status quo resulted. The Americans had their communications at the top and controlled the approaches below. In between lay the enemy. Both sides had what they wanted, and neither wanted to risk large casualties to seize what the other had. As Michael Call remembers, however, the status quo in November 1968 was uneasy and menacing:

Nui Ba Den was the only mountain for miles and miles in our area of operations. I mean, it sticks out like a sore thumb. It got everybody's attention, especially the VC. Seems like we had a whole load of communications equipment that was critical to the operations in the Saigon area and perhaps more than that. So we were assigned to handle the security for the radio jocks.

Roughly translated, Nui Ba Den means "Black Virgin Mountain." Well, the mountain is not black at all, except where napalm and artillery have scored her flanks. And by no means could she be considered a virgin; this mountain had fucked up many a troop. We in Bravo Company had heard about our sister company getting pounded pretty hard previously and also the story concerning the Special Forces group that got overrun up here in the past. So, needless to say, we were suffering a good deal of apprehension upon our arrival at the LZ. I could appreciate two things at that time: There were no mosquitoes, and it was really cool at that altitude, which was around 3,000 or 4,000 feet!

In the evenings, after the sun sets, the clouds move in and are below the summit. It was like looking upon a bed of cotton balls, and everything seems so peaceful. The only trouble is that Charlie owned the middle of this mountain, and we possessed the top and bottom somewhat precariously. While in our bunkers at night, we did "recon by fire" every hour, on the hour. In other words, every hour, we cut loose with everything we had down the mountainside with the idea of maybe discouraging Charlie from making a probe or an assault upon our defenses.

During the daylight hours, our group of six troops in our bunker would be split up; three would go down the mountainside with other members of the platoon for recon, while the others remained in the rear to reinforce the bunkers or other details. The recons down the lady's flank were somewhat chilling: There were so many caves and tunnels that survival during the night on top of the mountain became somewhat questionable.

At night, it was so impressive when there were no clouds to obscure the countryside below. We could watch the sunset and see various firefights among the troops below the mountain and the spectacular B-52 strikes. However, there was the thought that the night brings out the VC, and our vulnerability became foremost in our minds. We were so isolated, it was a hard time on the mountain. We began to believe it more safe to do recons down the mountain than to be in the bunker at night, trying to see through the clouds that clung to the very front of our position.

For several weeks, Jim Murphy helped operate the radio facilities on top of the Virgin. He shares his fond memories:

In April 1969, I went to the top of the Black Virgin Mountain, where the Division shared a relay facility with other units. It was the highest point in III Corps, 3,200 feet above sea level. It was a very beautiful view. You could see for miles. On a clear night, you could see the lights of Saigon. It was very lonesome; the only way we got resupplied was by air. It was a unique situation: We were on the top, and we were on the bottom; Charlie was in the middle. During the rainy season, that mountain was covered by a cloud. Nobody got in, and nobody got out. We'd be socked in for two, three weeks at a time. But still, the morale was pretty good. Everybody kind of stuck together. A situation like that kind of brings that out of people. Plus, we had our shifts to work on: on 12 hours, off 12 hours.

In June 1969, we got attacked. They came in and blew up a few pieces of equipment, and a few guys died. Needless to say, it was a very scary time for me. I remember when I heard the rounds coming in, I dragged myself out of the hooch. When I was alone, I was terrified. When I was with other people, it was okay.

Every veteran of the 25th Division remembers Nui Ba Den. He also remembers the massive enemy tunnel network that caused so much grief and frustration. Tunnels and field fortifications were common on all battlefields in Vietnam. Nowhere, however, had geology and geography conspired to make possible a tunnel network as large, sophisticated, and dangerous as the one the men of the Tropic Lightning Division found. The tunnels were worst in the wooded areas north of the Cu Chi base camp in northern Hau Nghia and southern Binh Duong provinces. The neighboring U.S. 1st Division confronted part of the same network in the Iron Triangle.

There were good reasons for the enemy to build the tunnels where they did. The terrain was slightly higher than the land to the south; consequently, the water table allowed them to dig stable tunnels. The terrain was rough and offered ideal cover from air strikes and surveillance. It was also just a few miles from the Saigon suburbs. Because the area was so ideal, the Viet Minh began constructing the tunnel zone during the French war, and this was one location that the Party retained during the Diem period. When open war broke out in the early 1960s, the Front expanded the network greatly. It protected its fighters from Diem's aircraft and posed a threat to the capital itself. When the United States intervened, the Front redoubled its efforts. Dug by hand, the miles upon miles of tunnels were a remarkable achievement of both cleverness and will.

As already noted, the men of the 25th confronted the tunnel system when they were first deployed. A small number of tunnels existed under the base camp itself. Apparently, Front snipers used them in the first days to shoot their new neighbors. Just to the north of the camp, however, the great network began. Some of the earliest patrols out of Cu Chi found out the hard way how difficult it was to deal with an enemy who could pop up out of a small and cleverly hidden entrance, fire a few rounds, and go back down, leaving a dead or wounded GI on the surface. The tunnels were a tactical obstacle that no one had considered at length: It was not American policy to occupy territory, so what should a unit do when it found a tunnel? Instinctively, it seemed that there must be an easy solution to a problem made of mud. The Army tried everything—tear gas, smoke, high explosives, bulldozers, and sensors. Del Plonka recalls that someone once got the bright idea of pumping water from the Saigon River into nearby tunnels. The result, according to Lieutenant Plonka, was that "before, only one man could move through them; when we were done, you could drive an oxcart through."

Ultimately, it dawned on the experts and Division engineers that there was no way to destroy the tunnels without diverting every engineer in the country there for an indefinite period. The Division, so it seemed, would have to live with the tunnels. But did that mean that men on operations should do nothing beyond dropping a grenade down every entrance they found? Obviously, there were things of value in the tunnels. If the Division could locate and trap anyone below, then they could bring in high explosives. In addition, firsthand intelligence was always scarce in Vietnam, and capturing an underground command post, whenever it happened, yielded splendid intelligence.

Unless the Division was willing to settle for passive acceptance of a tactical nightmare, the officers concluded there was only one countermeasure: to send soldiers down into the tunnels after the enemy. From this frustrating conclusion came the famous "tunnel rats" of the 25th Division. In 1967, Phil Boardman was an early practitioner of this dangerous specialty. He describes the simple techniques used to counter a bewildering problem:

I was a volunteer. I never heard of a tunnel rat that wasn't. We didn't get any privileges or anything, but I guess you always find someone to do something like that. We were twenty years old. Every company had one or two. When I volunteered in late 1967, they sent us to a tunnel warfare school at Cu Chi. I think the tunnels were American-made. You went down a tunnel and went in. It was about 10 feet long. Then you came out. That was it. Piece of cake. Some school.

Most of the tunnels I went into were in the Trang Bang area. There were also a lot of them in the Ho Bo Woods. We went into them looking for weapons, documents, or other supplies. We didn't go into them specifically looking for a contact. If you saw a VC go down a tunnel, you sure as hell didn't go down after him. That's when you would throw down a grenade or call in the engineers. Normally, of course, you wouldn't throw anything down: That would cave in the entrance. If you could see the entrance to the tunnel, a hole in the ground just sitting there, you knew it was abandoned: That defeated the whole purpose from the enemy's point of view. Usually, the entrances to the tunnels were carefully concealed and camouflaged. At the mouth, they were fairly large: maybe 2 feet by 2 feet. That was so the VC could jump back in on a run. Then they would narrow right away to maybe 1 foot by 1 foot. Vietnamese are really small, and they would make it a tight squeeze for them. I was thin, but there were tunnels I couldn't get into. Making it narrow like that would keep most GIs from going in after Charlie, as if they'd want to. A lot of GIs would go into a tunnel, look around for like 1 second and then come back out and say, "I checked it out thoroughly, sir! Nothing down there. Nothing at all." I could sure understand the attitude.

I went down with nothing but a .45-caliber pistol and a flashlight. About half the time, I went down with a buddy, half the time alone. I found bodies of VC killed in battle on the surface and dragged into the tunnels. But I never shot at anyone down there, and I'm damn glad. You can imagine how loud a .45 would be in a confined space. My buddy fired his sidearm once, and the concussion from the sound blew his eardrums out: They had to evacuate him to Japan. But you couldn't wear earplugs, obviously. You had to be able to hear what was going on. You might as well wear a blindfold.

The tunnel complexes were real low-tech warfare. If you had the people and you had the will, which the enemy did, you could put something together pretty quick, I think. But they could be elaborate. The biggest complex I was in included a small hospital or aid station. It was as big as a small living room, and you could stand up inside. The floors were earthen, but you could see undried blood all over them. Charlie got out just in time. He was probably long gone. Or maybe he wasn't. He could have been just a few feet away. Those complexes were just a maze. The tunnels themselves had branches. Any large chamber had two, three, or even four entrances or exits. Doesn't take long before you're talking about a real labyrinth. I always worried about getting lost in one. There weren't any signs saying, "This way out," or any light switches for you to turn on. None of us ever totally explored one of those complexes. They were just too big. They were hard to destroy, too. The engineers were always trying to think up ways to wreck them. What do you do? Fill them back in?

C. W. Bowman volunteered for the same job as Boardman. It was not an accident that both men began their accounts with brief explanations of why they did the job at all. Understandably, it was not a duty everyone relished:

Tunnel warfare was another war in itself, an underground war. People asked me if I had a death wish: Why would anybody want to go down into the tunnel? I don't know. I was eighteen, and you're not going to die, at least you think you're not going to die. You're invincible. I guess it was because I had a good sixth sense or whatever you'd call it.

They had tunnels of all sizes. In some, you had to crawl on your hands and knees, in some, you could stand up and walk, and in some, you could almost drive a truck through. Mostly, I ran tunnels around Cu Chi and the Iron Triangle. Most of them were what I called "hands-and-knees tunnels" because you had to crawl. Tunnels were cool inside—some went far underground—but you'd still be sweating. When you first entered, you'd look: Most of the tunnels dropped straight down and took off on a 90-degree turn. That way, you couldn't see what was down the tunnel until you dropped down into it. You couldn't throw a grenade down there or tear gas or anything else because then you couldn't go in. A grenade would eat up the oxygen. So a lot of times, depending on how the tunnel was dug, it would be like dropping straight down into it. You had a flashlight in one hand and a pistol in the other. You never knew if you were going to come eyeball to eyeball with somebody right then. There were all kinds of little things you had to look for. There were snakes down there, and the VC planted nests of fire ants. Now, fire ants would build a nest out of leaves, and if you hit one, they would just pour out of those leaves. Once they got on you, the only way you could get them off was to pull them off: If you brushed them, they still hung on to you. They would draw blood or take little pieces of meat as you pulled them off, and it would burn like fire. I guess that's why they called them fire ants.

Usually, my friend Gary and I went in tunnels. It gets strange down there; it's quiet. It's cool, but the sweat is running off your body—rivers of sweat running down your back, dripping off your shoulders and arms, running over your nose, into your eyes. I never really got claustrophobia. But sometimes, you think you hear something up ahead, and your heart starts pounding: Your chest hurts because your heart is pounding so hard. Sometimes, you could sense or feel there was something up ahead, but you couldn't really see it. You'd freeze in place, and you had to talk to your body to get it to move. Your arms and your legs feel about 1,000 pounds each, and at the same time, you feel so weak that you don't know if you had to if you could pull the trigger of your pistol or not. You want to back up and leave, and then you don't want to back up and leave because it's your job to go through the tunnel. The body sometimes feels like it's trying to tear itself in half. Part of it wants to go ahead because of the unknown, the challenge, but the other part, because of the fear and the unknown, wants to go back from where you came from. It wipes you out. When you come out of a tunnel, you are drained. You just have to sit down and pour some water over your head or whatever: take a break and regroup.

I've been in sandy tunnels, laterite tunnels. You'd get it all over you, and it would stick to you. We'd come up on trapdoors where we'd actually have to sit on the edge of the trapdoor, drop our legs through, and put our hands over our heads to narrow our shoulders so we could drop down. No telling what you'd find. We found medical equipment, surgical instruments, weapons, clothing, documents. Every tunnel was a little bit different. They had false floors in them booby-trapped with punji stakes, so you could fall through the floor and end up in a punji pit. They might ambush you when you stuck your head up a trapdoor and stab you with a pike. There were false walls in the tunnel: You'd go through the tunnel, and they'd be on the other side of the wall watching you through a peephole, and they could open fire on you. I was fortunate and lucky that a lot of this didn't happen to me. Still, Gary and I did run into the VC or NVA in the tunnels. We had our shoot-outs. I've seen in books where people had .22 or .38 pistols with silencers on them. But all we had were .45s, and when you start firing up a tunnel with a .45, the concussion damn near kills you. Gary and I both have come out of there with nosebleeds, and I ruptured my eardrums at least once. So it's a completely different world. And everything is fair game: If it moves, you can shoot. As a matter of fact, you better shoot. You can't take the time to say, "Halt, who goes there?" You just kill whatever you come up on. There is no place to run, no place to hide down there. You come face to face with somebody, either they're dead or you're dead.

I've seen guys break. They would go down into the tunnels, and then one day—maybe they had a dream or something—and they say, "No, no, no." The rule was, if you broke once, you never went down a tunnel again. There were all kinds of ways some guys broke. Some guys sat down and cried; some guys would drop down into the tunnel, and as soon as they dropped down, they'd start shooting, and that was it. Or you could just say, "Hey, I've had it, I can't do it any more." We had a lieutenant who thought he could order people down there. Once I went down a well, not a tunnel, and told Gary to pull me back because there wasn't any oxygen. The lieutenant called me all sorts of things, candyass and stuff. He told Gary to go down, and Gary told him to kiss his ass. I loved it. The lieutenant went crazy and was going to court-martial us, but the captain laughed at it. You'd find barracks-room types everywhere.

Gerry Schooler also went down. He stresses a commonly held sentiment on the part of tunnel rats and soldiers in general: respect for the people who built the maze. He is also skeptical about the value of his duty:

The tunnels were interesting. You could see how much work they put into them. That's when I first realized that these people were not lazy, that they were industrious and dedicated. They were able to do some impressive engineering with their hands and crude tools. I don't know how long it would take a platoon or company of Americans to dig tunnels like that, but it would be a long time. It was obvious they were dedicated and had been there for a lot longer than one or two years: These tunnels were big, complicated, and old.

I don't know what made me go down into some of them, except curiosity. Normally, you wouldn't find anything. Sometimes, you'd find 20 rifles or something, but they had enough advance information on us usually that they could get their stuff out. We never found huge caches. When you get down to it, in the bush, 1 man can carry 3 or 4 rifles. I never bought the idea of these big stockpiles of weapons. It always struck me that they had enough people to carry all the weapons. So maybe the stockpiling was more typical of 1965 or 1966, but when we were there, especially after Tet, there weren't any weapons to be found. There were plenty of people to carry them. There was no reason to leave huge numbers around. Once we found 20 or 25 brand-new AK47s covered in grease and wrapped in plastic. I saw that two or three times at the beginning, but after Tet, I never saw any weapons left around. If you got a weapon, it was usually because the guy was dead and was holding on to it. They carried as many of their dead off as they could. They were very efficient that way.

Ultimately, it was not the tunnel rats that defeated the tunnels. The enemy was present there from beginning to end. However, the value of the tunnels was reduced enormously, and many were turned into tombs for the living. The technique employed was a sustained series of massive B-52 strikes. The heavy bombers had often visited the areas in the past, but because the tunnels were a prime staging location for Tet, the Air Force moved to flatten the area.

The 25th's role was less direct but more important than that played by the Air Force. The tunnels were never totally destroyed, nor were they ever emptied. Yet, when the 25th left Vietnam, their significance was greatly reduced. The major reason for this was that there were far fewer people to put in them.

The tunnels were a Front stronghold. The NVA, on the other hand, preferred operating near its border bases. It was the followers of the Front in the South that had taken the lead in the great General Offensive. And it was they who fell under American guns. The Army completed this process in 1970 with the assault into Cambodia. Although a political calamity at home, the attack, in which several 25th Division units took part, was a great success. The Front's leadership was nearly captured and ultimately scattered across Cambodia. The logistic network that fed both Front and NVA forces was demolished.

When the 25th Division began returning to Hawaii late in 1970, the Front was on its knees in the Division's area of operations, and the NVA was dispersed. Saigon's political presence had expanded to a degree not seen since 1960. Although southern revolutionaries continued to struggle and tied down large numbers of South Vietnamese men, the war was increasingly a slugging match between ARVN and the NVA. The tunnels were quiet during the hammer blow of 1972. And ironically, the area that the 25th Division fought in, long a revolutionary stronghold, was one of the last to fall to the red banner in the onslaught of 1975. None of this was coincidence. Instead, it was the residual impact of the 25th Division's campaign in Vietnam.

It is the painful paradox of Vietnam that though the Army largely fulfilled its mission, the United States lost the war. In retrospect, it is not so surprising. It never was the Army's mission to win the war; its mission was to inflict pain on the opposition and drive the North to sue for peace. The enemy had too much strength and will to be defeated in the South. Furthermore, Saigon was never able to heal its own wounds, many self-inflicted.

The debacle in Vietnam was the result of monumental folly. Americans, if they think it would do any good, can point to a large number of people who bore responsibility for this. But not one of them wore the patch of the Tropic Lightning Division. When push came to shove, the men fought as well as their fathers had in World War II and their sons did in the Persian Gulf.

The price, however, was great. The 25th Division suffered 4,240 men killed and 30,000 wounded during the war, one of the highest totals among Army divisions. Considering the relatively small number of men actually at risk, the casualty rates were very high. This brings us to another paradox: Although the 25th Division was an excellent combat unit, the men showed the most courage when trying to save the lives of their injured comrades. When they did so, they were supported by a large, skilled, and tenacious medical apparatus based in the middle of the war zone—one of the few affirmative aspects of the Vietnam War. It is the matter we will turn to next.

5

WIA: Wounded in Action

WHEN COMPARED with past generations, most Americans in the late twentieth century go through their lives greatly insulated from pain and injury. The workplace is much safer, and government mandates have removed or lessened the causes of injury in a host of ways. If illness or injury strikes, medical professionals are normally close by, ready to ease pain and begin treatment. In particular, physicians have made great strides in treating trauma, and specialized wards exist in most city hospitals to give rapid care to the seriously injured. Thus, an injured person is often hospitalized, helped through the pain, given ongoing care, and, in most cases, granted medical leave from work. Tragedy, of course, still occurs and is devastating. Indeed, the emotional shock to those close to the victim is actually heightened because the occurrence of calamity is so rare.

As it was in so many ways, the world of combat soldiers in Vietnam was upside down from civilian life in regard to the occurrence of and attitudes toward injury. When talking to veterans, I am frequently astounded by the degree to which they accommodated themselves to a universe so utterly foreign to the one they knew before going to war. Some spoke of a drab and ugly dump like Cu Chi as though it were heaven. For them, of course, it was—a fact that says much about the alternatives facing field soldiers. Others spoke with relief about being given some boring, mindless duty that they would not even consider as real employment in civilian life. When things as commonplace and trivial as a cold can of soda become special treats, one is in a very warped world, indeed.

Nowhere is the twisted reality of war more evident than when veterans speak of injury. One frequently hears remarks like, "I was hit, too, but it wasn't anything special." The veteran's definition of "anything special" is a wartime one: In other words, compared to what happened to the guy next to him, the respondent was okay. But a specific description of his injury proves that this "scratch" or "flesh wound" would be an ugly highlight in the life of any civilian and cause for a great deal of anxiety. The Purple Heart is the most underrated decoration given by the military. No doubt, some men and women got one for little reason, but the vast majority of recipients received that decoration after suffering great pain and terrible fear.

One reason that combat soldiers speak so lightly of physical injury is that it was so common. A war zone is a dangerous place to be even in the absence of combat. No job in civilian life is remotely as dangerous in terms of accidents as the wartime military. And combat is, of course, much worse. Without more precise data, it is difficult to determine what the chances were for a combat soldier of the 25th Division to have been wounded during his tour, and the casualty rate varied according to date of tour. It is also difficult to take into consideration changes in field strength. Nevertheless, if field strength was 60 percent of paper strength, then a combat soldier would probably have had about a 75 percent chance of being killed or wounded. Wounded outnumbered the killed in Vietnam by about five to one.

Note, however, that unless a soldier's wound was very serious, the man went back to his unit after recovery. Therefore, many veterans were wounded twice or more. Nor would the statistics include the types of wounds that were treated in the field and forgotten about—the sort of injury that would send any civilian to the emergency ward immediately. A few men even talked of field wounds with a sense of relief. One Marine veteran related that he saw himself covered with blood, thought he was going to die, and then found out it was just an ugly gash caused by some shrapnel. He told me he almost kissed the medic when he found out. He was not even asked if he wanted to be evacuated, nor did he expect to be.

Despite the casual outward attitude toward injury and pain, the men deeply feared wounds. Every soldier in the field saw crippling and horrid injuries, and one can imagine the impact that had. Obviously, soldiers dreaded the unthinkable most of all. The Army is uniquely sensitive to these underlying but obvious fears. Although they do not often show it well, almost all commanders hate the idea of their men dying. And any decent commander knows that his soldiers' morale and fighting ability will be greatly improved if they know they will receive aid if wounded. Thus, it is no accident that military medicine, at its best, is extraordinarily good. It is also no accident that the Army utilized great resources during the Vietnam War to construct the best and most elaborate network of medical care ever to exist in wartime. Of all of the lies told about the war, one of the most noxious is the notion that the military treated wounded men with harshness and neglect. If the men that actually experienced the pain and fear coming from battlefield injury can be believed—and there were a great number of them—the exact opposite was true.

Wounds

Because the environment in Vietnam was so violent, wounds came in all sizes and types. Unless a man was desperate to leave the field, however, there was great peer pressure to treat and ignore small but ugly injuries that, in peacetime, would receive attention even in the military. All units had a medic who could do basic paramedical procedures. If the unit could not spare the wounded soldier, the medic might treat him on the spot and send him back to fight. Wounds that required care but not major treatment were often handled by corpsmen at the Division's own clinic. (More severe cases, as I shall discuss, were routed to a mobile hospital or the 12th Evac in Cu Chi.) Phil Boardman describes a "small" wound and the indifferent care he received for the field equivalent of a common cold:

I got hit twice. Once we were going down a river bank, probably the Vam Co, blowing up old VC firing positions—nothing more than big holes dug into the bank. Sure enough, Charlie decided to use one of them as an ammo cache. When we dropped in our grenade, there was a secondary explosion, and I took some shrapnel. It was no big deal, really. They sent me to Cu Chi, and some technician, who was kind of a jerk, sat there and probed my shoulder with this long needle.

Boardman returned to his unit immediately. His next injury was a little up the scale:

A few months later, I got hit again outside Trang Bang. We were on what they called a "roving patrol." Our company went out at night and, instead of setting up an ambush, kept moving around, looking for Charlie. Now, you couldn't see booby traps, so that meant you couldn't walk down the roads. So all we were doing was walking through the bush, making a lot of racket. It was a real stupid idea, and I didn't hear of many other "roving patrols." In any case, a dog and his handler were walking point, and I was right behind them. Right outside our perimeter, before we hardly got going, Charlie blew one of his command-detonated, homemade claymores. Then he opened up with small arms. The dog, the handler, and I were all hit by the claymore. It was wild. They brought in the gunships and artillery, and everybody was firing. They dusted the handler, but he died. They also dusted the dog, but I don't know what happened to him. There wasn't enough room for me, so I was left behind at the perimeter. The medics were there, and I wasn't hit real bad, but you have to wonder about the priorities.

The next morning, all bandaged up, I stuck out my thumb and caught a ride to Tay Ninh. Cu Chi was closer, but that's the way the convoy was going. The doctor at the aid station in Tay Ninh was great. He knew what he was doing, and he was nice to me. But I have to admit, he sure popped my bubble by being good at his job. A rough hunk of metal about the size of a big ball bearing was lodged in my shoulder. The doctor was probing for it and couldn't quite get it. He said they'd have to send me to surgery. I'm thinking, "That's wonderful!" Surgery would have meant at least three months off, and they might have evacuated me. Then he found the hunk of metal and pulled it out. I was cared for locally and was only out for three weeks. Then they reassigned me to a company that was being rebuilt after being annihilated during Tet. Bad luck all around. [Boardman was assigned to the new *Manchu* company constructed to replace the one demolished outside of Saigon.—EMB]

As one can see, the idea of the "million-dollar wound" was alive and well in Vietnam. No wonder Boardman was disappointed. Shoulder surgery was delicate and might have been a ticket to the rear, even though he was in no danger of dying or of facing a crippling injury. The ticket home, however, was normally reserved for people who received serious injuries that required prolonged care. Dan Vandenberg describes the events leading to his departure from Vietnam:

But like all good things, even luck runs out. On 7 April 1969, the whole company was going out. It took two flights of choppers to get us out in the field, so we stood around for a half hour with our thumb up our nose. Then we lined up in columns of two and moved out into these rice paddies. Up until this time, I often walked point, but this night, we had another squad taking point for a change, which was okay by me. Well, we went about 100 yards or so, and the point man from the other squad hit a booby trap. So that squad was ordered to stay in place: We figured the whole area was booby-trapped. They called in the Medevac. My squad and another were told to form a perimeter and face outward because when the choppers came in, Charlie liked to take a shot at them.

Soon, we moved, and I walked over a dike. I had gone about 30 yards when I felt something around my ankle. I knew it wasn't a vine, and I quickly figured out it was a wire. You've got approximately 2 or 2^1/$_2$ seconds once the pin is pulled on a hand grenade before it goes off. It took about 1^1/$_2$ seconds to figure out what I had tripped on, which left about a second. A lot of people ask me, why didn't you run, why didn't you dive? First of all, you don't know which way to run: You might run right into it; it could be anything from 2 to 4 feet away. Also, you're using part of that second of time to let sink into your head exactly what you've done. My first thought was, "Aw shit, I've blown it now." And for anybody out there wondering what it feels like to have a hand grenade go off at your feet, it's comparable to someone winding up with a baseball bat and rapping you in the face. Your whole body goes numb, it hurts like hell for the first 10 seconds, and after that, you can't move. At least, that was my experience.

I had to use great concentration and all of the strength that I had to reach up and scratch my nose. You can only have so many close calls for your luck to run out. Since the Medevac had already been called, it didn't take them long to get out there: I'd say 10 minutes, top. While I lay there, the squad leader came up and helped bandage me up and reassure me that all of my parts were still there. Once I realized that I wasn't going to die at the moment, we swapped jokes. I said I could get a job for Johnson & Johnson Band-Aids because I looked like a mummy when they got done wrapping me up. It's not funny now, but it was then. I'll always owe him a debt of gratitude because I was lying there with both my eyes bandaged, didn't know how badly I was hurt, and couldn't move, and he was there the whole time putting me at ease and reassuring me, telling me everything was fine. I was touched by the concern. We were good friends over there, but at a time like that, you find out how good your friends are.

I was put on a chopper and flown to Cu Chi base hospital. One thing I'd like to say that I haven't heard too much about: I can't praise the medical corps highly enough—medics, doctors, nurses, all of them. On a scale of 1 to 10, I'd say my care was a 10. They all went beyond just caring for me. They showed concern, you became a person again, you were no longer just a number. I can't imagine how those people managed to do their job day in and day out. I know I couldn't hack looking at the blood I saw, and that was something they had to do every damn day—bodies that were torn and mangled. I can't imagine doing something like that, but like the rest of us, they had a job to do, and they did it. Nobody asked you if you liked it or not.

All men feared catastrophic wounds. Because booby traps and mines were so common, there were an unusual number of amputees among Vietnam wounded. Worse yet, there was fire. During Tet, Gary Ernst's mechanized unit was in furious combat. He relates events from an afternoon when every track crewman's nightmare came true:

Leap year day was my last day in Vietnam. We started our day with our platoon sweeping the bush between the villages and had only sporadic contact, although one of the tracks was hit by an RPG, which caused a KIA. We kept finding more supplies and ammunition. About 1:30 p.m., my company hooked up with an infantry company. We soon flushed out a number of NVA or VC. We couldn't see them, but they were seen by an observation helicopter. A gunship was called in but was called back, and the VC got back in their holes. About 3:00 in the afternoon, one of our tanks took three RPG hits. And then, all hell broke loose.

We were moving along, going slow, but they were firing from one of the spider holes, and all of a sudden, there was a bang and explosion on the side of my APC. I just had the sensation of being hot. I looked down, and I'm on fire from the waist down. We had taken a hit on the fuel tank. I remember thinking, "My god, I'm on fire," jumping out of the APC and rolling on the ground, trying to get the flames out. Some grunts came up and put out the fire. A medic came up to me and said, "I think this thing is going to blow. Can you run?" I said, "Hell, yes!" We got up and ran about 50 yards, and I collapsed. At that moment, the track went sky high.

Many months later, I ran into a guy in my platoon who had taken a picture of the track later, and there was nothing left of it except for the bottom and a couple of wheels. I was the only injured; I was just in the wrong place at the wrong time. As I'm waiting there in shock, the medic gave me morphine, but the pain began. The helicopter picked me up. It was the only time I rode in a chopper during the war. The 12th Evac worked on me. Some of my friends visited me and told me later, at a recent reunion, that they didn't think I was going to make it. One of them just broke down crying. I was there in a time of the war when we still got on very well with our officers and NCOs. There was a lot of camaraderie and respect there. My treatment was superb. Nothing like *Born on the Fourth of July.*

Evacuation

Military medical personnel in recent wars have learned how important it is to dispense care to trauma victims as soon as possible. Frequently, they deal with shock and blood loss, either of which threatens lives, and minutes can make the difference between life and death. No matter how good the team at the 12th Evac was, a seriously wounded soldier had to arrive there alive if the professionals were to have an opportunity to practice their craft. In the field, medical treatment had two stages. The first was the critical care given on the spot by a medic or another soldier if a medic was not available. The second stage entailed getting the victim on a helicopter and off to the hospital.

Obviously, activity like this calls for cool and deliberate behavior under the best of circumstances. Unfortunately, though, when the medics and helicopter pilots had to swing into action, the enemy was either very close or a firefight was in progress.

Medics were extremely important members of any unit. Their training during wartime was not extremely intensive, but it included the essentials of handling trauma. In addition, soldiers normally carried bandages and received some paramedical training. The casualty rate among medics was high. The enemy knew they were important for morale and did not hesitate to shoot them, even if they were giving care. Naturally, the medics themselves did not wear any large identifying markers, and they were usually armed and practiced what one called "preventive medicine." But there were some exceptions. Eddie Madaris recalls that his unit's medic, who was very good at his dangerous job, was a conscientious objector and would not carry a weapon.

Beyond sharing the general hazards of the field, medics learned to treat men where they lay immediately. For a dedicated medic, this doctrine was dangerous. Although no one moved under aimed fire, the cry of a wounded soldier was a powerful incentive to react quickly. Thus, their jobs made medics more visible than many others—and more vulnerable, as well.

Lee Reynolds was a medic with a mechanized unit in the spring of 1970; he describes his job under extreme—but not unique—circumstances:

I became short about three days after I joined Alpha Company. We were working out of a little hard spot between Dau Tieng and Tay Ninh named Wood 3. Whenever you hear a name like that, you wonder what ever happened to Wood 1 and Wood 2. Headquarters company was in there doing fire missions on a suspected Viet Cong base camp in the Boi Loi Woods. That was one of those "Army intelligence" things we didn't have a lot of confidence in: "Viet Cong base camp? Oh sure." I went to the field with Alpha Company and a company of the *Wolfhounds*. We went into the Boi Loi Woods on a combined operation with some Ruff/Puffs. [Ruff/Puffs was a derogatory nickname for South Vietnamese militia known by the initials RF/PF—Revolutionary Forces/Popular Forces. They were not well thought of as soldiers by American troops.—EMB] All three American companies and the Ruff/Puffs were going to sweep through the wood line toward where the VC base camp was supposed to be. A combined operation with Ruff/Puffs: Surely, they wouldn't send us into any situation where we would get into actual combat? Right?

We were ordered to go through in line formation. We were supposed to go at a speed where the Ruff/Puffs could keep up with us. My platoon sergeant said we'd have to drive in reverse to do that. The wood line was too thick for us to stay on line. We ended up with three columns. Ours was on the right. Before we got to the wood line, they did some pretty impressive things. Some artillery batteries timed a barrage so everything hit the wood line at the same time: a nice piece of work. Air Force jets came in with bombs and napalm and put on a nice air show. Then they had the hunter-killer teams—a Cobra gunship and a Loach Lowbird—and they worked out: another good air show. The 105mm artillery was going to walk ahead of us as we approached the wood line. For some reason, we couldn't get the Ruff/Puffs to walk. We'd have to stop to get the artillery to adjust their fire because we weren't moving ahead steadily.

One time that we stopped, there was this explosion: It could have been a booby trap or a command-detonated mine, so we rock and rolled for a while ["Rock and roll" was slang for firing weapons at full automatic, laying down a wall of lead.—EMB], trying to clear things out. We decided it must have been a booby trap and went toward the track in the middle that had hit the booby trap. We had people wounded, so I ran over there from my platoon to try to help out. I was without a rifle.

I found out later that I could very easily have walked into the VC. The VC had gotten between our columns. I was subsequently shot at from people standing in exactly the same place that I had just come from. I saw some guy who was firing at some other people: He looked around and saw me and started to shift his aim, and I got down into the grass. He was right in the area that I had just come from.

When I got to the damaged track, the platoon leader was the most seriously wounded. We had one other guy slightly wounded. The senior medic was on R & R, and the guy that was there had some medical training but was in combat arms. He'd done his time in the field as a combat soldier, then got a rear job and subsequently volunteered to go back into the field as a medic. He was trying to evaluate the situation and give some help to the wounded. I told him that I thought we ought to get these guys back to the Little Angel. [This was the battalion's medical track: Angel is the code word for medic.—EMB] He decided to treat them where they lay, contrary to the first thing that you learn: You get your casualties out of danger first, before you do anything else. But what you really learn is to remove the danger from the casualty or the casualty from the danger. They're not the same. But he didn't do that, and he was my boss, so I didn't say anything more about it.

About that time, somebody opened up on us from behind with a Chicom machine gun at point-blank range. It killed the wounded lieutenant. The medic got shot twice in the back. The lightly wounded man was shot and killed. I got hit. Then nobody had a gun. Then people ran to help us, and we couldn't do anything, and everything was a complete mess. We were completely surrounded and cut off from the rest of our people. At that time, it didn't look as though we were going to get out of it alive. We had another medic there. When the shooting started, he tried to pull the wounded man to cover, but the man got shot out of his hands. The bullet took one of the medic's fingers off and killed the man he was trying to help. The medic also got hit in the leg. The track commander got hit. He had a BB-sized wound in his back that he died of: It must have gone into his heart. A BB-sized piece of shrapnel. If he'd been wearing his flak jacket, he wouldn't have even known he'd been hit. A bullet grazed my scalp and knocked me out. I was unconscious for a few minutes. When I woke up, I tried to start helping people again, and we started getting shot at again. I had an IV started on the track commander when Charlie opened up. I was using a bush to hold the IV bottle, and they shot the bottle down. The VC were paid an incentive to kill a medic, by the way. The other medic told me to take over for a while because he was real tired. Later on, in the track, I noticed he had a bullet wound in his leg. The exit wound at the back of his leg was so big that you could put your fist into it without touching the sides of the wound. It had just blown a massive hole in his leg. You could see the femur. He hadn't said anything about being wounded, but that's why he was tired. Tough little guy: a Japanese-Hawaiian and good.

We took fire in a strip between two areas that had been cleared by bulldozers. When the VC broke contact, we began to get control of the situation again after taking a number of killed and wounded. It was a real mess and the worst performance anyone could remember Alpha Company turning in. They had too many new guys: People panicked and made too many mistakes. When the VC broke contact, they went in the opposite direction from the way that we had come in. They were going through the plowed area that was at the other end of the wood line, and they ran head on into a Cobra gunship. He caught them out in the open with his minigun and did away with them.

As soon as possible, a radio operator would call in a helicopter to evacuate wounded. There were special helicopters prepared for medical evacuations. However, if time was of the essence—which was often the case—any helicopter close by was expected to perform a dust-off. This included command-and-control helicopters, as crewman Glenn Jeffers recalls:

We did a lot of Medevacs, especially on command-and-control missions. We were there on the spot and could get down very quickly, bim-bam-boom, and have them in. Being on the spot gave us a lot of versatility. Sometimes, we did mini-resupply. One night, we were flying back from a command-and-control mission late and spotted lights on the river. That was not usual. It was two of our riverboats that had been in contact with the enemy, and our people had been doing real well: But we had a lot of people shot up. So we landed in this area. There were many wounded. We loaded up the wounded in the helicopter, and they took all the room. So we two gunners, the colonel, and his assistant stayed on the ground while the pilot took the wounded back to the base camp. It was kind of odd. The officers had the big picture, but they didn't really have a good little picture and didn't really know where we were at. So we stood around in the dark there for about 45 minutes before the helicopter got back. It was a tense situation because we knew the other guys were in the area, and we were lightly armed. Everything came out for the best.

Jeffers rejects the notion, portrayed in some famous motion pictures, that helicopter crews abandoned American soldiers in danger. He describes the ethos of the crewmen:

Once in a while, we could put our two cents in, but normally, if someone said, go do this, we did it. If there was a dangerous situation on the ground, we did not think of saying no. The people who flew in our company were either brave or stupid. In *The Deer Hunter,* you saw a guy fall out of a helicopter, and they didn't go back and get him; they flew off and left him. That would have never happened, it just wouldn't have. Not with our unit anyway. I found that to be totally unbelievable. That was just amazing to me that they even put that into a movie. It wouldn't have fit into our mode of operation, the way our people thought. They were either brave or crazy. Some things have a certain amount of thrill, doing some things, and after you're over there in-country for a while, you can develop an attitude where you still have conscious fear but you can control it. That is, a person with the right attitude can control it.

To prove his point, Jeffers describes how he came to leave Vietnam:

I left the country on a negative note. This was after I had extended for six months because they had come out with this thing saying that if you extended for six months and you only had six months left, you could get an early out. I had got to where I had my fill of the Army and was at the point of preferring to stay over there in that dangerous atmosphere if it would get me out of the Army sooner.

My leaving occurred on a Friday the 13th, in June, about 11:00 in the evening. We had gone out to pick up a major and do an impromptu command-

and-control mission for some ground troops on a night laager. They would set up a mini–base camp with about 15 people in it. They would sit and watch. Well, they sat and watched, and 5 or 6 enemy came up, and they blew their perimeter defenses on these 5 or 6 people and made themselves real vulnerable. They didn't pay attention, and up came the rest of the enemy company. That's how the Vietnamese did it: They would send 5 or 6 in front of a larger group. If we were going to kill somebody, it would be these 5 or 6, and then the rest of the company would come walking up, and then there you were—defenseless. That's what had happened to these guys. When we got there, there were some gunships trying to support these people on the ground, and they were basically so screwed up they didn't know what was going on. They weren't prepared to do anything. They had several people wounded, and they had pulled back into a bad position. We made three approaches trying to get in and pick these people up, primarily because they had no way of identifying truly where they were at. They tried to bring us in with a cigarette lighter and eventually with a flashlight. And each time we came in, we came in with landing lights on.

Pretty soon, we landed, and Charlie opened up on us. They hit the aircraft with two RPGs: that's an antitank weapon that works real good on helicopters. One of them blew up on the base of the helicopter, and one of them blew up behind my head, and I took a whole lot of shrapnel in my back. I jumped out, the helicopter took off and crashed, and everybody crawled out. The fight continued on, and we were finally flown out. I spent two months in the hospital, then was sent to the States. I ended up spending another three months in Fort Rucker, Alabama, because I hadn't finished my six-month extension in Vietnam. It was kind of a joke.

Battalion commander Lt. Col. Carl Neilson was grateful to people like Jeffers and the medical apparatus behind him:

I was terribly impressed with the medical evacuation of casualties: the ability of the chopper to get in quickly, pick up wounded, and take them to relatively sophisticated medical facilities. We had a mobile army surgical hospital [MASH—EMB]—or the equivalent of it—at Tay Ninh. A soldier could be engaged in combat one minute and ten minutes later be on an operating table with a surgeon and a whole retinue of surgical support fighting to save his life.

Care

The mobile hospital at Tay Ninh was a busy place. Most helicopters, however, delivered their wounded to the 12th Evacuation Hospital at Cu Chi.

The 12th Evac lacked some of the amenities of the Mayo Clinic, but it was a formidable facility. Physical therapist William McDill was there in 1967, one of the first in his field to go to the front lines. He remembers the 12th Evac as it looked early in the war:

The 12th Evac occupied a rectangular piece of ground in the direction of the Cu Chi gate. Said real estate was probably 200 by 400 yards, bordered by the 125th Signal Battalion and an artillery battery of 8-inch guns. We occasionally questioned, unofficially, of course, the wisdom of setting a hospital down in between prime targets. The male officers' and enlisted men's hooches were wooden frame buildings. There was a fence between the women's hooches, which restricted entry to that area to the front doors of the buildings. The wards were Quonset huts. The hospital was a direct combat support facility, lacking only a neurosurgical capability. We could keep casualties that could be expected to return to duty within thirty days. If they were expected to be convalescing for more than this, we shipped them out. Over ninety days, they went to Japan. The hospital was designated as semimobile, which we figured meant it could be moved in a year or two. It was designated as a 250-bed hospital, although our actual capacity never approached this. We had somewhere in the area of 200 people assigned—this is a very rough figure.

Dr. Kenneth Swan served at the 12th Evac for several months during 1970 while on special assignment from the surgeon general. He saw the Evac at its most developed state:

The 12th Evacuation Hospital was a 360-bed semimobile but essentially fixed installation with concrete floors, wooden walls, and sheet metal for roofs. Like the other evacuation hospitals, it had a triage area near the helipad, and it was here that patients were brought into the hospital and sorted into walking wounded, expectant, and priority. There were approximately 30 physicians—radiology, pathology, internal medicine, psychiatry, etc. Surgical teams were organized with team leaders responding to a triage officer. A chief of professional services, in turn, responded to the hospital commander, who was a physician. The hospital could care for any surgical emergency, with the exception of cardiopulmonary bypass, which was not available; nor was renal dialysis. The triage area abutted an operating room area, which had six operating room suites, but usually only one, two, three, or four operating room suites were in action at any given time. Attached to this area was the surgical intensive care unit with about 20 beds, and in addition, an X-ray facility, a blood bank, and a preoperative holding area were all part of this complex. Walkways then led to convalescent wards, of which there were approximately eight, each capable of holding some 30 patients. The medical personnel lived in similar quarters, often occupying an abandoned ward, so that there might be 10 and 20 positioned together. The compound was protected by barbed wire.

In late 1967, cavalryman Gerald Kolb paid a visit to the 12th Evac. He noticed an odd mixture of businesslike behavior and profound concern:

I was walking through the village cemetery of Go Da Hau about 12:00 at night. There was a whitish-blue flash to my left. I felt a lot of something like sand hit me in my legs, but unfortunately, it wasn't sand, it was shrapnel. I didn't know it at the time. Immediately, I fell down, not so much from the impact but as a reaction to a possible ambush. We thought it was a command-detonated device, and it must have been. For whatever reason, there was nothing else but that one explosion. We dropped down, and everybody opened up with everything on the tracks and for maybe 30 seconds, and then we ceased fire. Then they noticed I was wounded. I didn't even know it. My legs were bleeding like crazy. They called the chopper to come in a little while later, and the next thing you know, I'm on the chopper and they're trying to get my clothes off me, cut my boots off, and cut through the bootstraps and the laces.

After I was maybe 5 to 10 minutes in the air going to the 12th Evac Hospital at Cu Chi, I noticed a pain in my back, and it was hard to breathe. That's when they realized I was hit back there, too. I got to Cu Chi. I was just about nude on the examining table. They wouldn't roll me over too much. They'd ask me some questions. I remember how cold it was compared to Vietnam. It was air-conditioned. It seemed like I was on the table too long. Maybe they cared, but I was just another GI wounded. It took maybe 45 minutes to get all the X rays. They didn't want to move me; I had to move myself because they didn't want to pierce any internal organs. I was going in and out of consciousness. Finally, that was over, and the next thing I knew, I was on an operating table. There was a caring doctor—a couple of doctors, actually—and a nurse. He said, "Gerald, we've got to clean these wounds out." Then he put a mask down, there was gas, and I went to sleep.

I woke up about noon on Saturday, 10 hours later. I couldn't eat. They brought me some food, and I couldn't look at it. I went back to sleep and woke up about 6:00. A few people from my unit came to see how I was doing. My left leg was hit in three places, my right leg once, and my back once. The shrapnel that caused the back wound pierced the flak jacket but stopped about a quarter inch away from my heart. There's still metal in there to this day, which I can't feel—at least, I don't think I can feel it. Both legs bother me sometimes. I was at 12th Evac for about a week or ten days. They figured there was some nerve damage. I do remember having to go to the bathroom, which was an outhouse. I had to leave the Quonset hut and hop along on crutches, across the muddy road, which trucks and jeeps would keep making muddier.

About a week later, I got to Japan. And that's when they sewed me up. I remember getting novocaine and painkillers, then they opened the wounds, and then they stitched it up. And that hurt. I was there convalescing for a couple of months. I do remember there were a lot of U.S. soldiers who felt they had to get back to Vietnam to finish unfinished business, as they said. There were a lot of sergeants. They felt bad because they left their buddies behind. And I didn't know which end was up. What's this all about? I saw some guys with some pretty bad wounds. I met a general's son who was shot in the head. He was trying hard to be normal. I remember writing a letter home for him. I saw another guy walking in the hallway, then he turned and looked at me, and he only had half a face. I remember young men lying in beds who had to be turned every hour or two, paralyzed. Even there, the morale was pretty high in that part of the war, late 1967. Helicopters were coming in constantly, bringing in guys from the Nam, ferrying people in from the airport at Japan. We were treated pretty well. The food was excellent in Japan. After I got better and hobbled around, I was able to tour Yokohama.

The world Kolb entered briefly and unwillingly was an extraordinary one. Alone among civilian occupations, practitioners of medicine have experience dealing with the essence of war: fear, pain, and death. The men and women at the 12th Evac, however, were very much a military unit, pushed to extremes by the violence all around them. They were reasonably safe, but no soldier saw the results of war as often and as closely as did the people at the evac. Herodotus once described war as unnatural because, in war, fathers bury their sons. It is not sentimental to state the obvious: The people laboring at the 12th Evac were fighting against the nature of war itself, and they did not enjoy losing. The result was an intense and volatile storm of action and emotion. Whether the protectors of life transcended the war, I cannot say. They were, however, certainly caught up in the manic pace of a place where war ruled.

Lily Adams, then Lily Lee, was a nurse at the 12th Evac in 1969. She gives a very interesting description of the general emotional climate at the evac and of people who knew their work was vital but who also dreaded the situations that required it:

The morale for us was very good. We felt very good about what we were doing. It was more constructive than destructive. When it was quiet, we all hungered for peace. A couple of the medics played guitar, and we would sit on the floor of the triage during night shift and sing war protest songs and songs of visions of peace. We never talked in detail about how we felt, but we expressed it like that. But when we had a real bad time, we were very supportive of each other. We would also get on each other's case if we got irritable. Sometimes, we were irritable because we were exhausted from the work of saving people. Sometimes, however, we were irritable during quiet times. You'd think we'd enjoy quiet times, but the time went very slowly, and we got on each other's nerves because we would be expecting the shit to hit the fan. So our time on duty was always very stressful, waiting for it to happen. It was almost like a sigh of relief when it did happen. But when the injured started coming in at a rapid pace, you prayed for quiet again.

Dr. Robert Hanson was a surgeon at Cu Chi during 1970. He describes concisely the swings in pace at the hospital:

Doctors were on 24-hour shifts: 24 on, 24 on call, 24 off. Not many people realize it, but we spent a lot of time doing general care and elective surgery, like hernias. Sometimes, the action was unbelievable, however. On two different occasions, I operated for 24 hours straight. At the end, you just don't know how to keep going, but you finish anyway. Every GI, in my opinion, received top-notch care. The surgeons, I thought, were excellent. Some of the interns were antiwar and didn't want to be there. The nurses worked 12-hour shifts, seven days a week, and were dedicated.

The pace at the 12th Evac, as might be expected, followed the unusual pace of combat in the field. On any given day, things were normally slow. Then, at a time totally unpredictable, the violence on the battlefield would send a stream of casualties toward Cu Chi. Lily Adams reflects on what it was like when the 12th Evac went into high gear:

The triage is one Quonset hut. The guys come in from the helipad—that's right outside. They are usually on litters that are hooked to the evac choppers and then unhooked after they land. Two litter bearers bring the litter into the hospital. I worked triage for about eight months. There are many signs about what kind of patient is coming into the triage room. One is how fast or how intense the chopper lands. It's like there's something in the air. Sometimes, you just know when a chopper is carrying a seriously wounded patient. Once on the heliport, you watch the litter bearers, and sometimes, they're running. That means it's something serious, and each second counts.

In triage, we work on the guys, tear off their clothes, and look for wounds on every part of their body, from head to toe. Zap them with tetanus vaccine, ask them if they're allergic to anything, get as much information as we can before they go unconscious. We need name, rank, serial number, and unit. We write the information down on an intake sheet. And we write the diagnosis: gunshot wound, amputation—right leg or left leg—shrapnel wounds to the face, things like that. We put an IV in them, and then it kind of depends. If they're hemorrhaging, we keep them and give them blood, and once their blood pressure is stable, we bring them into X ray, then on to the operating room. If the operating room is filled, they go to pre-op, which again is in a separate Quonset hut. They're kept there while they're being stabilized and watched over by nurses, medics, and, sometimes, doctors. From the operating room, they go to the recovery room, which is another Quonset hut. In the recovery room, it's decided whether to move them on to the ICU [intensive care unit—EMB] or another ward. If it's an amputation of one leg and that's it, then they'll just go to the surgical ward. If it's an amputation with a belly wound or a chest wound, more than likely he'll go to ICU.

There were times when we would get mass casualties, maybe 5 casualties every 5 minutes—they would just keep coming and coming. You know there is no way you can save everybody. You have to make these triage decisions; in other words, start deciding who is going to be in category 1—people who are going to have to wait a couple of days before surgery because their wounds are not life threatening; the other categories are the severely wounded, whom we can work on in short periods of time, and the "expectants," as we called them—men who were going to die no matter what we did or who did not have a good chance of making it through surgery. We needed to put those guys aside so we could help the patients who were in danger but had a better chance of survival.

The doctors and nurses had to develop defense mechanisms that were startlingly like those of combat soldiers to allow them to face their duty. Getting close to patients, like growing close to comrades, carried with it the danger of pain. Lily Adams discusses the topic:

Sometimes, there would be patients that would come in that would become known around the hospital. We had one who had lost both legs, one arm, and an eye, and he had chest or belly wounds. He had a son that was born a few days after he entered the hospital. His father came to visit about a week or two later. And then he died. That story went around the hospital. I remember how depressed we all were. We were hardened even more. You say to yourself, I don't want to get close to anybody, I don't want to get to know anything about them. Because if I do, I find myself getting drawn and attached to this person. I can't afford to lose more people like this because it will destroy me and I won't function.

A fellow nurse, facing a bizarre situation, reflected this reality in a deep way, as Adams relates:

For the nurses, there were four hooches with 15 women in each. There was also a married-quarters hooch in which, during my time, there were two couples. In both cases, one was a nurse and the husband was with the 25th Infantry Division. It was very difficult for these women, knowing their husbands were going out into the field. I remember, concerning one couple, that the wife was so freaked out she couldn't work. We really needed her, so they pulled her husband out of infantry and gave him a rear-echelon job. The nurse was more important: We were short staffed and couldn't afford to lose one person.

Despite the risk, humanity had a way of piercing the shell medical personnel tried to build around themselves. Just like the men in the field who could be moved profoundly—usually by tragedy—they, too, were vulnerable. Adams touches on this:

We saw men who came in who displayed feelings of love, gentleness, affection, closeness, and behavior we had never seen between two men before. Not in a homosexual way but in a brotherhood way—closer than brotherhood. Men coming in messed up telling us to work on their friends first. Guys concerned about each other. "See Smitty down there, how's Smitty doing?" Smitty might be fine compared to the guy who's asking, who might be dying. I miss seeing that. I see part of that today among the veterans' movement but never the intensity that I saw in Vietnam. To see two men love each other made me wonder why we can't be like that in the civilized world. Why does that only exist in the war zone? I'm just glad I was able to witness that side of the male species, that they really did have the ability to feel the way women feel and display in a normal society but that men can't. So men can't tell me that they can't show affection, can't be gentle, can't express their love.

Two pilots landed on our helipad. No one was allowed to do that because we have to keep it clear for Medevacs. Two choppers landed. The medics ran out there and told them they couldn't be there. The two pilots totally ignored them, got out of their choppers, and came into the triage. Only about 15 minutes before then, a chopper had landed, and a body was brought in of a major who got hit in the head. He died instantly. It was kind of sad to see. When we got a dead person, he was usually messed up—his body was really fucked up. On this pilot, it was one clean little wound in his head, and that wasted him. It was kind of sad, and we had brought his body out the back door and on to graves registration. Shortly afterwards, these two pilots came in and wanted to know about major so and so. Did he come through? Yes.

Was he dead? Yes. They both sat down and cried, cried their hearts out. It must have been 15 minutes. I remember the doctor, three other nurses, and myself standing there; there were about five medics and the radioman: this crowd of people standing there, watching these two pilots sob their hearts out. And I felt so helpless because I didn't know what to do. We were all looking at each other, trying to communicate the question, "What can we do?" What on earth could we do to relieve the pain these people were displaying? We knew how to deal with physical pain. How do you care for somebody who is psychologically in pain? There was nothing we could do. When they finished crying, they looked up—and I'll never forget this—and said, "Thank you, you were a great help." They left, got into their choppers, and flew off into the sunset. We just looked at each other because we had never experienced anything like that before. It wasn't in the books. It was an experience. They were expressing something they were feeling. But we couldn't express our feelings because we wouldn't have been able to function after that. Not only were they crying for themselves and the major, they were crying for the medical people who couldn't cry for the losses we had to deal with on a day-to-day basis.

The nurses at the 12th Evac were, of course, mostly women. As one might expect, this put them in an unusual situation in a combat zone. But there were other women working with the 25th. These were the Red Cross workers called "donut dollies" by the men, a name given by earlier soldiers to the women's counterparts in World Wars I and II. Apparently, some of them picked up the black humor of the front lines. Eddie Madaris recalls watching an air strike near the base with two Red Cross volunteers. They speculated that the pilots approaching low were single and that those dropping bombs from a higher altitude were married.

Naturally, the company of the nurses was much sought after by officers. Cu Chi, well stocked with civilian goods, had a vigorous social life, of a sort. More interesting, however, is the reaction of the line soldiers when they were able to meet the nurses or volunteers. According to Lily Adams, these women were seen as the physical embodiment of home and civilian life, a psychological breath of fresh air in a world that needed it:

For many of the men, they were only in a man's world. When they saw us American women, they went crazy. Not in a sexual sort of way but "My God, there's women here, I haven't talked to an American woman in months." They would come up to me and ask me to talk with them and say anything. Where do you come from, why are you here? They just wanted to hear the voice, smell the perfume. It would remind them of their girlfriends or wives.

I had a strong New York City accent, and the guys from New York would just say, keep on talking.

Like everyone in the base camps, nurses and doctors lived a risky life. Considering how often Cu Chi camp was shelled, the personnel at 12th Evac were extremely lucky and suffered very few casualties. But no one, of course, was free from the great stress that accompanies bombardment. Lawrence Obrist worked with the 25th Division's organic medical battalion. Although he was assigned to the mental health clinic, everyone in the medical apparatus was involved with casualtry treatment when violence picked up. During a trip to the mobile hospital in Tay Ninh during Tet 1968, Obrist saw that the people struggling against death could also become its victims:

Charlie had just hit Tay Ninh East, a Vietnamese troop compound with American advisers. The choppers were bringing in mass casualties. Thus, the doctors were busy treating these casualties. Charlie then scattered his rounds of mortar and 122mm rockets throughout the camp. It was one of these early rocket rounds that hit in front of the 45th MASH. The facilities were made of inflatable rubber. The rubber offered no protection when the rocket shrapnel crashed through and killed one doctor and two medics as they were treating patients. The unit deflated but was replaced by the end of the day. However, the personnel of the hospital were feeling the loss of their men. Little five-foot-two-inch nurses were still running around with steel pots and flak jackets on.

The medical personnel, no strangers to war's realities, were in an ideal position to observe two effects of the Vietnam War that have since become extremely controversial. The first is the emotional effect that the war in general and combat in particular had on the men. In the minds of many, to this day, a uniquely malignant war ruined everyone it touched. Pathological behavior exhibited later at home, many Americans believe, was caused by a pathological war. Much of this debate now surrounds the complicated issue of post-traumatic stress disorder (PTSD). I have no intention of drawing any conclusions concerning this complicated malady here, but only a fool would deny the incredible stress that combat puts on an individual. Furthermore, much of the impact of PTSD appeared long after the war. Yet, if soldiers in the field units were going berserk or falling apart, it was not apparent to the men and women who saw them daily under supreme stress. Both Dr. Swan and Lily Adams have interesting testimony, supported by additional expertise, for both have stayed connected with military medicine: Dr. Swan served in the Persian Gulf, and Lily Adams works with the Veterans Administration (VA).

Dr. Swan was with other units in Vietnam, in addition to the 12th Evac. He was at Cu Chi in 1970, a time when the Army was supposedly in disarray. His account does not fit that image:

> Most of the psychopathology that resulted from the Vietnam War was brought to Vietnam, in my opinion. With regard to "shell shock," or "combat fatigue" or "battle psychosis," I can only speak peripherally since, of course, I am not a psychiatrist. Most of our troops that were injured were treated promptly, and if they received any significant injury, they were evacuated out of the country. So the setting for prolonged exposure to combat was less than in other wars, in my experience. I did not, therefore, treat battle fatigue, but at the evacuation hospital level, it was not likely to be identified as a major problem. On the other hand, with the American division, working at battalion, brigade, and divisional levels of medical care, I only rarely encountered an individual with alleged battle fatigue. These individuals were supported psychologically with explanations of their problems and returned to their units as rapidly as possible since this had been determined to be the most satisfactory way of dealing with this problem. Rearward evacuation only intensifies the degree of psychosis or psychoneurosis. The best support group is the individual soldier's unit members up forward. His self-esteem is brought back to normal more rapidly by returning him to his unit.

Lily Adams has a somewhat different perspective. Note, however, that she, too, served when the Army was supposedly beginning to disintegrate:

> We didn't see much shell shock. We had some soldiers come in saying that they didn't want to go out in the field, that they just couldn't fight anymore. Most of the doctors were supporters of that. Some patients were malingerers who would make up anything just because they didn't want to go out into the field. I guess there was all of this macho bullshit—that you're supposed to be brave and be able to take it. Some of these guys, young boys, just couldn't handle it. They just didn't have it. I work for the VA, and sometimes, I wonder how some of these vets ended up in the service. Their IQ is so low. They just weren't Army material, but we used them anyway. There were a lot of guys who had stood before a judge somewhere and had had to choose between the Army or jail. So we had those types, as well. Shell shock did exist, but not the amount we are seeing today with the people with PTSD. I didn't deal with much alcoholism then, and 90 percent of the PTSD have a drinking problem. There were a lot of PTSD symptoms after Vietnam, but I didn't see a lot of it there.

The soldiers were hyperalert. You had to wake these kids up by shaking their toes. You didn't want to be close enough that they would grab your neck and kill you. These were warriors who were trained well and fought well, and their response was that of a warrior thinking he was getting attacked in the middle of his sleep.

The people working at the 12th Evac also were close to the issue of the Army's relationship with Vietnamese civilians. I shall consider the larger ramifications of this problem later. For now, the medical aspect is worth noting. The 12th Evac had a steady stream of Vietnamese patients. Yet, napalm wounds to civilians, almost archetypes of the cruelty of the Vietnam War, were conspicuous by their absence. William McDill, Lily Adams, Dr. Hanson, and Dr. Swan all noted that they did not see a single case of a napalm wound on a civilian, despite the fact that their tours, combined, spanned most of the war. (Napalm wounds did happen at tragic moments, however, as I will address later.)

It was American policy to give war-injured civilians care regardless of which side caused the wounds. When and if the patient was stabilized, he or she was transferred to Vietnamese facilities, which were greatly inferior. A large number of Vietnamese also came for acute treatment of major health problems. Many of them came in through the enormous Medical Civic Action Program (MEDCAP), which brought low-level care to the civilian population. Some found other connections. The Vietnamese knew that American medicine was far better than their own, and some even believed American doctors had nearly magical powers. If there was a way to get a sick relative under American care, many would take it. Naturally, too, there were Vietnamese working at the 12th Evac. Particularly when the battle action was down, Vietnamese might constitute a very large proportion of the patients, as Dr. Robert Hanson relates:

We treated mostly Vietnamese civilians during my tour. There were a few from friendly fire. I remember doing surgery on a twelve-year-old Cambodian girl during the invasion who had been shot through the chest by a helicopter gunship. Luckily, the wound was clean, and after a couple of operations, she was in pretty good shape. But nobody knew who she was, and no one spoke Cambodian. I think some of the Vietnamese knew but wouldn't admit it. They hated Cambodians and didn't treat the girl very well. I never saw any napalm wounds on civilians during my tour, although I did see some on NVA patients in a POW hospital. Most of the Vietnamese casualties, however, came from VC and NVA action. I remember once we got about 50 wounded at once. They were employees of the base camp; a sapper had managed to mine one of the gates, and one of the mama-sans blew it off. Booby traps hurt a lot of civilians. Also, Saigon started putting community television sets, painted the color of the South Vietnamese flag, right in the middle of some of the hamlets. People would assemble there. Sometimes, the VC would rocket or mortar these groups.

Dr. Swan, who also worked with many Vietnamese patients, notes an important fact: The general level of health among Vietnamese was very poor. Consequently, they were quite vulnerable to serious illness or injury:

I was involved in MEDCAPs, and these took a rudimentary form of primary care to the Vietnamese in their villages. This was fairly cosmetic in that often we passed out vitamins, toothpaste, and soap to the Vietnamese. On the other hand, the MEDCAPs that included dental operations (often called DENTCAPs) provided otherwise nonexistent dental care to rural Vietnamese. Likewise, on our MEDCAPs, we often identified the villager in extremis, such as advanced cancer and advanced hernias, and these patients we brought back to our evacuation hospitals and treated with elective surgery. In this case, the MEDCAPs were very successful. Above and beyond all that, however, they were fun and were an opportunity for the medical folks to get outside their compound. It was dangerous, and occasionally the teams fell into bad situations.

Diseases are always a big problem in any war. As a surgeon, I did not encounter disease except as it affected my combat casualties. Thus, all the parasitic diseases such as ascariasis, malaria, and typhoid existed to a greater or lesser degree in our patients. Virtually every Vietnamese shot in the belly had large *Ascaris lumbricoides* worms crawling out the bullet holes. This was incredibly nauseating until you became used to it. All of our Vietnamese patients were anemic from this intestinal parasite, as well as from malaria. I saw many patients with typhoid enteritis, tuberculous peritonitis, pulmonary tuberculosis, amebic abscesses of the liver, etc.

Lily Adams was also closely involved with the Vietnamese:

We took care of the Vietnamese. Sometimes, it's hard for people to understand who believe that My Lai was the menu of the day. A lot of nurses and doctors volunteered for MEDCAPs, where they would go out into the villages. Sometimes, the dentists would go out. We would reach the people who needed health care. If somebody had a foot infection, the doctor would cut it open and clean it out. If people needed hospitalization, they would be referred to the hospital. When we weren't tending to our GIs, when there wasn't a lot of action, we tended to go out and look for trouble, so to speak. These 12-hour shifts could get kind of boring. For us, it was kind of neat to have a villager come in who might have a tumor on the neck and have the doctors remove it and know she had a good possibility of a long and healthy life. Or care for a child with a cleft palate and change his life forever by fixing the defect.

We did a lot of good. One of the strategies was to win hearts and minds. And we did. Our MEDCAPs and involvement with the orphanage and with the villagers was encouraged. You wanted to make friends with these people so they wouldn't like the VC, right? The other reason I see us so involved, especially with the children, is the fact that we were in an adult world. We involved ourselves with the Vietnamese because there were women and children. Children's voices and their laughter—it's the same all over the world—kept us grounded because we were in an adult world. We were involved with war. Sometimes, you forget there's joy in the world at all, and then you listen to these kids teasing each other and there are babies crying and you realize that there is still life here. There is hope in the world. Dealing with the civilians was something we needed, whether the military knew it or not.

There was a Catholic orphanage called the Rose Orphanage, run by sisters. I remember getting involved on some of my days off. I would go down to the orphanage and provide care and bring supplies. I got involved with the orphanage as a result of one of the engineers. He brought in a baby with an abscess. We opened it up and drained it. The baby was fine. He came in a few more times with more babies: I asked him where he was getting all the babies, and why are there all of these abscesses? He didn't know why, so he invited us out to the orphanage. So that's how I got hooked. The nuns blamed it on flies. I got them surgical soap to use on wounds. I had one come in with pneumonic black plague; it was all in her chest. We had an X ray taken, and her lungs looked awful. She died, and we all ended up taking tetracycline. About five days later, I started to get sick, and some of the doctors were concerned that I might have the first stages of the plague. I was allergic to the medicine. There was a lot of TB.

If you've never been to war, you never realize that it's not soldier against soldier only. It's also civilians that get caught in the middle. More civilians died of war than soldiers. It's usually the women and children and old people that suffer. The old people were the worst. They're taken away on a chopper, come in to triage, and get their clothes torn away and stuck by needles—this machine, that machine. It is difficult for them to comprehend, even though we had interpreters.

So the Vietnamese joined the American victims of destruction and disease. Although the real world is never perfect and war no doubt caused events the medical personnel would like to forget, both groups found a haven at Cu Chi. There was, however, another Quonset hut adjacent to the 12th Evac where war mocked the efforts of the dedicated people next door. Lt. Richard Blanks remembers a visit:

When I was executive officer back in the rear, one of my responsibilities was to visit our troops if any were injured or hurt. I would go to the evac hospital and talk with them. I was over there one day to see two of our troops that had been wounded. One of our troops had been killed, I knew that. As I was leaving the hospital, there was this metal shed behind the hospital. Apparently, this was where they left the bodies before someone from graves registration could pick them up. The man who had been killed I had known briefly. He was a black soldier, an incredible physical specimen. Obviously an athlete, he was well over 6 feet tall and muscular. His body was lying in this shed, perfect in every way, with no flaws except this small hole in his chest where the bullet had hit him. But he was lying there dead, waiting for graves registration to come pick him up.

Fortunately, most people survived because of the excellent care they received. After a lifetime in civilian and military surgery, Dr. Swan believes he and his comrades have something to be proud of:

I think the thrust of any description of medical care in Vietnam was that it was awesome. Without a doubt, it was the finest combat casualty care ever rendered to a fighting soldier. In Vietnam, our doctors were exceedingly well trained, and we spent literally twelve years treating large numbers of casualties, so we were good at what we were doing.

Lily Adams witnessed an extraordinary moment that confirms Dr. Swan's opinion:

I met some people in Vietnam that were truly heroes. In quiet ways, like adopting an orphanage. In loud ways. But we all supported each other. I remember when Bob Hope came, the medical people went as a unit so we could keep an eye on the patients that were allowed to go. We were getting settled, and all of a sudden, there was this hooray, this ovation. I thought the show had started, then I realized that was their response to the medical personnel who had walked in. The doctor said, "They're cheering us." You know, we needed that. We got a lot of that from the 25th, and I'm grateful. I'm glad that I served with them.

And as the testimony of scores of Tropic Lightning veterans proves, the soldiers would applaud them once again today, twenty years after the fact.

6

The Vietnamese

In PAST WARS FOUGHT by men in the 25th Division, certain distinctions were clear. There were the battlefields and the rear. There were friends and enemies. There were civilians and combatants. Furthermore, the country in which operations took place served as a great stage, of sorts, with the inhabitants acting as extras in the great drama of war. The exact location— be it Guadalcanal, Korea, or any other land—was an accident of history and almost irrelevant to the nature of the experience.

In Vietnam, everything was different. The Vietnamese people themselves figured in every aspect of the war. Our allies were Vietnamese, and so were our opponents. Furthermore, the civilian presence was encompassing: Even if soldiers wished otherwise, it was impossible to avoid the Vietnamese. The 25th Division itself was frozen in place, operating for nearly five years in the same area with and against the same people. The people, the American soldiers, and the war itself were inextricably entwined. Ironically, in no previous war was the cultural divide between American soldier and indigenous population as wide as it was in Vietnam. And in no previous war were the consequences of this division so vital and so potentially tragic.

Before we consider this delicate and extremely important subject, two points are in order. First, the subject of relationships between the soldiers and the Vietnamese was one almost every respondent addressed in detail. It obviously touches an extremely raw nerve. Some men and women feel a profound and deep sorrow over events in rural Vietnam. Many others wanted to describe their views precisely to hammer home an important point: Human beings do not normally murder people, even if they bear them no affection. Other veterans tried to highlight another side of the picture altogether, pointing to many instances of kindness and affection between the two very different peoples that weighed, in a small way, against the grief and violence that permeated the world they shared. Many men, even those with feelings of sorrow and collective guilt, maintain that the truth, however ugly, did not come close to matching the perverse image created at home. My Lai was and is an albatross on the shoulder of every Vietnam veteran. Almost all of them resent this to some degree, and they are very right to do so. It is almost incomprehensible that so many Americans accepted the idea that the insane actions of one perverse junior officer (threatened twice with death by American soldiers on that horrid morning in My Lai) were representative of the entire U.S. Army. Comparing Vietnam with genuine acts of genocide in our time simultaneously mocks both a brave army in a bad war and the real victims of genuine malevolence. A people that cannot distinguish between tragedy and evil begs to be taught the difference.

Thus, different motives and experiences led to a great divergence in viewpoints. But another factor was at work that few enlisted men, officers, or experts in the field realized at the time or in the years that followed. Simply put, a soldier's attitudes toward the Vietnamese often were greatly influenced by pure accident. No soldier determined when and where he served. Yet, it was precisely these factors that would have a tremendous influence over his view of the Vietnamese.

Rural Vietnam was a complex and profoundly divided political cauldron, brutalized by a generation of civil war. There were, for instance, many hamlets in the 25th Division's AO that were solid, sincere, and long-time Front strongholds. Ironically, some of them were very close to the Cu Chi base camp. The Front ran dozens of hamlets in Hau Nghia and Binh Duong provinces day and night, until the 25th Division forcibly established a Saigon government presence. Some of these hamlets were what the Front called "combat hamlets," places specifically designed for an agonizing guerrilla war within the hamlet itself. Saigon's representatives might watch the streets during the day, but at night, they retreated to the local fort and the Front took over again. Other hamlets, perhaps half a mile away, might have an entirely different political orientation. Perhaps the Catholics or other religious sects were strong. Perhaps it was a more prosperous village, with more peasants owning land and fearful of revolution. Family loyalties, vendettas, and divisions, to make things even more cloudy, made friends of people that should have been enemies and vice versa. Consequently, there were many areas where the Front was feared and respected but not loved. People in some areas were intensely, profoundly anti-Communist. They might also dislike Saigon. But then, nothing was simple in Vietnam. In any case, if soldiers came into contact with these Vietnamese, the road was much easier. Furthermore, many men spent their tours in parts of the AO where there were few civilians. They probably lived in the best of all worlds for everyone's sake. Therefore, if the veterans' accounts differ, bear in mind that so did the setting. Sadly, very few soldiers ever realized this. To them—untrained and poorly prepared in this area—almost every nuance that spoke loudly to the Vietnamese was lost: Everyone looked the same, and everyone was potentially dangerous. It was the only war in American history where our own soldiers did not know and were not trained to know the very people that were or might have been their allies. The Army paid dearly for this policy of learned ignorance. So did many Vietnamese.

Civilians

There were very few American units in Vietnam that were put into closer and more sustained contact with rural Vietnamese than the 25th Division. For reasons not at all apparent in retrospect, the Army did almost nothing to prepare soldiers for the "culture shock"—and the term is a good one here—that almost all of them encountered when coming to Vietnam. A number of veterans, many just out of high school and not "senators' sons," as one put it, stressed how totally ignorant they were about the Vietnamese and their culture. They also were unprepared for the poverty of Vietnam. Initial reactions were usually a mixture of curiosity and disgust. Dan Vandenberg addresses this issue with candor. As luck would have it, Vandenberg's unit was based in Trang Bang, right in the middle of one of the strongest Front areas in South Vietnam:

I think one of the biggest disappointments over there was the attitude of the Vietnamese peasants. None of them seemed to give a shit about us. The feeling was mutual: We didn't even think they were people. Never once did they say, "Don't go over there—that trail is booby-trapped; don't go that way—there's a sniper." There was never a warning of any kind. Never one ounce of friendliness. On the other hand, I can understand why: If they'd have tipped us off, Charlie would have come that night and slit their throats. But it would have been nice to have seen them take a small risk for us once.

When you think about it, it was a total mismatch, like oil and water. We didn't have a clue about their language or their customs. I guess you're not supposed to pat their children on the head. I never knew that, but it was probably the first thing that we did. It was a sign of disrespect, we found out.

We'd eat their food but only out of desperation. We didn't know what the hell we were eating. They looked at us like we were giants: I sure ain't, but everybody in our Army was bigger than they were. They thought we were all rich. I got ambitious and worked it out, and we were making 20 cents an hour on a 24-hour day. We couldn't speak their language; they couldn't speak ours. We looked at them funny. There was a lot of wailing and screaming, which got on everybody's nerves. That's just the way they talked and acted, but it was something else. So we started losing our cool after a while. The Army could have prepared us a little bit better. A majority of us couldn't even say hello or good morning in Vietnamese. The only words we picked up were a mixture of French and Vietnamese, and you couldn't use any of them in polite company. The most frequently used phrase was *ditty mau,* which means, "Get the hell out of here."

Dr. Robert Hanson of the 12th Evac admired the Vietnamese but describes the sort of innocent scene that young Americans of limited experience did not understand:

Their culture was so different. Vietnamese hold hands with the people they are close to. Some patients would hold mine. It was the most incongruous sight. You'd see two ARVN soldiers, armed to the teeth, with a chicken in a cage slung over a shoulder, walking along holding hands.

Cultural misunderstanding exacerbated a far uglier reality. The Communists' concept of a people's war entailed a breakdown of the distinction between civilian and combatant. Front organizers had therefore spent years developing the military potential of sympathetic or contested hamlets throughout Vietnam. Villagers, whether supportive or fearful of the Front, knew they had to provide food, shelter, and intelligence to insurgents, and most hamlets had resident village guerrilla units capable of sniping or laying mines in front of approaching American troops. Tunnels, hiding places, and escape routes were carefully prepared to allow hit-and-run attacks. Guerrillas wore no uniforms and might be any age or either sex. Although American propaganda claimed that U.S. forces were in rural Vietnam to keep the VC away from the villagers, every GI knew that the enemy was already *in* the villages because he was *from* the villages. Thomas Giltner, a platoon leader in 1966, describes the result:

It was the hallmark of the war: You could never tell who was the enemy and who was not. Therefore, you treated everybody with suspicion and distrust. The enemy was everywhere and everybody at all times, and we were the foreigners in their country. We viewed the civilians as pathetic farmers caught in the middle of a tragic conflict that they did not understand, who really wanted to be left to follow their ancestral ways on their family farms. But we also knew that the VC infrastructure in South Vietnam was a part of this placid rural scene. We knew that the VC lived in the hamlets and that they stored caches of weapons, supplies, and rice there. And we knew that the farmers usually operated as local militia for the VC for purposes, at a minimum, of intelligence-gathering, observation of U.S. activities, ambushes, raids, and so on. It became imperative to assume that the people were either VC agents or sympathizers or somehow under their influence.

Any American veteran of Vietnam would echo Giltner's sentiments. However, the inherently bad situation between civilian and GI was particularly difficult for the men of the 25th. The Division's operational area included several longtime Viet Minh–Front strongholds. And if pacification missions and sweeps through villages usually entailed less risk than forays into hellholes like the Ho Bo Woods, they were dangerous, nevertheless. It was a nasty chemistry. Jay Lazarin, a rifleman in 1967, recalls the situation:

The "friendly" civilians were seen as no such thing. To us, there were no friendly civilians, only ones who posed no immediate threat. But because they were perceived as (at best) harmless for the moment, they were treated with relative ambivalence. We let our guard down with them a bit more, as we sat around their villages during area sweeps. The friendly villages around Duc Hoa were always a pleasure to sweep because we knew it was an easy operation with very low risk, compared to other areas we had been to. The vast open rice paddy country was considered beautiful because we imagined that we could see clear into Cambodia, and as we camped among the tree lines of the villages, we watched the spectacular sunsets knowing that we might get a good night's sleep. But even these friendly villagers slept in their underground bunkers when we were around, and as darkness came, our attitude toward them changed. We felt that they knew where the VC were and that they would never warn us if an attack of some sort was coming. So in the morning, even after an uneventful night, the villagers were always looked at in a different way, one that reinforced our mistrust of anything non-American and, in retrospect, one that reinforced our ignorance of their dilemma.

C. W. Bowman holds many of the same views as Lazarin, but he also stresses the ambivalence and confusion of 25th Division combat soldiers:

Our guys were mostly teenagers and thought most about whores. A lot of us didn't try to understand the people or make friends. Some of us hated them:

Everybody was a zip, gook, or animal. I think many of us wanted to be friends with the civilian population and get to know them, but you couldn't. You couldn't trust them. Well, some you could, but there were a lot you couldn't, and how do you know who was who? There were a lot of VC sympathizers. Many times when we approached a village, Chinese claymore mines would be blown off as we got close. You'd search the village, and there was nothing but old papa-san, mama-san, and young children. Somebody had to be detonating the mines. Sometimes, you wouldn't find things in the village, but sometimes you would. Not always weapons, but you'd go into a hooch and find 50 or 60 pairs of chopsticks: Who's using those? There would be other little signs to let you know that the VC were spending the nights in the village or the villagers were supporting them when they moved through.

Mostly the children in the village were great; they were smart. We felt sorry for them because we came from a country where people lived in mansions compared to the Vietnamese. They lived in straw hooches with dirt floors. You'd see little kids on a water buffalo out there in the rice paddy with smiles on their faces. Of course, they could cuss you out real quick. That was our fault—it was something we taught them to do. Usually, we'd give away all of our candy and throw it to the kids. After a while, later in the war, as a lot of your friends got killed by booby traps or sniper fire, this changed. You don't see your enemy, so the people you do see become your enemy. You become hardened. You could tell some of the old-timers because, instead of tossing their candy or C rations *to* the kids, they would throw it *at* them. I guess you would say it was hard-hearted, but that's what you had to be to survive over there.

The famous wartime rumor mill worked overtime in Vietnam. Many of the things that soldiers heard and believed, such as stories about old ladies or young children throwing hand grenades, were rarely, if ever, true. Some stories were total myth. Ignorance surrounded everything. Few soldiers, for instance, realized that the mines and booby traps that made life hell for them killed thousands of Vietnamese civilians, as well. Nor did guerrillas, much less Main Force units, tell civilians their military plans. A civilian might know these things but probably did not. Mario Tarin describes the attitude of many American soldiers:

A few GIs really got involved with the Vietnamese and tried to learn their language and customs, but most of us really didn't want anything to do with them. The only Vietnamese words we learned were the cusswords. The young kids did the same. They would curse at us in English, and we cursed them in Vietnamese. The Army did its best to keep us from associating with them because "all" civilians were potential VC and could toss a grenade at us at any moment; or if we bought a bottled soda from them, we might be drinking acid or powdered glass. Also, the whores might have razor blades in their vaginas, and we would have a hell of a time explaining to our wives why our pecker was split open like a banana; or we might get "blue balls" or some other type of incurable disease and be kept in a hospital in Japan until a cure was found. Consequently, we saw the gooks as subhumans and were prejudiced against them and downright hated their guts! Seeing a dead gook was no big deal. It only hurt when Americans got killed.

The struggle in Vietnam was extremely harsh, and acts of cruelty on the part of American soldiers toward civilians were common. Some men considered it sport to throw rocks or shoot slingshots at civilians. Many soldiers pushed around the slight Vietnamese, and some administered beatings. American interrogators working through their Vietnamese interpreters often employed physical intimidation and the threat of worse when questioning suspects. Men routinely shouted racial obscenities and insults. Some people on both sides mutilated the dead. Farm animals were shot for no reason: Officers instructed soldiers not to kill water buffalo, but some could not resist the temptation, probably not realizing that the material damage done might be worse than "torching a hooch."

The roadways were a particularly common site of cruelty and, sometimes, tragedy. Vietnamese roads were poor by American standards, and the U.S. Army used an astounding number of vehicles. Whether the vehicle in question was a truck or a tank, its driver was likely to be a young man. He might be exhausted, afraid, or merely cruel. The same might be true concerning any passengers. Because there were few roads, traffic was congested. Civilians traveled in every way imaginable—old cars, trilambrettas, motor scooters, oxcarts, or on foot. Sometimes, drivers could not resist the temptation to swerve slightly and run a cart or pedestrian off the road, even if injury was likely. Many men enjoyed chucking anything handy at Vietnamese along the roads. It was also a choice place to hurl racial insults and make obscene gestures, many of which the Vietnamese were quick to return. Simple accidents, however, were the worst cause of grief, and many Americans died this way. The Vietnamese frequently caused accidents with American vehicles, and Vietnamese vehicles, rarely well driven and never models of safety, often crashed into each other. Terrible sadness could easily result.

None of this was the norm, but, because the volume of both traffic and people was so large, the number of accidents and victims mounted very quickly. Unfortunately, on more than one occasion, tragedies were turned into something worse by malicious Americans. Michael Call witnessed one of these incidents:

Lieutenant "Smith" only had been in-country about five months. He was one of those people who thought they knew everything there was to know about survival in the Nam. Well, he did not know shit. We tried to help him get "in-country smart," but to no avail. He was returning from Tay Ninh City to Phuc Ninh, where Recon was based. As he was driving his jeep and *drunk,* he ran over a twelve-year-old girl riding her motorcycle from her home in Phuc Ninh. This happened just outside our outpost, and I went to the accident site and was a witness to this asshole bargaining with the parents of the little girl, who was dead, of course. After much haggling, the father of the little girl consented to a payment of around $55 to settle the matter. The sad thing about this transaction is that the $55 was not for the dead girl but for the cost of replacing the motorcycle. I think perhaps after witnessing this sorry episode, I finally realized that life was so very cheap and, if not only cheap, at least negotiable concerning the future of an American officer and the evidently low status of a pretty twelve-year-old Vietnamese girl. I can still see her to this day, lying beside the road, and the lieutenant making stupid remarks and showing no remorse. It crossed my mind that I just might want to blow his ass away.

Negotiating through this difficult world was sometimes made harder by gross cultural insensitivity on the part of American soldiers. Mechanized platoon leader Morgan Sincock provides a sad example:

Some of our other actions were clearly conceived and executed with indifference to the feelings of the populace. For example, the use of cemeteries for encampments was not uncommon. On several occasions during the wet season, we set up night defensive positions in cemeteries. We did this because the paddies were full and the village cemetery was often the highest ground at the edge of a village, thus offering good fields of fire (across the paddies), with only one flank (facing the village) affording the enemy concealed avenues of approach. The cemeteries were left in ruins when we drove off. I also can recall (unfortunately, very vividly) being ordered to open a grave in a cemetery. During Tet 1968, the VC/NVA had used mock funerals and cemeteries to move and conceal weapons. Therefore, when we came upon a freshly mounded grave with a 1958 date of death, it was suspicious. We had to dig up the coffin, open it, and confirm that it did not contain weapons. All we found was a ten-year-old corpse, and once we called that in on the radio, we were ordered to move out before the grave could be properly reclosed.

The men of the 25th Division also witnessed brutality toward the peasantry on the part of both the South Vietnamese government and the Front. C. W. Bowman describes the harsh environment that resulted:

You saw a lot of things and did a lot of things you didn't want to see or do because you had to. We didn't burn any villages. But if you found a hooch in the jungle in a place like the Iron Triangle or War Zone C, hell, yes, you'd burn it because you knew who was using it. As far as dealing with the hamlets, if we found people without an ID card, we'd hand them over to local forces. The local forces could be very tough. They'd take the people and beat the hell out of them. Once they caught a papa-san—it's hard to tell people's ages over there: You're either young or old. They thought he was a VC sympathizer. The local Vietnamese took this guy and tied his wrists to his ankles, slid a board underneath the small of his back, and lifted him up off the ground. They put a towel around his nose and mouth, and they wet the towel and lathered it with soap. This guy was trying to breathe with half the towel going down his throat. They were asking him questions, and if he didn't answer, one of the Vietnamese would punch him in the stomach and another one would throw a bucket of water on the towel at the same time so they'd be half choking him to death. This thing went on for maybe a half hour. They were beating on this guy. They finally gave up on him, gave him a case of C rations, and sent him home. That night, that old man was probably a VC sympathizer, and I probably would be, too.

The VC and the NVA were hard on the villagers, too. They'd go in and take out a whole village. Kill everyone—mama-san, baby-san, pigs, cows, water buffaloes, and chickens. They'd do that to set an example for the hamlets around the area. But most people in the United States never read about anything like that: They read about what the damn dumb GI did. There were things we did over there, sure—I don't condone them, and they weren't right. We didn't have any atrocities like My Lai. But there were an awful lot of things the VC did that were never heard about.

Although the atmosphere in rural Vietnam was tense, dangerous, and ugly, there is no evidence of willful murder of civilians by 25th Division soldiers. It is very possible, even likely, that murders took place. Yet, they were almost certainly rare. Many veterans are outraged by the image that still exists in some quarters today of the American soldier as an indiscriminate killer. Several of the men responding to this research eagerly confronted the issue and vehemently denied that any such thing took place in their units. Jim Ross comments on this serious matter:

I never heard of renegade squads or anything like that. My Lai was bizarre, an unusual aberration. Things like it were strictly for the movies. The average soldier fought hard and well.

Another typical response comes from Thomas Giltner:

I never saw any illegal killings. No man under my command or direction at any time committed any murders or rapes or engaged in any such activities. I'm certainly not saying it didn't happen in the annals of the Vietnam War, but not in my presence or my unit.

Tet veteran Larry Fontana puts his case very strongly:

Some units of the 25th operated in densely populated areas in Vietnam. Obviously, we were in contact with civilians. It was made clear to all the men I was with, when I first joined the 25th during our initial five-day training, that any soldier who intentionally harmed a civilian would have his skin hanging on the wall. During my year in Vietnam, I never saw an American soldier mistreat a civilian. Sometimes, we would have to get them out of their hooches, and a mama-san would give us some mouth, and we'd have to yell back and threaten. But it was all acting. We always took extra C rations with us on village-type patrols to give to the civilians. I believe most of us realized they were caught in the middle of this mess and didn't like the NVA any more than the United States fighting in their backyards. On one occasion, the civilians let us know there were 5 VC hiding in their village, and we found them hiding in a hollowed-out anthill. We got along great with the kids. They were all mesmerized by us as we came into the village. I can't remember ever being in a village where I felt a distinct hostility toward us. Some villages we would patrol through treated us with friendliness and respect. We would talk as best we could in our pidgin to them. We would not strut into villages as gods or conquerors. My platoons had a small share of borderline soldiers, but they were easily controlled by the other men and especially the sergeants. One of our newer guys burned down a hooch on his own while we were leaving a village. I guess he thought that's what he was supposed to do. Our captain ripped him apart unmercifully. I never saw a civilian killed by an American during my tour in Vietnam.

A vast majority of veterans insist that most American combat soldiers fought a very hard war honorably. This, they claim, was true even if most soldiers bore little affection toward the Vietnamese. The evidence strongly supports this claim. The 25th Division brass realized from the first day that friction with the civilians was inevitable; consequently, enlisted men were warned not to abuse civilians, and officers were cautioned to watch this matter.

Like all divisions, the 25th had a staff judge advocate's office that dealt with matters of military justice. Anthony Cavender was a young attorney when assigned to Cu Chi in 1966. His thoughts are of interest:

In a combat setting, we tried many cases of cowardice before the enemy and disobedience of orders. We also tried many cases of theft, larceny, and assault. Obviously, there were also several cases of AWOL and desertion. At that time, illegal drugs did not seem to be much of a problem.

I do not recall any cases of atrocities or war crimes during this time. We knew of the command's instructions to adhere to the Law of War, which was printed in the handbooks or guides for the troops. Vietnamese civilians were present in large numbers outside the base camp, and Vietnamese women worked as cleaning women inside the compound. There were a few rapes and/or sexual assaults against Vietnamese women but nothing, unfortunately, out of the ordinary. By this I mean nothing more than you would expect to happen when a large group of young men is set down in a confined area, whether in the States or overseas. I do not wish to be viewed as being insensitive to barbarous behavior.

Every legal officer that I knew was shocked by the My Lai killings and was pleased to see the Army prosecute these cases very vigorously.

In addition, independent lines of communication existed on these matters. South Vietnamese district and province officials, although often indifferent, sometimes confronted the 25th Division command very forcefully concerning violent incidents. American advisers stationed in the districts and provinces frequently complained about the 25th Division's use of firepower and undoubtedly had much to do with the gradual tightening of the Division's rules of engagement concerning its use. Cu Chi was close to Saigon, and reporters passed through frequently. As the war went on, many journalists eagerly sought atrocity stories. The news of My Lai itself shook the Army badly, and a repetition would have been a catastrophe. Consequently, later in the war, all divisions anxiously sought to identify and remove anyone like Lt. William Calley from their ranks.

Another military impulse that always operated during Vietnam was rarely considered by civilian commentators. Any commander worth a nickel during war realizes that a military unit, by definition, has the capability to wreak total havoc against civilians. He also realizes that allowing soldiers to do so would have a devastating impact on discipline and morale. Calley, after all, not only committed the worst war crime in American history but also destroyed his own unit's fighting ability. If soldiers are allowed to break the most elementary laws of human behavior, it is not easy to tell them where to stop. The entire group ethos of the warrior, which remains essential to the fighting ability of any army, presupposes that the violence soldiers dispense is for a higher good. That higher good might be something as simple as the survival of the group, but without it, the will to stand together dissolves. An army of murderers is not an army, and officers know this well.

Nevertheless, the best evidence that indiscriminate violence was very much the exception can be seen in the actions of some of the Vietnamese civilians themselves. American units in the field drew large numbers of small entrepreneurs wherever they went, and the hawkers and prostitutes, regardless of what they thought of American combat troops, obviously felt safe enough to be around them on a daily basis. Dan Vandenberg, a rifleman with the 2/12th, describes a typical road-clearing sweep outside of Trang Bang district town in 1969:

It was like a circus. Walking with us were girls and kids selling soda, beer, cigarettes, lighters, jackets, etc. You name it, they had it. If they didn't have it, and you asked for it, they'd have it the next day. Naturally, there was a "fun girls" contingent. It looked like a parade. But as soon as the Vietnamese civilians wouldn't go any further, we got uneasy real fast, I'll tell you. If we wanted to know what we were going to do the next day, we'd ask the civilians. They'd know before our commander knew.

Hamlets near American bases invariably grew greatly in size. This represented more than a desire to live in a safer area: Any government-controlled village or district town would do as well for that. Rather, it was due to a desire to make money off the U.S. Army. Economically and socially, this may have been a bad thing, but it was certainly not the action of a population terrified of wanton brutality on the part of American soldiers. Vietnamese were likewise eager to obtain the relatively high-paying jobs available at the 25th Division base camps, particularly Cu Chi. The Americans obliged by hiring hundreds of them, despite the fact that everyone knew that many were enemy sympathizers or agents. Mortar fire against Cu Chi, for instance, became more accurate when civilians were allowed into the center of the camp in early 1967.

Nihilistic mayhem was not the cause of death and destruction in Vietnam. Combat operations, however, frequently were. American units relied heavily on firepower both to accomplish their mission and to save the lives of U.S. troops. In the "boonies," the equation was simple because the mission was simply to "kill VC." Consequently, in places like the Ho Bo Woods or along the Cambodian border, officers employed firepower at will. The men encountered a painful contradiction when they operated in heavily populated areas. In theory, American troops on pacification duty were there to protect the villagers and aid Saigon's efforts to create political support, on one hand, and to kill VC with the least possible cost in American lives, on the other. American combat methods were well enough suited to the latter purpose, but they were woefully inadequate for the former. This was especially complicated because hamlets were excellent places from which the enemy could launch ambushes. In addition, American intelligence was convinced that Front guerrillas intentionally provoked firefights in populated areas, hoping that Americans would bring in their firepower, kill civilians, destroy property, and thus poison relations between the villagers and the South Vietnamese government.

The officers of the 25th Division were well aware of this dilemma, but they could find no good solution for it. It is difficult to generalize about the use of firepower by the 25th because so much was up to the officer on the spot. In addition, restrictions on firepower became tighter as the war progressed. Thomas Giltner gives a good description of the situation as it existed in late 1966:

Firepower was the biggest problem of all. We finally had to decide how to set priorities and deal with engagements in the field. This included engagements in or near a hamlet or village. The mission was "search and destroy." We were to engage the enemy troops, destroy them, and capture weapons, documents, and supplies. This was not only for a body count and to weaken enemy forces but to establish, maintain, and control our presence and influence over an area that we more or less permanently were assigned. The war was military, political, psychological, and logistical, all at the same time. There were no front lines, no terrain to capture, no clear military objective that would establish "victory" as it was known in past wars.

With these limitations, we decided to do the following. If we were approaching a hamlet, we presumed it was hostile. We did this whether it was believed friendly, neutral, or hostile. Unless we observed something, no fire was used. We certainly did not use reconnaissance by fire. [This is a common military tactic in which a unit directs fire toward a location where the enemy might be concealed, hoping that he will return fire and reveal his position. American units routinely used it in the boonies.—EMB] We didn't saturate the area with machine guns or shoot rockets into it or rake it with gunships or anything of that nature. No artillery or indirect fire. We just simply went through the area. We were very careful inside these villages, but that was all.

When we went through, we made whatever searches were deemed appropriate to the mission. Believe you me, we were careful inside these villages. We were careful of what we looked at, where we looked, where we stepped; we kept our eyes open in all directions. But that was all we did.

If fired upon, you tried to estimate how big the enemy unit was. But you never really knew unless you were very close. Under field conditions where the terrain is rugged and visibility limited, the size of any enemy force is difficult to estimate. You never really know until you get pretty close and it heats up. A lot of this depends upon how the enemy wants you to perceive his strength at any given time. You could usually tell if it was a very small or overwhelmingly large force. But you can't see the enemy: He is hidden and shooting at you from well-concealed positions. It is an "on-the-spot" judgment. At that time, we would use all force necessary, within reason. Most engagements were short: The enemy would hit us and run. The longer the engagement, the more firepower. Sometimes we had more firepower, and sometimes less. Sometimes we had tactical air for strafing, napalm—real tactical air support—but that was usually only with a battalion-sized force. Second were gunships. Sometimes gunships were right with us overhead or standing by. There would be Cobras and Hueys armed to the teeth with machine guns and rockets on call at Division. We could get them in just as quickly as we received dust-offs and Medevacs.

Third was indirect fire in the form of our mortars or artillery. On my operations, I not only had my radio, which was tuned in to battalion frequency, but I took with me the mortar forward observers so we could dial up anyone we needed. You had to know exactly where you were on the map: That was crucial for survival. If you don't know where you are on the map, you'd better find out, or you may already be dead. It is very easy in a small operation to get yourself in trouble very quickly and to need a lot of help very fast. Sometimes we used too much firepower, but we never really knew, when the shooting started, what we were up against, so we presumed the very worst.

We had no desire to harm any of the villagers—the innocent peasant farmers, if that's what they were—and this was true even though we believed them to be VC sympathizers or forced by the Viet Cong to support their activities. As Mao put it, they were the sea that the fish swam in. At the same time, we did what was necessary to carry out our mission. Obviously, a lot of people on both sides wound up getting hurt.

Giltner also expresses the common impression that Front guerrillas would exploit a reluctance to fire:

If and when the VC perceived our reluctance to fire on a certain area, they would exploit it to the hilt. They would hit us from a village or hamlet they thought we were reluctant to fire upon. Or else they would fire outside a village and retreat into a hamlet, thinking we wouldn't fire back. But on those occasions, they were badly mistaken. We would protect the local people if we could, but we were certain to protect our people and our mission.

Furthermore, Giltner doubts that the theoretically critical "village war" ever made genuine headway:

There were coordinated efforts of the U.S. military with the Vietnamese government to create a scheme or a plan to declare certain areas or hamlets "pacified." This was done by degrees. There was a color-coded chart of hamlets that had four or five categories. They were said to be either "pacified," "undergoing pacification," "secured," "undergoing clearing and securing," or "hostile." Make no mistake about it, this pacification plan and the chart with all of its color-coded territories never had any counterpart whatever in the world of reality. It was part of the overall briefing that everyone received who had to know what was going on in South Vietnam: It was the official U.S. explanation for what we were doing. It was known in Army parlance as the "dog and pony show."

Charles Albridge was a forward observer when Giltner served. Like many of the early arrivals, Albridge spent much time in and near the heavily populated areas of the AO. He recalls that officers were aware of the problem of stress between villagers and soldiers from the first day and tried to find an acceptable response:

We didn't trust civilians. Cu Chi village itself was supposed to be a safe area, yet there were a couple of times when men went there and were later found dead and mutilated. We didn't know if the people themselves did it or not, but it did cause problems. The question of populated hamlets comes from the My Lai thing. I can say from my personal experience I would call it an aberration. I don't doubt that My Lai happened; I just don't believe it happened with an extreme amount of regularity. When we went through an area on sweeps, we would be given data from intelligence as to whether any villages in the area were (1) friendly, (2) known to be unfriendly, or (3) questionable. It was all we had to go on. If we went into an area that was supposed to be friendly, we dealt with it in that light, unless we were attacked. If it was questionable, we would send in scouts and see if they could sniff anything out: If we had to go through the village or close to it, we would put out extra security.

If it was an enemy hamlet, the normal procedure was to avoid it if possible; but if we took fire from it, then, plain and simple, you just go in and take it. While the shooting is going on, especially when you are dealing with a populated village like that, if you're being fired at and you're shooting back, I am sure that civilians got killed. There is, unfortunately, no way to get around that, and it happens in any war. For the most part, once the firing stopped from the village, we stopped firing into it. I never personally saw civilians lined up and shot. We removed them from villages and moved them to camps. When we secured a specifically enemy hamlet or perhaps one declared questionable and moved the people out, especially if we were close to the Ho Bo or the Iron Triangle, we would destroy the village. This was a standing order. You destroyed any crops that were stockpiled. I never saw civilians killed deliberately. I may have killed people inadvertently myself when calling in mortars or artillery: I just don't know.

In the summer of 1968, Morgan Sincock had even more firepower available to support his platoon than Giltner had a year and a half before. Yet, the rules of engagement had been tightened, and Sincock had occasion to chafe under restrictions:

When we made contact with the enemy, we always had ample supporting firepower available to us. We always operated out of a fire support base (FSB), and our operations were never planned to extend beyond the range of the 105mm howitzers (usually 3 guns) in the FSB. We could get an artillery fire mission within moments. Helicopter gunships (as well as dust-offs) were usually available within 15 to 20 minutes. We could usually get an air strike on station (at our disposal) in about 30 minutes. About half of the time, the air strike would be coordinated by an FAC (forward air controller) in a small Piper Cub–sized plane. He could identify targets with a white phosphorous rocket. Two Phantoms would then make a series of "runs" on the target. They alternately dropped 250- and 500-pound bombs and napalm, strafed the target with their machine guns, and made occasional "dry" runs to try to get the enemy to poke his head up in the belief that the jets were out of ordnance.

We were free to use this firepower outside of populated areas. Many, although not all, officers shared my philosophy that it was wisest to use maximum firepower and minimum frontal assaults by infantry.

When we were in populated areas, we were often prohibited from using all of our available firepower. I recall two specific instances, one in Tay Ninh City and the other in a village a mile or so east of Trang Bang. In the latter case, during July 1968, we were going east on the road to the village, and the village residents were passing us loaded down with their household belongings, going west. It was obvious that they were fleeing an imminent battle. We did make contact with a platoon-sized element at the edge of the village. We pulled back about 100 meters and continued to put small-arms fire on the suspected positions. We were unsure of the exact enemy location. They had fired on us as we walked through a cornfield (déjà vu Antietam). The cornstalks obscured our vision, and we could not tell if the enemy positions were at the edge of the cornfield, in a house behind the cornfield, or along a hedgerow behind the house. We thought that at least one enemy position was in the house.

When the Cobra helicopter gunships came on station, I told them to rocket the house, but my battalion commander came on the radio and vetoed the order. He also canceled my request for an air strike. We continued to exchange fire with the enemy for the rest of the afternoon, and one of our other companies maneuvered to flank the enemy, but they sustained a number of wounded and had to draw back. I was reluctant to risk lives on a frontal assault because we were unable to use our firepower. In this case, we knew the civilian population had fled, so we were only "protecting" *property* by not using all of our firepower. As night fell, we could see and other allied positions could see numerous enemy fleeing the village. As I recall, even with enemy in the open, we did not bring in supporting fire in an effort to protect civilian property.

This situation is at great variance with the popular notion that Americans frequently burned villages to the ground. Such things just did not happen in my experience. I only heard of one village along Highway 1 that was said to have been burned to the ground by our troops during Tet, and I am aware of no documentation about that incident—only word of mouth, months after the fact. [Sincock is probably referring to Tan Phu Trung, a large village on Highway 1 near Hoc Mon. During Tet, an enemy battalion seized it, allowed the civilians to leave, and dug in, trying to cut the highway. Much of the village was leveled during days of American attacks before the enemy was destroyed.—EMB]

In the Tay Ninh incident, we encountered a large VC/NVA force dug in along the edge of a Cao Dai temple compound in the southern part of the city. This would have been around 20 August 1968. There were hundreds of civilians caught in the initial cross fire between our two mech companies and the entrenched enemy, but the civilians quickly dispersed. We had a positive fix on the enemy trench line. We called for gunships to rocket the trench line, but the request was vetoed. During a long afternoon of small-arms fire, we requested and were refused air strikes, artillery, and even our own supporting 81mm mortars.

Del Plonka had commanded a platoon in Tay Ninh the year before. He contends that Division policy was much the same as Sincock suggests:

In our case, our policy was: If it was gray, you did not fire into it; if it was white, you did not fire into it; if it was black, you asked for permission. [He refers to map codes: Gray indicated a contested area; white, a friendly area; and black, a Viet Cong area.—EMB] We did not mess with the villages—we stayed away from them as much as possible. These stories you hear about burning villages and atrocities come from the movies.

Sincock's attitude that it was best to fight the war with "bullets, not bodies" was shared by almost every combat soldier in Vietnam. Some partisans of the pacification campaign argued that firepower should always be minimized to avoid destruction: Their motto was, "In an insurgency, the bayonet is the best weapon, an air strike the worst." Yet, to the people on the ground, such sentiments reflected a military romanticism that threatened their lives. Jay Lazarin's thoughts were common enough:

When you are trying to survive, there is no such thing as too much firepower. We were not military tacticians or logistics people; we were infantrymen trying to kill them before they killed us.

Robert Conner expresses the same view:

I remember one time we had a colonel who said he did not believe in using soldiers where he could use artillery or air strikes: Hey, I like that. And we had the artillery and tanks and air strikes all the time. But somehow or another, he got promoted or moved, and we got another colonel in there who was just the opposite: He did not believe in artillery and air strikes when he could use manpower. How stupid.

Sincock is correct in stating that villages were rarely destroyed. In this regard, the term "free fire zone" has been very badly interpreted. Free fire zones were areas that American forces fired into at will. They were normally in the hinterlands and included the major Front redoubts. Implicit in the term, however, is a suggestion of its opposite. If one area is a free fire zone, then another area is not. Indeed, as the war progressed and public criticism of American tactics grew in the United States, the Army steadily tightened its rules of engagement.

Nevertheless, combat in or near hamlets was common enough. As I illustrated earlier, the enemy almost always took the first shot in Vietnam. Even the severest critics of Division policy among the men I contacted pointed out that American units did not employ "reconnaissance-by-fire" tactics near hamlets. Many soldiers argue that when Front forces ambushed an American unit inside a hamlet, they bore responsibility for what took place. Others found some bitter comfort in the knowledge that suffering was inflicted by the other side, also. American firepower was greater, but there was almost always ample warning of the approach of U.S. forces, giving villagers time to hide in the little shelters that were in virtually every peasant house. On the other hand, violent acts directed against civilians by the Communists were everyday events in Vietnam. And whether this violence took the form of assassinations, surprise mortar attacks on progovernment hamlets, or mines laid on the roads, it usually came without warning.

Yet, for many men of the 25th Division, such comparisons have little meaning. Many—probably most—of the combat veterans witnessed incidents of profound tragedy that they live with still. The horrifying events encountered by Jay Lazarin in early 1967 show a cruel war at its worst:

My first combat operation came a few days later. I either was too nervous to listen carefully or the information never reached my level of the platoon; anyway, I had no idea where I was going except that we were going in helicopters and landing outside a hostile village. My "rookie buddies" and I gave each other all sorts of secret looks of encouragement as we boarded the helicopters. The others in the squad were more serious looking and intense. We landed just outside a village that had been bombed by jets and was still being strafed by helicopter gunships. I was assigned as an ammo bearer for an M60 machine-gun team. I was so loaded down with ammo and so scared as we landed in the middle of the rocketing and machine-gunning of this village that as we jumped from the chopper, I leaned forward when I hit the ground and couldn't stop running when everyone else was lying on the dry rice paddy behind me. As I finally sprawled out about 30 feet from the rest of the platoon, I had images of being left there, amongst the deafening noises of the rockets exploding, and at that instant, I thought that those minutes were going to be the last ones I would ever see. Sheer panic took over, but my squad leader crawled up to where I was and had a smile on his face that made everything seem so easy and safe. When he stood up after the last helicopters left the area, I was amazed, assuming that all of the firing had come from both the gunships and the Viet Cong. I had no idea what was going on; I only had the rest of the squad to follow, nervously trying to absorb my new surroundings. Within minutes, I saw my first casualties of the war; they were Vietnamese.

Lying under bushes at the tree line were a father and two children; all had been hit by napalm. Their skin at various parts of their bodies was hanging off or, in the case of the badly burned girl, was dragging on the ground as they approached, the father gesturing with his two hands together in front of his face, as if in prayer. Myself and my "basic buddy" were told by my platoon sergeant to guard them as he motioned them to sit where they were. He and the rest of the platoon then started to search the tree line for other "Viet Cong."

I was horrified and curious at the same time; I couldn't keep my eyes off of them. I saw the damage that the napalm had done but didn't understand the mechanism that could cause such burns to still smolder as we sat opposite them. The children seemed to sleep but never cried. The father cried and continuously spoke to us and to himself. Neither I nor my buddy had any idea what he was saying. Through gestures, we offered him water, but he either didn't seem to understand or was not interested in our help. I asked a passing sergeant if we could help them in any way. "*Them?*" he said, pointing to the bushes where they sat. "Fuck 'em! That's Victor Charlie!" He quickly walked off toward the rest of the platoon. We sat there shocked and amazed. How could these people be Viet Cong, we asked each other, quietly, of course (we kept our thoughts between ourselves). More importantly, we didn't question the sergeant's reaction to our request to help them: He was experienced at this, we thought; he must know what he was talking about. We simply sat there for a least a half hour, listening to the sounds of men dropping grenades into bunkers and wells, firing shotguns at livestock, and then watching both the children die as the father vainly attempted to slap them both back to life as each one stopped breathing. I went for help after the first one seemed to go still. My platoon lieutenant came back with me and called a medic over the radio, who came as the father gasped for air in gulps, then fell over dead. Only then did we see that his entire back flesh had been completely burned through, exposing ribs and organs darkened from the burning. The medic looked at the children and walked away. He said nothing to us.

So, this was my first impression of the war itself. I didn't understand the scope of the whole action that had taken place and certainly didn't believe that these people were anything like my "enemy" was supposed to be. I had little sorrow at the time for them; maybe I was too busy trying to learn what I could about every move that the more experienced guys were doing that day. Those first casualties quickly faded from thought as we camped inside the village that evening and darkness engulfed us. (Yet, those same 3 people came back to my mind months later and continued to reappear, time and time again, over many years and still do, amongst "others." They, with the other particularly memorable ones, seem to be the real life symbols of our efforts in Vietnam.)

Gerry Schooler was in the middle of the bloody Tet Offensive of 1968. The Communist offensive brought the war into the densely populated areas around Saigon, and Front attacks demolished many hamlets. Whenever the North's men tried to stay, which was often, American or ARVN counterattack was certain. Schooler reflects on the results:

The thing that probably caused me more pain and anguish than anything else was just to see the civilians suffer, many times at our hands. I'm not talking about a My Lai–type of situation; I am talking about walking through a village and someone taking a potshot at you. You've probably heard this story a thousand times: It happened to every infantry unit over there. You take a sniper round or two—you may or may not be hit, but that's not really important. What's important is that the powers that were at that time thought it was more important to get that 1 sniper than it was not to get any of the 200 people in that village. They had no qualms about calling in air strikes and artillery right at the edge of a village or right in the village. I suppose all wars have been fought that way. I am sure that Hitler would have had no qualms. I don't think Patton would have. But the thing was that you would walk through afterwards and, in most cases, you still didn't have your sniper. But you did have little kids, women, old men lying around with their legs blown off, lying in the dirt making red mud. It is a horrible thing. That bothered me badly. You know, I never felt sorry for a VC, an NVA, or even one of our guys: We were the soldiers on both sides. If you are going to play that game, it is part of the rule book. But those kids didn't really have a say in it.

The other thing that bothered me about the people was the disdain shown for the average Vietnamese by the Americans. So many people had chips on their shoulders. If people had wives or girlfriends, someone else was screwing them back home. Their classmates were doing fine. But they were suffering. Who was to blame? They probably should have been blaming the government, but the handiest person around was the Vietnamese civilian. These were people that were about 4 feet 11 inches and very poor and ill equipped to deal with a hundred angry rifles and machine guns. That wore me down, too. I was raised to think we were on the other side, and I just couldn't see it. That doesn't mean everyone over there was bad, but if I would have been Vietnamese, I would have been a VC, even though I am an anti-Communist. I would not have been able to sit there and watch whole people's lives go up in smoke at the whim of a nineteen-year-old punk who blew away 2 or 3 people just because he was angry. It was like getting a lobotomy. I used to wonder, how could anyone do these horrible things that I read about concerning World War II, but I could see how it would happen. I bet half of our guys were capable of it. This is where good officers come in. They really have to keep their people from running amok. I think that's what happened in My Lai.

When walking through open rice paddy areas, I didn't feel as afraid. It was pretty open, so it would be hard for a battalion of NVA to hide there. But they were heavily booby-trapped, and you had to deal with the issue of who was the enemy. I guess it depends on your definition of fear. In my opinion, none of them were friendly. I didn't see how they could have been, going through with us what they were going through. My feeling was that everybody except people profitting from the war, like the whores and pimps, wanted us out of there, and they were probably spies, too.

It is very difficult to gauge the motivations of people in the midst of a dangerous situation. If the nurses at Cu Chi had to waken their patients by squeezing their toes to prevent the wounded from thinking they were being attacked in their sleep, one can imagine how deep combat experience conditions behavior. There were also many exhausted, hate-filled young men in the field. And it did not take much to provoke fire, especially from inexperienced soldiers. Although outright murder was certainly rare, the sort of incident described by Richard Blanks took place more than once:

There was another day when we were on patrol; I was 2d Platoon leader. My platoon was in the rear of the company that day. We heard M60 machine-gun fire from the front of the column, and I moved my platoon up to the flank of the company, but the fire had stopped by this time. When I moved up close, I could see what had happened. Apparently, a young Vietnamese girl had been walking in front of our company column. One of our men had yelled out a challenge to her. She ignored it and started running. One of the machine gunners shot her to death. There was this young Vietnamese girl, maybe sixteen years old, lying in the rice paddy dike, dead, with her eyes open, and it was starting to rain. Just lying there. The company commander just had us move on. Some of the Vietnamese in nearby hooches were watching the whole thing. It was one of those memories that stayed with me.

Yet, many soldiers of the 25th Division had a different type of experience. Tet veteran Ron Hart was in Tay Ninh and had much less contact with villagers. He describes an odd encounter that is moving testimony to the disorientation and sadness faced by many people in rural Vietnam:

I guess most GIs didn't pay enough attention to the people of South Vietnam; after all, this was their country. Nothing made me feel worse than a conversation I had with a girl, eight or nine years old, who lived in Soui Dau around the Black Virgin Mountain area. Her brother was taken away the night before to serve in some army. Which one? She didn't know—both the ARVN and VC "recruited." He was twelve years old. This was not that unusual. We had an interpreter, an ARVN staff sergeant who had been in the army six years. He was eighteen years old. They're just kids. In fact, the ARVNs had to be issued short M1 carbines. They couldn't handle anything else until they could get M16s.

Sgt. Maj. Jack Wood encountered confused and rootless people in a scene reminiscent of World War II:

We weren't around the civilian population. There were no incidents. At one time, southeast of Dau Tieng, we captured an oxcart platoon [a Viet Cong supply unit—EMB], and they had their women and children with them. We carried this oxcart group; some of the children were too small to walk, so we carried them back to Dau Tieng, which was probably about 7 kilometers. I remember carrying a little boy about five. He never made a sound the whole way: He probably thought we were going to kill him. When we got them back to Dau Tieng, we couldn't get rid of them. Their own people didn't want them. I suppose eventually the South Vietnamese took them because we didn't really have any place to keep them.

Lee Reynolds gives testimony on another aspect of the situation. Because he was a medic and went on frequent MEDCAP missions to the villages and because he served during a time when the 25th conducted many small operations with South Vietnamese units, he learned much about the local population. His observations concerning the inhabitants he knew are very perceptive:

It was our policy to try to marry the South Vietnamese people to their government. They loved their country and didn't seem to think too much of their government. They honored death the way we honored life. They didn't really have a word in their language for peace. They had a long phrase for cease-fire that didn't mean cease-fire but meant less fighting than normal. If you talked to them about peace, I mean an absence of war, they sort of went into brainlock. It was a concept they couldn't understand. They seemed to be believers in the philosophy that hard times make you strong. Throughout history, if you find a people that has suffered hard times, over time they develop a value system that says hard times are good for you, that it builds character, that enduring suffering is a virtue. They cultivate rice and are dependent on rain. We say that you save for a rainy day. For them, rainy is normal and good. They also think war is the natural state of things.

I'd ask the Vietnamese if they would want to go to America, and they would immediately say no. And I think they were honest. We talked about the United States as the world and Vietnam as another planet. You'd think they'd want to get away from the war. I think they thought this way for two reasons. One, they loved their country. Two, I think they really thought that in America, there would be even more Phantoms and gunships dispensing ordnance and napalm. They had a mindset, a military doctrine, that said, we'll be here when you leave. They used that with the Chinese, the Japanese, and the French, and they used it on us. When not fighting war, they fought the land: They thought the Viets were the people and Nam the land. Their whole historical existence was fighting. Although both religions were changed by the local culture, there seemed to be a big difference between Catholics and Buddhists. When someone was killed, Catholics would grieve and go into hysterics and then recover and persevere. We would recognize it because it was the way we responded. The Buddhists were different: They would just go stoic and had that kind of Oriental response to life that was so alien to us.

Reynolds ties these observations into an extremely common occurrence in Vietnam. Despite obvious risks, Vietnamese civilians frequently went into battle zones, searching for things of value. In other cases, farmers or fishermen went into areas they knew were dangerous to pursue their liveli-hoods or maybe just to take a shortcut. Civilians regularly violated curfews in very hazardous areas. According to Reynolds, this reflected an accom-modation on the part of the Vietnamese to a world perpetually at risk:

Free fire means there is no restriction on firepower because, at least we were led to believe, there were no civilians in that area. It is my understanding that many times we were misinformed concerning the location of Vietnam-ese civilians. Yet, on the other hand, because you are dealing with a culture that has known war as the norm for a thousand years, their attitude toward war was like our attitude toward driving down the freeway without a safety belt: You know it's dangerous, but you've grown up with it and you think you know how to handle it. A lot of times, they would be in free fire zones when they knew it was forbidden, but they felt, just in the course of their ev-eryday lives there was something to be gained by it. For instance, they did a lot of recovery and salvage of metal. They would collect items from blown-up personnel carriers or the brass from spent shell casings. Or whatever else they could find. They would go in and police a night defensive position to see if there were any C rations or anything. They knew it was dangerous, but they felt it was just a routine daily thing that you dealt with.

Reynolds experienced something else late in the war that was also com-mon if one was in the right area. Many people in rural Vietnam feared the Front for a great variety of reasons, and some hated it. Had this not been so, ARVN would have collapsed long before it did. And as Reynolds learned, not everyone in rural Vietnam looked at the Americans as enemies:

At the end in Long Binh province, we were in absolute control of our AO. We were dominating. The feeling was that the people wanted us there; they knew we were making it possible for them to live happy and peaceful lives and to live free. And they hated the VC. We had to protect POWs from the civilians: They would have ripped them to pieces if we would have let them. We were in absolute control. By the time I left, the VC had gotten down to the point in that area to where they virtually couldn't operate.

Company commander Henry Bergson's men did pacification duty in late 1969 in southern Hau Nghia province, near the Vam Co Dong River. The Front was very weak in this area because of its losses during the General Offensive. This was also near a large concentration of South Vietnamese forces. Violence, for Vietnam, was at a low level. His observations are close to those offered by Lee Reynolds:

During the late fall, we were pushing further and further out from the firebase toward the river. At the same time, I should comment that I remember that when I was first in-country, we could only drive from Cu Chi to Saigon in a heavily escorted convoy. By October, you could jump in a jeep, take a .45 with you just to hold your pants down, and drive alone across provincial roads to Saigon with no problem. There was a lot of civilian traffic. As we went further out toward the river, we began to pick up more enemy caches of arms and ammo, mortars, mines, and all sorts of supplies by the helicopter load. By this time, the VC were pretty much leaving the local villagers alone. The local villagers were quite friendly. If we brought food and stayed in one of the small villages, we'd get to know some of the people. We'd eat with them as a group and share rice and C rations. We'd pick up small pieces of intelligence about operations. The farther we pushed toward the river, the farmers would come in right behind us and reclaim these areas for fields. They were pretty happy with what we were doing. The men generally got on well with the civilian population. We tried to be respectful of them, and yet, because of the language barrier and the number of VC who had blended in with the locals, we were very wary. We had a real good Vietnamese scout with us for the last three months, and he provided excellent communications with the villagers.

Despite the violent, poisonous atmosphere, the human qualities of the soldiers and the rural Vietnamese mitigated some of the ugliness. Bridging the cultural divide, many friendships were made. Numerous soldiers fell in

244 / *The Vietnamese*

love with prostitutes, and the offer of "free snatch" was a likely sign that their feelings were reciprocated. Soldiers of the 25th Division "adopted" local street urchins, and some units took up collections to help children injured in war or born with birth defects to receive sophisticated medical treatment. Most U.S. units did some sort of civic action duty, aimed at raising local standards of living. Such missions were popular because they were usually safe, but many soldiers also genuinely appreciated the affirmative nature of this work. As already noted, the medical apparatus associated with the 25th Division was deeply involved with the civilian population. So were American civilians working to improve agricultural production and levels of general health. It is one of the ironies of the war that agricultural productivity in the southern portion of the country, very much assisted by American aid and knowledge during the war, has helped today's Vietnam—now a very poor and overpopulated country—avoid the worst consequences of the economic calamities the current regime has created.

The juxtaposition of what Americans called "nation building" with an inherently destructive struggle contributed significantly to the bizarre ambiance of the Vietnam War. Dale Canter, one of the first to serve in 1966, recounts a sad but interesting anecdote:

The relationship between U.S. personnel and the local population is a tough question because you were never completely sure. There was always a lack of trust there. We had ARVN interpreters that were assigned to our outfit, and I got to be very good friends with them. One of them was eventually killed. It was rare that you would find a family over there that didn't have someone killed because the war had lasted so long. The people we saw were the peasants out in the bush. I questioned whether it mattered to them who was running the country. I doubt that their way of life would have changed much under Communist rule, going from a democracy. The local politicians certainly said they liked the Americans because they needed our support.

The villagers were definitely VC sympathizers, if not VC themselves. When we first arrived in Cu Chi, in some of the hamlets you could see the hate in their eyes. But it was strange. I had a friend there named Robert Andrew Twing. In the daytime, we would go into Cu Chi on laundry runs, and the people were really friendly and genuinely liked us. Twing was killed in the field in Vietnam in December 1966, and when I was coming back into the village after that operation was over, people asked where "Mr. Twing" was; they always called him "Mr. Twing." We told them he had been killed.

They actually started to cry, they were so upset with this. But in reality, it was very possible that they had given information to the VC that we were going to go on this operation and that the VC used this information to set up the ambush that cost Twing his life. The villagers were probably a big part of his death. And yet, they were very touched by the fact that he had died. So, it was a confusing war on all sides. And of course, anyone who did cooperate with the Americans really couldn't be protected. The VC intelligence network was so good that they knew the people who would cooperate. The VC would retaliate by killing these people and using them as examples for the rest of the villagers, showing them not to deal with the Americans.

Roger McGill, also in Vietnam during 1966, served with the 3/4th Armored Cavalry. Mechanized units, because they were road bound and could carry so much gear, were given substantial civic action responsibilities that they carried out in the same areas in which they were seeking to destroy the enemy. McGill describes the result:

Once you got to know the people in the villages and hamlets, there were people who would come and give us intelligence and information. They would tell us when the VC would be in the villages. One particular incident happened to me. There was a boy I was teaching English to in Bac Ha II [a hamlet close to Cu Chi—EMB], and he would tell me what was going on. We worked in that hamlet an awful lot on pacification. One day, the boy wouldn't come up to me, so I told the major that something was up, that we were in deep shit. Sure enough, Charlie opened up on us from across the road. Luckily, we were able to warn people in enough time, and no one was hurt. We came back the next day, and the boy came and said, "I'm sorry, I'm sorry," but I told him he had done the right thing. He told me what had happened. The VC were coming into Bac Ha II at night more and more, and they were saying to the villagers that if they kept working with the Americans, they were going to kill one of the elders. The night before we came in, they had taken one of the elders and beheaded him.

We would be down in the daytime working with them and trying to help them out, showing them how to do things, giving them medical aid and treating their sick. Charlie would take over at night and do the opposite.

Undoubtedly, however, the cruel and ugly side of the war prevailed over acts of kindness or mercy. Indeed, with the basic division between combatant and civilian largely obscured, the war in rural Vietnam always teetered on the edge of brutality. It is a credit to the discipline and basic humanity of the American soldier that things were not far worse.

South Vietnamese Forces

The U.S. government claimed that American armed forces had been sent to Southeast Asia to defend an independent, sovereign South Vietnam from outside aggression. Because the United States decided to confine the war to South Vietnam, it was imperative from the beginning to build up both the South Vietnamese government and its armed forces. Westmoreland's "sword and shield" strategy after 1965 was designed to give GVN forces a respite that would allow them to rebuild and reenter the struggle when the military situation was stabilized. The later Vietnamization program implemented by General Abrams was a race against time to strengthen ARVN adequately before the American public demanded an end to the war. In both cases, strengthening the forces loyal to Saigon was central to the war effort.

Consequently, the 25th Division spent considerable time training and cooperating with South Vietnamese armed forces. Unfortunately for all concerned, this critical task was seriously compromised from beginning to end because the overwhelming majority of American fighting men were contemptuous of their Vietnamese "comrades in arms." This was true throughout the period of American involvement in ground combat. The reasons veterans cite for this animosity were remarkably similar: Essentially, they say, American soldiers believed that the South Vietnamese were unreliable troops who refused to do their share of the fighting.

The raw material with which to fashion an efficient fighting force was never in abundance in South Vietnam. John Pancrazio, an adviser with the South Vietnamese militia unit in Cu Chi in early 1966, describes the situation that existed when the 25th Division arrived:

The majority of the armed forces could have more easily been termed armed farces! They were very poor fighters, with the exception of the Rangers, and were much more eager to avoid combat than engage in it. When going on extended operations, they would carry live chickens to ensure they would have fresh meat, and they had absolutely no discipline, so that the enemy could avoid them. On one particular occasion, I was forced to pull my weapon on an ARVN lieutenant in order to force him to proceed to a night ambush. His reason for not wanting to go to the planned site was: "Beaucoup VC there. My *dai vi* [captain—EMB] will kill me if I go down there." My response was that he could die for sure right now or take his chances with his captain later. Needless to say, we proceeded to the ambush site, where ARVN "noise discipline" ensured there would be no enemy contact that night.

Botching a mission intentionally was one thing; American units did it more than once themselves. However, when ARVN timidity endangered American lives, 25th Division soldiers were enraged. Thomas Giltner relates that American soldiers quickly learned to distrust both the combat skills and the honesty of their ally:

The reports of ARVN sweeping through an area and encountering no VC were extremely dangerous to rely on. We were encouraged to run operations with the local ARVN units. They would be assigned an area to sweep, say at 0600 hours; a couple of hours later, we would follow in behind them and sweep the same area as part of the joint operation. We'd go in, and as soon as we'd arrive in the landing zone—well, you know the rest of the story: Sometimes we would meet hostile resistance, sometimes no resistance at all. We soon learned that these ARVN sweeps either never occurred or were "search and avoid" missions. They were telling us things we wanted to hear.

This sorry state of affairs was aggravated because the South Vietnamese unit operating most closely with the Tropic Lightning Division was the ARVN 25th Division, known throughout Vietnam for its incompetence. Gen. Phan Truong Chinh, its commander in 1966, was widely believed by Americans to be a Front agent. Michael Willis, who served two combat tours beginning in 1967, emphasizes the distrust felt toward ARVN:

They were losers. They didn't have any initiative whatsoever. I guess it would have been hard knowing you might shoot up your brother or uncle. The 25th ARVN morale was the lowest of the low: The whole division would run. Apparently, some of the spirit of the U.S. 25th rubbed off on them: I read that the ARVN 25th fought to the end in 1975. When we swept villages, ARVN would grab anyone and stick them on trucks, and off they'd go. Good work! They just drafted VC. The Chieu Hoi Program [a South Vietnamese program that allowed Front followers to surrender without punishment— EMB] could have been planned by Hanoi. Thousands of people surrendered and ended up in ARVN. Wouldn't that cause dissension? The corruption was incredible.

Tet veteran and tunnel rat Phil Boardman expresses the disgust he and his comrades felt:

We had absolutely no respect for ARVN. They wouldn't do a thing when we were around. They gave us some Kit Carson scouts: former VC who were supposed to act as guides for us. We never trusted them. Any way you looked at it, they were traitors to somebody. Hell, if ARVN could have fought, we wouldn't have been there.

During the fierce fighting of 1969, Dan Vandenberg developed a loathing for ARVN:

They were a joke. I despised the whole lot of them. They were all cowards. In the morning, their uniforms were spotless and their weapons clean. They'd look the same at the end of the day. We did all their work. We looked like tramps. For us to get new gear would take an act of Congress. The South Vietnamese always seemed to have a lot. We would rather go it alone: At least you only had to fight one enemy.

Alan Neill, who spent most of 1970 with the *Wolfhounds,* during a period when Vietnamization was in full swing, was only a bit more charitable:

ARVN did their thing, and we did ours. That was fine with us because the ARVN 25th was lousy. The fact was that we did a lot more fighting than they did. I have read a lot of books about the war in the last few years, so I know that ARVN could fight really well. But I never saw that side of them, and I never knew anyone that did. I think that when we were around, they'd let us fight the war. If we weren't around, they'd fight. We never really understood them.

Some men of the 25th got the opportunity to see South Vietnamese operations more closely. In 1967, for example, a small Combined Reconnaissance and Intelligence Platoon (CRIP) was formed and soon established a reputation as a tough outfit. Larger numbers of Americans were assigned to advisory duties on Mobile Advisory Teams (MATs). Morgan Sincock was given such duty:

When I was assigned to a MAT team in Long An, I spent six months living among ARVN and RF/PF [South Vietnamese militia—EMB] units. My attitude toward the Vietnamese changed as I developed personal friendships with a number of them. I also learned to empathize with them and see some of their actions in view of a nearly continuous war the previous thirty years.

Some of the younger soldiers had grown up with their world at war. Others dated their military careers back to the days of the French. The Vietnamese who commanded our ARVN unit (two infantry companies, as I recall) had jumped in (as a paratrooper) to Dien Ben Phu with the French. He also showed us the standard of the South Vietnamese leadership. On my first operation with him, he kept his command element a kilometer to the rear of his maneuver elements. We were so far to the rear of the infantry that I feared for our security. He was typical of the Vietnamese leader who led from afar, never endangered himself, and could not in any way inspire his men.

There was a tradition of privilege and family connections related to military commissions. There was also an aristocratic sense that some but not all of the South Vietnamese officers tried to project. Some of them grew long fingernails, which was meant to symbolize their position on the socioeconomic ladder, such that they did not have to work with their hands.

On my early operations with the ARVN, we would start around 3:30 A.M. and move to an assembly area adjacent to villages that we were to search. Around 4:30 to 5:00 A.M., we would move out. As the lead elements approached the village, usually walking right down the middle of the roadway, a single gunshot would be heard in the village, followed by a series of single shots at increasing distances. This was the VC signaling that we were moving into the area. Had we maneuvered through the paddies and stayed off of the road, we could have entered the first village unannounced.

We would continue our slow movement, with many stops, until nearly noon, at which time we would move to the home of a known VC to have his family feed the command element. Rice, tea, and a VC chicken or duck in a broth were served us by the hapless wife of the known VC. Few words were exchanged with her, and there was never real or threatened violence directed toward her by the South Vietnamese. Nevertheless, she was compelled to feed and serve us.

Right after lunch, the ARVN would pack it in and return to base camp. In 45 minutes to 1 hour, they would retrace the steps that it had taken the previous 6 hours to cover.

Sometimes, we would make contact with small elements or individual VC. I recall one time when we found 5 unarmed VC in a nippa-palm swamp. The South Vietnamese tied their arms behind their backs, and then one of the ARVN began to beat one of the prisoners with a stick. Our senior adviser was running around trying to get his counterpart to order a halt to the beating. I had a camera with me and was photographing the whole thing, which embarrassed the South Vietnamese and, I believe, caused them to stop.

I had met with several younger South Vietnamese officers who were truly fine men. They believed in their country and their cause. For some, their enthusiasm was tempered by the reality of the situation. These men were lieutenants and platoon leaders. They truly led men and exposed themselves to every bit as much danger as they asked their men to face. One of the two I recall in particular was killed in battle while I was there.

Some soldiers, by happenstance, found themselves briefly in the middle of the ugly village war that had torn Vietnam to shreds for years. The two sides had been murdering each other's leadership for decades. The Front, in particular, relied heavily upon a vicious campaign of terror against Saigon's officials, and many of the problems encountered by American troops were either caused or made worse by the Front's version of "revolutionary justice." The inefficiency and corruption of South Vietnamese officials was well known and commented on in American ranks. However, American soldiers did not properly understand that zealous, efficient, and honest government officials were top targets of the terror campaign. The Front was glad to leave inefficient and corrupt officials in place. The result of this reinforced a notion that ran very deep in Vietnam: the idea that the Front and the North would prevail in the end. It was a crippling handicap, and one that was never completely overcome. It was no coincidence, however, that ARVN troops fought at their best during the early 1970s when it looked, for a moment, as though they had a chance to prevail.

One result of the temporary battlefield superiority enjoyed by the South Vietnamese forces after the Americans and ARVN crushed the Front's General Offensive was a great expansion of Saigon's outward control of rural Vietnam. During this same period, the South Vietnamese leaders tried in their way to fight back against the Front's political apparatus. Thieu instituted a major land reform program and implicitly promised more reforms after victory. Aided by the CIA and the American provincial advisory teams, Saigon increased the pace of what the Americans called the Phoenix program. Although Phoenix was never the sort of massive assassination campaign that American critics alleged, it was an element of a very harsh part of the war. Several South Vietnamese strike teams were employed in Phoenix. In rural Vietnam, the most effective were the Provincial Reconnaissance Units (PRUs), which included some of the most fanatical anti-Communists in South Vietnam. Many had lost relatives to the Front's violence; a few were thugs and saw an opportunity for extortion. In general, they were a very tough bunch.

Normally, the South Vietnamese conducted Phoenix missions with their own resources. CIA advisers often accompanied them. On occasion, however, they asked for escort by 25th Division troops. Company commander Charles Boyd had that duty more than once:

My company would be given the mission of escorting the Phoenix team to a certain village. We were told they did a lot of research on people in the village to find a VC sympathizer. The Phoenix team would travel to a firebase, and this is where I would pick them up. The team would be made up of, say, a marine major, an army captain, and a high-ranking NCO, with weapons designed to make little noise when they were fired. This group would be fat, not accustomed to field duty or combat, and generally like a fish out of water. This group would join my company, and we would stop about 100 yards from a village. After this group screwed up their courage, they would move out of the security of an infantry company and move to the village. They would find a house with a male and kill him and return to our location, declaring their mission accomplished. There was no way to prove or disprove if they killed the person they had targeted.

It is not clear from Boyd's description whether this team was part of the PRU; the organization does not sound like it. Whatever the case, Lee Reynolds saw the genuine article at work a little later but with a rather different twist:

We provided transport to two PRUs who went into a village looking for two VC leaders. The PRU guys we picked up were definitely not the kind of guys you'd want to meet in a dark alley. They walked into the village and asked around. The people pointed and gave directions. One of my friends saw what happened. They went up to one hooch and called out. Someone came to the door, and each PRU emptied a full magazine into the guy at point-blank range. The dead man was the leader. His assistant was caught running across an open field, and the PRUs chopped him to bits with a couple of machetes. The interesting part of the story is that after it was all over, the people of the village pleaded and begged with these PRUs to stay. That was a big part of the South Vietnamese failure: They couldn't stay. If you could have put a couple of guys like that in every village, your problems would be over.

However, few fighting men of the 25th Division had the opportunity to see South Vietnamese units in action over a sustained period, and not many realized the great sacrifices ARVN endured in the same war. Only in 1968 did the number of Americans killed outnumber ARVN dead. ARVN was capable of stout resistance, but it did not usually fight well when American units were in proximity. As seemed to be the case in nearly every area, the two peoples did not see each other at their best. Consequently, few veterans were surprised by the ultimate military outcome of the war. Ironically, though, in a very strange way, U.S. soldiers did see the enemy at its best. Americans were insulated from the politics of Vietnam and did not have to deal with the very real fear of long-term Front retribution. Nor did they encounter the ruthless political side of the Front. What they did see was the undeniable courage and tenacity of the enemy. In more recent years, the Party has proven that it is incapable of running a country in peacetime, but twenty years ago, it was extremely good at war.

Charlie

Clearly, some of the animosity felt by American fighting men toward South Vietnamese soldiers reflected cultural bias and racial antipathy. Nevertheless, what was truly striking was the contrast between the general contempt felt by Americans for South Vietnamese soldiers and the nearly universal respect they had for their enemy. Almost every veteran I encountered expressed admiration for the cunning and courage of Charlie. They developed this respect on the battlefield. Indeed, many soldiers later complained about not being properly warned during training about the skill and resourcefulness of their battlefield opponents in Vietnam. As Michael Willis recalled, "We were told the VC were farmers by day and guerrillas by night. One day, at the end of an *8-hour* battle, I asked our lieutenant, 'When do these farmers go home to milk the cows?'" There was certainly no affection involved. As one man put it, "Your average VC was a tough little bastard, but no one was bothered by killing him." Yet, in a curious way, American soldiers affirmed their own skill and courage by acknowledging similar traits in their enemy.

Some of the same men who criticize ARVN in the earlier quotes simultaneously express very different views of their foes. A brief inspection of these views offers a splendid look at the asymmetrical nature of the attitudes held by most American fighting men toward their allies and adversaries. Concerning the opponents he faced in Cu Chi district in 1965–1966, John Pancrazio recalls, "The majority of the enemy were dedicated fighting men and women. They truly believed in their cause, and many of them, especially the NVA, were good and fierce fighters." Dan Vandenberg, who learned to detest ARVN while slogging through Trang Bang district in 1969, states that "Charlie was really good. Everyone at least respected his abilities. The NVA were damned good, and they wouldn't chicken out. They had to take more than we did. We didn't have to go through bombing and artillery. What they took was incredible."

Thomas Giltner, who had discovered that intelligence supplied by ARVN could endanger his own men, had studied Asian warfare at Fort Bragg before going to Vietnam. His opinions of the Front guerrillas he encountered in Hau Nghia were more informed than most, but they reflected those of his men:

We respected the enemy from day one. These people we were fighting in late 1966 were mostly the local VC. I mean, peasants with World War II weapons at best. They had no armor or air support and few supplies. They were taking on a modern, well-equipped army, the best in the world. This respect was not always expressed, but it was certainly there. The NVA units that came a short time later were better equipped and led, and we respected them, too, but for other reasons. I'm talking about the local VC. They received their training from the local cadres and their indoctrination from Mao Tse-tung, Ho Chi Minh, and Nguyen Vo Giap.

Following Sun Tsu's teachings, they always hit us where we were the weakest, always decided when, where, and how to fight us and when to break away and melt into the local populace or go down the tunnels. [Sun Tsu was a Chinese military writer in ancient times.—EMB] They decided when and where to conduct ambushes and raids, plant booby traps, employ snipers, infiltrate U.S. areas, and gather constant intelligence. They did an awful lot with an awful little.

These guys would go out with old and primitive weapons, wearing no more than black pajamas and sandals made out of old truck tires; they were lucky if they had a bolt-action rifle of some sort. They would ambush us, emerge from their spider holes, shoot down two or three of us at a time, and disappear very quickly. Just grind us down and harass us constantly. Of course, he spoke the local language and knew the local areas, so he had some definite tactical advantages. Let me give you some examples. We captured homemade weapons: I wish I had them today to show people. Rifles with stocks made out of fence posts, metal pipes, screws and nails, and anything that could be found. These weapons were very crude but very effective. I was literally amazed when I saw them.

In late October 1966, my platoon was called out as a reaction force. When we arrived, we found two platoons pinned down near the banks of a river near Trung Lap. Across the river, about 200 or 300 meters away, the local VC squad was shellacking us good. I immediately took two or three casualties and had a dust-off. I tried to get some indirect fire support, but the battalion commander was flying around surveying the battle, so we couldn't get clearance to shoot. We took more casualties while that was going on. I got my helmet blown off with a round and was cut up by a little shrapnel. In a battle like this, there is tremendous confusion. An engagement can last for an hour, but it seems like a day or two. It can last all afternoon or all night, but it seems like just a few minutes pass. It is impossible to judge how long a battle lasts unless you look at your watch, and who's going to do that? Finally, I was able, using the PRC25 field radio, to get a gunship to fly down low enough and locate what was going on. He was following our smoke. Of course, you had to watch your marking rounds. It has to be recognized from the air by color. You throw down a smoke grenade. If it is green, it will be identified. The reason you do this is that the enemy probably has his own

PRC25 and is listening in and will throw his own smoke grenade down to confuse the gunship. This happened in this instance, but the enemy guessed wrong on the color, and the gunship correctly recognized my grenade. The gunship strafed the tree lines and finally blew up the mortar crew with rockets, and the shelling finally stopped.

What we came to find out was that what the enemy was using for a 60mm mortar was a steel pipe about 3 feet long with a 16-penny nail embedded in the bottom for a firing pin. For a base plate, they used an old French helmet. They just scooped some mud into the helmet and stuck the mortar tube into it. They had some 60mm mortar rounds: That was our company weapon forty years ago. By Vietnam, we were using the 81mm. Lord knows where they got these rounds. They had to backpack them through the jungle, each man carrying as many as he could. Whenever the tube got hot, they'd just pick up the helmet and tie a wire on the other end and carry it off like a suitcase through the jungle. It was all fired by line of sight, of course. They just knew which direction they were supposed to shoot. It was mighty effective. Ingenious people, absolutely ingenious.

They would take any explosive material they could find, like a 750-pound bomb dud or a dud mortar or artillery shell, and make booby traps and hand grenades. Or they would use it to make small-arms ammunition. They had their own reloading benches down in the tunnels. All of us, from the lowliest private to the commanding general, lived in constant fear of the VC getting hold of a sophisticated weapon. Once, somebody lost a starlight scope. With this device, you can see at night just like you can in the daytime. The battalion commander, upon hearing that the starlight scope had been lost, ordered every company outside the perimeter that night to search the area where the scope had been lost, with orders not to come back without it. One of my men found it. But there was absolute fear that the VC would have a starlight. Claymore mines were to be strictly accounted for. On the perimeter at night, the VC would come in through our wire. We'd be there waiting, weapons at the ready, constantly observing the wire through starlight scopes from behind our sandbags 50 meters away at most. The VC would still slip under the wire, take our claymores, and turn them in our direction. One of the reasons that the United States never planted any mines, at least not to my knowledge—and we had lots of Bouncing Bettys and other antipersonnel mines—was that if our own men didn't step on them, the VC would dig them up and steal them. We knew everything stolen or discarded would somehow be used against us. Hell, we'd throw away our C ration cans, and they'd make explosives out of them. Our view very quickly became: They are not stupid, they're just poor.

American officers all knew that their men respected the people they were fighting. Some of them worried about the effect this situation had on morale and attempted to discourage what one soldier called "Charlie worship." Troop commander Jerry Headley recalls that such efforts were futile:

A lot of people talked about how good the enemy was. Some men called him Sir Charles or similar things. He was a very good fighter and very disciplined. He had been fighting, and his uncles and his fathers had been fighting, for years. Some officers didn't like us to honor the enemy, but we did anyway.

Many men of the Tropic Lightning Division single out North Vietnamese regulars for particular praise. They understand the conventional tactics that the NVA normally employed and greatly admire the courage required for the mass infantry assaults that were the hallmark of the big battles the two armies fought. They rarely distinguish between the NVA and the elite Main Force Front units that fought in a similar manner. Col. Duke Wolf, the 25th brigade commander responsible for the ultimately successful defense of Tay Ninh province during the harrowing NVA offensive in August 1968, wrote an interesting book about the campaign after the war. He dedicated it to the men of the 25th Division and to the soldiers of the NVA.

The men had somewhat different views of the Front guerrillas. The intense frustration caused by coping with guerrilla tactics was frequently translated into hatred. Jay Lazarin remembers the emotional distance that many soldiers put between themselves and the people they were fighting:

The "enemy" was mostly unseen and therefore didn't exist as a person. His weapons existed—his bullets, his mortars, his booby traps, his punji stick traps—but he himself didn't generally exist. VC was a name, a subject, an object that we were fighting. We didn't think of the individual VC; we only thought of the action and reaction that accompanied his attacks. We never tried to analyze his movements, his tactics, or his motivations. We weren't trained or required to do so; we were only there to engage him and kill him, whoever or whatever he might be. Since we made no overall tactical decisions, our purpose being so basic that it didn't matter to us who we were fighting, we only knew that whoever shot at us (or whoever was of potential harm) was our enemy and had to be eliminated.

We did, though, encounter an occasional "individual" VC/NVA who actually made some impression on us. Unfortunately for us, it was usually when we came against someone who had held off all of our men for some time or showed some weird sense of his moral commitment to their cause, such as blowing himself up as he charged at us, hoping to cause casualties. Or there were the particularly gruesome corpses, whose bodies became the butt of our fascination or jokes, or the wounded, whose severed body parts took the place of honor for the day propped up against some tree alongside the rest of the man's body in a cruel game we played. For many of us, myself included, these games were not in our individual nature, and as such, we observed but did not participate directly. But even so, we did not see them as people per se, only as objects. We did not speak their language, so we could not ask them their names, their home villages, or even if they were the same age as us. We were ignorant of their history or culture, so we had no idea if they were even Vietnamese, Cambodian, or possibly Chinese; to us, it didn't matter. One critical point has to be made here, and that is the presence of tremendous group pressure not to feel any compassion toward your enemy. If an individual GI had any pangs of compassion or showed that he wanted to treat the VC as an actual individual human being (after a capture), the fear that the less feeling (or emotional) men in the squad/platoon would ridicule him was too great. Many times, I saw small acts of compassion that were immediately counteracted by cruelty and deliberate steps taken to show the squad/platoon that to be human had no place in war. Of course, there was no official policy to this effect, but there was no shortage of GIs whose acts showed cruelty and wanton violence dispensed as haphazardly as possible.

As Lazarin's recollections vividly illustrate, Vietnam was always a harsh war. Nevertheless, the resourcefulness and courage of village guerrillas were acknowledged widely. As Lazarin's account shows, even hatred of the enemy was intermingled with a grudging respect:

The VC were good fighters, very good, not so much as individuals but as an enemy. They had a purpose, a seemingly homogeneous one that we couldn't match on an everyday basis. Our commanders were taking orders from a chain of command that was as remote from them as their daily existence was from the enemy they were fighting. We lived on C rations and hot food a few times a week, with beer and soda rations the norm, while the VC, we knew, lived on mostly rice and were half starved, eating local small animals if they could catch them. We watched a lone VC in a bunker last for an hour shooting at Phantom jets with a carbine rifle after each 250-pound bomb had missed its target. We knew he was something special, but after we found him, blown into small parts by a lucky bomb hit, he became another war story. But it all registered in our minds about the kind of enemy we were up against.

Platoon leader Del Plonka's opinion echoes that held by Lazarin:

The enemy was a terrific fighter. Of course, you couldn't beat the VC for their organization. The VC were dedicated. Any time you get people dedicated to a certain cause, a certain purpose, they're going to be a lot better than you.

Indeed, stories of the cleverness and tenacity of the Front forces are a staple among American combat veterans. During the Tet Offensive near Trang Bang, Bill Kestell witnessed a good example:

We had parked our track, *The Ugly American,* along the wall. It was just past sundown. I was in the hatch, and a friend was also up top. We were just talking when a sniper in a tree across the road took a shot at us. I can still see the muzzle flash. I think I loosed a short burst with the .50-caliber machine gun at the flash. I caught hell from the lieutenant for giving away our position! Really!

That night, we were mortared. Big deal—gooks dropped every single round short. Boy, these guys are really lousy shots. FNG [fucking new guy—EMB].

When we got south of Trang Bang Bridge, these same lousy shots took out *every important target in the compound—right from round 1.* When you have a fixed target that's known—plan your lines of fire—chcck this with short rounds—and when you're ready to, add 200 to 300 yards and fire for effect. They took out *TOC—commo—counter battery—the whole thing!*

Naturally, American soldiers tried to explain to themselves why their Vietnamese enemies on the battlefield routinely showed courage and tenacity while their Vietnamese allies frequently did not. The U.S. Army, as always was the case concerning larger issues of the war, was utterly mute on the subject. Racial or cultural explanations were worthless because there were Vietnamese on both sides. Consequently, American fighting men correctly interpreted the situation in political terms. They recognized that Front followers were fighting for a cause. Most U.S. soldiers did not really know what the cause was, although many recognized that hatred of the United States had much to do with it. American soldiers usually explained South Vietnamese military shortcomings in terms of bad leadership and corruption on the part of South Vietnamese officials and ARVN officers. This was not the whole story concerning Saigon and ARVN, yet the soldiers' impression was accurate enough.

It did not help the men's morale to have more respect for their enemy than they had for their ally. Although Front propaganda directed at Americans was crude and had little impact, some soldiers talked about being on the "wrong side." Others compared their role to that of the British redcoats during the American Revolution. Mostly, the political confusion increased the tendency on the part of American soldiers to shut out such concerns from their minds altogether and to fight the war for themselves and their immediate comrades. But Jerry Headley points out that even though his men were not politically sophisticated, they were troubled about these matters:

If there was a national strategy, it never filtered down to the regular soldier. Everyone knew that the South Vietnamese governments, no matter who they had in there, were all corrupt. We all wondered: Why do we want those guys in there? Are they any better than the guys we are fighting? There just seemed to be no goal. This was very distressing. I was surprised how much even the young soldiers were aware of this.

Headley's soldiers asked very good questions. Even with the benefit of twenty years of hindsight, the answers are not clear.

7

To Stand and Fight: Morale in the 25th Division

T HE SUBJECT OF THE military morale during the Vietnam War has probably preoccupied journalists, academics, and the makers of popular culture more than any other aspect of the conflict. They dwelt on the issue during the war and have done so ever since. And the cumulative result of this investigation, by and large, has been disgraceful. In the image created and advanced by many in the United States, the Army was contaminated by an evil enterprise, which caused a progressive destruction of the Army's morale and ability to fight. As the Army came unglued, its men descended into an amoral world of drug addiction, racial conflict, and murder. Often, the purveyors of this morality tale have singled out a few good individuals who fought to stay sane and moral against the growing tide of perverse evil. But according to this twisted screenplay, the Army was at war with itself. The result of this inner conflict was a generation of damaged veterans who, because of their horrid experiences and personal anguish, became neurotic or pathological wrecks. This image is so powerful that it has spawned a sad and ridiculous cottage industry that panders to phony veterans who try to look and act the part of the embittered Vietnam vet.

The fact that so many people who create what passes for culture in the United States have chosen to wage a sustained war on an entire generation of young men whose crime was serving their country in wartime does not speak well for America. Neither does the fact that the principal weapons employed in this effort have been lies and distortion. Whether motivated by greed or ignorance, the creators of this colossal lie deserve the contempt of anyone who respects historical truth. No "healing," no apologies, and no memorials can possibly compensate for the damage done and the pain inflicted on America's innocent children after the war. The only thing we can possibly do, twenty years too late, is try to tell the truth.

Morale in a large war like Vietnam is one of the most difficult and complex issues in the entire field of military affairs. Anyone hoping to understand this intricate matter must recognize two central facts. First, wartime morale is inevitably conditioned by the melancholy fact that any military's principal job is to kill other humans. And in pursuing this grim task, many of the military's own men will die in the process. It is a rare man who likes the idea of either killing or dying. Because of this, military organizations, regardless of cultural differences or the divide of time, have remarkable similarities. For instance, they must train and discipline their soldiers. And hierarchy is clear and strictly enforced. This is so for a very simple reason: Most humans, particularly if taken straight from civilian life, will follow instinct and flee if in danger. Soldiers must not only be taught what to do, they must be taught to do it in unison. That is why command and hierarchy are universal. Officers may applaud initiative in combat, but they know that uncoordinated activity leads to disaster. But who suffers the disaster? Armies will always do their best to convince their recruits that fighting well and aggressively is the safest thing to do, and often, they are right. Frequently, however, the truth is very different. In many instances, running from battle is, indeed, the safest course for an individual or a unit. But running, unless as part of a disciplined retreat, can easily condemn to death a man's own comrades down the line who are depending on him to keep the enemy from shooting them in the back.

Because of this dynamic, all armies stress a group ethos that has no counterpart in the civilian world. They also stress ceremony, patriotism, and, above all, the notions of duty and honor. It is critical for soldiers to feel that what they are doing is affirmative. The code of the warrior invariably revolves around the concept that risking one's own life or taking another man's during war is done for a higher good. A good army will instill this concept deeply into the heart of the group; a failure to do so explains those instances in military history when large and impressive armies on paper have folded in an instant when put to the test. The opposite is also true: A relatively small force stiffened by a genuine feeling of purpose will be an extremely formidable opponent.

Nevertheless, men can never completely resolve the tension between instinct and upbringing and the demands of war. There are, in my opinion, some men that enjoy war and combat. There is no way to prove such things, but I would guess they constitute 10 percent, at most, of any army. However, most men would at least consider an honorable and acceptable way out if it appeared before them. Accepting defeat, however, is a very different matter. As I shall later examine, one of the most powerful impulses driving wars forward is a desperate desire on the part of those who fight and suffer to believe that their sacrifice has been worth something. That something is victory—not a cause, at least not as a war progresses, but victory itself. In Vietnam, the U.S. troops' gradual realization that victory would not be theirs made the chemistry of morale in Vietnam even more intricate than normal.

The astute observer will also recognize a second point. Military morale is an extraordinarily multifaceted subject. Depending upon the area examined, morale could refer to something as relatively trivial as the quality of food or something as emotionally shattering as holding your best friend in your arms and watching him die. Consequently, formulating generalities concerning this issue is a precarious exercise. For example, it would be possible for the field morale of a unit to be very high and the political morale of the same men to be at rock bottom. In Vietnam, this situation was not only possible, it was probably the norm. Leadership is another variable. A well-led unit might possess high field morale, whereas a poorly led but otherwise similar unit is crippled. Furthermore, morale will rise and fall according to immediate circumstances. Obviously, if the enemy pounds a unit in battle, the men's morale will fall. Conversely, if they fight and are hurt but shatter their opponents in the process, some men will find solace. If they are on a roll and no one is getting hurt, the men are temporarily living in the best of all possible worlds.

In addition, for many aspects of morale, timing is also important. In every war, political morale and, frequently, fighting morale are at their peak at the beginning. But, as Thucydides reminded us, "war is a stern master." Violence over time transforms the psychological chemistry of any army. Naïveté concerning combat is the first casualty. Political morale, unless it deals with an absolutely clear case of national extinction, will likewise change. Clichés do not live long in combat. Stress between men who are at risk and those that are not inevitably appears, and this invariably manifests itself in an uneasy relationship between front-line soldiers and support troops. It can also evolve into a very tense relationship between front-line soldiers and young men who are safe at home. Ironically, however, at the same time that some elements of morale are changing for the worse, the group cohesion of the men at risk can actually rise. Because men must depend on their comrades in battle, soldiers in a fighting unit confront a critical point early. Simply put, the men find out if their fellows can be trusted to stand if the others are in peril. If the answer is no, the group falls apart. If the answer is yes, a relationship develops that is so deep it can only be described as a type of love. After his victory at the battle of Fredericksburg, General Lee wisely remarked that "it is well that war is so terrible, or we should grow too fond of it."

Political Motivation

All soldiers, regardless of how poorly schooled or apolitical they might be in civilian life, realize that a connection exists between war and politics. In concrete terms, however, the U.S. Army did very little to indoctrinate their Vietnam-bound troops. There is a long tradition of apolitical behavior in the Army. In addition, officers such as George Patton or Douglas MacArthur who dabbled in politics while in uniform had skirted ruin. That lesson was not lost on the Vietnam-era officer corps. Officers did not systematically use the issue of anticommunism, even though the government employed it to convince the American public that the war was justified.

In this regard, the contrast between U.S. forces and the enemy was great. The Front and Hanoi assigned political commissars to all units. These men administered continual political indoctrination and conducted the numerous and numbing "self-criticism" sessions all troops had to endure. Political cadres stressed the connection between personal self-sacrifice and political goals. In the North, where the government had been in power long enough to raise a generation of young men, military indoctrination was part of a systematic and ceaseless propaganda offensive that began in elementary school and never stopped. Although the urban elites in the North had a more realistic attitude toward the struggle and would move heaven and earth to get foreign scholarships in Eastern Bloc countries for their sons, the rural population of that poor country was totally at the mercy of the Party's propaganda lords. In the South, supporters of the Front inevitably heard propaganda coming from Saigon. Consequently, the Front cadres developed an even more disciplined and tightly organized system of indoctrination and revolutionary discipline. As American soldiers found out quickly, their enemy was well disciplined, highly motivated, and extremely formidable. In retrospect, we can also see that they were the victims of what developed into a monumental lie and shed their blood only to create a miserable government. Courage is admirable in the proper context. When betrayed, it is the stuff of tragedy.

Indoctrination at the beginning of U.S. involvement probably was not necessary for American soldiers. The U.S. Army was a good combination of citizen soldiers and professionals in 1965, and conscription was an accepted fact of life for those not lucky enough to get one of the various deferments. (The college deferment that later caused so much anguish was a provisional one. Before 1965, college graduates served when eventually drafted.) Although specific propaganda was notably absent, general appeals and ceremonies aimed at creating group cohesion and an identification between the soldiers and the flag and country were an important part of military training. The extraordinary prosperity of the period reinforced an informal type of indoctrination that influenced almost all Americans. There have been few, if any, periods in U.S. history when so many people believed that the United States was the greatest nation on earth.

Furthermore, a very important historical coincidence took place at this time. By 1965, two decades had passed since the end of World War II. Consequently, a very high percentage of American soldiers on the eve of Vietnam had fathers or immediate family who served during that war. As anyone who lived through the time can attest, there was a very strong feeling among countless young men that, whether they liked it or not, it was their turn to serve.

Lastly, inexperienced young men thinking of battle are often foolish or innocent. As has happened so often in the past, few men, from generals to privates, had a proper appreciation for the staggering difficulties that the Army would face in Southeast Asia. The officers and NCOs, many of them combat veterans, knew that war would challenge their young soldiers vigorously. But they, too, were in the dark about Vietnam. The combination of anxiety and enthusiasm, so typical of a young army going off to war, existed in full measure in 1965. What was lacking was a clear and unmistakable reason for their mission. At the beginning, they did not need one. And ultimately, the 25th learned to fight without one.

In retrospect, we can plainly see that the political morale of the 25th Division largely paralleled that of the country. An indistinct sense of purpose existed on the surface initially. Very quickly, however, as the soldiers themselves learned the frustrating realities of Vietnam, political enthusiasm for the American cause, vague at the best of times, declined steadily.

Dale Canter was one of the first to arrive in Vietnam with the 25th, and his opinions of the war were widely held among his comrades at arms and Americans as a whole:

My perspective is that of a soldier serving in 1966. As the war progressed, I believed the views and attitudes of the soldiers serving changed dramatically. In 1966, we went to Vietnam fully expecting to win the war and defeat communism. The 25th Division was staffed with top-notch career professional officers. With the constant rotation of personnel and political turmoil over the years, that situation changed. We fought the war with a different army every year.

Robert Conner, like many of the earliest arrivals, came by ship. Although already a trained infantryman, his debarkation was delayed by the Division until April 1966 so he could pass his eighteenth birthday and thus become eligible for combat. He recalls a situation similar to the one Canter describes, but stresses the ignorance of the common soldier concerning the coming ordeal:

We thought we were tough and streetwise, but we were really ignorant at eighteen years of age. Most of us didn't really know where Vietnam was. If we were going to the Far East, why did we keep sailing west? In the distance, land was breaking. As we looked, we wondered why were we coming to a country like this. We sat in the harbor for two days. Back in training, they had told us the VC wore black pajamas. There were sampans all around the ship, and everyone wore black pajamas. Were they all the enemy?

Col. Thomas Ferguson remembers the earliest days with unmistakable and understandable nostalgia:

There was a total willingness on everyone's part to sacrifice the prerogatives of the normally separate commands for the common purpose. We all knew each other and treated each other like equals. We were able to throw individual mission statements out the window and subordinate our individual interests to the common good. General Weyand had a strong positive attitude and helped us face every problem. In Hawaii, we had developed realistic operational procedures that lessened the need for detailed orders. We all had a great latitude for action. Our officers and NCOs were outstanding. A trust existed among ourselves that is hard to put into words today.

C. W. Bowman arrived in 1967 and, like many newcomers, felt some of the same reflexive enthusiasm that the first men deployed had:

Morale was good then. It was early in the war. Everybody had a cause. We were fighting the Communists. But everybody I was with over there out in the field were poor white, black, or Chicano men: eighteen or nineteen years old. I was eighteen then, but I guess if you're fighting somebody and killing him or he's trying to kill you, I don't know if that makes you a man or not, but we had to do a lot of things a lot of men I know wouldn't do. Didn't see any senators' sons or doctors' sons or lawyers' sons or upper-middle-class children. Everybody I talked to had a daddy who was a coal miner or share-cropper or something along that avenue. But morale was high. Most of the guys had been brought up patriotically. Their daddies had fought in World War II, and their granddaddies fought in World War I. Everybody talked about winning the war, and a lot of them were afraid it would be over before they got to fight. A lot of men thought Charlie was inferior: He had inferior weapons, and he didn't know how to fight Americans. But he changed a lot of our minds.

Mario Tarin, on the other hand, arrived in late 1969. He notes that the sense of purpose evident earlier had faded dramatically:

By the time I made it to Nam—5 October 1969—everybody was pretty disil-lusioned with the whole war effort. There was a lot of talk about Vietnamization—let the gooks defend their own country—and black GIs were getting more militant, so morale was pretty low. I guess you've heard it all by now, but by this time, we no longer wanted to win but just get out alive!

Dan Breeding came to Vietnam in early 1970. By that point, in Breed-ing's opinion, the Army's political morale had disappeared:

This was the time when we were reading about all of the upheaval going on in the United States, on the college campuses and so forth. No one really gave a damn. I recall when I first came in-country at Cam Ranh Bay, they gave me guard duty at night. Some guys were out smoking pot. One guy came up to me; he knew I was new in-country, gave me a joint, and said, "Enjoy yourself, this is all that goes on." I soon found out that was a lot of what went on. In the firebases a lot of times, it was sheer boredom. You could only fill so many sandbags. During 1970, a lot of the GIs would just flat refuse to do anything like that. They would flat refuse to go out in the field. They would flat refuse to do anything in the rear. They would just ask the NCOs, "What are you going to do, send me to Vietnam?"

There were several reasons for the decline in political morale. In many respects, the men of the 25th lost their feeling of mission for the same reasons that the American people steadily ceased to support the war. One vital factor was shared by soldiers and civilians: Though support for the war at the beginning was wide, it was also very thin. Countless men like Robert Conner and C. W. Bowman went to do their duty, feeling it was the right thing to do, and intuitively trusted the U.S. government. The Johnson administration, however, refused to develop a compelling rationale for the war. As we know now, the administration, afraid that its domestic agenda would suffer, did not want to rouse the country. The resulting attempt to keep a long war on a short leash was political madness. It totally ignored the metamorphosis of blood that accompanies every serious conflict. The will to win and thereby vindicate the blood sacrifice made by the nation inevitably overwhelms specific political goals. Johnson's belief that he could treat a war as large and long-lasting as Vietnam as a political act ranks with the greatest follies in American history. Not since 1860, when James Buchanan sat crying in the White House as the Union fell apart, has the United States been led so incompetently. The collapse of political will in the United States ultimately had nothing to do with a change in political perceptions toward Southeast Asia or America's role in the world. The first was never understood by supporters of the war, and the latter was only vaguely accepted by the population. The collapse of domestic support for the war took place when the citizenry realized that the United States was not going to win. Even ideological supporters of the war turned their backs when it was clear that Washington had no intention of taking the risks necessary to obtain victory. In short, Americans increasingly viewed the war as a violent and futile exercise that was leading nowhere.

If American citizens safe at home came to believe that the war effort was a huge and tragic waste, one can imagine how much more quickly this realization struck the men who knew Vietnam best: the combat troops of the U.S. Army. It is striking how rapidly the men sensed that something was wrong and that their mission, politically, was dubious, at best. Richard Mengelkoch served in 1966 and detected an erosion of political will almost immediately:

People accepted the fact that we were there and had a job to do. We would follow orders, go out and search the countryside, and do what we had to do. Since we weren't engaged in heavy, severe combat, it just didn't become so oppressive. However, the subtle objective for the men was to stay alive and count the days. You didn't count the days the first six months, but as you started getting down into that last six months, then you started thinking

more about it. It was always a subject of somebody's conversation, but it became more and more a subject of your conversation.

C. W. Bowman, who believed the government's message as a recruit, soon learned a different reality in the field:

What did the men think they were doing over there? Just surviving. Making that 365 days. Your family was your squad, and that's who you looked after, that's who you took care of. Mom and apple pie and stuff, that was out the window. You were fighting for each other. You were trying to keep each other alive so you could make it home.

As a junior officer for the 3/4th Armored Cavalry, Jerry Headley was thirty years old, one of the oldest men in his unit. He also established a superb combat record while serving in a most perilous time. Yet, it was precisely men like Headley, the most professional and experienced, who best appreciated that something was dreadfully wrong with the conduct of the war. The frustration Headley expresses was felt by many:

There wasn't anything different in Vietnam from the day I arrived to the day I left. We were still fighting over the same terrain, the same areas. Where an ambush or a fight had been a month before, you were fighting again. You never, never held anything. You'd fight in an area one day and come back again and fight on another. It was very frustrating to know that it didn't matter what you did or how many of the enemy you killed or how many you captured. He was going to be there again tomorrow. And so the more you did this, you kept wondering, what the hell am I doing here? I'm not getting anywhere. It's just the same thing over and over again.

Infantryman Jay Lazarin has almost identical views concerning his tour:

Over my one-year tour, my unit went to two areas along the Vam Co in Duc Hue district numerous times and made serious contact with the VC. We sustained many casualties from both firefights and booby traps, yet we never stayed put there long enough to keep the area clear of the enemy or to block his travel routes. So, as the year wore on, each time we knew we were going back to these places, we (the experienced ones) mumbled out loud about going back for the express purpose of trying to see who could kill more of each other. We were certainly not ashamed of what we were doing and went about all our operations trying to do our best. Yet, the most troubling aspect was always the knowledge that as soon as we left, they would be back, and most likely, so would we. Each time we took casualties, they became our priorities and Medevac missions took first place in most thinking on the scene. I am not saying that this was bad, from a grunt's point of view; that's how we stayed alive or survived injuries. It just didn't seem aggressive enough then or, certainly, now. I'm not now sorry for it; this kind of tactic probably kept most of us alive.

None of these examples are intended to show that the soldiers of the 25th Division were "antiwar" in the way the term was understood in the United States. Certainly, few of them shared the beliefs of the New Left that they were fighting for a malignant, racist, power-mad imperialist power. Some men did, in retrospect, remark that they felt like redcoats. In the previous chapter, I examined the nearly universal contempt felt for the South Vietnamese army and government on the part of U.S. troops. Far more common, however, was the feeling that the war was going to turn out badly no matter what they did. Furthermore, everyone realized what was taking place in the United States. If the country did not care about the outcome of the war, why, the men felt, should they?

Although the slide in political morale was evident from the beginning, it was greatly accelerated by two events. One was the bombing halt that followed the Tet Offensive. The other was Vietnamization and the withdrawal of American troops. If the war seemed aimless before these events, after them, it was obvious that the United States was looking for a way out of Vietnam that would mean, at best, some sort of indistinct conclusion to the conflict. Therefore, even if the soldiers wanted to believe in some greater purpose for their efforts—and most did—a feeling of utter waste steadily embittered the men on the spearpoint. Inexorably, the 25th Division ceased fighting the war for the United States. Instead, they began to fight it for themselves. Most accepted their role and did their duty. But survival became the aim, not victory.

Thomas Giltner remembers the impact of events in America on the soldiers' sense of mission:

Comparing Vietnam with World War II is like comparing apples and tangerines.

The Vietnam War had a lot of faces to it. It got almost comical in certain respects. For example, we had been out on a big operation for two weeks. Then the men would come back after two weeks in the field and have a chance to do their laundry, get spare parts for the weapons, take an account of everything. They would go into their hooches at night and watch Vic Morrow in "Combat." And they watched the 6:00 news; they'd watch everything from a Jane Fonda protest to a John Wayne World War II epic. This isn't the sort of spirit the soldiers had in England in 1944 as they trained and prayed and sharpened their bayonets, waiting to cross the channel and fight the mighty German Wehrmacht.

How's it all going to end? Was there an equivalent of capturing Berlin that would lead to a victorious conclusion to the war? And, granted, in late 1966, we had some difficulty in explaining this to the troops. We looked for ways to describe our mission. In late 1966, free elections were going to be held in Saigon. We went to the troops telling them that their job and our job was to make the place safe for democracy, so people could come down and not be afraid to vote or cast their ballots like we do in America. That sounds reasonable enough, and it was true at the time. But as the antiwar movement ground on and it became more and more uncertain what the mission was, the political framework certainly became more shaky. And I'm sure there was much debate over indoctrination when the troops in military training could go in the day room, turn on the television set at night, see Jane Fonda and Tom Hayden, and hear the hawks and doves debate each other in Congress over the issue of whether or not we would continue with the Vietnam War or pull out.

Sgt. Rick Lewis was a young noncom with the mechanized infantry when Nixon announced the beginning of troop withdrawals. As he relates, the reality was rather different from the promise and was not appreciated by those involved:

Richard M. Nixon's plan of Vietnamization caused a lot of hope in the war zone. The 25th Division was one of the units targeted to be sent home in 1969, and we were all ecstatic about the news. Later, to our disappointment, we were to learn only the colors [ceremonial flags—EMB] would leave the country. The troops would be reassigned to other units. So, as preparations were being made to move the headquarters company and its staff back to Hawaii, we were left to worry about the rest of our tour of duty in the tropical paradise. With this slick political maneuver, Washington had proof to show to the American public that, in fact, the administration was pulling whole divisions out of this unpopular war, and in reality, the only move made was changing the signpost in front of the headquarters buildings. Due to this bad situation, the Army now had a bunch of twenty-year-old soldiers that never trusted the news media or the political machine in Washington again. We were already much wiser, thanks to the lessons we learned in war and by being burned by the very people we were there to defend. [Sergeant Lewis's point is valid, but I should clarify the time frame. The 25th did not leave Cu Chi until 15 December 1970. By that time, many men had been rotated back. Others who were early in their tour were reassigned. The 2d Brigade stayed on until April 1971.—EMB]

Lee Reynolds explains some of the ambivalence the men felt toward the press. On one hand, by 1970, when Reynolds served, everyone was eager to leave quickly: No one wanted to be the last to die in Vietnam. On the other, the soldiers were bitter at the way they were portrayed in the media:

We came across a village during the Cambodian operation where a lot of civilians had been murdered. It was done by the North Vietnamese and not the Americans, but that is not the sort of story you hear. ABC, NBC, and CBS were there and grinding out films for the 6:00 news, but they didn't report it. They were in the night defensive positions, trying to find the dumbest guy they could find to do an interview with to try and make the Vietnam soldier look like an idiot. I've got mixed feelings about media coverage. Every night on the news, they would report casualty figures of Americans killed every week, which put pressure on our leadership to keep losses down, and that helped us. But I don't like the way the Vietnam soldier has been presented or characterized by the media, even to this day. Lieutenant Calley is an albatross that the Vietnam soldier must carry around his neck.

Thomas Giltner points out how much more available and widespread media coverage was in Vietnam in comparison with earlier periods:

Don't forget that the media in Vietnam, in the 1960s, was much more pervasive than in the 1940s. The troops had radios, and if they got back to their hooches, they had television. They could hear or see more on the evening news than when they were in the field. They saw their leaders, Lyndon Johnson and General Westmoreland, on television. But as the war went on, they also saw Jane Fonda and Abbie Hoffman and the protest movement back in the United States. They were raised on Walter Cronkite and Eric Severeid, who gave them impressions on the war. So, information was much more prevalent in those days. And that also helped shape the soldier's attitude toward his superiors. I was in-country in late 1966 when LBJ came to Vietnam. It's always impressive when a president of the United States visits a battlefield, no matter what war you're in. But the troops just weren't interested in it.

Other men were simply bitter. Sidney Stone, who was older and better educated than most soldiers, expresses the commonly held view among troops in Vietnam that the antiwar movement aided the enemy and killed Americans:

I still won't go see Jane Fonda. I know she thought she was a great American for pointing out the evils of the war. But what she did affected my morale and other people's, too. We were doing our duty and carrying out the foreign policy of the United States, we hoped for the welfare of our country, and then we had people who would not support it. When I grew up, the generation before me served in World War II, and the generation before them served in World War I. It seemed like every generation had a war, and this was my time to serve. I never did question that idea. It is very difficult to justify a war. However, today, after studying the war more objectively than some of the critics, I believe that had we been able to accomplish our goals in Vietnam, we would have a stronger nation and a more peaceful world.

Larry Fontana is even more blunt:

We never lost the war militarily. To a man, I think we all hated the peace marchers and hippies. Some of us were college graduates; some were professionals, farmers, laborers, mostly sons of middle-class families, with high school diplomas. Even we knew that the protesters would make it harder on us by giving the NVA hope. We didn't want bombing halts anywhere. Our necks were stuck out there, and nobody really gave a damn about us except for our own immediate families. There were questionable soldiers serving there, but, by far, the majority of the infantrymen were good, decent men who were doing their jobs the best way they could.

Dan Vandenberg's infantry unit was in the field for most of his tour. He does not recall a media barrage in the bush. Nevertheless, the cynicism and bitterness he expresses were not his alone:

Basically, we felt pretty isolated. People at home were not really affected by the war. The majority of our friends were in college, doing their bit to stop the war, which we were quite grateful for. If you can believe that, I've got some swampland I'd like to sell you. We thought they were a bunch of long-haired, pussy, chicken-shit assholes. But we really didn't get that much news from the States, unless somebody got a hometown newspaper or mail. Armed Forces Radio sure didn't tell us anything. Plus, we didn't have much time to listen to the radio. I can only remember a few instances when we had both time and someone who had a radio so we could listen to it.

There was never any discussion about whether the war was right or wrong. We all agreed that it was being fought in a real Mickey Mouse way. There was never any effort to hold ground. You would see how high a body count you could get, how many enemy you could kill. If there was more enemy killed than you lost, it was a great week. It was pointless. The government could just as easily have taken every nineteen-year-old male in the

United States, lined them up, and shot every tenth man and have accomplished as much. Maybe that sounds bitter, but it's realistic and makes about as much sense as what we did.

Many men also bitterly resented the draft as practiced in the United States. Kenneth Stumpf expresses these resentments forcefully:

That fucking draft. How unfair that damn thing was. We young people didn't know any better. We just went on. But I can't believe that older people would let a draft work like that. It was so obvious. If you had money or connections, you could get out or join the National Guard or reserves. I have more respect for the people who went to Canada than I do for the people who went into the reserves: They were the draft-dodgers. At least the people who went to Canada knew they might be punished.

Vietnamization added fuel to the fire when American soldiers looked beyond their own immediate concerns. Most men welcomed the withdrawal of combat forces and hoped they would be among the lucky ones to return home quickly. However, most also believed that when they left, their enemies would triumph and the war would end as a complete waste.

Dan Vandenberg and his comrades in 1969 had no illusions about the outcome of the war and apparently not very much concern:

We could give a shit what happened to the country after we left. We had 365 days to spend there, and then we didn't give a damn what happened. All we wanted to do was make it through our time alive and get the hell out of there. As far as pulling out of that country, we all agreed that as soon as the United States pulled out, that country was gone because the Vietnamese weren't going to fight for it. They weren't fighting for it when we were there backing them up; they sure weren't going to fight for it when we left. I am bitter. I guess mainly because it was all wasted. There was no effort to win. Nobody back here gave a shit.

Dan Breeding served even later. With troop withdrawals in full swing by 1970, Breeding and his friends had neither hope nor concern for the outcome of the war:

When I arrived in-country in February 1970, I thought there was a purpose. But it didn't take long to rub off on me that the way the war had been waged, it wasn't going anywhere except to hand it over to ARVN. It was a shame it was dragging on like it did. Politics was playing into it. I don't think anyone thought we were going to leave the country and say we won or contributed to a victory. There may have been a token few that thought we were really accomplishing anything. Maybe if we had the backing of the people back home, we would have felt differently. For the most part, people thought it was a waste.

The GIs were very lax. They knew that some divisions were being pulled out and that we were giving a lot of the base camps over to ARVN. A lot of guys resented that because we would always have to spit-shine the places when they were given over. We found that the ARVN were more of a lazy, cocky bunch. We resented them because we were over there and they didn't seem to be doing their fair share. The only contact I had with South Vietnamese was the interpreter each company had assigned. We had the Chieu Hois, who were once NVA or Viet Cong and had rallied over to our side, but you couldn't trust them. Everyone despised the South Vietnamese soldiers in our units.

Jim Ross served at the same time as Breeding. He describes well the combination of relief and disappointment felt by American soldiers as they departed, fully expecting the war to end in defeat:

It was a relief for all of those going home; on the other hand, it was very distressing, very discouraging, to think of turning over the entire area of operations of the 25th Infantry Division to the South Vietnamese army. We couldn't help but feel that it had all been for nothing, that nothing had been gained, that no forward progress had been made, and that things were basically about the way things were when we got there. The war was still going on, and the Americans were withdrawing. The reality of the combat situation within South Vietnam was worsening. All of the political talk—"peace with honor" and such things—had very little meaning in South Vietnam because everyone knew that with each step we took to withdraw, the North Vietnamese and the VC were doubling their efforts to take over the country. We knew that when we left, the country would be overwhelmed by the VC and the North Vietnamese.

It is evident that the soldiers of the 25th Division were left at sea by their government concerning the purpose of their sacrifice. Students of the war, however, must be very careful in what deeper conclusions they draw from this fact. Intense political motivation is extremely rare in war. The fear of combat's consequences, however, is a given. So is the realization that individual survival is connected to the welfare of the group. As a combat unit, the men of the 25th Division were not fighting for the United States. Nor were they fighting for victory. No doubt many men wanted to fight for both. They were, however, fighting for themselves. Ultimately, despite strains of all sorts, this proved sufficient not only to keep the Division in the field but also to make it an extremely formidable presence on the battlefield until the bitter end.

Day by Day

Commanders always try to compartmentalize the world of an army at war. Soldiers have often thought of themselves as passive components in a machine or "just numbers," as several men told me. Leaders typically expect a soldier to tend to his task and do not encourage him to look beyond it. The hierarchy that has characterized every army in history is predicated on the assumption that men can be trained to act in a certain way very quickly and without question.

Without doubt, this dovetails very nicely with human nature. Men may need to learn an unusually rigid form of discipline in the military, but it is not difficult to convince most people to tend their own garden. This is particularly true during wartime because of the press of events. Every soldier in history has complained of periods of boredom, but as should be very evident, men on or near the spearpoint have much to do and think about. Consequently, the world of most soldiers is a small one. Depending upon their job, it consists largely of a relatively small number of people that share their surroundings. Jim Ross was speaking for himself on this subject, but soldiers throughout history have undoubtedly voiced similar sentiments:

People were tired of hearing about the war, they were tired of thinking about it, and they were tired of listening to the politicians and their rhetoric. It was like people getting tired of getting their taxes raised. They just throw up their hands and say to themselves that there is nothing they can do about it. So they just roll with the punches because it doesn't do any good to worry about it. You had the same situation in Vietnam. People were sick of the whole mess, but they still had to put up with it. They didn't spend their days and nights worrying about what the outcome was going to be and when it was going to happen. They focused more on their own individual needs, not only on surviving their tour in Vietnam but also on their day-to-day existence.

The multitude of factors that constituted the day-by-day existence of the men of the 25th Division make precise generalizations impossible. Some men were crushed by the war; others view their service with great pride and plainly miss the intensity of the war and the depth of human relationships that were formed because of it. In between the extremes are as many way stations as there are veterans of the war. It is possible, however, to at least identify some of the major components of daily morale.

As I have just illustrated, the Vietnam soldiers' feelings toward the United States ranged from bitterness to indifference. But personal ties to home remained strong. Naturally, the most important people at home for every soldier were his loved ones. Recognizing this, the Army did much to see that the men could maintain vital personal contacts. [Here is one area where soldiers on the other side were treated brutally. Their mail was rare, and Hanoi frequently did not even inform families that their sons had died—EMB] Even in an army that expended great resources to this end, the 25th Division had earlier earned a reputation for having excellent mail service. It is not clear why this was so. One 25th Division vet of Korea speculated that because the Division was based in Hawaii and many of its men came from the mainland, mail received unusual priority in the days before inexpensive telephone service. In any case, the Division went to great lengths to get mail to the men at camp and in the field as quickly as possible. It is difficult to overstate the importance of this policy, as Richard Mengelkoch points out:

Mail service was good. I don't recall that we had a problem with first-class mail, but packages took a little longer. Mail—and this is no revelation—without a doubt is the most important thing to a soldier in that environment. It is important to any soldier, especially to a combat soldier in another part of the world. It's that tie that holds you. I was fortunate. I got mail from my girlfriend, who later became my wife, and from my mother and from my brothers and sisters and my friends.

Platoon leader Del Plonka cites an incident showing the importance of mail to the soldiers under his command:

The best part of the whole day was mail call. That was something the Division tried to maintain. We talk about morale, but believe me, if you don't have mail call, you don't have morale. Once, we were assigned to another company. Its commander cared only for his mission, not his men. For five days, we pulled ambush patrol. We didn't get any mail. We were used to getting mail every day in the field. My men were getting very, very touchy. We had a good sergeant. That evening, he approached me and said, "Sir, where's our mail?" I said, "We don't have any." He said, "My men aren't going out until they get their mail." I reminded him that I didn't have any control over the mail, and he recognized that. I said, "Let's just do our job." He said, "No." Right about the time we were discussing the mail, here it came. Later, they went on ambush patrol, and everybody was happy.

If mail did not come from home, the military itself periodically filled in. The Army tried to sweeten the pot by disbursing what the men called "poggie packets," small packages containing cigarettes, toothpaste, and such things. The soldiers doubtlessly appreciated the trinkets, but they did elicit a frequent complaint from men in the field. It seems that somewhere in the pipeline between Cu Chi and the bush, either all the desirable brands of cigarettes were gone or the packets disappeared entirely. Morale in the 25th Division certainly did not stand or fall on cigarettes and toothpaste. However, this apparently minor matter reflected a far deeper and integral part of warfare: the tension between field soldiers and support troops.

In theory, of course, no such tension existed: Everyone was part of the same team and working for the same ends. The reality was different. The base camps were not safe places, in the normal sense of the word. Hundreds of men of all categories were killed and wounded during innumerable enemy mortar and rocket attacks on these camps. Perimeter guard could likewise be hazardous. Yet, in comparison with field duty, the camps were havens of security and comfort. The men and women that served there were not only safer but also far more numerous.

The relationship between front and rear was ironic in two ways. Although it is impossible to prove, it is reasonable to speculate that some of the resentment felt by combat soldiers in Vietnam toward their fellows in the camps was a spillover from a wider alienation they felt from those even safer at home. The word often used by fighting men to describe those in supporting roles—REMFs (rear echelon mother fuckers)—is reminiscent of the various references directed toward college protesters. Despite the fact that life in Cu Chi or a similar location was infinitely more dangerous and uncomfortable than that led by a prosperous civilian, the soldiers serving in the camps were close and visible targets for the resentments of the combat troops. On the other hand, though the men in the field might have resented the inequality of risk, they greatly enjoyed the fruits of the massive pipeline operated by the support troops.

Platoon commander Thomas Giltner, who served both in the field and at Cu Chi, describes this aspect of the situation:

We had at least two convoys a day coming in from Saigon all the way to Cu Chi. You know what they were bringing? They were bringing cases upon cases of soft drinks, cases and cases of beer, and cases and cases of whiskey and other types of liquor for the officers', NCO, and enlisted men's clubs. They brought cameras, tape recorders, and all kinds of electronic devices the troops could buy with the script money they drew once a month. There were books, magazines, *Playboy* magazines—everything that you would need to stock a club or a bar or a PX was brought out. Except for rare situations, there was never a time when we troops in the field didn't have all the beer and soft drinks we wanted. They brought out the USO shows, and the Red Cross dollies would come out and put on a show. The Army thought that troop morale would be at its best if the troops had reminders of home. The soldiers wanted that stuff whether or not it dampened a warlike spirit, which it probably did.

No Army in history has ever received the sort of creature comforts in the field that the U.S. Army did in Vietnam. When possible, hot meals were lifted out in helicopters. The choppers also delivered ice cream. As noted by Giltner, every trooper had a daily ration of two beers or sodas, easily supplemented by purchases from local entrepreneurs. It is difficult to imagine what a man on the front lines in Guadalcanal would have paid for some ice—another luxury usually available in Vietnam.

The Army also put much effort into entertaining the men. Most bases had swimming pools, athletic facilities, and the like. Ad hoc movie theaters were established wherever possible. In addition, Cu Chi was close to Saigon and received a steady stream of VIPs, such as Spiro Agnew. Most men never saw these visitors, but the entertainment celebrities were decidedly popular. Although mocked by self-righteous antiwar protesters at home, the efforts of people like Danny Kaye and Ann-Margret, who came in 1966 when Cu Chi must have seemed a dingy nightclub, were appreciated by the soldiers. World War II veterans claimed that Kaye's show was the same one he put on twenty years before. They also were happy when Bob Hope brought his nationally televised Christmas show to Cu Chi in 1968. He was, after all, one of the richest men in California and hardly needed the publicity for his career. Lest one think that Hope's assemblage performed in utter safety, I should note that less than one month later, the Cu Chi camp was penetrated by NVA sappers and damaged badly during what proved to be the opening gun of the 1969 Tet Offensive. Maj. Robert Broyles, who was responsible for preparing for the Hope show, illustrates how the Division often used its manpower:

I organized the 1968 Bob Hope Christmas show, and it was a hell of an operation. I never dreamed it would be as big as it was. I was given the assignment in October 1968, and thank God, I had some good young officers and NCOs because the lion's share of my time was taken up by the show. Among other things, we were told that if the show was coming to Cu Chi, we had to provide a proper facility. But we didn't have one. We had to construct what became known as the Lightning Bowl, a major amphitheater. We had to hollow out the bowl with the engineers. The show wasn't just for the Cu Chi guys but for everyone in the whole area. It paid off because we got a lot of airtime on television.

Another strange feature of the Vietnam War was the ten-day leave given to every soldier in the year-long tour. During the famous Vietnam R & R leave, the Army would transport soldiers to almost anywhere in the Pacific, including Hawaii. Few passed up the opportunity, but for combat soldiers, it was an ambivalent experience in retrospect. Sgt. Charles Albridge, who arrived with the Division, expresses these mixed feelings:

R & R was part and parcel of the Vietnam War experience. It was a tension reliever in more ways than one. Obviously, we were on the loose for a week someplace where we could do almost anything to excess. That ran the gamut from simply sleeping to pigging out on food to excess booze and women. There were buying sprees: Some things were very cheap in Asia at that time. I went to Japan, but other people went to Bangkok, Hong Kong, Manila, Taiwan, or Seoul. A few, mostly married guys, went to Hawaii and met their wives there. It was a relaxing thing in one respect, but it was also a little bit debilitating. I'm not sure it wouldn't have been better to keep people in that combat zone for a whole year. It's awfully hard going back into the bush, knowing you're going to get shot at, after you've been away from it for a while.

Jerry Headley believed that Cu Chi itself had developed into the equivalent of R & R and therefore had a negative impact on morale in the long run:

I don't think the men felt isolated or let down. Guys could even call home if they wanted to. If you could get to Saigon, at the USO they had pay phones where you could call home. If you were in your unit, you might get a call through to home via a ham radio operator. You had PXs on the main base camps. You certainly weren't isolated. It was weird, really; you'd be out in the bush for two or three weeks or longer and come in for a stand down. You could have a cookout, go to the PX, see movies at night. It was almost like being back in the world. I personally could never get used to that, and to me, it was one of the problems. We were deceiving ourselves. If we were going to fight the war and win it, let's fight the war and win it and go home. But this artificial living and the continual rotation of troops through the meat grinder was beyond me. It may have kept the troops entertained, but it prevented them from focusing on what we were there for.

Although the field soldiers enjoyed what little luxuries Cu Chi provided them, there was, nevertheless, a very deep feeling of antipathy on the part of most fighting men toward "housecats," another name given those in the rear. No doubt, the inequality of risk played a large part in this. However, as usual in Vietnam, the situation was more complex than it appears at first glance. As Thomas Giltner points out, there was a strong degree of envy on the part of many soldiers who wished that they, too, could become REMFs:

Think what a rifle company coming in looked like. You'd see a couple of guys severely wounded, a couple of them taken in with a leg blown off, bandages around their heads, ponchos over the KIAs, and another guy white-faced because he's been in-country two or three weeks and he has eleven months to serve. The men would be tired, filthy, angry, and terrified for their lives. If some idiot from the media sticks a microphone in your face and asks if you would rather be somewhere else, I think you know the response you'd get. And I don't believe those responses would be exclusive to soldiers fighting in Vietnam. And if you asked them, at the same time, if they believed the soldiers in the rear echelon positions had it better off, I don't have to tell you what those answers might be. When you go out there and live in that mud and rain and buffalo dung and you're exposed to danger constantly, even for a short period of time, duty in the city looks attractive. Some men prayed constantly day or night to be given a rear echelon job. I promise you that every man who has taken fire, who has heard bullets coming his way, if he has any sense at all, wishes he were somewhere else.

Giltner's point is both important and most understandable. The Army recognized the great yearning for safety. Indeed, if a man was willing to risk the contempt of his peers and perhaps disciplinary action, it was normally possible to get thrown out of a field unit. But the Army also made allowances for good men who had served in the field with skill and honor. It was military policy, unwritten but altered only in extreme circumstances and with great risk to morale, to allow a field soldier who was "short"—who was within a few weeks of the end of his tour—to finish his stay in Vietnam in the rear. Unless prevented by cruel necessity, most armies in the past have had a similar policy. Although dangerous for everyone, it is common under the best of circumstances for men to crack in battle. And most soldiers, even very good ones, reach a point where they might not just crack but break. It is a process that can be contagious and lead to horrible results. Far better for everyone, as the Army knew, to relieve these men of their final few weeks of agony. Robert Conner, a battle-hardened nineteen-year-old NCO, speaks of the day when he received the word:

I was a short-timer. When I got my orders to leave, we were in an outpost in the Mekong Delta. I had gone to get a haircut in the village that day and got back about four. I sat down on my cot in the tent. I knew that night I had an ambush patrol. The guys looked at me and said, "Boy, you're lucky." I said, "Why, because I've got ambush patrol tonight?" Then they told me the lieutenant had just been there looking for me and had said I was going home. I said, "Sure, uh-huh." I thought they were kidding. But I found the lieutenant, and he told me I was going home the next day. He assigned another sergeant to take out the patrol and told me to stay back. I could have reached up and kissed that man. Good Lord, the thrill and hope that ran through me. Going home. The next morning, bright and early, I packed up my stuff and walked down to the chopper pad. But it was a Sunday. Only one or two choppers came in that day, and they weren't going back to Cu Chi. But I stayed down at that helicopter pad until I knew it was too late for them to send me out on ambush patrol that night. I was scared they'd need me for patrol. The next morning was Monday, and we flew back to Cu Chi.

Mario Tarin describes something similar to Conner's thoughts, but he also points out the consequences that ensued if the policy was not followed:

If you're lucky enough to start getting short enough to dare think that you might be able to complete your tour and get out in one piece, then you start getting *paranoid.* You'll be goddamned if you're going to become a casualty after having survived almost a year of this hell. You think of all of the close calls you've had and all the guys who never got to finish their tour for one reason or another. Everybody has heard the horror stories—true or not—of guys who bought it on their last mission. So guys that are that short start wearing the protective gear again [the heavy and hot flak jacket—EMB], the hell with the heat or the inconvenience. You again start taking that orange horse pill to prevent malaria, even though it gives you the shits like it did when you first got in-country. You put in for a nice "housecat" job at the rear, and if you don't get it (and chances are you won't), then you try to convince the sergeant to let you stay and do KP instead of going out on missions the last few days or weeks. Unless they were really hard up, they would let short people stay behind. Sometimes, the brass would mess with a short-timer for whatever reason, and he would be kept out in the boonies until the end. You talk about a pissed-off grunt! If he is black or a minority, he starts believing that "the man" is discriminating, and you hear talk of "fragging" someone.

Another factor was also at work to sour relations between front and rear. The combat soldiers, understandably, felt they were doing the Army's real job and should receive respect and honorable treatment when they went into Cu Chi for one of their all-too-infrequent stand downs. Instead, they found themselves treated with indifference and an odd hostility. All the soldiers, regardless of duties, tended to form cliques and groups. Anyone outside them was just one of the herd. One might also speculate that despite the fact that few rushed to volunteer for field duty (although that certainly happened on occasion), the men in camp may have felt a degree of guilt for their safety. Whatever the case, Thomas Giltner, a man who had been on both sides of the fence, makes a keen observation:

Some of the Special Forces soldiers and others might say, "Yea, we like it out here; send us more VC." Some men actually liked field duty and would rather be out there fighting. But if the soldiers preferred to be in the field fighting or preferred to be combat infantry, they certainly believed that they were better and should have more prestige. They felt they should be honored not only by their fellow soldiers but by the people at home. Lack of recognition, support, and appreciation is a devastating blow to a soldier's morale.

Phil Boardman, who served as a combat infantryman and volunteer tunnel rat in 1968, admits that given the opportunity when he arrived, he gladly would have taken a rear job. After a time in the field, his attitude changed. His recollections are a strong support for Giltner's observation:

Once you're out there, it just wouldn't have felt right to take a rear job. That would have been letting someone down. And there really was a kind of "them and us" attitude between the "legs" in the field and the people in the rear. We felt we were better than they were. I don't know what they felt. I don't think we were well treated back in base camp. We had to do perimeter guard. We never really felt at home in the NCO and enlisted men's clubs at camp. When we were in, we'd go to our little area in the camp and hang out there.

C. W. Bowman also remembers his time at the rear with animosity and sadness. Unfortunately, as he notes, unknown to him and countless of his comrades, it was a melancholy preview of what was to come when he returned home:

The sad thing about it was that we felt more at home out in the field than in base camp. In base camp, we were the animals and the outcasts. It was two different worlds. A lot of us were treated the same way when we got back to the States: Nobody wanted to have anything to do with us, and nobody wanted to help us out that much. Gary and I had to go to base finance one time. They flew us back in from the field, and you could probably smell us a mile away. We were virtually skin and bones. We noticed when we went into finance that everybody was strong and healthy. They had some guys pounding on typewriters that looked like they could bench-press 800 pounds. We told each other that those big guys were the ones we needed out in the field. But everyone out in the boonies was skinny and worn out. It was just unreal at times.

We'd come in, and the mess hall would be closed, and they wouldn't feed us. But you could walk down the road, and there would be the mess sergeant and the supply sergeant cooking steaks. And the clerks were great: We'd try to get new fatigues and boots, but they never had our sizes. But all the people back in base camp were wearing new boots and pressed fatigues. And when we came out of the field, we always had to go back down to the bunker line and pull perimeter guard. A lot of guys didn't like that, and I didn't like it, either. It was something we had to do, though. We always thought the cooks and clerks should do that because they were the ones who stayed in camp all of the time. So we were the outcasts, the animals. It was really strange. It was almost like when I came back to the world here.

To some unfortunate soldier thrashing through the bush, Cu Chi or one of the other big camps must have summoned an image of Oz. But the daily life at camp, in reality, was a little less blissful. Most of the men that served there put in long hours and took their jobs seriously. Nevertheless, the unusual but powerful glue that bound combat units was not present at camp. Furthermore, as previously noted, many soldiers who were discipline problems and malcontents found jobs there, and a good number of these jobs were very unpleasant. There was also more tedium and boredom in camp than in the field. As a whole, life in camp would be considered desirable only in the context of wartime conditions: Judged by any other standard, civilian or military, Cu Chi was an ugly place. Compared to the sort of life led by men stationed in one of the big cities or one of the giant bases, like Bien Hoa, any camp in the 25th Division's area was a hardship spot.

Ironically, as the war progressed and the military tide moved in the direction of the 25th Division, Cu Chi and Tay Ninh camps became steadily more secure. By 1970, rocket and mortar attacks were extremely rare. This was certainly welcome news for the men and women there, but removing danger also served to emphasize the drab tedium. In addition, the people at camp had daily access to television and radio and were thus very well informed on the catastrophe developing in the United States for virtually every political leader associated with the Vietnam War.

Yet, though the people in camp were far safer than the men in the field, it is ironic that morale at Cu Chi and places like it was, in many ways, lower than in the field. Certainly, the standards of behavior were very different and reflected the enormous difference in circumstances between the relentless violence of field duty and the dreary apathy of camp. Drug use, for instance, which has grown to be as much a symbol of the war as the M16 to the misinformed American public, was much more common at base than in the field. Availability of marijuana was not a problem. It is an odd coincidence that the marijuana craze in the United States began just as an Army was deployed to an area of the world where the plant grows in astounding abundance, is widely consumed, and is extremely strong. So many locals sold it that the price was ridiculously low.

It took a little while for soldiers to realize this, and the earliest arrivals, many of whom had never heard of the drug, were not heavy users. Richard Mengelkoch served in 1966 and expresses a certain relief that his tour was not confused by the additional pressures coming from social rebellion or ethnic mistrust:

I was there at a fortunate time. I was there before drugs played a major impact. I was there before race was a divisive factor within the military. Morale was high. At the time, we thought this was what we should be doing. We were treated pretty well and lived pretty well under the conditions. But the conditions had not yet deteriorated into the heavy combat or the problems at home that came on in later years.

Professional soldier Charles Albridge arrived with the Division and has similar recollections concerning the earliest newcomers. He does, however, also mention a change in attitude on the part of the "Class of '67":

We had a pretty large number of troops coming over in early 1967 who were not there voluntarily. They had been exposed to the protest movement stateside. They brought these attitudes with them. The problems were really not all that heavy at the time, although I understand it got worse later. One of things I've heard a lot about is the stereotypical "massive" use of drugs by the troops over there. Frankly, I never saw it. I'm not saying it didn't go on. It certainly didn't go on to a large enough degree to come to my attention. If it would have been widespread, we would have known about it. Drug use was very minimal in my experience. Unfortunately, the media had a predilection to play on the bad. It seemed to get them better ratings or sales of their magazines.

In 1968, marijuana use was becoming much more common. Morgan Sincock, who commanded a company of mechanized infantry, states that it was common in camp but rare in the field:

There was no heroin in the Army in 1968. Apparently, that came later. There was marijuana. I never saw it used in our unit in the field. Again, it seemed to be an aspect of base camp life. When we prepared our company for an inspection in September 1968, we found enough marijuana stashed in the barracks buildings to fill a GI wastebasket (about 5 gallons).

Bill Noyes also served in a mechanized infantry unit, a little later than Sincock. He challenges the accusation that drugs debilitated the fighting ability of the Division but also charges the Army with insensitivity on the issue:

To some, any drugs are a problem, but in my estimation, my company did not have a drug problem in the field during the time I was there because I saw no significant result upon the war from the drug use I witnessed. Sure, the 25th might have lost some man-hours, and some guys performed less or inadequately at times, but overall, the parade kept on marching pretty much in step.

We had a spunky, proud, black squad leader who was decorated at least twice during his hard year of service. While on a reward leave to the resort of Vung Tau, he was busted for dope and court-martialed. Some reward the Division gave him for doing a job well that few others would do—busted for trying to enjoy himself a little during some off-hours. I suppose someone in the inspector general's office or wherever might have received a promotion out of it. But if that man's bust could somehow help America win the war, I'll be damned if I can understand how. Sometimes—maybe often—it seemed that the greatest predator was not the enemy but the paper-pushing system that decided what image their army would pursue. If anyone might have a complaint about the drug use, it was not then and should not now be the Division command. Perhaps it was the Division who owed the common soldiers greater sensitivity concerning the issue, rather than the soldiers who owed the Division drug-free service.

At the time of Robert Julian's tour during 1971, the Army's morale, according to the script written by journalists and others, was at rock bottom, and drug use was epidemic. Julian, however, bitterly challenges that characterization:

There weren't any drugs in my platoon out in the field. It just did not happen, and we wouldn't have let it happen if a new guy would have brought drugs with him. I never saw any fraggings: I heard of incidents of them, but I never saw any of them. People were reading about insubordination, mutiny, and failure to obey orders. It's true that no infantryman looked forward to or enjoyed combat: I certainly didn't. But we gave better than we got whenever it happened. It's true that the joke was—and I want to emphasize it was a joke—that rather than on search and destroy missions, we were on search and avoid missions. The fact is, we never refused an order or refused a fight.

Clearly, exceptions abounded, but it is difficult to challenge the assertion of so many veterans that serious substance abuse in the field was rare. There were, of course, very practical reasons for this, as C. W. Bowman relates:

I know a lot of the vets are depicted as drug addicts and junkies. But when I was there, nobody did drugs or alcohol in the field. That was the wrong time and place. You needed everything you had to stay alive, and doing drugs wasn't one of them. Word was that if you were doing drugs, you might get shot out in the field during a firefight. They didn't need to have you screw up and maybe get the whole squad killed.

Few civilians can appreciate the narrow edge that existed between life and death in Vietnam. As it was, thousands of men died through absolutely no fault of their own. Yet, contacts with the enemy were very frequent, and the stream of dead and wounded comrades was unending. Only a fool would jeopardize himself further by anesthetizing his senses. And if someone wished to play the role of the fool, there were comrades to remind him that it was a very bad idea. Fatigue and exhaustion were enemies enough. Nor did men enjoy being near someone stoned who was playing with death-dealing devices. As Morgan Sincock notes, drugs and combat zones were a bad mix:

When I was an adviser to a Vietnamese unit in 1969, I had to Medevac a couple of the 9th Infantry Division soldiers who had smoked marijuana on guard duty. They were on a barge tied up at a bridge and were supposed to toss a quarter-stick of C4 plastic explosive into the river every 15 to 20 minutes to discourage underwater sabotage. After a few marijuana cigarettes, one of the men became fascinated watching the fuse burn down on the C4. He lost one or both hands, plus he had other blast injuries.

A final word on drugs comes from medic Lee Reynolds, another man who served a late tour. His point is basic and hard to dispute. In 1970, Reynolds correctly reminds us, drug use in the United States was very heavy. In

Vietnam, where there was the equivalent of an American city of half a million young males, some drug use was inevitable. As Reynolds puts it:

Concerning drugs, there was less abuse in my battalion in Vietnam than there is in your college. What I say is true about almost any school or workplace in America today. I never saw drug abuse among our soldiers to a level that it degraded their ability to do their job.

The subject of racial relations is more complex and difficult to deal with. It is one of several topics regarding Vietnam that needs another clear look, hopefully unencumbered with preconceptions. Although I cannot examine this important issue with the detail it deserves here, some of the components of the mosaic are clear enough. In the first place, the Army had played a central role in the story of racial relations in the United States since World War II. The discrimination suffered by black soldiers during that war and the fierce reaction to it became a major part of the civil rights movement. Because the Army was in the limelight on this issue, perceptions of what was done and what should be done in this realm became intermingled. Compared to most U.S. institutions, public and private, the Army took a progressive position on racial matters. By 1965, there were a large number of black officers commanding troops of all races. The tough black NCO was no myth, and black soldiers served in all areas of the Army. The Army fully integrated combat units nearly twenty years before Vietnam. For all of these reasons, the Army was understandably proud and more than a little self-congratulatory.

It is one thing, however, to say that the Army was a progressive institution relative to others in the United States and another to say that racial discrimination did not persist there. The reality, unfortunately, was quite different. There were many black soldiers in 1965. A good number had enlisted because, whatever its imperfections, the Army offered a better avenue than most available to them in the States for a dignified and successful life. And many young black men, like their counterparts in all racial groups, were drafted. However, although sensitive officers, with reason, might point out that time and larger social changes in the United States were required before a numerical balance of authority would occur, the Army of 1965 was still run overwhelmingly by white officers. The most desirable rear positions tended to go to men with better educations, and the converse was likewise true. Most black soldiers, like most American soldiers, served in support positions. But because the majority of black soldiers had been denied the opportunity to develop sophisticated skills at home, the army assigned all too many to the menial positions that had been the traditional lot of black soldiers in the past. There were many exceptions, but most black combat soldiers served under white officers.

Another point is obvious. Although the soldiers in Vietnam were making the history of their time, they were also reacting to it. The political chemistry concerning the war, as I have tried to show, both anticipated and reflected domestic currents. The youth culture of the 1960s found continual expression in Vietnam. Racial matters worked themselves out the same way. The 25th Division was not isolated from the larger world, and in the United States during the late 1960s, the relationship between the races was simultaneously improving and deteriorating, depending upon the realm explored.

Like a majority of Americans, most blacks in the United States instinctively supported the war effort in its initial stage. But over time, doubts about the war appeared in full measure in the black community. The racial disturbances starting in Watts in 1965 precipitated a historic crisis among black Americans, and the National Guard and, later, federal troops in many cases restored order. The Muhammad Ali case stirred many young men very deeply. Soon, the idea that the black man's enemy was in the United States and not Vietnam was easy enough to accept. The thoughts, rhetoric, and symbolism of the various manifestations of "black power" all found their way to Vietnam. Undoubtedly, all the makings existed for an extremely tense situation.

As in many things, the reality of race relations was complex in Vietnam. Perhaps it would be better to ask whether racial relations in Vietnam were better or worse than those existing in the United States. Obviously, generalizations are dangerous. Furthermore, race is a sensitive issue and one that the men I interviewed might have held back on to avoid having their descriptions of the past interpreted as their present opinions. In addition, one must be careful in dealing with anecdotes: Uninformed observers of the war have been quick to make sweeping comments based on very flimsy evidence. With these caveats duly recorded, I will attempt to draw some conclusions concerning racial relations in the 25th Division, based on what was told to me—but also on what was not.

It is clear that racial tension was a fact of life. It is also clear that the tension was at it worst at the base camps. Both support and combat units had their own pieces of turf in camp. Beyond that, the Army made no effort to require men in camp to share hooches according to the smaller units they belonged to. What developed was a form of voluntary segregation. Looking back, company commander Morgan Sincock thinks that the Army made a serious error in allowing this to develop. He also makes the assertion, supported by scores of men, that this was a problem either confined to or far more serious in camp:

Some racial tension existed in 1968 base camps but not in the field. Some companies had black hooches in base camps. These were the exclusive domain (by choice) of black enlisted men. Occasionally, white soldiers (officer or enlisted) who walked close to these hooches at night would be taunted. Allowing these hooches was a mistake, and we failed to exercise proper leadership by not requiring men to hooch by platoon. In the field, there was zero racial tension. Everyone relied on every other person.

Henry Bergson commanded his infantry company in late 1969. His recollections echo Sincock's:

In my company, race was never a question. We had some blacks, Hispanics, and Orientals, but for the most part, the company was white from all across the United States. We had a good cross section of high school grads, some college kids, and some that got caught up in the draft. For all intents and purposes, a really great group of people. I think that all of the crap took place in the base camp. That's where the drug problems and the black power groups and all of the rest of that junk was. But by the time you're out in the field facing the elephant, as it were, you weren't involved with this political foolishness.

From December 1969 to February 1970, I was assigned a position at Cu Chi. There, I started to see some of the problems that you read about in some of the books. I got involved with a number of drug problems, sleeping on guard, insubordination, black power groups, and some military justice investigations. By the time my orders came through to return to the States, I was ready to go.

No doubt, the racial composition of individual units played a role in the problem. Racially, the 25th Division reflected the numerical ratios of young men existing in the United States at the time. Most soldiers, consequently, were white. If, however, a large percentage of a unit was a racial minority, some of the segregation existing at camp spilled over into the field. Richard Blanks, a platoon leader in 1970, describes the mix in his unit:

When I was 2d Platoon leader, the platoon broke down one-third white, one-third Hispanic, and one-third black. The blacks fairly well tended to stick to themselves, as I recall. I had two machine-gun teams—one was all black, one was all white. In the late 1960s, the black power movement was going strong.

I remember the black troops giving each other the ritual handshakes. They sort of stuck together.

Yet, forming voluntary groups and cliques, especially among young men who are extremely prone to doing this in any case, is not the same as expressing racial hatred or declaring a racial cold war. C. W. Bowman's reflections on the subject are insightful and have the ring of truth:

Back in camp, we had a few problems with black and white relationships. Some of the black soldiers yelled black power slogans at us, and they would congregate together. And there were some arguments, but they never really got into any big fights. One of the things combat vets told the new guys was, don't make any enemies in your unit because you had enough of them out in the field. When we did go out in the field, everything that went on back in base camp was left there because we had to depend on each other too much.

Many soldiers went out of their way to deal with the racial issue and were eager to point out the many deep friendships made between men of different backgrounds or the many times when a soldier of one race risked all to help one of another. Rick Lewis describes his track crew:

As far as racial problems, we had none in the field. My squad of grunts that rode on our track consisted of an Italian, a Mexican, a Hawaiian, a black, a Jew, and three token WASPs. Now, I don't know what some would call racial problems, but I would follow and defend this crew to the end. When I was shot on 5 June 1969, every one of these guys was right there with me, putting me on the Medevac chopper, and twenty-one years later, I still remember every sweaty, grimy face as we silently said good-bye to each other. They all knew my party was over, and I hope they all will finally know that their sergeant is still alive and kicking. I know I would dearly like to know the fate of each and every one of them. This is the saddest part of the war, simply not knowing what happened to these guys.

Ronald Hart served in a mechanized unit throughout 1967 and shares Lewis's thoughts:

I've heard a lot of talk about prejudice in Vietnam. Here's what I think about that. The first time I was involved in a firefight, I was crouching in a ditch, trying to figure out what the hell I was firing at. So as I fired into the bush, my M16 jammed. My platoon sergeant ran over and took my rifle, unjammed it, made sure it fired, and gave it back to me with a smile. I'm white, he was black. Enough said.

I think that it is also important to record what was not said. I have communicated with hundreds of Vietnam veterans, not all with the 25th Division, in the course of research for two books. They have included men from every racial group. Accounts of uneasy, tense relations were common. More men described what I would characterize as uncomfortable relationships. Several recalled incidents of racial slights, insults, and fistfights. Yet, at the same time, many men—frequently the same people who related sad aspects of the situation—also recalled that this was one time in their lives that they worked, lived, and were close to fellow countrymen of another race. Not one man related a first-person account of serious racial violence. Not one man described an environment where men from different racial groups were eager to get at each other's throat. Aloofness or dislike is not the same thing as hatred. Indeed, it may well be that racial relations in the 25th Division were better than they were in the United States. It would be difficult to prove that they were worse. As far as the soldiers are concerned, there are thousands of individuals throughout America who, like Sergeant Lewis, have deep feelings for the men with the "sweaty, grimy" faces, regardless of race, who lived and fought beside them, and they wish them well. Surely that is a good thing.

Field Morale

Field morale is the most complicated subject in the study of warfare. A great number of history's finest artists and thinkers have attempted to portray and explain the behavior of men facing battle, and it is easy to understand why they have done so. The battlefield is a cauldron of intense and conflicting emotions and actions. Thus, it serves as a splendid laboratory in which to explore the human spirit when pushed to the extremities of experience. There, the simplest actions can have extraordinary stakes. A mistake in judgment, whether due to bad fortune or incompetence, is not something that looks bad on your efficiency rating. Instead, it leads to dead or maimed comrades at your feet. Human relationships, which are made and severed with relative ease in civilian life, take on an entirely different hue. Trust and trust betrayed are matters of life and death. And always, the "fog of war" enshrouds the battlefield. This fog has been studied by many military thinkers. It symbolizes the uncertainty and chaos inherent in the exchange of fire. An uncertain situation with extremely high stakes is a powerful drama, but the drama, which is very real, can obscure what is truly important and vital to understand. The essence of battle is not dreadful uncertainty or high drama—it is fear. The fear of the battlefield is not the dread of something vague or internal. It is the blood-chilling fear of what is real and immediate. It is the fear of physical pain, the fear of grief, the fear of death. Yet, the combat soldiers of the 25th Division, like countless others before them, found ways to cope and persevere in a malignant and lethal environment.

For most soldiers, the field was a small world. Group identity was largely reserved for small units. Some men, however, found pride in serving in the 25th Division. Although it did not have the famous public reputation of some of the units thrust into dramatic actions during World War II, the 25th had a strong reputation within the Army. As a new recruit, Michael Butash knew the Division's reputation and wanted no part of it. Yet, in retrospect, he believes his assignment to the 25th was a stroke of luck:

When I went through basic training at Fort Bragg and advanced infantry training, a lot of the drill instructors were wearing the Tropic Lightning patch. The 25th was perceived to be one of the greatest combat units in the Army. I understand that the 25th took more casualties in Vietnam than any other unit. The perception was that it was a kick-ass unit. When I was at the replacement battalion and they said the 25th Division, I was not a happy cowboy. But I grew to have confidence in the machine, in the unit. I think that, for the most part, the relationships between the men, junior officers, and NCOs were very good. You were made to feel that you mattered, that you were an asset, that you were of value. The lowest private was made to feel that he mattered. It sounds kind of corny, but we all knew we depended on each other.

Infantryman Mike Miller had an early tour in Vietnam. He was with the 25th Division brigade sent to the Central Highlands and later attached to the 4th Division in exchange for its brigade stationed in Tay Ninh. The move made geographic sense, but Miller and his friends did not like it:

When I got my orders to go to Vietnam, there were three units I wanted to serve with; one of them was the 25th. When I got my orders to go to the 25th, I was a happy person. The switch to the 4th Division upset a lot of us. A friend of mine described the 4th Division as "Keystone Cops." I don't know if that was really fair, but we didn't want to be with them. We had the choice of wearing either the 25th or 4th division patch, and we all chose the 25th. I'm sure the 4th was a good division, and I don't want to knock them. But we were with the 25th and wanted to stay with them. It was upsetting. I am very proud to have served with the 25th and would rank it as one of the best or the best division in Vietnam.

Kenneth Stumpf was one of Miller's comrades and shared his feelings on the subject:

We all considered ourselves members of the 25th Division. I was sick to death when they told us we had to wear the 4th Division patch. I still wear the 25th Division patch. We wanted to be 25th. That was us. We did a lot of things, but the togetherness and things like that taught me a lot.

However, for most soldiers, it was not past reputation that was important. Their identity with their unit—and much of field morale in general—was very much a factor of leadership. The relationship between a soldier and his leaders is, like so many relationships in war, complex. Junior officers and NCOs, the leaders closest to combat soldiers on a daily basis, are the men who give immediate orders during battle. Therefore, they are a critical cog in any war machine. Soldiers must respond to orders during the chaos of battle, or the fighting unit suffers a great decline in combat effectiveness. While under fire, some degradation is inevitable. Some soldiers will freeze, some will be wounded, others will not hear the orders given. Yet, if a unit is badly led, this will compound its difficulties greatly. If a combat leader lacks the tactical competence and intangible requirements necessary to lead, he will harm the unit's spirit. And the importance of spirit and morale can hardly be understated. Every unit met tragedy at some time or another in Vietnam. If there was a reservoir of strength to draw upon, the unit could recover and face further danger intact. If the reservoir was dry, a unit could be so badly damaged that major surgery would be required to get it back into operation.

What characteristics should a good junior officer or a good noncom possess? The answer to this question is complicated and largely depends upon whether one is looking from the top of the ladder of rank down or from the bottom up. This dichotomy is a natural reflection of the unusual situation that faces men who lead others in war. To some degree, regardless of rank, they confront an agonizing contradiction. An important part of any officer's job is to guard the welfare of the men under his command. But he must also accomplish the military mission assigned him, and undertaking this mission will mean death and injury to some of the men he is supposed to care for. Obviously, an unavoidable and extremely painful tension results.

Because they were closest to the men, NCOs and junior officers in Vietnam and all wars faced this tension most directly. Even if an individual cultivated an intentional reserve and distance from the enlisted men, the powerful personal bonds of a combat unit ensnared the small-unit leaders over time. They, after all, were in the bush or in the tracks and under great risk themselves. Soldiers did not expect perfection from their leaders, but it made a big difference to know that if a lieutenant made a mistake, he would have to face the consequences along with everyone else. In addition, because a powerful political motivation was notably lacking in Vietnam, soldiers were quick to equate an officer's skill with his ability to avoid casualties. He could do this in one of two ways: first, through the mastery of complex combat techniques that relied heavily on firepower from supporting arms and, second, by conducting operations with the utmost caution, sacrificing some vaguely defined mission for the immediate safety of his men.

Thomas Giltner was a second lieutenant in the field and was forced to face the horrible dichotomy of combat leadership:

It's true that in the soldier's mind, his superiors are sitting back in nice warm quarters having a life of ease. And compared to the way he lives and the dangers he's exposed to, that's exactly correct. Sometimes, a soldier appreciates the weight of the responsibility of his officers' burden, and sometimes he doesn't. Usually, a soldier in the field has just one thing on his mind, and that's survival and getting the job over with so he can return home. There is maybe a little difference between the combat officer and an officer in the rear echelon. I was a rifle platoon leader out in the field, sharing the same hardships. One vet mentioned that he never saw an officer above captain in the field after dark. I suppose for the most part that was true. A major and above commands a battalion-sized operation, and most of the operations in Vietnam were smaller. They were led by captains and lieutenants. It wasn't often that a major would go out on field operations at night. I can also believe that the soldiers didn't know the name of the division commander: Hell, they probably didn't care. Certainly they didn't care if he got promoted to a higher rank or whether he was famous. They had their minds on the day-to-day combat operations. That's true in all wars.

You just have to do whatever it takes in those situations to show that there is some leadership going on. And I think they respect that. Then, if you get into a situation where you screw up and make a mistake in the field, they're ready to cut you some slack. If they think you're scared, that's all right. In combat situations, being scared is perfectly all right: Everybody's supposed to be scared. Giving in to it is another matter. Of course, one of the things that makes it so hard on the small-unit leader is that when you do get into a situation where people die, even if it's bad fortune, you either get yourself killed or wounded or some of your men become casualties and you feel responsible. You blame yourself for their deaths. You can't help it, even if you know in your heart of hearts you were not at fault. You've heard many times the term "acceptable losses." They're not acceptable to the leader. It happens that way, and you have to accept it, but there's a difference in being compelled to accept something and finding something acceptable. The point I'm trying to make is that the combat officer has a lot on his mind. He's certainly scared for his own well-being and worried about the well-being of his troops, but he's also got his own performance as an officer on the line, his knowledge as a soldier on the line, and, foremost, he's got the accomplishment of his mission at stake. His professional competency is being tested by the minute. I honestly believe that unless the officer's a complete dud, the men still like to have him around.

Jerry Headley was in a somewhat different position than Giltner. Like Giltner, he was a platoon leader, but he later took over his troop (company, in regular infantry parlance) as a captain. The 3/4th Armored Cavalry was the Division's most versatile and powerful unit, and it compiled a distinguished field record. During a running fight, Division command frequently sent elements of the 3/4th to the rescue of another unit in danger. As noted earlier, Headley's men were no more politically motivated than any others in the Division, but the power of the unit and its obvious importance clearly helped its officers maintain good field morale. Headley describes the situation as it existed in early 1969, a period of intense combat:

I can only speak of my little microworld, but I felt the morale was very good. I had a lot of men reenlist or extend to stay in the unit. You would wonder about this. Perhaps it was due to leadership or to the camaraderie of the men; I don't really know what it was. At least in my troop—and I think this was true throughout the squadron—their morale was very high. There were a few things they were usually teed off about. Obviously, the riots and marches by the college kids back in the States had a deep effect. They resented this, and they didn't understand it. The typical remark was: If they want to riot and fight, why don't they get their asses over here? We'll give them something to riot and fight about. When you are so removed from one another, it is hard to understand who is right or wrong. I was thirty and probably the oldest troop commander. With the exception of a few of the sergeants, the rest of the guys were, at most, twenty-three years old. You had a much younger fighting force in the field than you did in either World War II or Korea, and these young fellas performed admirably. I think relationships with NCOs and junior officers went well. I can only focus on me. I got along well with the men, and I think the men liked me. For the most part, they respected their officers and NCOs. In one case, one of the platoon leaders, a college graduate, was an intelligent fellow, but he couldn't pour water out of a boot. The men came to me and said something had to be done. They didn't have to do that because it didn't take long to figure whether you were going to cut it out in the field. Indeed, I had the lieutenant relieved, and he was put in Division headquarters, where he did a nice job. It didn't bother him because he knew he couldn't do it, and it helped the men because you looked out for their welfare, too. I was offended by the movie *Platoon* because it implied that the platoon leader was a "weak Willie" and that the two dominant NCOs ran everything. I'm not going to say that it didn't happen, and I'm not going to say it didn't happen in the 25th Division, the division represented in the movie. I am going to say that it did not happen in the 3d Squadron of the 4th Cavalry, and I wasn't aware of it happening in other units. I don't know if it was the license to steal by the author or what. It greatly offended me.

Like Headley, Morgan Sincock commanded both a platoon and a company. As members of the "class of '68," Sincock and his men were in the middle of the most violent period of the war for the 25th Division. He speaks of the divided loyalties that plagued combat officers in Vietnam:

Infantry officers are taught to prioritize their situation, with their mission taking priority over their men. This is the necessary philosophy to wage war. Men do get killed and wounded. To put the men first diminishes the chance of accomplishing the mission. In war, you risk lives. To many of us, the risk became unacceptable when we were unable to utilize the resources at our disposal. Some battles were fought with timidity and caution rather than abandon and commitment because we could not rationalize the sacrifice of men's lives in order to protect civilian property.

When we made contact with the enemy, we always had ample supporting firepower available to us. We were free to use this firepower outside of populated areas. Many, although not all, officers shared my philosophy that it was wisest to use maximum firepower and minimum frontal assaults by infantry. We would often make contact, pull back a few meters, and continue to engage the enemy with small-arms fire while we began a massive pounding of the enemy positions with all available firepower. Once the enemy positions had been pulverized by ordnance, we would assault and sweep the positions. Some enemy bunkers were so well built that they withstood all but a direct hit. Occasionally, the bunkers survived intact, but the occupants had been killed by the concussion of the heavier bombs dropped adjacent to the bunker.

There developed, among those who could exert some control over events on the ground, a great respect and affection for the men we commanded and a powerful reluctance to shed their blood. Our overall effectiveness as a fighting force was diminished in this situation. This should not be interpreted to mean that the men and their leaders could not and would not fight with heroic ferocity when the circumstances were right. I saw our men perform best when we got the maximum supporting firepower available, when going to the rescue of another unit, when defending positions and each other, and when inspired by extraordinary leadership.

Sincock's reflections are very accurate. Recall, however, that in most engagements, whether U.S. units were on the defensive or the offensive, it was the other side that took the first shot. Consequently, "the circumstances were right" for fierce battle very frequently. As Sincock further illustrates, a wise officer also knew when the immediate situation on the ground required caution, regardless of what those higher up the command line believed:

An incident along the slopes of Nui Ba Den illustrates an occasional attitude and action of the ground commander. In this case, we were ordered to move up the gradual slope of Nui Ba Den and then, with one platoon deployed on the 45-degree slope of the mountain, sweep around the perimeter of the mountain for several kilometers. This struck us as a bad tactical idea to start with since the terrain was thick and rocky. Going was tough, and we feared being fired down on from NVA defensive positions. Most operations on this mountain involved landing troops on the peak and having them work their way down. This was also known to be a major enemy base camp and staging area. Our doubts were confirmed as we moved in the open to the base of the mountain and immediately discovered a hastily abandoned campsite, with water still boiling in a tin teakettle over a campfire. Within moments of our finding the camp, the NVA blew a claymore on us and opened fire from above.

We were able to use all our firepower after we withdrew to evacuate our wounded. We were ordered to resume the maneuver later in the afternoon. The captain commanding the company thought the whole plan reckless. He had us move back up the gentle slope of the mountain and sweep—but about 20 meters away from the dramatic 45-degree slope of the mountain, well concealed by forest canopy. He called our location in as if we were on the mountainside, but we weren't there.

The attitude of the fighting men toward their officers obviously varied somewhat depending upon the individual. But generally speaking, the degree of respect they felt declined as the leader's rank rose. In other words, the NCOs and junior officers who shared the men's risks were, by and large, well thought of. But with officers higher and higher up the ladder of rank, there was an increasing tendency either to view them as hostile or to not think about them at all. This reaction, well known to students of military history, also has a powerful inner logic. As noted, the equation in battle is mission and men. Leaders within gunshot range of the enemy, regardless of their feelings of compassion toward their own soldiers, have an obvious interest in not ordering their units to move toward oblivion. But field-grade officers are professionals, have careers to consider, and are trained to put the mission first; many of these men consider battle a rite of passage. A very high percentage of field-grade officers in Vietnam were combat veterans of earlier wars. They therefore believed that the passage of time and the mastery of the skills necessary to command larger and larger units put them in a different position and gave them a different role than that of the younger officers. Few of the brass were intentionally reckless with their men's lives, and a lost battle or an unusually large number of American casualties meant not only a damaged career but also bad dreams. Yet from above—and there was always someone above—there was constant pressure for results. Results in Vietnam were equated with activity, whether purposeful or not, or with enemy dead—the famous body count—whether real or not. Most soldiers could not have cared less about either. It was not a good mix.

None of this is intended to be a criticism of the 25th Division's leadership. Much of the difficult situation I am trying to analyze is inherent in warfare. Some of it was unique to Vietnam, but nothing was uniquely true of the 25th Division. Many thoughtful soldiers were aware of this. Charles Albridge, an experienced NCO, gives a very commonsense opinion of the Division's officers:

We didn't have much contact with them because we were off with our own units. We assumed that they knew what they were doing. Since they weren't doing any really stupid things that were getting people killed, we didn't really pay that much attention to them. The highest-ranking officer we usually had to deal with was the company commander. Every once in a while, the battalion commander was around but not often. As far as the junior officers were concerned, there were good and bad. Relationships between junior officers and NCOs and the men were pretty good when I was over there. We would get green second lieutenants assigned who would have to be taught the ropes. But they usually learned pretty quick or got dead pretty quick. As far as the quality of military leadership in the U.S. Army in Vietnam, there is just no way to generalize: It ran the gamut from outstanding to total duds.

Jim Ross was there four years later and voices similar opinions about the overall quality of the people above him:

We never saw the commanding general, although most of us knew his name. We never saw the man and didn't really know his job description or what he did on a day-to-day basis. We knew he lived in a very nice facility and that he had a very nice office in Cu Chi. The man was virtually invisible. He was too far up for us to know what he did and why he did it. We did get good support in the field—resupply, air support, artillery support—and I think we got good support in the way operations were conducted, the way we went about our business. We were allowed to protect ourselves, and we had policies within the Division that were very compatible with what our mission was and how we went about trying to accomplish that mission. I think the brass were pretty well respected. We had virtually no contact with the brigade commander, a full colonel. We did have some contact with the battalion commander, a lieutenant colonel. We had daily contact with our company commander and our platoon leader. Considering the situation, I have no real complaints.

Perhaps he had no complaints, but Ross makes the distinction that was typical in Vietnam between the leaders that faced risk and those the men believed did not:

Junior officers and NCOs were our coworkers. Our relations—and I can only speak from my experience—were very good. Squad leaders, on the whole, were very good. Some were very young, some very cocky. Some were a little less than highly intelligent. But overall, pretty good. Everybody made a lot of noise about "shake-and-bake" NCOs, but I tell you something, I spent some time where they were trained, and it was not a joke. Most of them were top-notch. The junior officers received excellent training. No one incompetent or inept completed officers' training. It was a tough school, requiring intelligence and leadership abilities. The physical demands were incredible; the discipline was almost beyond belief. There were bad officers and NCOs, but you're going to have that, it's part of life. I didn't see anything like you see in the movies, with the officers shooting themselves in the foot and too stupid to make a decision. Or where some well-muscled NCO or enlisted man from the streets of Chicago ran things. It just wasn't that way. Overall, we had good leadership. Our lieutenant was twenty-six years old and out of OCS. He was a three-year enlistment guy with no intention of making the military his career. He was down to earth and wasn't pretentious, and you could talk to the guy. He'd pull guard with you and help fill sandbags; he had a hell of a sense of humor and a sharp wit. I can't say anything bad. The other junior officers I was around were the same story.

In a certain sense, no news was good news if it concerned the attitudes of combat soldiers toward the brass. The men of the 25th Division did enjoy good support. As in any war, there were a number of debatable decisions made by the various commanding generals of the Division. There were also incidents of undeniable tactical skill. The Army recognized this and promoted an unusual number of the 25th's Vietnam-era officers to extremely high rank in the following decades. Moreover, the Division, when hard pressed, won all its engagements. In my research on the 25th, I have never encountered the sort of blind, intense, and understandable hatred that some World War II veterans (of several nations) expressed for divisional commanders who made incompetent decisions that led to slaughter and defeat.

Robert Julian was part of the Division's 2d Brigade, which had the questionable honor of staying behind in Vietnam for an extra six months as an independent unit. He mentions the invigorating effect of a change of command in his unit:

Morale was quite good, as a whole. Fortunately, I was attached to an excellent platoon with excellent leaders. The men, as young as they were, were very professional. I must say, the battalion commander when I got there was not very popular with the men in the ranks. His chopper crashed in early 1971, he was wounded, and we got a new commander. Things changed right away. We noticed some little things we hadn't seen before. Previously, when we received supplies, all we got was ammunition, C rations, and bug spray. The new commander would send out hot meals on each chopper, which we all enjoyed, and even sent ice cream out, on occasion. We got our mail much more regularly; he would even send out rubber bladders of water. The other commander told us to get our own water and use iodine pills; you know what those streams were like. He also met with us frequently. Whenever we made contact, he would fly out and stay with the platoon for a while, maybe overnight. Whenever we were in a rear area, he would get with us and tell us what was going on and pass on the intelligence to us. The new commander did an excellent job, and morale rose quite high when he was in command. Once, during a contact, our commander was flying overhead, dropping grenades from his helicopter on the enemy position and drawing fire. It was really unusual to see a lieutenant colonel out in the field like that.

Relations between soldiers and officers were greatly influenced by a policy that was unique to Vietnam and touched every aspect of field morale:

the one-year tour of duty. The Pentagon decided, early in the war, that soldiers would be rotated home after one-year tours of duty in Vietnam, and this decision has been controversial ever since. Many officers believed it showed a lack of political resolve that the enemy would exploit. It was better, they believed, to follow the World War II policy of serving for the duration of the conflict. Other officers did not quarrel with the idea of rotation but objected to the Pentagon's way of implementing it. Units in Vietnam stayed in place and, after the initial deployments, received a steady trickle of replacements as needed through the supply pipeline. It would have been preferable, many military men argued, to follow the Australian policy in Vietnam or the German policy during World War II and rotate entire battalions. That way, men would go into battle after training together and acquiring a ready-made cohesion. A battalion that moved out would be rested and fleshed out with new personnel. At that point, soldiers not wishing further combat service would be transferred, although it was hoped that enough would stay on to give the rebuilt unit the added advantage of having a battle-hardened cadre of men and officers.

The issue of rotation policy in Vietnam was difficult to address at the time, and no easy answer appears in retrospect. Clearly, some sort of rotation was essential: The people then arguing for service through the duration could not foresee the length or nature of the war, and those who have held that position since the war evidence a great lack of empathy for what the soldiers on the spearpoint faced. Anyone who thinks morale would have improved if the line soldiers had thought they were stuck in Vietnam for eternity is dreaming. In fact, the rotation policy was probably the one thing Washington did that made the fate of the combat soldier bearable. Individuals well versed in the intricacies of logistics are best able to judge whether unit rotation was feasible, but certainly, undeniable morale advantages would have emerged.

However, the Pentagon simultaneously made a calamitous error that revealed a shocking lack of judgment at the top of the American war effort. To military leaders trained to think in terms of a monumental struggle to the death with the Soviet Union, Vietnam was military small change. It was an opportunity to try out some new weapons and a chance to give a large number of officers command in the field. The march of time combined with astounding bureaucratic blindness in the high command. Leaders believed, with some reason, that combat experience was a tremendous advantage for officers, and after Korea and World War II, the Army steadily lost officers who had commanded troops in battle. Soon, the officer corps would have no combat experience of any sort. The officers themselves also knew that a combat command was vital for the climb up the promotion ladder. Therefore, Washington decided to assign these men six months in the field and six months in the rear. In practice, the rotation period was even faster, so great was the lust for career officers to get their "tickets punched."

This policy was so bad it could have been created in Hanoi. It was guaranteed to create dissent in the ranks and hinder the development of good officers. In past wars, marksmen would intentionally aim for enemy officers. Revolutionary troops in Vietnam no doubt did also, without thinking the matter through. But beyond the fact that any dead American was good for North Vietnam, officers actually would have had no particular significance. After all, if they were good, the Army was going to pull them out of the field just as they were acquiring the practical experience that would complement the courage and good training most of them already had. And if they were bad, why not leave them in place? This line of reasoning is not mine: It came, in one form or another, from about a dozen 25th Division veterans.

Enlisted men were not the only ones who resented the inequality of risk. Lt. Col. Carl Quickmire, who served two tours with the 25th Division separated by many years, gives an opinion held by countless officers:

Perhaps one of the dumbest policies we had was the six-month rotation of commanders, so everybody could get in and punch their ticket. The poor soldier and, in many cases, the lower-ranking NCOs were there for their whole tours and never had the luxury of rotating out to a safe and secure assignment or a semisecure assignment, such as the one I had in Saigon after my six months in the field were up. Extremely dumb policy, in my opinion, and very bad for morale.

Gary Ernst served with the 3/4th Armored Cavalry until severely wounded during the Tet Offensive. He recalls with affection the unexpected kindness of his platoon commander. He also contrasts it with the attitudes of those higher up:

When I got back to the hospital in Texas when I was just about done with my treatment, I got some recuperative leave for a month, went home to California, and came back. I was really stunned when I got off the airplane in San Antonio and here is my lieutenant: You could have knocked me over with a feather. His home was in the area, so he tracked me down and picked me up at the airport, took me home, and we visited his mom. He was a captain then. It was quite impressive.

Higher up from that, there were a lot of problems. From general on up, or even lower, I'm not impressed with the leadership we had over there. One thing that struck me was that the Army had gone several years without a war before Vietnam came along. We had an officer corps without combat experience, and they were worried that the war might end too soon. So, they instituted this policy of rotating the officers to make sure that more officers got combat experience. Little did they know the war was going to last ten years. After six months, officers went from combat to administrative positions. This caused resentment with a lot of guys. It really hurt with the experience factor. It took a while to learn things, and they would rotate people just when they were getting the hang of things. Then you would get a new officer, who may or may not have had the ability to pick things up quickly. So, especially later in the war when the NCO corps had been decimated by people going back for multiple tours, etc., I think there was a drop-off of the lower-level leadership in Vietnam. But when I was there, it was very good.

Kenneth Stumpf is in accord with Ernst, but he puts the case more strongly:

We had gutless politicians and, worse yet, gutless general officers. The young lieutenants and captains I served with in the infantry were right there with me, and they have my utmost respect; they did an outstanding job under the conditions. Above that, I never saw any field-grade officers out in the field. I have very little respect or very little to say about them. I saw an article a few years ago where forty former generals and admirals from Vietnam, now retired, were interviewed about Vietnam. They all said they knew the war was being fought wrong but couldn't do anything about it, to protect their careers. I thought, you dirty sons of bitches. We've got these young soldiers dying on the battlefield, and you want to protect your career? Loyalty is a very important part of the military, and I've got twenty-four years in right now, but when it comes down to life and death for your soldiers, these goddamn general officers had a moral obligation to stand up and say something. I mean, who's going to listen to us? When I went back from my first tour, a teacher asked me if we were going to win in Vietnam, and I said, "Hell, no! Not the way it's going right now. All we're doing is going from this mountain to that mountain, firefights here, firefights there, and then we'd go somewhere else." When your soldiers are going to die on the battlefield, you must say something, and the general officers didn't. I have no respect for any general officer. Priority one is promotion; priority two is their social status. They could care less about that young private down there. If there is any blame at all for defeat in Vietnam, it was our general officer leadership.

Dan Vandenberg expresses intense bitterness toward his leadership. His judgment is more severe than most, but nearly every combat infantryman I interviewed would have agreed heartily with one element or another of Vandenberg's assessment:

As far as I know, there were very few officers over there. Everything was run by NCOs. The ones I came across were damned good. They were the same age as I, but they were operating squads or platoons with a hell of a lot more courage and efficiency than I would have had. Some of the very few officers I came into contact with were totally incompetent. They were more concerned with how you looked, how your uniform was, or how your hair was cut. The petty, chicken-shit stuff that they tried in the United States they tried to enforce in Nam—which is a way to get a bullet in your back. We had enough to worry about staying alive. As far as shaving, we were lucky enough to have water to drink, much less waste it on what few whiskers we were able to grow. If somebody offered me $500,000 to give my company commander's name, I wouldn't have a chance: I never saw the guy. I had very little contact with our platoon leader, a second lieutenant.

There was one colonel we all hated with a passion. I never met the guy, and I have no idea what his name was, but he spent his whole time in Vietnam flying a chopper right above us telling us to move 4 clicks over there. We'd get there, and he'd change his mind and have us walk 5 clicks over there. This all looks very easy from the air. But when it's roughly 100 degrees and you're loaded down with gear, you're hungry, you're tired, and this guy keeps changing his mind and sending you all over the countryside on a whim, while he's nice and cool up in the air, you want to kick somebody in the ass. Plus, we knew when his day was done, he'd go back to Cu Chi and sit around in an air-conditioned officers' club and have a nice steak dinner with a couple of drinks. He'd tell his buddies how he was doing his best to win the war. At the same time, we'd be eating our cold rations, sleeping in the dirt, and fighting off mosquitoes in some godforsaken spot he sent us to for no reason that we could decipher. If there were any firefights, he'd be there right after it was over, fly around, check out the battlefield, and then go back for the glory. I know once he showed up at our firebase and wanted a meeting with some of the officers. We just came in from a bitch of a patrol, tired and cranky as usual. All we wanted was a cup of hot coffee and to sit in the mess hall, which was screened from mosquitoes, for a minute. It didn't seem as though we were asking for the world. But the word drifted down the line that we weren't allowed in the mess hall during the meeting, so we had to grab our coffee and go sit out in back in the dirt and dust, with the bugs falling all around us. It's very hard to put down the feeling we had, but it was just another case of being shit on. Now, it sounds like a very minor thing. But our feeling was, this guy doesn't even want us in his sight. His comfort and the comfort of his officers came first, and the men, well, they could go eat dirt for all he gave a shit. Like to meet the guy someday so he could tell me how he won the war. But he wasn't the only guy. Most of the higher officers got their medals and ribbons for doing basically nothing.

The last point that Vandenberg raised is a very sensitive one among veterans today. The attitude of combat soldiers toward medals and recognition took me by surprise. Several men expressed bitterness at the ease with which brass picked up medals and then asked me not to quote them on it. It was the only subject in my research where this happened. Furthermore, with the exception of a Medal of Honor winner (whose citation is a matter of public record), no one ever mentioned a personal award, although they frequently cited those given to others. One of the respondents received six Silver Stars (two on consecutive days), but someone else had to tell me about it. In retrospect, I can tie this matter to something else I observed. Combat soldiers never discussed their own courageous acts. They described the courage of others—even that of their enemy—but never their own. It was almost as if it was bad form to discuss personal bravery. The men who showed sensitivity toward being quoted on this matter undoubtedly feared that they would sound like either spoilsports or braggarts. Nevertheless, if a combat soldier received a medal for bravery, he almost certainly deserved it. If a field-grade officer received one, even one of a higher order, it might mean nothing. There is no question that military awards were degraded in Vietnam by the same impulse that put officers into six-month rotations. The veterans on the spearpoint know this better than anyone, and they do not like it.

Fortunately, Medal of Honor winner Kenneth Stumpf was more than willing to speak out. His award was no secret—and no fluke. Many veterans would applaud Stumpf's candor and agree with him completely:

The awards system was another thing that sucked. Even though I got a Medal of Honor, I'm talking about the other soldiers I was with. They kicked ass. But the officers walked away with the nice big awards for doing shit and the enlisted man got nothing—maybe a letter or some damn thing.

The people who were making decisions were not out in the field. They made decisions from back in the firebases and base camps. I totally disagreed with that. You have to be in control of your unit, and you have to know your men and know their capabilities, and the only way you're going to know their capabilities is to live with them, fight with them. Officers would be out in the field six months. Six months! It took two to three months to break in a lieutenant, and then they'd be with the soldiers another two to three months, and then they'd be gone. But the poor old enlisted guys, we had to make it through 365 days. I thought, what a bunch of crap.

Even under the best of leaders, stress and fear were inevitable companions in the field, and soldiers developed several methods of coping with them. GIs cultivated a black sense of humor that is impossible to relay but fascinating to hear in person. Many units adopted dogs, cats, or sometimes even Vietnamese children as mascots. And some used liquor or dope for short-term relief.

On a deeper level, many men found comfort in religion. Justice Selth was one of the Division's nineteen chaplains and was assigned to artillery. He spent much time visiting firebases and giving services in the field. He describes his duties in mid-1968:

Services were well attended. I would say attendance was usually somewhere around 40 to 45 percent. At one battery, we asked the sergeant to announce services. I said, I'll be in gunpit 1, the priest will be in gunpit 7. I listened in on the sergeant's conversation in one of the gunpits. He said something like this: "Listen up, fellas. The chaplains are here. All you Protestants go to gunpit 1, all you Catholics go to gunpit 7. The rest of you go to hell." We had almost 100 percent attendance at that battery for quite a while. We had memorial services when people were killed. There was intense fighting that year, so we had quite a few of them.

Dale Canter, one of the first men sent over, remembers that memorial ceremonies were important even when morale was at its peak:

Morale seemed high. The mission was to kill the enemy and win the war, and that's what we were going to do. It was amazing how you could lose track of time. I rarely knew the date or even day. Every day was the same. However, I do remember when the first church service ended with taps for dead comrades. I was very moved and remember it to this day.

Jim Murphy served on top of Nui Ba Den for several months during early 1969, helping to tend the communications facility on the peak. It was a hazardous place, for the enemy controlled the slopes. Murphy recalls that religious services boosted morale:

Most of us would attend services. There was no chapel per se, but the Division would fly up a chaplain, and he would hold services. Nothing fancy, but it meant a lot. After all, there are no atheists in foxholes.

Deep personal faith was instrumental for many men. Dan Breeding speaks of the importance of prayer for him:

I want to talk more about how we coped with fear. I did a lot of praying. I carried a small Bible in the breast pocket of my fatigues. I tucked it in a plastic bag. I read my Bible occasionally. That gave me strength. When I read the Bible, I would always think about back home and think about my Mom and Dad, who were good church-going people, active in their church, and I knew that they were constantly praying for me. That gave me encouragement and strength, as well. Looking back twenty years, now having children myself, that probably meant the most, knowing that my immediate family did care. There were prayers going up for me. That's all you could ask for. It's a shame that not everyone had that hope. And I'm sure that a lot of guys didn't have the prayers that I had. That helped me cope with a lot of everything. And of course, the letters from my girlfriend at the time, who later became my wife; I could count on a letter every day. That meant a lot.

Infantryman Mike Miller also found great solace in his faith:

The best friend you have is God. If you never heard of Him or knew Him before you went to war, you sure knew him by the time you came home. You become so close to Him. No matter what faith you have, no matter what color you are, you all worship him the same.

Ultimately, however, the men had to depend upon each other for physical and emotional survival. The bond between individuals that holds a combat unit together has long been written about. It is a factor in every war. In Vietnam, however, some unique components intruded that should be mentioned. First of all was the matter of the fixed tour of duty. Within a year and a half or so of deployment, the number of replacements due to combat casualties, illnesses, and other causes resulted in units that were increasingly a mix of FNGs, experienced soldiers, and men who were short. And how many days a man had crossed off his personal calendar greatly influenced his morale. Morgan Sincock recalls the situation:

Morale varied. Keep in mind that with totally asynchronous tours, we had no group orientation to our DEROS [date estimated to return from overseas—EMB]. Some men who were close to going home were nearly euphoric. Others who faced 200 or 300 more days were less delighted.

In addition, we are discussing an *American* army. Blind discipline—as George Washington's drillmaster, Baron von Steuben, found out—is not characteristic of American soldiers. Furthermore, the Army in Vietnam was the best educated in history. It lacked the sons of America's elites, but every other group was well represented.

The bush skills of the soldiers were good, considering the circumstances. Moreover, there was a certain advantage in operating in the same area for years on end. The Division accumulated a detailed knowledge of the terrain and, through bitter experience, a detailed knowledge of what was required to survive. Medic Lee Reynolds makes the point, unquestionably valid to some degree, that much of what uninformed and hostile observers took to be a lack of discipline and a lack of spirit was, instead, a reflection of the skills of the American soldier in the bush:

It really gets me how the media and the movies beat up on the Vietnam soldier. It really irritates me to see the soldiers portrayed as drug-crazed, psychopathic murders, losers, idiots, and cowards. From what I saw over there, nothing could be farther from the truth for the vast majority of Vietnam soldiers. They weren't any of those things. They were very skillful, very professional, probably the most knowledgeable soldiers that our military has ever put on a battlefield. They were very knowledgeable about tactics and about evaluating the status and capability of the enemy, to be able to know the enemy. There was a lot of knowledge at a very low level.

This leads me to something very important: the absence of blind obedience in Vietnam. In other wars, if a colonel or a captain gave a bad order, you would have 100 or 200 or 1,000 troops just blindly obeying the order, like Gallipoli with its suicide charges. There was nothing like that in Vietnam. There were situations when you had mutinies and refusals. The kind of spin the media put on that was cowardice or lack of discipline or motivation, whatever negative connotation you want. These incidents were caused when some officer gave a stupid order. Because of the level of knowledge that was common among the troops, the men would refuse to carry out that order. That happened over and over again. They knew their jobs and refused to carry out stupid orders or suicidal orders just because some officer with doodads on his collar said so. There was a tremendous amount of bush wisdom and courage. I admired my fellow soldiers very much. I thought they were very fine people.

Reynolds, in my opinion, is quite correct about the quality of the American soldiers in the 25th Division. An officer who tried to order an exhausted unit into a dangerous situation without obvious reason risked a sit-down by even the best unit. The daily grind of patrols at day and ambush at night pushed many units to the edge of destruction, and it was not at all unusual for the men to take things into their own hands, as Dan Vandenberg relates:

Sometimes, we "sandbagged" a night ambush. We would head for a friendly ARVN compound, give them a case of C rations, and stay there all night. We just had to make our hourly radio checks. That way, we could get some sleep for a change. That was a great luxury. Every outfit over there was sandbagging. You had to make sure you came back in the same direction, and heaven help you if you got caught sandbagging. We sure didn't do it most of the time.

If even good soldiers bent the rules for the sake of safety and survival, they also knew that, above all, they depended on their comrades for mutual safety and support. The depth of personal bonds formed under fire is the one thing that virtually all respondents to this research emphasized. It is key to the explanation of why the Division's field morale, by and large, held up to the end, despite the fact that its political morale had disappeared long before.

If wartime relationships were intense, they were also inevitably narrow. The soldiers made deep friendships with their comrades, but their groups were invariably small. To a certain extent, this reflected reality. As previously noted, the world of most men in Vietnam was a small one. But the exclusive nature of their group-building also reflected the fear that permeated everything near the battlefield. And breaking into a group was not easy. Although more seasoned soldiers no doubt helped a newcomer out in practical ways, they also wanted to see if the new soldier was going to be an asset. To a large extent, this was self-interest. But it also reflected a fear of grief. C. W. Bowman describes the process facing new men:

There was no gung ho. When you got there, they put you in a squad. New guys didn't get much help. Nobody wanted anything to do with you because they figured that if you lived through the first ninety days, you'd make it through Nam. Your first ninety days and last ninety days were your hardest: the first ninety days because you didn't know anything and the last ninety days because you knew you were short and going home and were overcautious. In between those times, you'd do pretty well. But you didn't really want to make any friends. You were friends with the guys you came in with. Other than that, with the people that came in after you, you knew their names, but you didn't want to know them because if they got blown away that was fine: It wasn't you, and you didn't know them. It didn't mess you up too bad.

Michael Call's memories echo Bowman's:

I recall attempting to shy away from making close friends after our initial engagement. I did not want to really know their hometowns, kids' names, wives' names. The less you knew about them, the less you suffered when they died. However, it was inevitable that I became close to certain people. In future engagements with the enemy, I found myself actually being more concerned with the safety of people I had let myself get close to. I am not saying I was not concerned with other troops in our unit because I was. You must understand that if you have been in the boonies with certain people for months, you are going to be more aware of them as compared to a "cherry" fresh into the unit. Sad but true.

I think the majority of combat soldiers would go to any length to help a fellow grunt. This is particularly true when a buddy is wounded. The degree of how much you, as a soldier, are willing to sacrifice in the aid of a friend depends somehow on how close he is to you physically as well as mentally. I would have a tendency to put my life at more of a risk for a member of my squad or platoon as compared to someone of another platoon or company. I was very close to the guys in my platoon and did not hesitate to let it all hang out when one of them was hurt or in some other manner in need of help. When a small group of people spend night and day together, suffering all the horrors of war and also depending on one another to stay alive, we come closer than brothers. Sometimes, you don't even know their last names or cannot stand to be around them while out of the boonies and back in base camp, but when together in the field, there is a common bond of survival that prevails.

Obviously, Call is describing a necessary self-defense mechanism. Death surrounded the men in the field, and they required some distance from its horrid impact if they were to persevere and survive. To new recruits, this attitude seemed callous, although virtually all of them came to share it to some degree. Todd Dexter recalls the shock he suffered when he first witnessed the results of war and one of his more experienced comrade's reaction to it:

We began an inch-by-inch search of the area. I did my share, and as I walked, I spotted something in the trampled trees and stopped and grasped it. As I picked up the helmet, I heard a sound similar to an apple rolling around the inside of a wash basin. When I turned the helmet over, a chunk of a head fell out. The helmet belonged to the first American I had seen killed: the one we tried to pull back from the wood line last night. He had been hit in the skull by one round of small-arms fire, fallen from the tank, and then been run over. He was missing a leg from the knee, one arm at the elbow, and an ear.

The small chopper lifted rapidly off the ground, wafting the stench of death back into my face. The smell filled my nostrils and lungs and was very nauseating. I stared blankly, contemplating the ominous dark fly that crawled through the tacky, viscous fluid that was oozing from the hole in the young soldier's head. I examined the helmet again and noticed the trite saying he had scrawled on the camouflage cover. It was now his epitaph: "Don't shoot me, I bleed!" Someone muttered, "Why don't they at least cover him up?" "What the hell for? He's dead, ain't he?" came the answer.

When he first arrived, Dan Vandenberg went through a similar experience:

We were on a company-sized patrol and had gone about a click when we heard a bang up in front. Somebody had tripped a booby trap. Being a new guy, this was the first time I'd come into contact with any sort of action at all. I started asking questions like, Who was it? as if I'd know him: I only knew the guys in my squad and then only half of them. Then you'd get the word down the line of the column how bad the guy was, and I looked around, and nobody else seemed to give a damn. They were sitting down. It was a chance to quit walking and rest. They'd break out the canteens and smoke a cigarette, and some took naps, but nobody really gave a damn. I thought, that's a really callous attitude. There is a guy lying up there full of holes.

Then, about a week later, the same thing happened again. We were out on patrol, a guy walked into a hooch, and there was a booby trap about head high with a little wire strung across the doorway and a grenade on it. When he hit that wire, it pretty much tore his head off, but he was still alive. Again, I got a bit antsy as everybody sat down and took a break. Whenever something like that happens, everything comes to a stop, and everybody gets what rest they can. Once again, I started with the questions: "Hey, are they going to get this guy out of here? Where's the chopper?" The only answer I got was, the guy's a goner and just a vegetable, so there's no need to get all shook up about it. Again I thought it was a pretty callous attitude.

After about five or six times like this, I noticed that I wasn't asking questions anymore. You heard a bang, and if it didn't concern your squad, the 6 or 7 guys that were closest to you, you didn't think much about it. It's not like you didn't care, but you just took care of your own little group. There was nothing you could do about it anyhow. I found I was plopping down, I was whipping out the canteens, lighting up a cigarette, or even managing to catch a little precious sleep. I thought nothing of it, and this went on for the rest of the time I was there. Unless there was actually somebody I knew personally, it just didn't get to you anymore: You just kind of blocked it out. You cared about the person; you sure didn't want to see anyone get hurt, and if they did, you wanted them to come out of it ok. But you just couldn't get worked up every time somebody got zapped. And you don't even realize that you're feeling that way at the time. Then, at some time, you look back on it and think about how you felt. In a way, you feel like a total ass. But in another way, it was the only way you were going to get through the day. Otherwise, you'd be a wreck after just a couple of days over there.

Vandenberg's thoughts on this tragic subject show rare insight and honesty. In a strange way, the violence around the soldier, if it did not touch him directly, actually confirmed an inner belief that he himself was invulnerable:

There's an attitude you develop over there. You never think you're the one who is going to get hit. It may be your buddy who shares a foxhole with you or Joe Blow over here or a guy over there, but it's never going to be you. You sure don't wish these guys harm, and you wish the best for them and all that. But in order to keep your sanity, you always have to keep figuring that it will be somebody else. If you walked around every day thinking this is the day I'm going to get it, your mind would be fried in a hurry. You also wonder, at times, how much luck you can use up. I had a few close calls that make you wonder when your time is going to come.

Jim Ross makes the same point in his sophisticated description of the soldier's reaction to fear:

How did the men cope with fear? I can think of three kinds of fear that men over there experienced. The most prevalent and lowest level of fear was just knowing that by virtue of being in Vietnam, you could be killed. You were sitting nice and cozy in Cu Chi, and it was conceivable that a rocket could land right on top of you and send you on your way. If a bullet had your name on it and found you, that was it. It didn't matter who you were or what you were doing at the time.

The next level up of fear is what I would describe as anticipatory fear. That's the kind of fear you feel—and it can be pretty intense—when you are in a high-risk situation, for instance, when you're in the leading APC, going into an area that you know is heavily booby-trapped or that you know is subject to ambush. We had a lot of this kind of fear in Cambodia. We were ambushed so many times that it reached the point where the guys riding point were really under a lot of stress. The lead element is ordinarily the one that is ambushed. It can be a false fear a lot of times. But it can be a pretty intense level of fear.

Naturally, the highest level of fear is the terrifying fear when you're actually under fire. That almost can't be described. It is utter terror. What is so difficult about it is not only the intense fear, the sense of imminent injury or death to yourself, but that you can't get away, you can't avoid it. You just have to accept the fact that something bad is going to happen. In addition, you've got to somehow keep enough sense about yourself to do what you have to do to prevent it from happening. It's very difficult to describe. It's utter terror; when it's over, if you survived, the relief is almost impossible to describe.

It wasn't the kind of thing that you spent all day thinking about. As a matter of fact, you did basically the opposite. There was a lot of denial involved. It was the same old story: You don't think it's going to happen to you. You know it can happen, and you see it happening all around you, but somewhere deep in your consciousness, there is a little voice saying that this stuff happens to other people. You see it, but it won't happen to you because you're special. But when you get under fire, all of that goes out the window. For those few moments, it not only is that it can happen but that it is probably going to happen. The terror and the anguish are unbelievable. Once you've survived, that little voice comes back and says, "See, it happens to other people." It's a very complex subject. It involves elements of both panic and heroism. Sometimes, those two words are interchangeable. You cope with it on a gut level. Whatever is in your mind, your psyche is set up to handle it: It is not a voluntary thing. It's something that just happens. It's a psychological and physiological process that happens at the moment. Low levels of fear you can think about and try to deal with. Certain types of fear you just react to: How you react is dictated by the situation. You're really powerless to have any control over it at all. Different people did it different ways. Mostly, you didn't see it, it was suppressed, but everybody knew it was there.

For most men, their closest friends were the most crucial support available in Vietnam. This phenomenon was described so often that it must have been almost universal among fighting men who survived the war. As Jim Murphy commented, "This was the only time of my life that I saw men bond together the way women do." James Cipolla reflects on how important it was to have the support of others:

Slowly, you became a member of the group. You were still new, and there was a certain shyness toward you from the others. I found out later this was because you had the greatest chance of being killed. There was one nice thing over there. I got some bad news from home once, and my friend Mack came up to me and said, "Hey, man," and I just told him to get the fuck away from me, real nasty-like. And he did, he understood. A while later, he came back and asked if he could help. He knew I needed a friend. We got that close with the people around us. You put your life in the hands of a few strangers, and they didn't betray you. That's a unique situation. You all wore the same clothes. And you wore your hair any way you wanted it. You didn't have anybody to impress. Of those people close to me, there's not one of them that I wouldn't give the keys to my car, my checkbook, anything. That's how much I trust them.

Larry Fontana remembers the constant turmoil. Booze came in handy, but, ultimately, it was his comrades that got him through:

Emotionally, for myself, Vietnam was a combination of a roller coaster and a runaway train. To be nineteen and see friends killed and wounded, to kill and wound the enemy, to fear being killed at any moment was hard, to say the least. One day, you may be the hero of the platoon, fighting in close quarters with the NVA and doing daring deeds, and two nights later, you could be in a bunker, crying while the mortars explode outside. Emotions came and went constantly, and you had to be as strong as you possibly could to keep a handle on yourself. Like all humans, some had no problem, while others did. We each had a way of searching for our own separate peace.

The biggest stress reducers were ourselves. We all communicated with each other, and we all belonged to different groups within the platoon that would provide the support we needed to climb out of the rut. I learned that to keep my sanity, I just had to let it out with somebody. I guess the overall view and attitude was "them against us."

Gary Ernst comments simply,

I was nineteen but the youngest one in my platoon. They called me Teeny Bopper. There were several college graduates and career NCOs. There was a true brotherhood. It's amazing how intense that is. In combat, everything is magnified, and friendships or hatreds can develop overnight and last a lifetime. In my experience, it was the camaraderie and friendship that developed.

Dan Vandenberg, who had few pleasant memories of the war, also recalls the bond that held his squad together:

You've got Charlie, and he definitely doesn't like us, and we don't like him. The majority of the people back home, our so-called peers, have absolutely no use for us because we're baby killers and drug addicts. To the Army, we were just numbers. So it was definitely just us: your buddy next to you and yourself against the rest of the world.

It's kind of funny, I still feel close to the members of my squad. I really didn't know them that well, and I was really with them for a short time. Yet, I feel closer to them than I do to anyone I knew before then or since then. You really can't explain the camaraderie or whatever word you want to use for what develops. It's something that's got to be experienced. I'm not saying that I wanted to be lifelong friends with everyone in the squad or that I even liked all of them. But I respected the fact that they were out there putting themselves on the line, and I knew they were watching my ass and I was watching theirs. Each guy in the squad had the others guys' lives in his hands. You don't think of it at the time, but you look back on it now and it's an awesome responsibility. I mean, we were all just kids. To us, everything was still a game. Then we saw a few guys shot or blown up, and then it became real.

But the intense comradeship, so necessary in times of danger, carried with it a tremendous emotional risk. If someone truly close was killed or mutilated, a soldier faced extraordinary emotional damage. Michael Call meditates on this matter:

I would think anyone could understand the tremendous emotional shock of witnessing the death of a friend in combat. It is comparable to losing a member of your family. Even in the death of a buddy in combat, you must force yourself to continue doing your job as other friends are depending on you. The grieving comes later. There were times in a firefight when a kid right near would catch "the big one," and I remember thinking "thank God it wasn't me" but, at the same time, feeling very sad. Sometimes, the emotions get all mixed up during the heat of combat. I don't believe a person ever gets used to death, especially violent death. I may have become somewhat callused and tried to think of it as a natural result of war, but no, I can truly say I never got used to death.

Eddie Madaris, a tough veteran of Tet, feels that the death of his best friend was a blow as damaging as a wound:

Mike was the point man. They shot him in the stomach. The colonel brought his little chopper in there and got him, but it was too late. They said his last words were, "I can't breathe." When Mike got killed, it took something out of me that's never come back. I wanted out of that field. I wanted to leave that place. I didn't think I was ever going to leave. I was going to try to go all the way through my tour without going on R & R, without spending the money. But I wrote home to my family and asked them to send me enough money to go on R & R. When I got back, I functioned and did my duty, but it was real hard. I wanted out of that field; I wanted a housecat job. I saw so many come and go.

As I write this, a good thing is taking place. For years after the war, many of the men, for reasons internal or external, did their best to drive the war from their minds. Several of the respondents commented that my research had prompted them to talk about Vietnam for the first time. However, around the country, thousands of veterans are doing that and more. Vietnam veterans are joining the divisional associations and veterans groups in large numbers. The 25th Division has a large and vigorous association, and on an informal level, smaller units have held reunions. Some men have simply reestablished ties via phone or post. Many choose to remain aloof, and their former comrades understand. Yet, many others are trying successfully to salvage some part of the only good thing that came to most of them from a harsh and cruel war. I wish them all good luck and Godspeed.

Epilogue: Last Thoughts from Three Veterans of the Tropic Lightning Division

Dennis Hackin

Now, I was one of the old-timers. The guys who survived Tet became very hard-core. It was almost a badge of honor. My squad had a lot of old-timers. A few new kids came in. It was hard now to let people in. But one thing about the squad: We had a bunch of guys with great senses of humor. If the ammo was plenty, so were the laughs.

When I look back on the war, I do think of the Vietnamese people and how much they suffered. I sometimes ask myself, did we do more harm than good? I wish I had the answer. I do believe they were the pawns in this ugly game.

Our platoon continued to be the hard-luck platoon of Charlie Company. In May 1968, a second offensive started. Once again, we were brought down to work the surrounding areas of Saigon and Cu Chi. Once again, we got hit. And once again, friends were wounded and killed.

To this day, it hurts to think about those guys who never got the chances in life that I did. Why did I live, and they didn't? Surely, I wasn't a better person, nor a better soldier. When it's your time, it's your time. I believe that.

In my outfit, there were guys who made it on God, beer, pot, and Coca-Cola. But I think what really got us all through was the bond of friendship. To this day, nothing compares to that bond. It's not often friendship is tested under fire. Ours was.

And then there was the third offensive up in the Tay Ninh area. By the end of August, I was one of the oldest guys in the company. Except for a handful of guys, I didn't want to get to know anybody very close. That handful of guys was my lifeline.

Charlie Company drove into a **U**-shaped ambush during the offensive. Although my platoon took some wounded, it was 1st Platoon that went down bloody. One of my best friends received the Distinguished Service Cross. Another soldier was awarded the Congressional Medal of Honor. Both posthumously.

That night, word came down that I was going home on emergency leave. They didn't tell me what the problem was at home. It was the longest night of my life. Emergency leave didn't come easy. I knew somebody was hurting at home.

I was flown out of Tay Ninh on an ammo plane. Back at Cu Chi, I was taken to the Red Cross office. The man at Red Cross told me that my kid brother had been killed in a motor scooter accident on the road where our ranch was. He also told me, and I will always remember this, "You know about death. They don't. You're going to have to be strong."

I flew home on one of those huge C-34 cargo planes. Aluminum caskets with KIAs were stacked. It was a long, cold flight. It was strange. I had been warm all year. And now, I felt as cold as the guys in those caskets.

Looking back after all these years, I know how lucky I am. I still don't know why I lived and my buddies didn't. Why I lived and my kid brother was killed. I try to think that my buddies are watching over my kid brother up in Heaven.

It hurts to think that the guys I knew and those I didn't who were killed in Nam died in vain. I hope the lessons learned from Vietnam will make our country a stronger and better place to live. That the Vietnam War will not make us weak and scared.

There is an old saying about Vietnam: I wouldn't give up the experience for a million bucks, but I wouldn't take a million bucks to do it again. I don't prescribe it for everybody. Did I get my merit badge of manhood? It doesn't matter. One doesn't have to go to war to get a merit badge of humanity. That comes with trying to live life each day the best you can. To give a little to those who have less.

My friend David Drake, who I went over to Vietnam with? He's 100 percent disabled, but he made it out alive, and we were together last week, smiling together.

Last year, I reconnected with seven of my buddies from 2d Platoon. We met in Washington, D.C., and went to the wall to visit old friends. The bond of friendship, tested under fire, was as strong as ever. I kept thinking as I looked at my friends, the guys are safe. And as I looked at the wall, I saw my own name reflected in the pain of others. Let us never forget their sacrifice. It was truly the ultimate sacrifice!

A prayer to their families!

Robert Conner

I was eighteen years old. I should have been home getting ready to take a pretty girl to the prom. Getting my car cleaned up, getting on my tux, putting on some English Leather. Instead, for some reason, I didn't know why, I was in South Vietnam. We were supposed to be fighting communism, but I couldn't have told you exactly what communism was at the time. All I knew was that some little guy with a black hat was shooting at me. Looking back, I bet he didn't really know why he was shooting at me either. The whole period I was over there, all I saw was escalation. The more we'd fight, the worse it got.

We fought in a war that not too many people can explain. I have never heard a reason why we were actually over there, what we were supposed to accomplish over there. I was glad to see us out of Vietnam, but I didn't understand why we were out. Why we went over under one president, then another president pulls us out. Why? I believe one of these days, those generals, congressmen, and presidents are going to have to give an account to Almighty God for making that stupid mistake. I mean, it's the same Vietnam today as in 1965. Why aren't we still over there fighting?

I read the book *Close Quarters* lately, and it brought back bad memories. In a way, I'm glad I did read it, but in a way, I wish I hadn't. It brought back memories I thought I had put out of my mind. It brought back those painful nights as I lay shivering on those ambush patrols, mosquitoes eating me up, praying to God that no Viet Cong would come along. Those hot summer days of walking through the jungle saying, "Please God, don't let us run into any Viet Cong today, don't let Charlie be out here today." But he would be there, and someone would get shot and killed. Some mother's son would have to be buried.

After I came home from Vietnam, I still had a year in the service. I was stationed in upstate New York. One of our duties was to be an honor guard for the dead. I probably went to ten funerals. We were the ones who would stand back and fire the salute. The MPs would fold up the flag and present it. The guy in the corner would blow taps. You'd hear the moaning and groaning of some mom or dad of some eighteen-, nineteen-, or twenty-year-old son, husband, or even daddy. And they had killed him. The Army had taken us up and mowed us down. There had to be a better reason than for a war that killed innocent people. I hope I never live to see another Vietnam or hear about another one.

C. W. Bowman

I was eighteen, and as corny as it sounds, I thought it was my duty, my patriotic duty. It was my turn to go. My father was in World War II, my grandfather was in World War I. It was time to pay my dues and prove that I was a man. But I went. When I got there, I felt I did my job. At times, I didn't and had mortal terror and fear in me. But I went. A lot of us went, and a lot of us didn't make it back. Whether it was right or wrong, we went. When we got back, it wasn't the place we left. I was a second-class citizen, the scum of the earth because I went. I want people to know that it seemed like the newspapers and the media and everybody labeled us all as drug-crazed killers. But there were so many of us that weren't. Yes, some came back hooked on drugs, but they were mostly in the rear. We didn't have time to do drugs. We were trying to stay alive, trying to keep others alive.

When we came back, it was tough. People wouldn't talk to us; you had nobody to talk to about your problems. It took me a long time to get over it all, ten or fifteen years. That's just the big problems. I still have my nightmares, and I still have strange feelings at times when I try to understand why I made it and so many of my buddies didn't. It took me a while to cleanse my soul and get my heart back. When I got back, I'd think about Vietnam and I'd start shaking, hear my heart pounding in my ears. I don't know if it was fear or delayed reaction or what. But that wasn't as bad as trying to go out in the world and make it and have somebody find out you're a vet and say, "You're one of those." Well, a lot of us came back and went through that and made it. I did good. A lot of that was hard work, and some of it was luck. That's what I want people to understand. Many of us have come back, and we've done good in life, and we've contributed to society, and we've made something of ourselves.

Whenever I go to any Vietnam function, it seems like the news media picks out the dirtiest, nastiest-looking vet they can find, and they use him to represent us. But that's not us. That's a small part of us, but it's not us. Here it is, twenty years later, and it's the thing to have been a vet. I've had people tell me that they wanted to go, but they had flat feet or they went to college. They're laying all of their guilt on me. I don't want to hear it. If they wanted to go, I'm sure they could have found a way to go. I don't feel for them. That's their problem. Now it's popular to have served. They have parades, and everybody marches through town. That's nice: They gave us parades and stuff twenty years later, and I appreciate the efforts. But much of that has taken place because of vets. We built our own memorial, we organized our own parades. And now some people want to know how we feel now that the American people are accepting us. What the hell do they have to accept me for? I went and did my job. If they want to burn someone, burn their congressman or whoever. No matter what they do today, no matter who pats me on the back, I'll always remember when I came home, and I'll always remember how they treated me. I will never forget that. I'm not saying I will never forgive, but I will never forget.

It's taken me a long time to get a lot of my feelings straightened out. I know the first time I went to the wall when it was dedicated, I cried. The second time I went there, I cried. It's like they're all standing there in the wall—not in the wall, but they're there, you can feel them. It's really strange. I went to the wall one time and wrote a little letter to three childhood friends that were killed over there. I wrote to them to straighten my head out. It was addressed to Joey, Freddy, and Barry:

> I remember when we were growing up in Boardentown, New Jersey, how we played football in the streets and chased girls and drank beer together. I remember when you guys would come to my house, when we would meet on the river and camp in the woods; I remember when we were drafted and went our separate ways. I remember when we went to Vietnam. Joey, I'll always remember Memorial Day because that's the day you died in 1967 in a lonely place called the A Shau Valley. I miss you. Freddy, you died in 1968. You were an MIA for several months. You're buried now in the Midwest with the rest of your platoon because they didn't know who was who. And I miss you. Barry, you died in 1968 in Saigon. Shot in the chest by a Viet Cong. You were an only child and didn't have to go. But now you're gone, and I miss you. I survived the mortars, the bombs, the bullets. At times, death was so close I would have tears in my eyes. I lay in the mud, the rain, and the dust of Vietnam. I listened to the crying of the dying. And I survived. Now you are together and I am alone, still trying to survive in a country that didn't want me or any veteran when we got home. There were times when I really wanted to join you. Someday, God willing, we will all be together again playing football, chasing girls, and drinking beer. Until then, so that I may survive, I must say good-bye and that I miss you. Love, Reds.

There is one big asinine question people always ask me when they find out I'm a vet. The big question is, did you ever kill anybody? A lot of times, I don't know how to answer that, and I walk away from people. Or I just tell them, "What the hell do you think you do in a war?" Why don't they ask me how many people I saved, instead of how many people I killed? Maybe that would count for something better.

Appendix: A Roster of the 25th Infantry Division

THIS IS A ROSTER OF the 25th Division as it was constituted during the Vietnam War. Veterans who served with the 25th before or after Vietnam will notice some familiar names missing and some unfamiliar ones present. This was due to the brigade switch that took place between the 4th and 25th divisions. Although the respective units maintained their original divisional attachment until August 1967, in practice both brigades functioned as parts of the division to which they were finally assigned. Therefore, the 4th Division battalions deployed to Tay Ninh were always under the operational control of Cu Chi. The list here is of the 25th as it actually existed throughout most of the war.

Nevertheless, nothing is simple during war. At different times, the 25th Division command exercised operational control over units from a number of different divisions. Conversely, on a few occasions, 25th Division units were commanded by other headquarters on an ad hoc basis. There were also independent units that became part of the 25th Division's world. An Air Force contingent, for instance, served at Cu Chi. The most important of these independent units was the 12th Evacuation Hospital at Cu Chi. The 25th also had its own medical battalion.

Many of the regiments had nicknames, which are listed in parentheses. An asterisk signifies battalions transferred to the 25th Division from the 4th Division in August 1967. The full Division roster that follows was derived from Shelby Stanton's *Vietnam Order of Battle* (New York: Galahad Books), 1987.

Infantry

1st Battalion, 5th Infantry {Mechanized}
4th Battalion, 9th Infantry (*Manchu*)
2d Battalion, 12th Infantry*
2d Battalion, 14th Infantry (*Golden Dragons*)

2d Battalion, 22d Infantry* {Mechanized}
3d Battalion, 22d Infantry*
4th Battalion, 23d Infantry {Mechanized} (*Tomahawks*)
1st Battalion, 27th Infantry (*Wolfhounds*)
2d Battalion, 27th Infantry (*Wolfhounds*)

Armor and Reconnaissance

2d Battalion, 34th Armor*
3d Squadron, 4th Cavalry {Armored}
Company F, 50th Infantry {Long-range Patrol}

Aviation

25th Aviation Battalion

Artillery

1st Battalion, 8th Artillery {105mm} (*Automatic Eighth*)
7th Battalion, 11th Artillery {105mm} (*Dragon Regiment*)
3d Battalion, 13th Artillery {155mm} (*The Clan*)
2d Battalion, 77th Artillery {105mm}
6th Battalion, 77th Artillery {105mm}

Support

1st Support Battalion {Provisional}
2d Support Battalion {Provisional}
3d Support Battalion {Provisional}
25th Medical Battalion
25th Supply and Transport Battalion
65th Engineer Battalion
125th Signal Battalion
725th Maintenance Battalion
25th Administration Company
25th Military Police Company
372d Army Security Agency Company
9th Chemical Detachment
25th Military Intelligence Company

18th Military History Detachment
15th Public Information Detachment
20th Public Information Detachment

Dates of Service

25th Infantry Division Headquarters: 28 March 1966–8 December 1970
2d Brigade, 25th Infantry Division (Separate): 8 November 1970–30 April
   1971

Commanding Generals and Dates They Assumed Command

Maj. Gen. Frederick Weyand, January 1966
Maj. Gen. John C. F. Tilson III, March 1967
Maj. Gen. Fillmore K. Mearns, August 1967
Maj. Gen. Ellis W. Williamson, August 1968
Maj. Gen. Harris W. Hollis, September 1969
Maj. Gen. Edward Bautz, Jr., April 1970

2d Brigade, 25th Infantry Division (Separate): Col. Joseph R. Ulatoski, December 1970

Terms, Abbreviations, and Acronyms

ACAV	armored cavalry assault vehicle
AFV	armored fighting vehicle
AO	area of operations
APC	armored personnel carrier
ARVN	Army, Republic of Vietnam
AWACS	radar-carrying aircraft
AWOL	absent without leave
Bde	brigade
C & C	command-and-control
CO	commanding officer
CRIP	Combined Reconnaissance and Intelligence Platoon
DENTCAP	dental civic action program
DEROS	date estimated to return from overseas
DMZ	demilitarized zone
DRV	Democratic Republic of Vietnam (North)
FAC	forward air controller
FAO	forward air observer
FDAC	computer-controlled artillery
FNG	fucking new guy
FO	forward observer
Front	National Liberation Front
FSB	fire support base
GVN	Government of Vietnam (South)
H & I	harassment and interdiction
HE	high-explosive

HQ	headquarters
ICU	intensive care unit
KIA	killed in action
LAW	light antitank weapon
LCLC	Lightning Combat Leadership Course
LO	liaison officer
LZ	landing zone
MACV	Military Assistance Command, Vietnam
MASH	mobile army surgical hospital
MAT	Mobile Advisory Team
MEDCAP	Medical Civic Action Program
MP	military police
NATO	North Atlantic Treaty Organization
NCO	noncommissioned officer
NVA	North Vietnamese Army
OCS	officer candidate school
POW	prisoner of war
PRU	Provincial Reconnaissance Unit
PTSD	post-traumatic stress disorder
PX	post exchange
R & R	rest and recreation
REMF	rear echelon mother fucker
RF/PF	Revolutionary Forces/Popular Forces
RPG	rocket propelled grenade
USO	United Service Organization
VA	Veterans Administration
VC	Viet Cong
WIA	wounded in action